MARKET ACCESS ISSUES IN INTERNATIONAL FOOD TRADE

MARKET ACCESS ISSUES IN INTERNATIONAL FOOD TRADE

Shrimp Exports from Benin to the EU

A. Kévine KINDJI GASPARD

intersentia
Cambridge – Antwerp – Portland

Intersentia Ltd
Sheraton House | Castle Park
Cambridge | CB3 0AX | United Kingdom
Tel.: +44 1223 370 170 | Email: mail@intersentia.co.uk

Distribution for the UK:
NBN International
Airport Business Centre, 10 Thornbury Road
Plymouth, PL6 7 PP
United Kingdom
Tel.: +44 1752 202 301 | Fax: +44 1752 202 331
Email: orders@nbninternational.com

Distribution for the USA and Canada:
International Specialized Book Services
920 NE 58th Ave. Suite 300
Portland, OR 97213
USA
Tel.: +1 800 944 6190 (toll free)
Email: info@isbs.com

Distribution for Austria:
Neuer Wissenschaftlicher Verlag
Argentinierstraße 42/6
1040 Wien
Austria
Tel.: +43 1 535 61 03 24
Email: office@nwv.at

Distribution for other countries:
Intersentia Publishing nv
Groenstraat 31
2640 Mortsel
Belgium
Tel.: +32 3 680 15 50
Email: mail@intersentia.be

Market Access Issues in International Food Trade. Shrimp Exports from Benin to the EU
A. Kévine Kindji Gaspard

ISBN 978-1-78068-328-7
D/2015/7849/67
NUR 828

British Library Cataloguing in Publication Data. A catalogue record for this book is available from the British Library.

CONTENTS

ACKNOWLEDGEMENTS

At the end of the seemingly lonely journey of writing a PhD dissertation, I realised that I met great people who tremendously enlightened my path and enriched my experiences in the most striking ways. I owe my deepest gratitude to all these people who have made the completion of this book possible.

First and foremost, I would like to express my profound gratitude to the Netherlands Organisation for International Cooperation in Higher Education and Research (NUFFIC) which funded this research through its South-North cooperation programme NPT 262 in Benin. I am grateful to Dr. Martin Gbeboutin, Dr. Pieter Windmeijer and Noel Djivoh for their remarkable work in this programme.

I would also like to sincerely thank the Maastricht University Centre for International Cooperation in Academic Development (Mundo) which took care of all finance-related issues. Special thanks go to Han Aarts, Martine Prins, Hennie Sijen and Jan Ploum. Your availability, understanding and your all time support were a great comfort during my research.

I am much indebted to Prof. Michael Faure, my main supervisor. Already during my somewhat 'unusual' selection, he trusted my ability to carry out this research in fields that were totally unknown to me. Similarly, throughout the years, his patience, his sound judgment and his exceptional knowledge of many disciplines could always give me renewed energy and inspiration to face my various challenges. His constant childlike cheerfulness and his readiness to also advise on private life issues were the 'icing on the cake'. You have truly been to me the perfect supervisor.

I am also grateful to Dr. Leïla Choukroune for her enthusiasm, her commitment and her concern for precision. My gratitude also goes to Prof. Barnabé Gbago for his spontaneous approval to supervise this research.

I owe my deep gratitude to the members of my doctoral assessment committee for patiently and thoroughly reviewing the manuscript: Prof. Peter van de Bossche (Chair), Prof. Patrick Van Damme, Dr Denise Prévost and Dr. Paul Ingenbleek. I owe additional thanks to Prof Van den Bossche and Dr Prévost, who assisted me already in the beginning of my research. Your priceless advice were exactly what I needed at times when I did not even know where to start from. I would also like to express my sincere gratitude to Prof. dr. Ellen Vos, Dr. Tetty Havinga and Prof. Pedro Santos, who have agreed to sit in my public defence committee.

My sincere thanks are also due to the team of the Institute for Transnational Legal Research (METRO): Yleen Simonis, Chantal Kuypers, Marina Jodogne, Marjo Mullers and Elke Hundhausen. I owe special thanks to Yleen Simonis, whose assistance these last months was of great help for the completion of this book and all procedures leading to the public defence. I also thank the "METRO family" for all the wonderful memories we shared through the years. I am particularly grateful to Jing Liu, Wenqing Liao and Charles Ibikounlé who have been my closest and most supportive friends.

I must also express my gratitude to the Institute for Globalisation and International Regulation (IGIR) and the Ius Commune Research School for all the inspiring seminars, master classes and conferences.

I was also honoured with the assistance of several people who contribute at specific times to my wonderful stay and my work in Maastricht. I would like to thank Arouna Lassissi, Djalalou-Dine Arinloye, Rhylwann Alassane, Elissavet Malathouni, Arkadiy Kudryavtsev, Katharina Eisele, Viorelia Gasca, Emma Sihite, Souléïmane Adekambi, Sylvain Dabadé and Fernande Honfo.

I gratefully acknowledge many people who have contributed a lot to my research by giving me much needed information. I would like to thank Sylvain Tossou, Benoit Adéké, Kevin Kinkpé (Directorate of Fisheries, Benin), Vincent Ogui (FSG, Benin), Richard Gnimavo (ADEFIH, Benin), Dr. Pascal Gbénou (SAIN, Benin), Claude Laleyè (National Technical Coordinator WAQP, Benin), Koffi Gnakadja, Maria Luisa Ferreira, Cléophas B. Houngbédji, Lucie Rose Tiémoko Kabran, Maïmouna Drave, Josita Nadia Adanle Hountondji, Marcel Gbaguidi, Aka Jean Joseph Kouassi and Théodore Domagni (UEMOA, Burkina Faso), Diène Faye (Seafood Factories Direction, Senegal), Samba Seck, Charles Bakundakwita, Marie Madeleine Gomez (WADAF, Senegal), Aboubacry Baro (National Technical Coordinator WAQP, Senegal). Your warm welcome, your availability and your insight on your daily work experiences were much valuable to give me a better understanding of my subject.

My heartfelt gratitude also goes to Daniel Strijdhagen. Your care and support during my time of sickness was much appreciated and helped me carry on. I also thank Guillaume and Antoine Strijdhagen for the joy and love they gave me these last years.

Last but not least, I am particularly grateful to my family: my father Constant Kindji, my mother Clémentine Agbossaga, my brothers Oswald and Bérenger Kindji, and my sister Lynette Kindji. Your unfailing support gave me the necessary strength to hold on steadfastly to the goal that led me away from home and the warm family comfort.

LIST OF ABBREVIATIONS

ACP	African, Caribbean and Pacific Group of States
AFSCA	Belgian Federal Agency for the Safety of the Food Chain
AFSEC	African Electrotechnical Standardization Commission
AIMAEP	Project of Institutional Support to the Ministry of Agriculture, Livestock and Fisheries
ASPS	Project for the Improvement of the Sanitary and Phytosanitary Quality of Agricultural and Food Products
BFSA	Beninese Food safety Authority
BIP	Border Inspection Post
BOC	Base of Compulsory Check
BSE	Bovine Spongiform Encephalopathy
BTC	Belgian Technical Cooperation
BTSF	Better Training for Safer Food
CA	Competent Authority
CAP	Common Agricultural Policy
CCP	Common Commercial Policy
CCP	Critical Control Point
CCT	Common Customs Tariff
CEN	European Committee for Standardization
CENELEC	European Committee for Electrotechnical Standardization
CIP	Common Industrial Policy
COFRAC	French Accreditation Committee
CREQ	Regional Committee for Quality
CU	Customs Union
CVED	Common Veterinary Entry Document
DANA	Directorate of Food and Applied Nutrition
DG SANCO	Directorate-General for Health and Consumers
DSU	Dispute Settlement Understanding
EBA	Everything but Arm
ECJ	European Court of Justice
ECOWAS	Economic Community Of West African States
EEA	European Environmental Agency
EEC	European Economic Community
EEZ	Exclusive Economic Zone
EFSA	European Food Safety Authority

EMEA	European Medicines Agency
EPA	Economic Partnership Agreement
EU	European Union
FAO	Food and Agriculture Organization
FBO	Food Business Operator
FTA	Free Trade Agreements
FVO	Food and Veterinary Office
GATT	General Agreement on Tariffs and Trade
GDP	Gross Domestic Product
GPSD	General Product Safety Directive
GFL	General Food Law
GHP	Good Hygiene Practices
GLP	Good Laboratory Practices
GMP	Good Manufacturing Practices
GSP	Generalized System of Preferences
HACCP	Hazard Analysis Critical Control Point
HIPC	Heavily Indebted Poor Countries
IEC	International Electrotechnical Commission
IMF	International Monetary Fund
INSAE	National Institute of Statistics and Economic Analysis
IPPC	International Plant Protection Convention
ISO	International Standardization Organization
JICA	Japanese Cooperation
JRC	Joint Research Centre
LCSSA	Central Laboratory for Food Safety
LDC	Least Developed Country
LNSP	National Laboratory of Public Health
LSSEE	Laboratory of Soil, Water and Environment Sciences
MAEP	Ministry of Agriculture, Livestock and Fisheries
MCA-Benin	Millennium Challenge Account – Benin
MFN	Most Favoured Nation
MLA	Multilateral recognition agreements or arrangements
MRA	Mutual Recognition Agreement
NGO	Non Governmental Organization
NORMCERQ	Regional Secretariat of Standardization, Certification and Quality Promotion
NSB	National Standards Body
OCBN	Common Benin-Niger Organization
OCT	Overseas Countries and Territories
OIE	World Organization for Animal Health
ORAN	African Regional Organization for Standardization
PAEX	Support Program for Expertise of the government of Benin

PAH	Polycyclic Aromatic Hydrocarbons
PASP	Project of Support to the Private Sector
PAU	Agricultural Policy of the Union
PFT	Platform of Transfer
PPMs	Process and Production Methods
PSRSA	Special Regional Program for Food Security
PTB	German Metrology Organization
RAPEX	Rapid Alert System for non-food consumer products
RASFF	Rapid Alert System for Food and Feed
SCFCAH	Standing Committee on the Food Chain and Animal Health
SDoC	Suppliers Declaration of Conformity
SDT	Special and Differential Treatment
SEA	Single European Act
SFP	Strengthening Fishery Products Health Conditions in ACP/OCT Countries
SHEA	Section Hygiene, Waters and Food
SOAC	West African System of Accreditation
SOAMET	Regional Metrology Organization called the West African System of Metrology
SPS Agreement	Agreement on the Application of Sanitary and Phytosanitary Measures
STC	Specific Trade Concern
STOA	Scientific and Technical Options Assessment group in the European Parliament
SYCOPAS	System of Sanitary Control of Fishery Product
TBT Agreement	Agreement on Technical Barriers to Trade
TEU	Treaty on the European Union
TFEU	Treaty on the Functioning of the European Union
TVB-N	Total Volatile Basic Nitrogen
UEMOA	West African Economic and Monetary Union
UMOA	West African Monetary Union
UNDP	United Nations Development Programme
UNIDO	United Nations Industrial Development Organization
WHO	World Health Organization
WTO	World Trade Organization

LIST OF TABLES

LIST OF BOXES

LIST OF FIGURES

CHAPTER I
INTRODUCTION

1.1. BACKGROUND

Foodborne diseases are a major global issue that require attention due to their impact on human life and health and their economic implications. While there is no precise and consistent data on the burden posed by foodborne diseases, most countries with systems for recording foodborne diseases have reported significant increases in the incidence of foodborne diseases caused by pathogenic micro-organisms in food over the past few decades.[1] It is estimated that one in three people worldwide suffers annually from at least one foodborne disease, whereas 1.8 million die from severe foodborne and waterborne diarrhoea.[2] Adverse effects can come from the natural contamination or cross-contamination by the introduction into food of several kinds of biological or chemical agents.[3] Growing international trade, migration and travel accelerate the spread across borders of contaminated foods and food products, making foodborne diseases a major challenge to global public health.[4]

Consequently, food safety occupies a predominant place within international trade, although scientists generally agree that food safety risks have a low impact relative to many human health problems such as cancer or heart disease.[5] But whether it is justified or not, the fact remains that the growing interest granted to that concept reflects the will of people to protect and safeguard humankind from threats of extinction. According to the Food and Agriculture Organization (FAO), food safety is defined as a scientific discipline describing the handling, preparation, and storage of food in ways that prevent foodborne illnesses.[6]

The risk of food contamination or adulteration is increased by the fragmentation of the marketing channel. This phenomenon is more severe in developing countries where food supply systems involve a multitude of

1 Slorach 2002, p1.

2 Othman 2007, p83.

3 Unnevehr, 2003, IFPRI Focus 10, Brief 1.

4 Kuchenmüller et al. 2013, p459.

5 Buzby and Unnevehr 2003, p1.

6 FAO 1999, The Importance of Food Quality and Safety for Developing Countries, 25th session of Committee on World Food Security, available at www.fao.org/docrep/meeting/x1845e.htm, visited October 2014.

middlemen, leading to an increase in fraudulent practices and subsequent food risks.[7] This observation holds all the more true for the sector of fishery products that involves not only fishermen and processors, but also many other stakeholders, including fishmongers, collectors, transport operators, distributors, as well as governments in their role in the protection of public health. The multiplicity of stakeholders adds complexity to the management of fishery products risks, especially in countries like Benin where many of these stakeholders are small-scale operators, which are predominantly illiterate and unaware of the minimum basic hygiene measures. To overcome these issues, there is a trend towards a preventative approach involving a twofold requirement. First, fishery products must be processed in certified plants and establishments and the industry must take responsibility in fisheries' safety control, and implement HACCP-based in-plant quality control programmes.[8] Secondly, a regulatory competent authority must be in charge of certifying fish plants and establishments, with the understanding that, in case of export, an additional control can be exercised by the importing party, including an audit of the national control system of the exporting country to ensure that the latter meets the requirements of the importing country.

Considering that there is a correlation between the length of the production cycle and the probability of the occurrence of a risk of contamination[9], the features of a long food chain increase the possibility of contamination, because a harmful agent may enter the food at any stage of production. Moreover, fishery products are particularly prone to pathogenic contamination, resulting mainly from unhygienic handling during and after harvest, insufficient refrigeration, substandard processing, and poor packaging.[10] Therefore, already in 1980, there was an international drive to reform fish inspection systems and to move away from end-product sampling and inspection into preventative Hazard Analysis Critical Control Point (HACCP)-based safety and quality systems.[11]

Due to the risks associated with fishery products, these products have long received particular attention from policymakers in the European Union (EU). Directive 91/493 already instituted strict hygiene rules for their production and a system of prior approval for third countries intending to export to the EU.[12] In addition, with the media attention received by sanitary crises, such as Bovine Spongiform Encephalopathy (BSE) and dioxin contamination of animal feed, food risk regulation has become a core policy objective in the EU. Accordingly,

7 Idem.
8 Caswell & Hooker 1996, p778.
9 Unnevehr 2003, IFPRI Focus 10, brief 1.
10 Abila 2003, IFPRI Focus 10, brief 8.
11 Ababouch et al. 2005, p5.
12 Directive 91/493, Articles 3 through 9 laying down general provisions for the production and the placing on the market of fishery products for human consumption.

the EU adopted a comprehensive and holistic approach to food safety regulation covering the entire distribution chain 'from farm-to-fork'.[13]

1.2. MARKET ACCESS ISSUES RELATED TO FOOD SAFETY MEASURES

The recent increased emphasis on food safety regulation may have many advantages not only for the quality of life, but also at the economic level. Standards and regulations advanced trade in food in many ways by establishing requirements, compliance with which operates as a key to access to relevant markets. An optimistic vision acknowledges the potential benefits that can be accrued for countries if necessary steps are taken to follow the international risk regulation pace. The mere fact of aiming at compliance with strict food safety standards has the potential to trigger a capacity building process that would ultimately enhance the efficacy of institutional structures.[14] In this respect, many scholars support the view of standards as catalysts because they could potentially increase efficiency and thereby increase competitive advantages, modernise export-oriented chains and hence improve health standards at the national level, with positive spillovers on domestic food safety systems and economic growth.[15] Improved food safety results in enhanced consumer well-being and increased life expectancy, greater productivity levels and reduced health care costs as foodborne illness declines[16], and improvements in the livelihoods of food chain actors.[17]

Keeping in mind that standards are a necessary bridge between increasingly demanding consumer requirements and the participation of international suppliers[18], it becomes obvious that food business operators need to comply with standards to ensure their competitiveness so as to safeguard sustainable access to the international food market. In this regard, international standards can generate economies of scale and production efficiencies, reduce transaction costs, and facilitate international trade, thereby improving regulatory convergence.[19] This helps improve the quality of food and enables greater opportunities to trade with high-value markets. At a more operational level, food safety and product requirements can improve transparency and simplify control procedures by

[13] European Commission 2004, p3.
[14] Henson & Jaffee 2006a, p602.
[15] In this regard, see for example Charnovitz 2002, Roberts & Unnevehr 2005, Jaffee & Henson 2004.
[16] Unnevehr et al. 2003, IFPRI Focus 10, brief 17.
[17] Jaffee & Henson 2004, p3.
[18] Jaffee & Henson 2004, p3.
[19] WTO Agreement Series TBT 2014, p22.

averting duplicate control systems. In this way, these requirements enable a substantial reduction in costs and time for both importers and exporters.

Despite actual and potential benefits generally acknowledged, there is an ongoing controversy surrounding the adoption and the increased stringency of food safety and product requirements. The polemic is more than ever justified considering the current level of globalisation that virtually eliminates borders, facilitating trade, but also contributing significantly to the spread of food risks.

1.2.1. CHALLENGES FOR DEVELOPING COUNTRIES

Compliance with the food safety requirements of importers has become the key to gaining market access, regardless of existing preferential trade agreements. In this regard, food safety is no longer simply a public health concern, but it has become a market development issue.[20] Reaching their commercial development objectives has led developing countries to integrate food legislation within their national policy objectives, with the aim of competitive repositioning and enhanced performance.

However, the determinants of market access are manifold. As regards food or agricultural products, market access is conditioned by several factors reflecting marketing costs, tariffs, costs of complying with both public and private standards, and government regulations.[21] Products must conform to regulations and possibly adhere to standards.[22] In fact, the combination of the structural and financial problems of developing countries, generalised globalisation and the current safety standards of developed countries contributes to ejecting developing countries from the international trade scene.

In this regard, there is a general perception, in particular among developing countries, that food safety and product requirements are rather serious impediments to trade. The trade effects created by these requirements are difficult to assess and estimate.[23] But some evidence, such as total or partial import bans, contribute to fuelling the debate because they sustain the view that a lack of compliance often leads directly to marginalisation. In addition, even if compliance could be achieved at a national level, the administrative, technical and financial burden on small players might still contribute to their marginalisation.[24] Further marginalisation would even result from the combined effect of institutional weaknesses and rising costs of compliance for various weaker economic players, including small/poor countries, small and

---

20 Unnevehr et al. 2003, IFPRI Focus 10, Brief 17.
21 Josling & Roberts 2011, p1.
22 Zarrilli 1999, p1.
23 Josling & Roberts 2011, p1.
24 Jayasuriya et al. 2006, p1.

medium-sized businesses and small-holder farmers.[25] Prohibitive costs of compliance to stringent requirements of exporters feature among the range of most quoted factors that affect market access for food and agricultural products, leading to increased costs of production and reduced export competitiveness. Other factors may include tariffs and marketing costs.[26]

Moreover, the evolving character of food safety measures creates continuing challenges for producers and policymakers in exporting countries. As international food trade develops, the increased stringency of food safety and product requirements for many hazards have the potential to influence market access because they can raise the costs of imports or prohibit entirely imports[27] from certain countries or some of their processing plants. This is even more so because it is nowadays well acknowledged that, for many high-value foods like fish, international competitiveness depends more on food safety concerns than price and basic quality parameters.[28] The complexity of food safety and product requirements sustains among developing countries the view that several standards and methods of enforcement are protectionist and discriminatory[29], because they are thought to be more stringent than necessary to reach the appropriate level of protection or the policy objectives of the importer. Moreover, even beyond all discriminatory intentions towards imports, this growing intricacy of food safety and product requirements and the lack of harmonisation might still impede developing countries' trading efforts.[30]

The debate between developed and developing countries is exacerbated by the fact that many developing countries are unable to meet minimum and basic requirements, such as hygiene, in the production process. As a result, food safety and its related issues are somehow embryonic in several developing economies. Many of these countries lack adequate food security and therefore having effective food control systems appears not to be a priority. In many developing countries there is a weak emphasis on food legislation, its administration and enforcement, because these countries lack the technical infrastructure necessary to effectively develop and design regulations, standards and conformity assessment procedures.[31] Likewise, developing countries also lack the laboratories and accredited certification bodies to test and certify compliance against a certain standard.[32] Furthermore, poverty coupled with poor environmental hygiene and sanitation, rapid and unplanned proliferation of street food vending sites, poor public health funding, inadequate human

25 Jaffee & Henson 2004, p3 & 15.
26 Josling & Roberts 2011, p1.
27 Roberts & Unnevehr 2005, p470.
28 Jaffee & Henson 2004, p1.
29 Jayasuriya et al. 2006, p2.
30 Jaffee & Henson 2004, p3.
31 World Trade Report 2012, p153.
32 Idem.

resources and expertise, civil strife, boarder conflicts, droughts, and floods constitute recurring problems which reduce the capacity of developing countries to offer safe food.

This compliance issue is also increased by the absence of a strong demand by domestic consumers for food safety regulations, which translates into obsolete and outdated food safety control systems. But, in view of the increasing stringency of food safety standards at the international level, lots of developing countries that opted to participate in international food trade can no longer afford to maintain insufficiently regulated food systems. However, the mere willingness to comply is generally not enough to make food safety regulation an effective reality in developing countries.

Food safety and product requirements mainly become an issue because the capacity to comply seems closely linked to the level of development and the organisation of production in a given country. In this respect, the lower the level of development is, the lower the capacity for compliance is[33], and the longer the compliance period will be. The cost of compliance is therefore often determinative of the ability of developing countries to upgrade to a satisfactory level. The higher the costs of compliance in developing countries depend on the initial food safety capacity and regulations that tend to be less strict.[34] Compliance with food safety standards requires big investments, technological skills and a well-functioning institutional framework.[35] However, costs of compliance do not affect all the countries equally, because structural differences are not homogeneous across countries. Therefore, major disparities may appear in standard setting and implementation. This is an important determining factor in the reactivity of countries in the light of changes in standards at the international level, particularly when costs of compliance are high. While least developed countries have a low capacity, other countries like Kenya have a modest capacity, and more advanced countries like South Africa have adequate capacity.[36]

In Sub-Saharan Africa, pre-existing technological gaps and weak food chain organisation is a major constraint in a country's ability to respond to market signals, increased competition, and emerging standards.[37] But a closer analysis reveals that the reactivity of countries in the face of compliance issues is also largely dependent upon the trade interests at stake for a particular country. Looking through a few cases in the West African region, it can be observed that, while some countries like Senegal and Ivory Coast tend to have a better reactivity in relation to non-compliance detected by the FVO, others like Benin and Togo are slower in undertaking reforms. These two groups of countries

33 Idem.
34 Kadigi et al. 2007, p5.
35 Kadigi et al. 2007, p3.
36 Nyangito 2002, p10 & 12.
37 Rios & Jaffee 2008, p69.

share some common features. First, with regard to traded volume, Senegal and Ivory Coast exported respectively 43,000 and 25,000 tons of fishery products in 2011.[38] Before Benin put a voluntary moratorium in place in 2002, in its best year, in 2001, Benin exported only about 700 tons of fishery products, while neighbouring Togo exported 1,500 tons in the same year.[39]

With regard to compliance, the systems in both Senegal and Ivory Coast were found compliant with the EU system already in 1997. Although compliance issues were reported later by the FVO, both countries managed to take the necessary steps to upgrade their systems to a satisfactory level.[40] In contrast, the deficiencies in Benin and Togo were much harder to overcome. In response to severe shortcomings reported in 2002, both countries decided to suspend their shrimp exports to the EU in 2003 and to apply for EU funding to undertake regulatory and institutional reforms. Despite the EU assistance, the outcome of the upgrading process is not very positive. Benin's shrimp exports slowed down in the aftermath of the voluntary moratorium and ultimately led to the collapse of the shrimp export industry. Similarly, the production and certification system in Togo remained impaired by serious deficiencies, leading the EU to put in place an official import ban on fishery products, except live lobsters. These examples are illustrative of the fact that when the stakes are high, the reactivity and the commitment of domestic stakeholders also tend to be higher, resulting in a better outcome. High-quality food safety standards then become catalysts, contributing to building capacity to ensure higher safety standards of fishery products for the export supply chain, which might later result in positive spillovers on the domestic market. However, standards will act as barriers for smaller industries, especially when they rely heavily on only one outlet market like Benin.

Some of the reasons for the difficulty in meeting standards are the low quality and availability of raw material, the high cost of laboratories, testing and certification and financial constraints, and issues with waste disposal and antibiotics.[41] For example, border rejections of fish consignments were often associated with filth, microbiological contamination and decomposition. More than 50% of the rejections of consignments from African countries are attributed to a lack of basic food hygiene and a failure to meet labelling requirements.[42] In Benin, some food business operators were abusing the use of chlorine to remedy

---

38 Ivory Coast also exported about 100,000 tons directly transshipped in the EU from freezer vessels flying the flag of either a third country or an EU Member. See respectively Commission Européenne 2013a, p2; Commission Européenne 2013b, p2.

39 Another 1,000 tons were transshipped in the EU. See Commission Européenne 2002, p4.

40 However, it should be noted that the FVO reported in 2013 that doubts remain about the reliability of the results of laboratory analysis in Ivory Coast. Likewise, some shortcomings were pointed out in the control system and some recommendations from earlier FVO reports had yet to be applied.

41 Jayasuriya et al. 2006, p4.

42 FAO/WHO 2004, p1.

the problems related to the low quality of fresh shrimps. It is also important to underline that the competitiveness of African agricultural exports is impeded by a number of factors, among which market access has the most important share (37.8%). However, supply constraints rank nearly as high (32.4%). Other factors are of less importance: poor governance and institutions: 16.2%; rules of origin: 8.1%; others: 5.4%.[43] However, if costs of compliance are high, the cost of lack of compliance is even higher due to the loss of exports and the adverse socioeconomic effects on the actors involved in the exporting country.[44]

Another challenge with regard to food risk management lies in the fact that the awareness of food safety concerns varies widely from one area to another, and depends generally on the local culture and development level. The perception of risk and the regulatory response to it can vary greatly between different countries or societies[45] leading sometimes to frictions between trading partners.

In any case, the failure of many developing countries to meet basic hygiene requirements supports the suspicions that compliance with standards requiring more sophisticated and costly techniques such as heavy metals would be quite challenging.[46] In this context, developed countries consider it to be legitimate to take appropriate regulatory steps to prevent low quality or unsafe foods from invading their markets, with the potential to endanger the health and life of their consumers. Understanding the synergies between the development of the domestic food system and food export industries is therefore essential for policymakers in developing countries.[47] This is a *sine qua non* condition for developing countries to remain actors in the international food trade, because the combined effects of institutional weaknesses and rising compliance costs could contribute to the further marginalisation of weaker economic players, including poor countries, small businesses and artisanal fishers and boat owners.[48]

1.2.2. CHALLENGES RELATED TO THE NATURE OF FOOD SAFETY AND PRODUCT REQUIREMENTS

The fact remains that the proliferation of sanitary standards is not entirely new in the international trade arena since, well before the WTO, there was already a certain regulation of technical standards through the standard codes. Since 1995, there have been two specific agreements that regulate the sanitary and

43 Economic Commission for Africa/African Union 2007, p96.
44 Idem.
45 Zleptnig 2010, p332.
46 Henson & Loader 2001, p91.
47 Unnevehr et al. 2003, IFPRI Focus 10, Brief 17.
48 Kadigi et al. 2007, p2.

technical standards that might affect trade liberalisation more specifically, namely the Agreement on the Application of Sanitary and Phytosanitary Measures (hereinafter SPS Agreement) and the Agreement on Technical Barriers to Trade (hereinafter TBT Agreement). The SPS Agreement establishes the principles that enable WTO Members to legitimately take measures to protect human health or life from risks arising from international trade in food. The TBT Agreement focuses on the provisions that govern the obligations Members are under while adopting technical regulations, standards and conformity assessment procedures. While the SPS and TBT Agreements have different scopes of application according to the objectives of the covered measures, they both have the potential to fuel contention.

According to studies, Non-Tariff Measures (NTMs) almost double the level of trade restrictiveness imposed by tariffs, while recent evidence suggests that, with falling tariffs, the contribution of NTMs to overall trade restrictiveness is likely to have increased even more.[49] There is a widespread suspicion that the core of the trade contention related to health measures lies mostly in the SPS agreement and to a lesser extent in the TBT Agreement. WTO notifications suggest an upward trend in SPS/TBT measures that are the most frequently encountered NTMs and considered among the most relevant impediments to exports.[50] Some countries in Africa claim that the SPS agreement is not implemented well, essentially due to the lack of adequate SPS information about their targeted markets, the arbitrary or discriminatory application of SPS measures, the use of SPS measures to disguise trade restrictions, and the lack of efforts from developed countries to monitor the extraterritorial effect of their SPS measures.[51]

While governments are often obliged to take measures motivated by genuine health concerns, other considerations, such as the protection of domestic producers against foreign competition[52] or political pressure from consumers, might sometimes lead governments to adopt measures that are more stringent than necessary to protect only human health. In fact, sheer complexity results from separating legitimate differentiation from non-legitimate discrimination because, in most circumstances, alleged protectionism exists concomitantly with at least partial safety and health issues.[53] Both public interests and protectionist interests are often combined in a single measure.[54] Similarly, the mere existence of stringent measures engenders regulatory divergence and might translate into artificial trade barriers.[55]

49 World Trade Report 2012, p9.
50 World Trade Report 2012, p8.
51 Nyangito 2002, p8.
52 Roberts & Unnevehr 2005, p470.
53 Jaffee & Henson 2004, p5; Stephenson, 1997, p12.
54 Baldwin 2000, p241.
55 Alemanno 2013, p3.

Food safety and product requirements are both sub-sets of technical measures that may take different forms. These requirements are SPS measures for example when they address food contamination or refer to allowable levels of substances such as heavy metal in food products. Generally, the TBT Agreement addresses quality and packaging attributes.

It is also worth making the distinction between product certification and the certification of quality systems. Product certification refers to the intrinsic quality of the product, while the certification of quality systems relates to the validation of safety or quality criteria such as the validation of a food safety or quality system, procedures or technical requirements. The covered agreement mainly depends on the particular concerns assessed for the certification. When product certification or certification of a system relate to a safety concern or the ability of the system to ensure food safety, it then falls under the SPS Agreement. Certifications referring to food quality concerns fall under the TBT Agreement. Likewise, non-food product safety and quality are usually considered TBT issues. In this regard, certification and accreditation are fundamental tools, which add credibility to the implementation of food safety measures.

The effect on trade is typically dependent upon the level and nature of national food safety requirements.[56] The forms of the product requirements are decisive of their easy implementation or the ability to assess their effect on trade properly. For instance, as regards governmental policy instruments, requirements can be classified according to the level of intervention involved. The most interventionist measures are import bans that translate a significant and acute risk and/or great uncertainty about a hazard. Total bans are applied when no cost-effective mitigation measures are available to control the risks, while partial bans still permit trade only in certain seasons or to/from certain countries or regions.[57] The most widely applied measures are technical specifications that allow imports when there is compliance with certain pre-specified requirements. Lastly, the least interventionist measures are information requirements that submit imports to appropriate labelling.[58]

From another viewpoint, one can distinguish national performance requirements (such as maximum residue levels for pesticides) and process requirements (such as the required use of filters for irrigation water), which may alter the cost of foreign supplies relative to domestic production.[59] Performance requirements require the attainment of an objective without specifying in detail all the elements that must be developed and implemented. Performance requirements are product-based requirements, which focus on the final product

56 Henson & Jaffee 2006, p 594.
57 Jaffee & Henson 2004, p16.
58 Henson et al. 2000a, p16.
59 Roberts & Unnevehr 2005, p470.

characteristics. In contrast, process requirements stipulate particular details in the process of production.

While performance requirements are thought to be more amenable to harmonisation across countries and more conducive to facilitating trade[60], process requirements are considered to have more potential to fuel contention in international trade.[61] The implementation of an HACCP system, for example, is primarily a performance requirement resulting from the voluntary adoption of a management tool to attain a performance goal of a safe product. But when HACCP becomes a government regulatory requirement, its qualification is no longer so straightforward. HACCP remains a performance requirement if regulators require companies to develop and implement a HACCP plan, but they do not specify its elements in detail. If particular details are specified (e.g. carcass chilling temperatures in the processing plant), it becomes a process requirement.[62] Irrespective of the type of measure, food safety and product requirements become trade impediments when they create unjustified different requirements in different markets, unnecessary costly or time-consuming tests, or duplicate conformity assessment procedures.[63]

Undeniably, building capacity for a modern and competitive agro-food system can be quite challenging and costly since it requires a vast array of functions. As regards SPS, these functions include the capacity to detect the presence or demonstrate the absence of biological, chemical or physical hazards, undertake the scientific analysis of hazards, monitor hazards throughout the production process, ensure traceability, and implement an effective monitoring and surveillance system so as to inform decision-making processes and ensure adequate reactivity in advance of emerging hazards and outbreaks.[64] TBT-related functions include certification and accreditation[65], which are not affordable for many single countries.

1.2.3. CHALLENGES RELATED TO THE NATURE OF THE PRODUCT

For products such as fisheries that are considered extremely sensitive due to their ability to carry diseases or the likelihood of the occurrence of cross-contamination during the production process, the sole capacity of processing

60 Caswell & Hooker 1996, p777.
61 Roberts & Unnevehr 2005, p 494.
62 Caswell & Hooker 1996, p777.
63 Zarrilli 1999, p1.
64 Jaffee & Henson 2004, p10.
65 Codex (1997b) defines official accreditation as the procedure by which a government agency having jurisdiction formally recognises the competence of an inspection and/or certification body to provide inspection and certification services.

plants to ensure compliance with exporters' standards is no longer sufficient to attest to their reliability to supply foreign markets. According to the FAO, fish and shellfish pose a health risk and become hazardous to the consumer because of contamination from the environment in which they grow and live, their inherent chemical composition, cross-contamination during handling and processing and inadequate processing, and poor storage, distribution and marketing practices.[66] Moreover, the WHO reported that heavy metals – such as lead, cadmium, arsenic, or mercury present in soil, coastal and continental waters – can accumulate in seafood, especially in bottom-feeder and predatory fish, shellfish or crustaceans.[67] The capacity of national authorities to certify compliance then becomes a key factor in ensuring access to the market for these sensitive food products. Consequently, the lack of an adequate regulatory framework and quality infrastructure may become an effective impediment to trade.[68] In such a way, building capacity throughout the entire food chain is knowledge-intensive and requires time and training for its implementation.[69] In the shrimp-processing sector in Benin, many individuals are involved and work on a small-scale level to provide fresh shrimps to processing plants. In this context, the low level of literacy and the lack of means of accessing information also constitute important factors that make capacity building even more challenging.

With regard to the EU, the tendency to an overly cautious approach seems to take precedence over the allegations of protectionism in the fishery sector.[70] In many cases, the EU has founded its measures on suspicions of health issues, such as a cholera outbreak in East Africa, rather than actual health risks related to fishery products. As a result, some countries suffered from EU bans on grounds that were later proven to be unsubstantiated. In other cases, EU trade restrictions were based on dysfunctions in the production and certification system of developing countries, on the assumption that reasonable doubts remain about the ability of such systems to provide end products that comply with EU requirements.

1.3. PROBLEM DEFINITION AND RESEARCH QUESTIONS

From 1994 to 2002, the shrimp industry in Benin was a growing sector comprising of three processing plants, namely CRUSTAMER, Froid Surgelés

66 FAO 2009, p13.
67 WHO 2004, p96.
68 Roberts & Unnevehr 2005, p470.
69 Shafaeddin 2007, TWN briefing paper 38.
70 Ponte 2007, p57.

Glaces (FSG) and Société Béninoise de Pêche (SOBEP). These three companies used to export exclusively to the EU on the basis of bilateral agreements with food business operators in EU Member States. Following severe deficiencies revealed in 2002 in the production and certification system by the EU's Food and Veterinary Office (FVO), a voluntary suspension of shrimp exports was decided in 2003 by the authorities in Benin to undertake remedial actions to ensure compliance with EU requirements. In fact, Benin then adopted an approach followed by many developing countries consisting in gradually adopting or adapting legislative food safety models that were initially established in developed countries or by international organisations, such as the Codex Alimentarius.[71] In Benin, this process resulted in the transplant of the EU food legislation into the national legal order, followed by steps to develop the necessary institutional framework with the support of the EU. The legal transplant was a response to the pressure of an imminent EU ban, considering the seriousness of the shortcomings of the former production and certification system in Benin.

Transplanting the EU food law amounted to abiding by a high-quality law, which in the EU context was the result of an evolutionary process. The configuration of the EU legislation developed following the evolution of the European market and its structural and institutional changes. Adjustments occurred in the EU food legislation progressively in the light of measures that were necessary to eliminate trade barriers between EU Member States. EU measures contributed to furthering the harmonisation scheme aiming at the completion of a single EU market. Likewise, diverse food crises led to the strengthening of the food law to help to provide an enhanced level of protection on the EU market.

Considering the magnitude of the flaws revealed by the FVO in the former law and system of production and certification in Benin, substantial investments were needed both for processing plants and the competent authority to upgrade to be in conformity with the EU law. The recurring lack of resources at the national level therefore made it a great challenge for Benin to move from a virtual absence of law to adopting high-quality legislation, such as the EU food law. In this context, the assistance of many donors was required to carry out the capacity building process. As a result, the development of the current food safety system was only possible with this external assistance.

The lack of resources was and remains an issue for an effective food risk management. Despite some improvements, the process of regulatory and institutional reforms eventually had some finance-related difficulties and delays that led to the collapse of the shrimp export industry.[72] Under these

71 Snyder 2006, p149.

72 The FVO inspections in Benin and subsequent reforms to ensure compliance with the EU food law will be detailed in chapter IV.

circumstances, questions arise as to whether Benin, at its current level of socio-economic development, will be able to ensure the implementation and enforcement of the transplanted law and to safeguard the sustainability of the food safety system as developed in the aftermath of the voluntary export suspension.

Furthermore, given the stakes, the steps to implement the transplanted food law essentially focused on the supply chain leading to exports to the EU. In the absence of a domestic demand for an intricate food safety law, the system developed from 2003 is not very concerned with the supply chain intended for the domestic market and it is disconnected from local realities. The development of these two supply chains in the same fishery sector is an issue that casts doubts on the reliability of the food safety system. This factor also raises the issue of the viability of such a food safety system, especially in the context of the collapse of the shrimp export industry.

Considering this unusual development of a food safety law and system merely for compliance purposes to regain the market share, it becomes essential to analyse whether EU food safety expectations with regard to third countries like Benin are overly ambitious. Seen from a different perspective, one might also ask whether Benin itself was not too ambitious in the regulatory steps it took to comply with EU law.

In any case, at the international level, the WTO acknowledges the sovereignty of Members in deciding the appropriate level of protection they deem necessary in their own territory with regard to managing food risks. However, the WTO also sets up provisions to circumscribe the regulatory autonomy of Members to avoid that this freedom serves the purpose of protectionism or excessively precautious approaches to food safety regulations.

Members' sovereignty is subject to the disciplines of Article 5.5 that requires consistency in approach, with the understanding that Members should avoid arbitrary and unjustifiable distinctions, in particular when the latter result in discrimination or a disguised restriction on international trade. Similarly, Members are entitled to an undisputable right to adopt measures meeting their level of protection of human life or health. However, this right must be balanced by the obligation laid down in Article 5.6 pursuant to which Members should ensure that the measures they establish or maintain are not more trade restrictive than necessary to achieve their appropriate level of protection, taking into account technical and economic feasibility.

In the exercise of this regulatory autonomy, legitimate differences between nations' safety requirements could appear, because countries have different levels of tolerance for food safety risks, different costs of producing safer food, different levels of accidental contamination[73], and even different levels of protection. These differences may even be supported by factors that are as instable as non-scientific

73 Mitchell 2003, p10.

issues such as consumer preferences or consumer risk perceptions.[74] The SPS Agreement underlined in Annex A(5) that many Members refer to the concept of Appropriate Level of Protection as the 'acceptable level of risk'. In this respect, while the determination of the Appropriate Level of Protection could take into account quantitative information, Members could also integrate societal factors such as consumers' risk perception.

To sum up, this research aims at identifying the food law in two different contexts. On the one hand, we will consider the context of a developing country (i.e. Benin), weakened by its lack of resources and which consistently faces a lot of difficulties to meet international sanitary requirements. On the other hand, we will focus on the context of a regional economic organisation (i.e the EU), which establishes its own standards that condition access to its markets. While examining the interactions between these two systems of food safety regulations, it is essential to integrate the requirements of the WTO as an international organisation that fixes the rules with which both Benin and the EU must comply.

The main general research question is hence: Are there conflicts between food laws at the EU, Benin and WTO's levels of governance and, if so, is it possible to reconcile these divergent requirements? In searching for an answer to this fundamental question, it should be possible to address two sub-questions: To what extent is there compliance between the food laws in the EU and in Benin? How could WTO rules be used as leverage to avert a potential 'overregulation' from the EU while enabling the EU to legislate to the level necessary to avoid adverse effects from an overly lax food safety system in Benin?

This research aims at studying the legal systems of Benin and the EU vis-à-vis WTO law in order to analyse how Benin could better regulate food safety through a law suited to its political, legal and economic situation, while at the same time being able to meet international requirements. The utility of such a study is to ensure the sustainability of the shrimp export industry, given its social and economic importance for the country, while at the same time fostering a national framework for an effective implementation and enforcement of the food law on the domestic market.

Studying the EU's food law in the context of this research also explains how EU requirements have influenced the process of food law development in Benin in the aftermath of the first FVO mission in 2002. This step is necessary to find out whether alternative avenues could have legally been sought to ensure compliance with EU's food law, while better accommodating the needs arising from the socio-economic development in Benin. Ultimately, the research aims at establishing whether the EU approach to food safety regulation is consistent with relevant provisions of the SPS and TBT Agreements.

In order to accurately achieve these goals, it is important to choose a suitable research methodology.

74 Buzby & Unnevehr 2004, p5.

1.4. METHODOLOGY

The initial hypothesis of this research is that the EU has adopted an uncompromising approach towards Benin. To verify this hypothesis and to reach the objectives, the research will be conducted through a threefold methodological approach. First, EU and Benin laws will be examined using a historical perspective to give a foundation to the research. In the EU's food law, the evolution of the law with regard to the experiences and the need for the common market will be explained. Particular attention will be given to the fishery products' sector legislation and the need for specific standards in that field will be explained. With regard to Benin, the research intends essentially to examine the conditions for the adoption and implementation of food legislation. Looking at the historical development is therefore required to explain why and how obsolete laws could remain in force unimpeded. Furthermore, this step helps to better explain the rationale behind the ultimate legal transplant.

Second, a comparative study is used in this research to examine how food safety risks are managed in the EU and in Benin. The description of the positive law in the two systems implicitly requires a critical analysis of the food laws that lead to the analysis of their integration. The primary and secondary sources of the food laws as well as their application will be highlighted. Moreover, this method is used to find responses in other jurisdictions to specific problems encountered by Benin. This search is directed mainly towards other West African countries that share common features with Benin, particularly the level of development and the main reliance on the EU market. Lastly, this method is useful to analyse the development of a food safety framework at the regional level by the West African Economic and Monetary Union (UEMOA). This makes it possible to clarify certain issues taking the example of the development of the EU food law, which has become *de facto* a law of reference for most UEMOA Member States.

Thirdly, a mixed method approach has been adopted. This refers essentially to a critical documentary analysis and semi-directive interviews. The use of such an approach is justified by the necessity to provide sufficient information on the shrimp export trade while highlighting the administrative and institutional mechanisms pertaining to the implementation and enforcement of the law and their influence on the trade relationship between the EU and Benin. In this regard, the documentary analysis refers to a thorough review of relevant academic literature, as well as reports from the FVO, the Rapid Alert System for Food and Feed (RASFF) to collect data underlining bans, consignment border rejections, the monitoring of fishery products on the EU market, WTO documents, relevant WTO jurisprudence, etc. First, the primary focus was on the laws and practices in Benin with regard to food safety,

The literature review focused on market access restrictions, whether in the form of total or partial or *de facto* bans, to shed some light on the motivations leading to trade restrictive measures. This step is necessary to understand how actual or perceived food safety risks have been impeding trade and the responses given to these trade impediments both by importing and exporting countries. With regard to the EU, this stage focused on the development of the food law to enable a narrative of the challenges and incentives reaching the current high-quality law. In fact this analysis was important considering that the current EU law was transplanted by Benin. Also, the analysis focused on the mechanisms used by the EU to implement and enforce its food law, particularly with regard to third countries, as well as the influence of these instruments on policies both in the EU and in its trading partners. The research focused on the role of institutions such as the European Food Safety Authority (EFSA), for its role in policymaking and risk communication, and the FVO, for its control missions in third countries. Extensive use was made of FVO reports on many developing countries in West Africa and FVO's annual reports. Furthermore, the RASFF system was considered for its essential importance for market surveillance and reactivity to food risks within the EU. In fact, focusing on the functioning of these EU institutions was also crucial because, along with the legal transplant, Benin also undertook to replicate similar institutions in its own context. Therefore, a better understanding of the EU institutions was important to assess the efficacy and the sustainability of such initiatives in Benin.

The literature review then put an emphasis on concepts such as discrimination, harmonisation and equivalence for their importance in assessing the legitimacy of food safety measures at the international level. In this regard, provisions of the GATT, and the SPS and TBT Agreements were examined, particularly to assess whether these international agreements could have helped Benin avoid or curb the effects of EU food safety requirements on its shrimp export flow. Furthermore, the data on compliance costs in Benin were collected, both as regards the competent authority and processing plants. With regard to the WTO, SPS/TBT-related documents were used, including material on the work of the SPS and TBT Committees and other relevant materials referring to cases brought before the Committees. Moreover, the work of the Codex Alimentarius was considered because of the importance given to the latter by the SPS Agreement as far as food safety international standard-setting is concerned.

Lastly, interviews were carried out, specifically in Benin, Senegal and at the headquarters of the UEMOA in Burkina Faso. Interviews were conducted with staff of the Directorate of Fisheries (competent authority), processing plants, technical assistance programmes, and law departments at the UEMOA. These interviews were mostly used to gather qualitative information about the law in practice and to provide support for the findings in the literature. Specifically, this stage made it possible to get a better understanding of the challenges faced by diverse stakeholders in Benin in the aftermath of the first FVO mission in 2002.

With regard to the UEMOA, interviews provided data and information for a twofold analysis. First, it was essential to determine the importance of developing legal and institutional food safety frameworks at the UEMOA level, in support of initiatives at the Member State levels. In this respect, the progress of these regional institutions and/or the hindrances to their completion could be better ascertained. Secondly, information and data could be collected as regards the UEMOA Quality Program, which played a key role in the capacity building process in Benin's fishing sector. As such, the main incentives for the strategic choices made within the framework of this regional support to Benin could be better explained and analysed.

With regard to Senegal, qualitative information was mainly gathered to provide grounds for comparison between the challenges faced by stakeholders in both Benin and Senegal. The choice of Senegal was motivated by the importance of its fishing sector and the fact that this country also exports mainly to the EU and therefore faces, in principle, similar challenges as Benin. Furthermore, as a Member of the UEMOA, Senegal is also involved in the development of regional infrastructures. Therefore, it was useful to compare the experiences and involvement of both countries and their stakeholders with regard to the work of the UEMOA. Likewise, this stage made it possible to evaluate whether in practice there were synergies between UEMOA countries to facilitate the work of the UEMOA.

All this information enabled a critical analysis of WTO consistency of EU requirements imposed on Benin shrimp exports, focusing on the Agreement on the Application of Sanitary and Phytosanitary Measures (SPS Agreement) and the Agreement on Technical Barriers to Trade (TBT Agreement).

1.5. STRUCTURE

The structure of this research is designed to reach the objectives previously defined. Chapter I provides an introduction to the research. This introduction explains the background to the research and gives an overview of market access issues as they relate to food safety regulations and their impact on developing countries' trade and regulatory activity.

Chapter II gives an economic background of Benin and the shrimp export industry. It further provides information on the two FVO missions in Benin and their main findings.

Chapter III provides an overview of the EU food law. It focuses especially on the gradual development of mechanisms such as harmonization to eliminate trade barriers in the EU in order to attain the internal market. This chapter intends to highlight the extraterritorial application of the subsequent trade measures.

Chapter IV focuses on food safety regulation in Benin. It gives an overview of the former law and explains the next steps taken to comply with EU requirements. The chapter aims specifically at studying how and why the food law in Benin was adopted, emphasising the specific influence of the EU food law. The chapter intends to shed some light on the reasons for the underdevelopment of the food safety regulation in Benin.

Chapter V explains the compliance issues and the steps taken by Benin to upgrade both the law and related institutions. This chapter analyses the steps taken in the aftermath of the legal transplant. It examines the way the capacity building was performed and the results achieved. This chapter aims at explaining the process of law making and capacity building in order to assess the sustainability of the food production and certification system in Benin.

Chapter VI analyses the development of a food safety framework at the regional level. It explains how the UEMOA intends to legislate in order to raise the food safety level among its Member States by ensuring cooperation that combines their respective strengths to reach a better implementation of national food laws. The UEMOA intends to invest specifically in the field of capacity building, which is a major impediment for its Member States.

Chapter VII draws upon the SPS and TBT Agreements to outline the influence of EU food safety requirements on the development of a food law in Benin and subsequent institutional reforms. This chapter ultimately provides a compliance study of the EU law with regard to these agreements in order to answer whether or not the EU is abusing its regulatory autonomy in relation to food risks.

Chapter VIII provides some concluding remarks on the main issues addressed in the research. It focuses on the assessment of compliance strategies, technical assistance, and regional cooperation. Moreover, the chapter provides observations on the legitimacy of EU and Benin approaches, as well as the importance of WTO rules in this particular context.

CHAPTER II

BACKGROUND ON BENIN AND ITS SHRIMP SECTOR

2.1. INTRODUCTION

Benin, like most countries in the West African sub-region, is renowned on the international market for the export of one main agricultural product, in particular cotton. Cotton accounts for 90% of exported agricultural product revenues and over 45% of total foreign exchange earnings.[75] Agriculture occupies almost 56% of the labour force and contributes almost one third of the GDP, but most agricultural production remains oriented towards self-sufficiency or local consumption, with low and sporadic exports.[76] Export diversification policies have not yet enabled an effective integration in international trade. In this context, fishery products contribute barely 4% to overall GDP and fish exports, mainly shrimps to the EU, represent 1% of the GDP.[77] The shrimp export sector that started in 1994 grew rapidly, suggesting promising economic perspectives. However, the abrupt voluntary moratorium on shrimp exports to the EU in 2003 for safety concerns had significant impacts on Benin's economy in general and, at a lower level, on individuals and processing plants in terms of job losses, loss of foreign exchange and the termination of activities.

Benin's government sought immediate solutions to curb the likely effects of the suspension of shrimp exports and to ensure that the crisis would not last long. In this regard, the cooperation with the EU and the West African Economic and Monetary Union (UEMOA) to build capacity in Benin from 2003 onwards failed to achieve the expected results due to a combination of factors ranging from a lack of resources to poor commitment by the stakeholders.

This chapter intends to shed some light on the economic background of Benin in order to attempt to understand the failure to implement an adequate food safety law effectively.

The second section (2.2) will briefly present Benin and its economy. The third section (2.3) will present the fishing sector and its importance in Benin's

[75] STDF 2008, p2.
[76] Idem.
[77] Idem.

economy. The next section (2.4) details more specifically the shrimp fishing activity and export. The fifth section (2.5) will succinctly outline the context and findings of FVO inspection missions to Benin. The last section (2.6) will conclude the chapter.

2.2. PRESENTATION OF BENIN

Benin[78], a small country situated in West Africa, is bordered by Togo to the west, Burkina Faso and Niger to the north, Nigeria to the east, and the Bight of Benin to the south. With a total surface area of 114,763 km^2, of which 2,000 km^2 are internal waters, Benin has neither a natural port nor islands. The city of Cotonou is considered to be Benin's economic capital because it regroups the headquarters of most public administrations and private companies and hosts the only port and airport of the country. As a result, almost the entire national economic activity is concentrated there. Porto Novo, the official capital, enjoys less obvious fame and only the Parliament is located in that city.

Benin has an underdeveloped economy. Unfavourable economic indicators result from several political and economic upheavals faced by Benin after reaching its independence in 1960. Benin was one of the nations which was "gifted" after colonisation with an elite of diversely knowledgeable scholars and a well-organised civil administration managed by high-class civil servants.[79] Nevertheless, Benin had seen rather rapid and ceaseless changes of political systems and coups, which finally ended in 1972 by the accession to power of a new regime that governed for eighteen years.[80] The previous Marxism-Leninism regime plunged the country into an economic lethargy characterised by severe economic imbalances, which resulted in political and social tensions.[81] A salutary outcome was found to that national crisis through the organisation of

78 Different names have been used throughout history to describe this country, which is now the "Republic of Benin". Originally called "Kingdom of Dahomey", the country became part of French West Africa from 1894–1960. The country gained its independence in 1960 as the "Republic of Dahomey". In 1975, it was re-named "The People's Republic of Benin". After the advent of democracy in 1990, the country became and remains to date the "Republic of Benin". For convenience, only the current name of the country will be used in this research, even when referring to times when it was known under a different name.

79 Business Africa 2011. The republic of Benin Briefs, Newsletter ISSN 1563–4108.

80 Mathieu Kérékou took power then and ruled the country until 1990.

81 Maldonado (1998) redrew the main troubles, which were damaging Benin's economy during the Marxist period. According to him, the "socialist" option led to the ascendancy of the State in productive and financial sectors to the detriment of the private sector, conferring a comfortable monopoly to the nationalised companies and suppressing private investments by the intervention "of a yoke of binding regulations and subjected to social harassment". Combined with these factors and other exogenous factors, the freezing of banks deposits and wages by the government and the general incapacity to manage public finances greatly damaged the social climate with inevitable economical repercussions.

the Conference of the Active Forces of the Nation that led to the advent in 1990 of a pluralist democratic State subject to the rule of law[82] and the adoption of a constitution, still in force, that totally abides by international human rights principles.[83]

2.2.1. ECONOMIC SECTOR

Benin's population is estimated at 10,160,556.[84] The country has an under-diversified economy based on agriculture. Approximately 57% of the population resides in rural areas[85] and is devoted essentially to subsistence agriculture, using traditional techniques. Agricultural performances depend on natural conditions. As a whole, agriculture accounts for 31.6% of GDP[86] and employs 70% of the working population.[87] Local producers face increased competition from imports, which makes the local market less attractive for domestic producers. These problems in the agricultural sector discourage most farmers, resulting in a search for other activities. Local producers face increased competition from imports, which makes the local market less attractive for domestic producers. Unfortunately, economic opportunities in rural areas are few, and prospects for conversion to more profitable activities are limited. Ultimately, this situation results in the depopulation of rural areas. The suitability of the land for diversified agriculture and the richness of the subsoil in natural resources are essential assets for the development of the still embryonic industrial sector.

Industrialisation is still emerging and provides the country with a few products such as textiles, construction materials and cement. Benin's industries represented 12.9% of the total GDP in 2013.[88] These industries include mostly the sugar refining factory of Savè, the breweries in Cotonou, the cement factories located in Pobé and Onigbolo, and textile and cotton mills located in the northern regions of the country. In general, the development of industry is impeded by many factors. On the one hand, the secondary sector is dominated by the informal sector. The latter accounts for about 60% to the GDP and its development is essentially due to fiscal pressure, administrative complexities and

82 Constitution of the Republic of Benin, Law 90-32, preamble.

83 As a matter of fact, the Constitution of Benin expressly recognised in its preamble some international texts as an integral part of the Constitution and, moreover, these texts have a value superior to the internal law. These texts are the Charter of the United Nations (1945), the Universal Declaration of Human Rights (1948), and the African Charter on Human and Peoples' Rights (1981).

84 CIA 2014, People and Society-Benin, available at https://www.cia.gov/library/publications/the-world-factbook/geos/bn.html, visited October 2014.

85 WTO, Trade Policy Review, Report by Benin, Burkina Faso and Mali 2010, p9.

86 CIA 2014. Economy – Benin.

87 WTO, Trade Policy Review, Report by Benin, Burkina Faso and Mali 2010, p7.

88 CIA 2014, Economy – Benin.

the lack of respect for contracts.[89] The importance of the informal sector is very detrimental to the economy since it prevents the collection of taxes and duties and endangers the solvency of the government, considering that revenues from taxes mostly fund public expenses. For instance, from 2008 to 2009, the decline in customs revenues was estimated at 7%.[90] On the other hand, construction and energy, which are essential for industrial development, contribute very little to the GDP (4.4% and 1.1%, respectively in 2010).[91]

Due to the economic liberalisation and fiscal reforms in Benin, the service sector grew rapidly. This sector's average share of GDP was 55.6% in 2013[92] and the sector employed 21% of the working population in 2010.[93]

2.2.2. GENERAL ECONOMIC TRENDS

Democracy inferred a new political stability in Benin, but it failed to introduce an economic recovery. After a few years of growth, the economy slowed down again. It then became imperative to search for appropriate solutions to avoid falling into economic lethargy again. This initiative resulted in progress at the macro-economic level, characterised by a yearly economic growth of 5% from 1991 to 2002, while between 2003 and 2005 growth was just over 3% a year.[94] After 2006, Benin experienced inconvenient power cuts with severe repercussions on companies and the economy as a whole. Combined with the extreme sensitivity to exogenous shocks, these issues resulted in a slowdown in growth. Nevertheless, the real growth rate was estimated at 5% GDP in 2013.[95]

Benin's trade balance is negative. Imports of goods and services are estimated at 26%, while exports accounted for 13.2% of the GDP in 2013. The trade deficit in Benin was estimated at XOF 300 million in 2008[96], while the current account remained structurally deficient.[97] This is because imports are increasingly taking precedence over exports, not only due to the dependence on a limited number of export products and the decline in these products' export, but also and largely due to the demographic growth.

---

89 Index of economic freedom, Benin, The heritage Foundation and the Wall Street Journal, 2011.

90 Africa Research Bulletin 2011, Benin: Challenges ahead. Africa Research Bulletin: Economic, financial and Technical Series. Vol 48, Issues 4, 19081A-19081C.

91 African Economy Outlook, Benin 2011 available at www.africaneconomicoutlook.org/en/countries/west-africa/benin/#/macro_economic_policy visited on 15/08/2011.

92 CIA 2014, Economy – Benin.

93 WTO, Trade Policy Review, Report by Benin, Burkina Faso and Mali 2010, p8.

94 République du Bénin – PNUD Bénin 2008, p9.

95 CIA 2014, Economy – Benin.

96 Africa Research Bulletin 2011, Benin: Challenges ahead. Africa Research Bulletin: Economic, financial and Technical Series. Vol 48, Issues 4, 19081A-19081C.

97 BafD/OECD 2008, p154.

On the one hand, Benin imports capital goods, petroleum products and most of its food. Quite paradoxically, although the country has fertile soil and a climate favourable to agriculture, most consumed fresh products are also imported from countries of the Sahel like Burkina Faso. On the other hand, Benin does not have a broad product range to offer on the export market, even though agricultural products represent 80% of Benin's official exports.[98] Benin exports products such as cotton, cashews, shea butter, textiles, palm products, and seafood. However, cotton is the only commodity that offers real export potentialities. The cotton sector benefited in the past from the general economic recovery that followed democracy in 1990. Cotton's export share in the total export revenue increased at that time from 51.3% to 80.6% respectively during the periods 1983–1990 and 1991–2001.[99] However, recent years have witnessed a vertiginous decline of cotton exports, falling from 67.9% in 2003 to 29.6% in 2009.[100] This downward trend is justified by the dependence of Benin on international market prices, the lack of governmental subsidies, the vast informal and re-exportation trade with Nigeria, and the entire dependence on other countries with regard to energy supply.

It is worth noting that the poor intra-regional trade also contributes to the structural trade imbalance. The fact remains that Benin is located in Sub-Saharan Africa, which is renowned for being one of the poorest regions in the world and comprises the majority of Least Developed Countries (LDCs).[101] In this regard, most of Benin's neighbouring countries are facing similar challenges and are focused on developed markets for their imports.

Despite these unfavourable economic indicators, Benin is endowed with many advantages that could be beneficial to its development. First, Benin's geographical position could potentially become a strategic location for the development of transports, tourism and transit with landlocked neighbouring countries such as Burkina Faso, Niger and Mali. Unfortunately, road and railroad infrastructures that are necessary for the development of these sectors are either non-existent or poorly maintained. First, the development of a common railroad network connecting Benin and Niger was never completed according to the ambitions of the initiators of the Common Benin-Niger Organization (OCBN). The railroad, which begins in Cotonou, stops regrettably in Parakou, the first big city in the north of Benin. Moreover, existing trains are few and decrepit. It follows that solutions must be found to transport goods to destinations in Niger. However, while roadways cover 16,000 km, only 1,400 km of these roads were paved in 2006.[102] Therefore, conveying goods by road is expensive and

98 WTO, Trade Policy Review, Report by Benin, Burkina Faso and Mali 2010, p71.
99 Decaluwe & Robichaud 2008, p6.
100 WTO, Trade Policy Review, Report by Benin, Burkina Faso and Mali 2010, p16.
101 UNCTAD 2008, p5.
102 CIA 2014, Economy – Benin.

cumbersome. Moreover, the excessive number of checkpoints and corruption on main highways are severe impediments to trade with neighbouring countries.

Second, real potentialities exist to take advantage of the chronic insecurity reigning in the port of Nigeria and to build an organised transit sector focussed on that vast country. Undoubtedly, the market of re-exportation towards Nigeria exists and develops constantly, but the other side of the coin is the development of informal trade between both countries, ranging from household electrical appliances and food products to the fraudulent trade of oil products transported through fields or by the canal of lakes and lagoons.

Third, thanks to its membership to the XOF franc, Benin has relative currency stability likely to attract private and public external investments. Furthermore, Benin benefits from aid from several international institutions, organisations and bilateral donors. The EU, the African Development Bank, the World Bank, and the United Nations agencies are in this regard key partners in aid coordination for Benin. Many international NGOs are active in the country in order to help it improve its situation, and to achieve poverty reduction and a sustainable development. In reality, private foreign direct investment is small in the country and foreign aid accounts for the majority of investment in infrastructure projects.[103] Contrary to other countries of the West African Economic and Monetary Union (UEMOA), Benin did not have recourse to the emission of Treasury bonds and bills to finance its public deficit and resorted mainly to external financing.[104] This is in fact a reflection of the lack of resources at the national level. Benin is recognised as a Heavily Indebted Poor Country[105] and even benefited from several international debt reliefs.[106] Nevertheless, the external debt was still estimated at 987 billion euro in 2013.[107]

A number of initiatives are being implemented to overcome these challenges. Fiscal reforms are implemented to promote employment growth and secure the commercial environment to encourage private initiatives and to attract more foreign investors, so as to improve revenue collection and create a new dynamic for public investments. Furthermore, Benin envisages placing more emphasis on tourism, facilitating the development of new food processing systems and agricultural products, and encouraging new information and communication technology.[108] The current trend reveals the privatisation of State-owned companies, completely in line with Benin's commitments with international financial institutions, mainly the International Monetary Fund (IMF). Benin

---

[103] CIA 2014, Economy – Benin.

[104] BafD/OECD 2006, p153.

[105] International Monetary Fund, Debt Relief Under the Heavily Indebted Poor Countries (HIPC) Initiative.

[106] CIA 2014, Economy – Benin.

[107] Idem.

[108] Idem.

already disengaged from the sectors of cotton, banking, wood, and cement, and has started a procedure for the privatisation of telecommunication and energy.

However, these initiatives are not yet completely effective considering several structural factors, in particular administrative red tape and the lack of an appropriate framework for the protection of property rights. The public administration is renowned for its lack of ethics and the unrestrained personal appropriation of the *res publica*.[109] Corruption is widespread in the public administration and its effects even extend to the judicial system. According to the report of Transparency International, Benin is classified 110th out of 178 countries in 2010. The freedom from corruption rate, which is approximately 30%, slightly increased in 2006 before declining again since 2008.[110]

It is worth underlining that, through regional bodies such as the Economic Community of West African States (ECOWAS) and mainly the UEMOA, West African States created favourable conditions that must support regional trade development through the creation of a common market. The latter could result in the elimination of tariff barriers, the adoption of a Common External Tariff and common positions as regards international trade.

The UEMOA is at present working actively for the development of a harmonious legal framework of its Member States for their own common good and for their integration in world food trade. Concerning food safety, this translates largely into progressively updating common regional law and assistance through development projects for institutional capacity building to comply with international standards.

2.3. FISHING SECTOR

2.3.1. ECONOMIC IMPORTANCE OF THE FISHING SECTOR

The fishing sector in Benin shows promising development prospects due to its social impact in poverty eradication within its rural population. Fishing binds the waterside populations to fishing areas[111], contributing therefore to limiting the movement of populations from rural to urban areas, the rejection of traditional activities, the reduction of demographic problems, and water draining problems noticeable in Cotonou. The activity plays an important economic role because it generates employment, taxes and export revenues. Fishery products contribute about 12% of the agricultural GDP[112] and constitute

109 Système des Nations Unies Benin 2008, p12.
110 Transparency International 2010. Corruption Perception Index 2010 Results, Transparency International, 2010.
111 FAO 2008, p4.
112 PAM 2009, p21.

the second export product after cotton. However, this importance must be considered in context, taking into account differences in the classification of activities with regard to national accounts. While fishing itself is classified in the primary sector, processing activities are classified in the secondary sector and the marketing of fishery products is considered in the tertiary sector. It follows that the effective integration of all related activities would reflect more accurately the actual contribution of fishing to Benin's economy. In that respect, a survey conducted in 2003 estimated that fishing contributes 3% to the GDP.[113]

Generally speaking, fishery products correspond to 50% of consumed animal proteins.[114] National production covers only 31.9% of needs in animal protein and imports are relied upon to cover the deficit. Considering the population growth, imported quantities are rapidly increasing, while the national production stagnates. During the period 1998–2005, the production stagnated around 40,000 tons a year, whereas imports increased from 20,000 tons in 2001 to 45,000 tons in 2006.[115] 15% of the workforce is active in fishing and represents 25% of the labour force in agriculture. In terms of numbers of workers, there are around 50,000 fishermen and 20,000 wholesale fish merchants[116], which operate in the sector that provides employment to approximately 600,000 people. These figures include not only the fishing population itself, but also all the people involved in activities directly connected to fishing, such as the processing and marketing, and ultimately activities indirectly related such as the manufacturing or repair of fishing equipment. The population of fishermen is around 100 to 125 fishermen per square kilometre, while the density allowed is 9 to 11 fishermen per square kilometres. This reflects the dependence of local populations on this activity and their inability to turn to other sectors easily. In fact, most of these people have received no further education, are illiterate and generation after generation become fisherman.

At another level, the fishing industry creates some incidental revenue receipts for the government through economic incentives, fishing licenses and the collection of various taxes.

2.3.2. POTENTIALITIES OF EXPLOITATION OF HALIEUTIC RESOURCES

Benin benefits from an opening to the sea that grants the country a sandy facade extending 120 km from the Nigerian border to the Togolese border and an Exclusive Economic Zone (EEZ) of about 27,750 km^2. This enables the

---

113 Houndekon et al. 2003, p38.

114 Commission Européenne 2006, p22.

115 République du Bénin/Ministère du Développement Rural 2000, p8.

116 Idem.

development of fishing activities on 3,100 km^2. Considered as a whole, the water coverage is insignificant compared with other countries in similar climatic zones.[117] In general, the hydrological network is made up of lagoons, lakes, streams, rivers, swamps, floodplains, and reservoirs.

The river system comprises permanent and regular streams belonging to three main drainage areas[118] of which the coastal area gathers the longest rivers namely the Ouémé, the Mono and the Couffo. In the South, the network has an opening to the Atlantic Ocean. The great majority of halieutic resources are found in these southern regions from Lake Ahémé (8,500 ha), Lake Nokoué (15,000 ha) and to a lesser extent from the lagoon of Porto-Novo (3,000 ha).

Fishing activities are essentially concentrated in internal fresh waters, which provide 80% of the national production. The main species caught in southern waters are Cichlidae (40%), Clupeidae (15%), crustaceans (15%), crabs (15%), Mugilidae, Claridae, Bagridae, Heterotis, Chrysichtys (13%), and other species (2%).[119]

Fishermen use different fishing techniques depending on the targeted species. These techniques can be grouped into four main categories: traps (traps, channel nets, dams), nets (cast nets, gill nets, shrimp nets, frame nets, crab balance), lines, and gear grips (arrows, harpoons).[120] Concerns were raised with regard to questionable fishing practices used by some fishermen. Due to the limited water coverage and the rarefaction of resources, fishermen resort to the use of nets with meshes that are too small and prohibited fishing machines, leading to the capture of fish below their size of first sexual maturity (more than 90% of captured fish is immature).[121]

Fishing is divided into three sub-sectors of variable importance: maritime fishing, inland fishing and aquaculture. The results of each sector depend not only on the natural wealth of the rivers in resources or potentialities, but results are even more dependent on means and techniques used by fishermen in the category considered.

Maritime fishing is subdivided into maritime artisanal fishing and the maritime industrial fishing that must in principle be carried out in limited fishing zones.[122] Approximately 4,000 fishermen, a half of which comprises

117 Dominguez & Foster 2011, p20.

118 This refers essentially to the drainage area of Niger (38,000 km^2), the one of Volta (45,000 km^2) and the Coastal drainage area (45,000 km^2).

119 Houndekon 1992, Proceedings of the symposium on post-harvest fish technology, FAO.

120 Idem.

121 Commission Européenne 2006, p22. It is worth noting that issues related to responsible fishing and sustainability are outside the scope of this research.

122 The maritime artisanal fishing is carried out below five marine miles, whereas the maritime industrial fishing must be beyond this limit. However, considering the bad state of the boats of industrial maritime fishermen and numerous related problems, the latter prefer sometimes to fish in the zone devoted to the artisanal maritime fishermen, therefore creating a lot of conflicts between fishermen on both sides.

foreigners, carry out maritime artisanal fishing. These fishermen use a fleet consisting of 850 wooden dugouts, mostly from Ghana, of which 45% are motorised.[123] As for the maritime industrial fishing, not having its own fleet, Benin authorised a few foreign boats, (trawlers, shrimp trawlers, shrimp boats), to capture fishery products in its waters with the obligation to off-load their catch in the Industrial Port of Fishing in Cotonou. This activity developed in an uneven fashion, consisting of eight to fifteen boats, unloading around 800 tons of products, less than 10% of the entire production of the maritime fishing.[124] Maritime fishing is not particularly relevant for shrimp fishing. Generally, the decrepit boats go out to sea for indefinite periods and reappear with insignificant catch.[125] Sea fishing produces barely 20 tons of shrimps, but strong suspicions exist about Nigerian ships operating in Benin's territorial waters without landing their catch in Benin.[126]

As far as aquaculture is concerned, despite real potentialities of permanent streams suitable for fish farming, private promoters' initiatives and the existence of few public projects, aquaculture never developed because of organisational problems, lack of technical abilities and financial means.[127] In Benin, aquaculture is performed using semi-extensive or extensive fish farming methods such as ponds, nets, enclosures, and floating cages. However, this activity consists essentially of extensive fish farming made by brush parks named "*acadjas*" and fish holes. The *acadja* is a traditional system of fishing by trap by which an artificial habitat is created by gathering leafy branches in the lagoon that attract the fish. The *acadja* is very conducive to the safety, reproduction and growth of fish. However, that method is currently the subject of controversy because it leaves wood residues in rivers that contribute to the degradation of the fishing environment and threaten sustainability.

Continental fishing is primarily the privilege of waterside communities. Mainly performed in Benin's Southern region, continental fishing off-loads approximately 30,000 tons of fish, representing 75% of the national production.[128] Continental fishing therefore represents the most productive sub-sector for the halieutic sector in general and thus for shrimp production. It follows that most people who engage in fishing-related activities are also greatly involved in this sub-sector. Approximately 300,000 people participate in these related activities and are mostly fishing tackle salesmen, dugouts manufacturers and women fish retailers.[129]

---

123 Degbey 2004, p5.
124 FAO 2008, p6.
125 Idem.
126 République du Bénin/Délégation de la Commission Européenne au Bénin 2009, p6.
127 République du Bénin/Ministère du Développement Rural 2000, p12.
128 FAO 2008, p1.
129 Idem.

Continental fishing is practiced in a total surface of 130,000 hectares of water, of which at least 333 km^2 are brackish waters and 700 linear kilometres of rivers.[130]

2.4. SHRIMP FISHING

Statistical directories state that there are several thousands of people involved mainly or occasionally in shrimp fishing in Benin. This activity is essentially carried out in brackish waters, as salinity creates the biological environment favourable to the growth of young shrimps. The exchange of waters between the sea and inland rivers is made possible in the dry season during which water levels are relatively low. Therefore, the shrimp life cycle means that shrimp fishing is a seasonal activity par excellence, which lasts on average eight consecutive months a year, from February until October.

Shrimps are essentially captured in Lakes Ahémé and Nokoué and, to a lesser extent, in the lagoon of Porto-Novo. The greatest proportion of shrimps is captured in Lake Nokoué, which, due to its geographical situation and some natural factors, is more exposed to contaminants likely to negatively influence the quality of its shrimps. Lake Nokoué is integrated in a network of continental and marine interactions. Therefore this lake receives seasonal salt water from the Atlantic Ocean and fresh water from the Ouémé and Sô rivers. This situation potentially results in Lake Nokoué collecting waste from these various sources. Also, the shore of the lake is essentially swampy, since household waste pours into it from waterside populations for backfilling purposes. Last, the illegal transportation of petroleum from Nigeria exposes the lake to chemical contaminants.

Based only on an organoleptic analysis, a considerable visual difference can be noticed between Lake Nokoué's shrimps and the shrimps from Lake Ahémé. The latter shows a more whitish and clear texture that testifies to the better quality of the water in which they were captured. This does not mean that Lake Nokoué's shrimps are unfit for consumption, but they will require more treatment than the others to achieve the same level of compliance to safety and quality standards.

Statistics show that, on average, 3,000 tons of shrimps are produced every year.[131] Two-thirds of this production comes from Lake Nokoué. About 1,000 tons enter the export processing chain[132], suggesting that the difference would go to the local market or the sub-regional market. No data exists about intra-regional trade, considering the porosity of physical borders. However, one can

130 Idem.

131 République du Bénin/Délégation de la Commission Européenne au Bénin 2009, p6.

132 Idem.

assert with very little uncertainty that shrimps sold in traditional markets are mainly smoked shrimps considering the relatively short life cycle of the commodity and the absence of a proper cold chain. Fresh shrimps are a relatively expensive food for average households and are therefore rarely consumed on a daily basis. Smoked shrimp powder is widely used to enhance flavours in the cuisine of certain populations of the South.

Shrimps offer enormous processing possibilities. This characteristic decreases the risks related to its fragility. In Benin, there are two main types of shrimps, namely the pink shrimp (*Penaeus duorarum*) and the tiger shrimp (*Penaeus Monodon*), commonly called "black Tiger". These species are wild-caught shrimps renowned for their high collagen rate, which makes them a high-quality choice of product for people concerned about the nutritional value of the food they sell or consume. Furthermore, shrimps caught in the wild in West Africa benefit from the image of a product having an exceptional taste and texture.[133] These factors give Benin's shrimps a prominent place on the market and enables exporters to get good prices for them.

Briefly schematised, the life cycle of the *penaeus duorarum* includes several phases. First, the eggs are laid at sea and their number varies with the size of the female, the water temperature and moon phase. The larvae develop at sea before entering the lagoon or estuary when their shells reach about 7.5 to 8 millimetres. When their shells are about 28 millimetres, they return to the sea where they carry out the end of the growth, maturity and the laying of eggs. Post-larvae shrimps and juvenile shrimps need a salinity of at least 0.5 per mille without which they would not survive. In Benin, they adapt to a wide range of salinities and growth takes place easily in water containing 0.5 to 40 g of salt per litre.[134] The low productivity of marine shrimp fishing can be explained by natural phenomena. Muddy and sandy areas coexist in parallel strips along the coast of Benin. However, muddy areas that are most conducive to the growth of shrimp are not found until 45 meters from the coast.[135]

Fresh shrimps can break easily and, if they are not put at once in isothermal boxes after their capture in order to protect their quality, a process of decomposition starts and they begin to rot from their head. The same effects can be observed when, for one reason or another, the cold chain is not maintained along the marketing channel. In such instances, when the decomposition is still at an early stage, the head can be rapidly cut off and that does not impair the quality of the product. Therefore, shrimps can appear under several forms in sale circuits depending on the possibilities offered by the initial product. The presentation of the final product can also meet existing needs in the market, including consumers' expectations. In this area, Benin's processing plants export

133 OECD 2006, p15.

134 Crosnier & De Bondy 1967, p15.

135 Idem.

the following varieties: frozen whole shrimps, frozen shrimp tails and a tiny quantity of frozen cooked shrimps.

2.4.1. CHARACTERISTICS OF THE SHRIMP FOOD CHAIN

The length of the production chain is a decisive factor for security guarantees offered by the finished product. The safety of the finished product implies that each player must ensure that they comply with hygiene and safety requirements. This is especially true in the shrimp fishing industry that involves many actors before fresh shrimps are delivered to the processing plants carrying out the ultimate transformation and packaging for export.

The length of the shrimp food chain differs according to the envisaged nature of the finished product. Shrimps destined for the domestic market enter a shorter food chain. In any case, involved actors are all likely to influence the safety of the finished product, whether with regard to mere hygiene requirements or contamination risks from diverse potentially harmful germs. As such, their role and the importance of their intervention in the shrimp sector deserve to be underlined.

Figure 2.1. Benin's shrimp supply chain

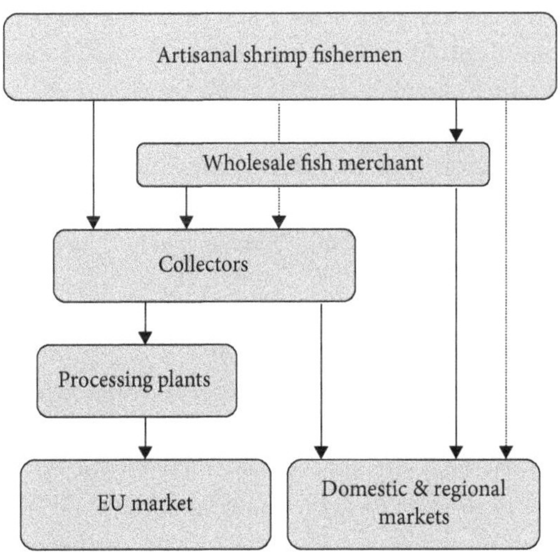

a. Fishermen

Fishing is often the privilege of waterside populations. On some old lagoons, including Toho, Todougba, Ahouangan, Dati, the exploitation of water resources has even been reserved as a right for indigenous resident fishermen while "foreign people" had to request a fishing permit. This permit is renewable annually and is subject to the issuance of a card obtained against payment of one thousand XOF, slightly less than two euro.[136]

Fishermen represent the foundation of all shrimp processing activities, as they make available the raw materials. For the greater part, they are illiterate and have no professional qualifications. Operating alone, fishermen use rudimentary means and traditional techniques. The fishing vessels are generally light narrow wooden canoes propelled by paddles. Within the fishermen's population, the better off fishermen own canoes, while others participate actively and regularly in fishing activities without owning their own canoes.

Given the relative importance of catches, fishing is a purely commercial activity involving all family members at diverse levels. There is a strict task distribution, which is sometimes qualified as "sexual division of work"[137] in fishermen's households. While men are often in charge of the fishing itself and some related activities such as making fishing machines, post-capture activities like preservation and marketing are especially the work of women.

b. *Wholesale fish merchants*

Wholesale fish merchants operate as middlemen to supply both the traditional retail supply chain and the processing chain. Most of them are fishermen's wives and receive freshly captured shrimp from their partners to ensure the distribution. Over the years, the sector was modernised and other women who do not live at the shores of lakes or lagoons and are not fishermen's wives were also involved. These women take their supplies directly from the fishermen as wholesale fish merchants.

A system of reciprocal trust exists between fishermen and wholesale merchants and prices are sometimes negotiated after the sale of the shrimps to the final consumer, taking into account constraints faced by the wholesale merchants on the market. Official statistics show 7,500 formally identified wholesale fish merchants but, given the population of fishermen, one could estimate the actual number at around 18,500 women.[138]

The highly perishable character limits the consumption of fresh fishery products and leads to the necessity of preservation methods, such as smoking, frying and salt-drying. Such activities are specific to shrimps for local consumption and are performed by women, whether they are wholesale fish merchants or simply other retailers in the marketing chain. These shrimps do not pass through the network of collectors.

---

136 Ordinance No 070/MDR/DC/CC/CP of 12 march 1997 on fishing regulations on the old lagoons (Toho – Todougba – Ahouangan – Dati).

137 Houndekon 1992, Proceedings of the symposium on post-harvest fish technology, FAO.

138 PASP 2007, p4.

c. *Collectors*

Collectors intervene in the processing chain and serve as middlemen between wholesale fish merchants and industrial units. In that respect, they move along fishing zones' borders to collect fresh shrimps, which they forward to processing plants. Considering that collectors usually handle large quantities, they often have isothermal boxes in order to preserve the freshness and quality of the shrimps. Most of the time, collectors maintain privileged relations with processing plants and every plant has its own collectors' network. These middlemen were estimated at 150 people. The following table shows an estimate of these actors in 2002.

Table 2.1. Categories and numbers of actors in the fishing sector

Activity category	Permanent or seasonal jobs
Fishermen	21,000
Wholesale fish merchants	18,500
Collectors	150
Salaried plant employees	50
Seasonal employees	1,200
Total shrimp export industry	40,900

Source: République du Bénin/Délégation de la Commission Européenne au Bénin 2009

d. *Processing companies*

The information presented in this section is related to shrimp processing plants before the first FVO inspection, and the subsequent exports suspension. That inspection took place in October 2002 and disturbed the "routine" established in the sector, bringing drastic changes. It will be considered in this analysis that this FVO inspection and its immediate effects up until the auto-suspension in 2003 was a "crisis" in the export-oriented shrimp fishing sector. The periods before and after the crisis will be referred to as the "pre-crisis" and "post-crisis" periods.

Few processing plants operate in the shrimp-processing sector. The development of these plants started in 1993. All of the processing plants were focused on the export market, as they dedicated all of their production to the supply of the EU market. During its period of prosperity, the sector had three active plants, each of them within the limits of its financial resources and the specific agreements with trading partners. In 2014, the industry amounts to the export of a tiny quantity made by a company which was created after the "crisis", whereas the three other plants are practically closing down business.

Processing plants conducted their activities with a limited number of people, which increases by tenfold during processing periods. The combined permanent plants workforce was estimated at 50 people, while they may employ up to 1,200 seasonal employees, mainly women, to carry out the production.

1° "Pre-crisis" processing plants 5

Registered under Benin law, the three shrimp processing plants were formerly quite prosperous and used to participate actively in the export of shrimp. The table below provides an overview of the three plants.

Table 2.2. Overview of shrimp processing plants

Designation	CRUSTAMER	FSG	SOBEP
Legal form	LLC	LLC	LC
Date of creation	1997	1994	1993
Capital (MXOF)	170	100	110
Turnover 2002 (MXOF)	1.319	1.066	792
Turnover 2002 (M€)	2.00	1.62	1.20
Permanent employees	35	20	20

Source: PASP 2007

A. CRUSTAMER

The last processing plant to be established in the sector was CRUSTAMER in 1997, and it quickly grew bigger than its predecessors. This plant certainly benefited from the experience of its founder whose relatives were also renowned in the fishery products processing sector in Senegal, another West-African country in which shrimp exports represent more than 50% of official export receipts. CRUSTAMER was established as a Limited Liability Company with a capital of 170 million XOF, approximately 260,000 euro, for the refrigerated industry, the preparation and the treatment of sea products. Over the years, CRUSTAMER grew and its turnover in 2002 exceeded 2 million euro. However, the former fame of CRUSTAMER did not prevent this company from being very harshly affected by the crisis. Not only is the company closing down, but also its premises are being seized by tax authorities.

B. FSG (Frais – Surgelés – Glaces)

FSG was established in 1994 as a Limited Liability Company with a capital of approximately 168,000 euro. FSG was registered as specialising in the export of sea products. This processing plant proved to be successful in that field and managed to qualify as the second most important shrimp exporting company to the EU. In 2002, FSG had a turnover of about 1.62 million euro.

c. SOBEP (Société Béninoise de Pêche)

SOBEP, a pioneering company in the shrimp processing sector, was established in 1993 as a Limited Company with a capital of 110 million XOF francs, approximately 168,000 euro. SOBEP was registered for the treatment and the export of fishery products. The company was a subsidiary of a regional group named "Pêche Azur", which operates in Ivory Coast and Senegal. SOBEP's turnover in 2002 amounted to 1.2 million euro.

Studies state that SOBEP is not autonomous in its decision making towards the group.[139] This could justify why, despite its importance in the sector, its turnover has never equalled that of its competitors and it is the only company to date to have officially ceased all activities.

2° "Post-crisis" processing plant: DIAX

DIAX, a Limited Liability Company with a capital of 85 million XOF, approximately 130,000 euro, was registered in 2003, the year of the suspension of shrimp exports. DIAX is more known for fresh fish exports and ships only a tiny quantity of shrimps by air. However, this processing plant benefited in the same way as its competitors from the advantages connected to upgrading standards, given that this process was implemented for fishery products as a whole.

2.4.2. SHRIMP EXPORT TRENDS

Data on shrimp exports goes back to 1994, because the first export-oriented processing plant was created in 1993. In total, three companies made up the sector until 2002. These processing plants exported an average of 350 tons from 1994 to 1997. Exports, which dropped to 250 tons in 1997, increased to 453 tons in 1998 and, from then on, an upward trend was observed, reaching over 700 tons in 2001.

Significant differences were found between statistics of the Fisheries' Administration and those published by the National Institute of Statistics and Applied Economy (INSAE). These discrepancies are the result of shrimp sales on the regional market, which are not within the control of border customs

139 Union Européenne- Afrique de l'Ouest 2002, p16.

checkpoints. However, European statistics also recorded the export of 607.7 tons of shrimps in 2001.[140]

The following table shows the evolution of shrimp exports from 1994 to 2001.

Table 2.3. Evolution of shrimp exports in Benin (quantities)

Year	1996	1997	1998	1999	2000	2001	Total
Shrimp exports (tons)	312	250	453	306	456.2	733.12	2510.32

Source: Fishery Directorate

The next table summarises the evolution of fish production in Benin from 2002 to 2008.

Table 2.4. Evolution of the halieutic production in Benin – Quantity

Year	Fish production (tons)
2002	40,670.48
2003	41,617.62
2004	40,077.09
2005	38,696.88
2006	39,614.00
2007	36,386.42
2008	37,494.58
Total	274,557.07

Source: Fishery Directorate

The following table represents the value of Benin shrimp exports from 1999 to 2003.

Table 2.5. Evolution of halieutic production in Benin – FOB Value (XOF)

Year	1999	2000	2001	2002	2003
Frozen shrimps	557,747,980	1,062,804,768	1,933,233,708	2,151,554,625	1,082,552,930

Source: INSAE/DSEE/SEC of 23/08/04

This data confirms the hypothesis that the national production of fishery products in general was not strongly affected by the voluntary suspension. Only the shrimp export industry was adversely affected by the consequences of non-compliance.

[140] Commission Européenne 2003, p5.

2.4.3. IMPACT OF THE 'CRISIS'

Studies estimate that more than 60,000 people suddenly lost their jobs and, at the same time, they emphasise the development of parallel sale channels, focusing on the supply of more shrimps to domestic markets.[141] It therefore appears necessary to present the issue from a different perspective. In effect, while the local market absorbed quantities usually delivered to the processing plants, it would be wrong to dwell upon the direct impact on fishing communities in terms of job loss. Considering that the overall fish production did not decline significantly, data suggests that fishermen found alternative ways to maintain their activity despite the suspension of shrimp exports.

However, it is undeniable that the export suspension resulted in unemployment for collectors and the employees of shrimp processing plants. It remains also true that the crisis generated huge losses for processing plants and financial institutions. As previously described, despite substantial investments, processing plants are still unable to carry on their activities. However, if national and international experts' reports strongly emphasise the difficulties faced by processing plants and the losses they incurred, there is little interest in the consequences for financial institutions, which suddenly had bad debts in their portfolios.

As for the economy, reports have always depicted the vulnerability and the slowdown in growth over the period 2000–2006 as a result of the dependence on cotton and re-exports to Nigeria.[142] However, no correlation was established between that slowdown and the suspension of shrimp exports in 2003 and its ongoing consequences. Could this suspension be an aggravating factor or a negligible one? Nevertheless, this adds credence to theories that fisheries have a marginal impact in the countries of sub-Saharan Africa. Even at the national level, no one has ever linked the decline in growth to the effects of the sudden interruption of the shrimp industry.

In any case, real potentialities exist to enable the export sector to collect more shrimps for processing, due to the large quantities sold on local and regional markets. Redirecting more shrimps to the processing sector is of particular interest, because individual retailers run the domestic food chain and escape control by the public administrations. Therefore their activity is considered to be in the informal sector and does not enable government tax collection. Similarly, no tax is levied on quantities conveyed to the regional market because these transactions are not carried out within a well-organised supply chain. In this way, shrimps exported to neighbouring countries also escape governmental

141 PASP 2007, p6.

142 WTO, Trade Policy Review, Report by Benin, Burkina Faso and Mali, Annex 1 Benin 2010, p77.

oversight. It follows that the revival of the shrimp export industry could have both social and economic benefits for stakeholders.

Considering these prospects, the government, professional organisations and processors are all mobilised to find appropriate solutions to overcome the "crisis". Studies were carried out and diverse very optimistic scenarios were envisaged for the revival of the processing plants' activities. The initial idea consisted of finding the best ways possible to restructure the processing plants' debts and re-establish their financing. The plans also take into account the seasonality of the activity, and consider the introduction of additional activities to enable the use of the full business potential. Funding by the government and/or international financial backers is envisaged as the ultimate solution to end the "crisis", given that local banks lost confidence in all three companies due to their failure to pay off the loans that they received before the suspension of exports. To reinforce donors' funding plans, the additional scenario would be a partial discharge of debts by the banks.[143]

2.5. INSPECTION MISSIONS IN BENIN AND THEIR FINDINGS

2.5.1. FIRST MISSION: EXAMINATION OF THE SYSTEM OF SHRIMP PRODUCTION

The 2002 inspection, which was carried out as part of the schedule of missions of the FVO, was the first of its kind in the area of fishery products in Benin. This inspection followed the registration of Benin for the import of fishery products on 30 June 1998 on part II of the list annexed to Decision 97/296/EC, after a documentary assessment of the application for approval sent to the Commission. The FVO mission was intended to evaluate the equivalence of the legislation of Benin with corresponding Community requirements and performance of national authorities for the control of conditions of production and export of fishery products to the EU.[144] To this end, all sectors were scrutinised, from the natural environment to processing plants, as well as the competent authority and laboratories. Various deficiencies were pointed out at each level.

At first glance, the highlighted dysfunctions referred to the legislation, as law is the support of all actions and responsibilities of all actors involved in the food chain. The seven statutory instruments relating to fishery products were then mere drafts and lacked certain basic requirements such as setting maximum

143 Reforms following the crisis are explained in chapter V.
144 Commission Européenne 2003, p4.

limits for contaminants in the natural environment[145], limits for histamine[146] and additives used in foodstuffs, especially sulphites, the list of materials authorised to come into contact with food, permitted cleaning and disinfection products, and the list of authorised cleaning and disinfection products. It follows that essential analyses for these elements were not carried out. This situation increased risks related to the natural environment of shrimp, in this case inland waters that are partly stagnant and potentially contaminated by sewage from riparian cities sewage and upstream cultures. However, it was stressed that the annual microbiological water analysis is sufficient, while no results of a physico-chemical analysis were provided to the inspection team.

These failures led the FVO inspection team to conclude that the Competent Authority (CA) for fishery products in Benin had no legal basis to set up a monitoring system to ensure and certify the export of products conform with EU requirements.[147] The FVO report further mentioned that harvested shrimps were landed in and transported inappropriately in wooden canoes. This practice presented substantial product contamination risks, which were aggravated by the lack of a microbiological analysis of fresh shrimps. Furthermore, the report pointed to the lack of a list or map of fishing grounds. The lack of hygienic conditions was even worsened since the required organoleptic tests were not being carried out on all landed grounds. Transporting products to processing plants also suffered from some breaches. The network of collectors was not well-organised and failed to maintain the cold chain properly.

Given all these factors, fresh shrimps delivered to processing plants were considered not to be free from contamination. The FVO inspection team revealed in its report that some of the analyses showed that there was significant bacterial contamination. To overcome this issue, processing plants resorted to questionable methods, such as the use of chlorine not suitable for food products and the use of additives in an uncontrolled manner. Moreover, although all processing plants were equipped with HACCP manuals, their HACCP plans were neither complete, nor applied.

As regards premises, processing plants were structurally acceptable, but some issues were underlined about their equipment. Due to their structure, most equipment could not be properly cleaned and were therefore very dirty and covered with rust spots. In general, the condition of certain materials such as

---

145 Contaminants of the natural environment referred more specifically to heavy metals (mercury, lead and cadmium) and organohalogen substances, mainly pesticides.

146 The FVO report had then specified that the definition of maximum limits for histamine was not necessary given that Benin did not export any fish belonging to the Scombridae, Clupeidae, Engraulidae and Coryphaenida families. Therefore, as long as that would remain the case, it would not be necessary to investigate the rate of histamine.

147 Commission Européenne 2003, p6.

bulbs or ceilings did not meet the minimum hygiene conditions or left room for easy contamination.

As far as the CA was concerned, deficiencies were highlighted in the evaluation and approval of HACCP plans. Likewise, there was no record of inspections carried out in the processing plants. Consequently, there was no real basis for the approval and renewal of licenses given to processing plants.

Finally, with regard to the end product, no residue research was performed despite their heavy use in processing plants. In this regard, microbiological testing was conducted with sufficient frequency but, if the microbiological testing revealed negative results, no documented corrective actions were found to have occurred.

Lastly, the laboratories were not accredited or approved or did not belong to networks of laboratories with which comparative tests could be carried out. There was no laboratory capable of performing physico-chemical analyses of the shrimp and water. Yet, existing laboratories had adequate equipment and appropriate testing materials.

Despite all these aspects, the inspection team noted the great efforts being made by Benin's CA to make the official control system of Benin equivalent to EU requirements. However, it had to conclude that Benin was then unable to guarantee and certify the compliance of products exported to the EU with the requirements of Directive 91/493/EEC concerning the production and placing on the market of fishery products.[148]

At the end of the mission, recommendations were addressed to correct the deficiencies identified in the process of the production and control of fishery products intended for export to the EU. In this regard, draft regulations on fishery products had to be adopted, published and sent to the EU Commission, taking into account the omitted information mentioned. Recommendations were also made to improve or correct each shortcoming revealed during the FVO inspection.

Beninese authorities responded immediately by establishing an array of corrective measures aiming to serve as a guarantee that the FVO recommendations would be addressed effectively. This action plan was presented as a timeline that specified, for most recommendations, the corrective actions planned and the actors in charge of their implementation.

In the same logic, an application for funding was sent to the EU Commission within the framework of a project entitled "Improving the health of fishery products in Benin", which would undertake some corrective measures of the action plan.

Overall, the report of the FVO inspection team was not really helpful to Benin. However, one may refer to some of the positive points from the report that could substantiate the claim that administrative authorities and those in

[148] Commission Européenne 2003, p9.

charge of processing plants were not completely unaware of the need to put safe food on the market. For example, the existence of HACCP plans in all three processing plants was a rather positive fact. Similarly, the CA had a guide of inspection practices which they brought to the attention of control inspectors and laboratories. Even if the guide was not applied, it had the merit of describing the ideal manner for carrying out control tasks. Finally, governmental authorities realised, well before the FVO inspection, the necessity of revising their food safety laws and had already begun updating more accurate drafts that were submitted for consideration to FVO inspectors.

Notwithstanding the recommendations and Benin's subsequent action plans, FVO inspectors suggested to the EU Commission to "consider the need to take protective measures proportional to the deficiencies identified". This did not exclude that guarantees provided by Benin's CA would be evaluated later, with the understanding that their positive assessment would result in a new FVO inspection.

In any case, the guarantee measures immediately suggested by Benin's authorities were considered insufficient to overcome the identified weaknesses. A few months later, in August 2003, Benin decided to temporarily suspend all shrimp exports to the EU to improve the production and certification conditions of shrimp somewhat. This measure was taken in response to an injunction of DG SANCO, allowing Benin to avoid an official EU ban.[149] This voluntary moratorium on shrimp exports was maintained for 18 months. Meanwhile, processing plants were urged to destroy all stocks still in their possession. 189 tons of shrimps, valued at 700 million XOF francs, equivalent to more than one million euro, were destroyed early 2005. After this last step, the EU gave approval to Benin in February 2005 for the export of fishery products to the EU.

Given the consequences of the suspension and the destruction of stocks, processing plants were not able to benefit from the measure ending the suspension. Exports were never really revived. While 175 tons of shrimp were nevertheless exported in 2005, exports fell to 32 tons in 2006. The following years were not more successful with respectively 54.6 and 6.2 tons exported in 2007 and 2008.

Table 2.6. Evolution of shrimp exports to the EU from 2002 to 2008

Year	2002	2003	2004	2005	2006	2007	2008	Total
Shrimp exports (tons)	680.45	366.91	0	175	32	54.6	6.2	1315.16

Source: Fishery Directorate/Commission Européenne 2003

149 Blanc 2003, p10.

Figure 2.2. Evolution of Benin's shrimp exports from 1996 to 2010

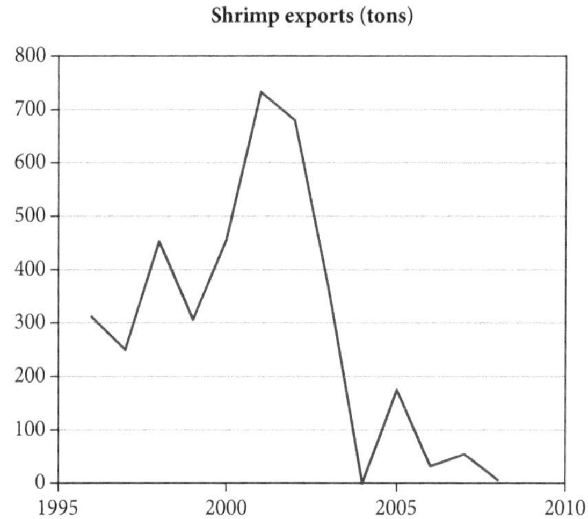

Despite the decrease in exported quantities, alerts were raised about Benin's shrimps within the framework of the RASFF. These notifications, three in 2005 and one in 2006, were all about excessive rates of sulphite in frozen whole raw shrimps. Paradoxically, no such problems were raised earlier when production conditions were assumed to be much worse. However, one could infer that the notification of these undesirable substances was the result of tighter EU controls and the improvement of control methods. In any case, neither Benin nor the EU decided on a further suspension until the second FVO inspection in 2009.

2.5.2. SECOND MISSION: ASSESSMENT OF THE IMPLEMENTATION OF UPGRADING MEASURES

The second FVO mission in 2009 also aimed to assess whether official controls by Benin's CA could ensure that the production and certification conditions for fishery products were equivalent to EU requirements. This second FVO mission acknowledged significant improvements in the sector since the previous mission in 2002.

Overall, the inspection team reported that the Beninese legislation could be considered equivalent to EU requirements, although some texts were not yet published in the Official Journal. Efforts were made to train the staff of the CA, which had been sufficiently reinforced to implement the necessary controls. The CA established documented control procedures for the registration and approval of establishments.

However, the fact remains that deficiencies were also detected in the new production and certification system. Prior to the processing, although a census was carried out with regard to fishermen, there was no system to prevent unregistered fishermen from also supplying shrimps to collectors. This raised doubts about the origin and safety of processing plants' supplies. Furthermore, poor sanitation persisted at landing sites, even though they are considered compulsory unloading facilities for fresh shrimps.

As regards the CA, controls were not regularly and sufficiently carried out in accordance with their schedule and following the rules designed for this purpose in the intern manual of inspection. The control system itself did not enable the CA to certify all entries listed in the health certificate. This deficiency also raised concerns in several respects. Firstly, only four companies were expected to be active in the sector and, therefore, failure to ensure the proper implementation of a control schedule could not be blamed on an excessive workload, even though this argument should also not be used as an excuse to neglect food safety. For this reason, the insufficiency of controls reflected either an apparent inability to establish a well-organised monitoring system or a serious lack of will to perform the tasks required in the control procedure. Secondly, some important tests were not carried out, such as the analysis of water and ice used in shrimp processing plants and the control of the sulphite content of baths used for dipping shrimps. In principle, performing these tests should have called for greater care because of the sensitivity of this issue, resulting from the first FVO's mission and the RASFF alerts afterwards involving Benin shrimps.

By contrast, the FVO report revealed a poor transcription of analysis results and disorganised practices as to the use of control documents including the Base of Compulsory Check and the Platform of Transfer.[150] As a result, the control system was considered not to be equivalent to the relevant part of EU food law, in particular the first chapter of Annex III of Regulation 854/2004.

Moreover, due to the inactivity of processing plants, the CA's inspectors did not identify obvious deficiencies in their control system. For example, FVO inspectors could notice shortcomings in the implementation of HACCP plans, poor knowledge of conditions of use of preservatives or additives, and hygienic handling defects. The FVO inspection team also noted that procedures did not provide for the suspension of approval for establishments out of business, violating Article 12 of EU Regulation 854/2004. Given all these weaknesses, the functioning of factories was also deemed not to be equivalent to relevant rules of EU law.[151]

In conclusion, FVO inspectors found that one could not consider that the organisation of the CA and the implementation of national provisions on which

150 These infrastructures were developed within the framework of measures put in place by Benin to comply with new standards. The role of these infrastructures will be explained in the chapter V.

151 Regulation 853/2004, Annex III, Section VIII, Chapter III; Regulation 852/2004, Article 5.

the control of fishery products intended for export to the EU is based were at least equivalent to EU requirements.[152]

2.6. CONCLUSION

Benin's economic indicators are not very favourable. Agriculture is essential for subsistence and the country relies heavily on imports. Moreover, assistance from donors is crucial to undertake important reforms. This has an important impact on life in general, but it is also decisive for policymaking, due to the Benin's inability to allocate substantial resources to specific areas which do not address priority issues. While the shrimp export sector contributes to employment, foreign exchange earnings and tax collection, the regulation and control of the sector by State departments was found deficient by the EU, the only export market. Severe deficiencies highlighted in 2002 casted some doubt on the ability of the country to provide safe shrimps. It appeared therefore of major importance to undertake both legal and institutional reforms to ensure the sustainability of the shrimp export sector.

152 Commission Européenne 2009, p15.

CHAPTER III
FOOD SAFETY REGULATION IN THE EUROPEAN UNION

3.1. INTRODUCTION

Market access for goods refers to the conditions, tariff and non-tariff measures, agreed by WTO Members for the entry of specific goods into their markets.[153] Within the European Union (EU), market access conditions evolved following the needs that arose for the creation of an internal market. Numerous reforms, at structural, institutional as well as legal levels, were carried out. Both at the level of the Member States and in their relations with third countries, market access conditions have been strictly connected to the creation of the common market and the mechanisms set up for its completion. The implementation of EU policies is oriented towards the fulfilment of the famous 'four freedoms', namely the free movement of goods, persons, services, and capital.[154] Economic purposes were primarily at the forefront of policymaking.

Health and safety regulations have evolved on two fronts, being part of both an internal market development policy and a consumer protection policy.[155] With the passing of time, problems inherent to the functioning of the common market and social factors gradually introduced other priorities in the definition of policies. Differences existing in legislation at the level of Member States began to act as trade barriers, threatening the smooth functioning of the common market and its completion. Consequently, food sector regulation was developed in conjunction with the efforts to eliminate trade barriers arising from different domestic legislation in order to establish a unified market.[156] In the same way, food safety matters, which up until then appeared in Community law on an accidental and infrequent basis[157], began to receive more attention due to the

153 WTO 2012, Market Access Conditions for Non-Agricultural Goods, p1.

154 Treaty of Rome, Article 3. The free movement of goods was previously laid down in Article 3(1)(c) and Articles 23–31 EC Treaty. Currently, see Articles 28–37 of the Treaty on the Functioning of the European Union (TFEU).

155 Vos 1999, p11.

156 Alemanno 2006, p1.

157 Broberg 2009, p4.

increased awareness of food consumption risks by the general public and the rising interest consumers showed accordingly in food safety regulation.

Moreover, diverse food crises in the 1990s disrupted this trend and showed that food safety policies could no longer be considered measures that are secondary to policies aiming at the realisation of the common market. As a result, the Community became aware that to regulate the food sector only through the economic lens of the internal market would be inadequate to address the new challenges brought by the rather new perception of risk.[158] Most importantly, the experience acquired from the food crises allowed the main deficiencies of the food safety control system to be identified. These deficiencies included the lack of a common approach to food safety, contradictory opinions of the Commission's scientific committees and national agencies, vagueness in certain Member States to take precautionary food safety measures, and a failure to manage communication appropriately.[159] These diverse parameters were at the origin of the current EU food legislation, which is designed to guarantee a harmonised legal framework throughout the food supply chain and across the EU as a whole. Based upon a risk-based approach, the EU's legislation promotes comprehensive and transparent policies and offers the advantage to be coherently applicable to all types of food, whether the latter are domestic or foreign products.

From another perspective, the creation of a commercial bloc had an influence on the implementation of the Community's external trade policy. As such, public health and consumer protection policies could not be restricted to the limits of the Community. Therefore, policymaking also aimed at ensuring that products coming from third countries could comply with the Community's policy, so as to provide the same level of protection. In this regard, international trade rules were also considered in the Community's policymaking to avoid discrimination. Furthermore, thanks to its position in world trade, the Community could exert powerful leverage with its trade policy.[160] In this way, particular relations were developed with certain developing countries whereby, over the course of history, these relations influenced Community policymaking.

This chapter aims at outlining the evolution of EU food safety legislation and identifying its influence on access to the EU market. This will make it possible specifically to highlight the impact of the successive changes in the trade relations with third countries. The second section (3.2) presents the creation of the single market, its policy implications, the difficulties encountered to eliminate trade barriers, and the consequences on policymaking, as well as the international dimension of EU policymaking. The third section (3.3) underlines how food safety became a priority in the EU's

158 Alemanno 2006, p1.

159 Marre 2001, p65.

160 Brown 2005, p2.

political agenda and how the policies the EU were adopted to attain a high level of public health and consumer protection with regard to both EU products and imported products. The fourth (3.4) section presents the current EU food safety framework. The fifth section (3.5) explains EU mechanisms to enforce its food law with regard to third countries. The last section (3.6) provides some concluding remarks.

3.2. EUROPEAN FOOD LAW: BETWEEN THE SINGLE MARKET AND THE INTERNATIONAL MARKET

The establishment of the common market and reforms necessary for its completion led the Community to a gradual and increased involvement in food safety regulation. The first attempts consisted in harmonising food standards and were primarily implemented for the facilitation of the free movement of goods. Further developments revealed the need to make adjustments to the different approaches of harmonisation by using principles like the mutual recognition principle and adopting control policies on sensitive products such as products of animal origin. Despite all the instruments implemented within the Community, trade barriers continued to exist and were exacerbated by the dioxin crisis in 1999. These aspects were the precursors of the current EU food law, which is an innovative approach to the development of a clear and coherent policy based on the principles arising from the White Paper on Food Safety.

The table below gives an overview of the treaties mentioned in this chapter.

Table 3.1. List of treaties relevant to the development of EU food law[161]

Signature	Entry into force	Title	Comments
25 March 1957	1 January 1958	Treaty of Rome or Treaty establishing the European Economic Community (TEEC)	The Treaty of Rome established the European Economic Community (EEC). The main objective of the Treaty was the creation of a single European economic area based on a common market. Article 2 of the TEEC laid down that "the Community shall have as its task, by establishing a common market and progressively approximating the economic policies of Member States, to promote throughout the Community a harmonious development of economic activities, a continuous and balanced expansion, an increase in stability, an accelerated raising of the standard of living and closer relations between the States belonging to it".
17 February 1986	1 July 1987	Single European Act (SEA)	The SEA is the first major amendment to the Treaty of Rome. The objective was to establish the internal market by 31 December 1992. The internal market is now set out in Article 26(2) TFEU as "an area without internal frontiers in which the free movement of goods, persons, services and capital is ensured in accordance with the provisions of the Treaties". No explicit reference to public health or consumer protection was made in the Treaty of Rome until the adoption of the SEA in 1986 and the subsequent adoption of the Treaty of Maastricht in 1992.[162]
7 February 1992	1 November 1993	Treaty of Maastricht or Treaty on European Union (TEU)	With the entry into force of the Treaty of Maastricht, the EEC was renamed the European Community (EC). This treaty also established the European Union. The main goals of the treaty were to strengthen the democratic legitimacy of the institutions, improve their effectiveness, establish economic and monetary union, develop the Community social dimension, and establish a common foreign and security policy.

161 Other treaties such as the Treaty of Amsterdam (1997) and the Treaty of Nice (2001) are not mentioned in this table because they were not relevant for the analysis in this section.

162 Alemanno 2006, p3.

Signature	Entry into force	Title	Comments
			The Treaty of Maastricht established consumer protection as an essential mission in regulatory decision making. In this regard, the Community was urged to take specific actions, which support and supplement the policies pursued by Member States in order to protect consumers' health, safety and economic interests, and to provide consumers with adequate health information.
13 December 2007	1 December 2009	Treaty of Lisbon	The Treaty of Lisbon created two new treaties to replace the previous framework, namely the Treaty on European Union and the Treaty on the Functioning of the European Union (TFEU). While the TEU sets out a number of policies such as the mission and values of the EU, the democratic principles of the Union, the composition and central functions of the EU institutions, the TFEU sets out the explicit competences of the Union and, with the exception of external action, the detailed procedures to be used in each policy field. In legislative style, the TFEU is similar to the existing EC Treaty[163].

3.2.1. THE TREATY OF ROME: ESTABLISHMENT OF THE COMMON MARKET AND ACCESS CONDITIONS

The Treaty of Rome[164] was signed in 1957 with the objective to create a 'United Europe' and is the original agreement that established the EEC. It pursued objectives oriented towards the economic development of its Member States. The Treaty of Rome intended to cover a rather broad range of measures, including social and agricultural initiatives. The fundamental goal was clearly the creation of a common market that would provide Member States with economic gains resulting from the free movement of goods.[165] The Treaty of Rome clearly sets the realisation of the "four freedoms" within Member States as the central pillars for the combination of their respective efforts. In this respect, the free movement of goods, services, persons, and capital governed the adoption and the coordination of common policies, as well as governmental action to complete the common market according to the original vision.

163 For more details, see Chalmers et al. 2010, p38–39.

164 Treaty establishing the European Economic Community, EEC Treaty of 25/03/1957, not published in the Official Journal.

165 Ex Article 3(1)(c) and Articles 23–31 TEC. Currently, Articles 28–37 TFEU.

The general architecture of the Treaty of Rome underlined a cooperation which would result in the creation of a space without internal trade barriers. Therefore, all physical, technical and fiscal barriers that would be likely to create discriminatory restrictions between Member States were prohibited. Physical trade barriers consist of stopping and checking mechanisms set up to supervise goods moving from one territory to another. Fiscal barriers constitute all tariffs or other indirect taxes imposed on exports, imports or goods in transit. As for technical barriers, they represent all quantitative restrictions or measures having an equivalent effect which impede the free movement of goods.

The expansion of the intra-Community trade was more directed at the elimination of quantitative restrictions and customs duties[166] than the suppression of non-tariff barriers to trade. While Free Trade Agreements (FTA) and Customs Unions (CU) focus solely on the free movement of products, a common market enables the free movement of production factors as well as goods. In this respect, the free movement of goods is only one of the EC's objectives for achieving the creation of an internal market.[167] Hence, a good coordination of various provisions was necessary to ensure a suitable integration of the diverse instruments.

To reach this level of integration, a twofold system was developed. First, there were negative integration rules, which include a set of prohibitions aimed at eliminating a number of impediments to the proper operation of an integrated area, such as the common market. Secondly, positive integration measures were adopted to enable the creation of new policies.[168]

Negative integration rules were mainly adopted within the meaning of Article 28 TEC[169], and prohibited quantitative restrictions on imports and all measures having equivalent effect between Member States. The free movement of goods promoted on these grounds aimed at the elimination of all kinds of trade restrictions dealing with goods produced by Member States, but it also left room for the free movement of goods imported from third countries. Imported products benefited therefore from the creation of a Customs Union, which was linked with the creation of one external customs frontier that created the same conditions all along the common external border for the entry of goods from the world outside the borders of the Customs Union.[170] In this regard, once third countries' goods were imported into a Member State's territory, these products should enjoy the free movement provisions and were subject to the common external customs duties.[171] Moreover, these imported goods should be allowed to circulate freely within the Community without the payment of any further customs duties.

166 Ex Articles 28–31 TEC, now Articles 34–37 TFEU.
167 Alemanno 2007, p 35.
168 Idem.
169 Now, Article 34 TFEU.
170 Van der Meulen & van der Velde 2008, p217.
171 Ex Article 23 TEC, now Article 28 TFEU.

Member States were allowed to maintain national measures that could impede trade for several reasons, which were laid down as exceptions[172] to the principle of free movement of goods. The protection of health and life of human, animals or plants could be a valid exception to free trade as long as it did not constitute a means of arbitrary discrimination or a disguised restriction on trade between Member States. The other exceptions laid down referred to public morality, public policy or public security; the protection of national treasures possessing artistic, historic or archaeological value; or the protection of industrial and commercial property.

Positive integration rules were developed to neutralise the effects of disparities in national legislation. The active cooperation of each Member State was required to adopt measures at the national level aiming at the proper functioning of the common market while the Commission would 'contribute' to the attainment of a high level of health protection and the strengthening of consumer protection.[173] As stated by Article 152 TEC[174], the main concern for the implementation of the Community's contribution to public health would target the scourges of that time such as drug consumption. Therefore, food safety did not occupy a prominent place. However, the Community did not define the main specifications of a consistent policy. Therefore, the Community conferred full authority on the Member States to legislate on food safety and to take measures they deem appropriate to protect their own consumers. Since such measures could constitute legitimate obstacles to trade, the only way to remove trade barriers was through 'positive integration' by Community legislation. The Community's harmonisation activities in this and other fields tended to blur the traditionally strict distinction between 'negative' and 'positive' integration. By harmonising the health and safety aspects of products, the Community intended to eliminate trade barriers (i.e. negative integration), while at the same time positively contributing to the development of a policy to protect consumers' health and safety (i.e. positive integration).[175]

3.2.2. FAILURE OF POLICY IMPLEMENTATION

a. *Emergence of trade barriers within the Community*

In its earliest years, the Community's policymaking consisted of harmonising national foodstuffs legislation in order to realise the free movement of goods. For the attainment of harmonisation, two approaches were adopted: horizontal

172 Ex Article 30 TEC, now Article 36 TFEU.
173 Ex Articles 152–153 TEC, now Articles 168–169 TFEU.
174 Now Article 168 TFEU.
175 Vos 1999, p19.

harmonisation covered all types of foodstuffs, while vertical harmonisation enabled the Commission to define detailed specifications for a specific type of foodstuff. The failure to harmonise national legislation gave acute evidence that trade obstacles continued to exist within the Community and led to increased product quality and identity policies. From this perspective, and inspired by its General Programme for the Elimination of Technical Barriers to Trade, the 'traditional approach' to harmonisation was launched. The implementation of the 'traditional approach' was to be done by the Commission through vertical legislation. This measure is certainly at the origin of 'recipe law' and directives laying down compositional and technical standards for individual products. The first product affected by this approach was chocolate.[176] The 'recipe laws', adopted according to the traditional approach, laid down detailed specifications for all European-made foodstuffs.[177] For example, Directive 73/437/EEC[178] was designed to lay down definitions and common rules on the manufacturing characteristics, packaging and labelling of certain sugars intended for human consumption to ensure their free movement within the Community. Likewise, Directive 74/409/EEC[179] provided definitions and rules for honey offered for sale.

Unlike these types of measures, which referred exclusively to a specific product or category of products, positive harmonisation was used to set up similar standards in all Member States. Positive harmonisation therefore applied to all food.

By the virtue of the traditional approach, specific Member State products should have the same technical specifications. Very detailed directives were issued aiming at describing individual requirements for each product category. In principle, every national product needed a Community measure to ensure the free circulation of goods.[180]

Given the limited success of this approach, it was supplemented in 1973 by the 'Industrial Policy Programme'[181], which fixed a new timetable for the removal of technical barriers to trade in foodstuffs. Several categories of foodstuffs were identified and the Commission was required to submit relevant proposals accordingly. To take but one example, concerning fish and fish products, the proposals had to be adopted by the Council by 1 January 1978.[182]

176 Council Directive 73/241/EEC, 1973 OJ L 228/23 replaced by Directive 2000/36.
177 Alemanno 2007, p53.
178 Council Directive 73/437/EEC on the approximation of the laws of the Member States concerning certain sugars intended for human consumption.
179 Council Directive 74/409/EEC on the harmonization of the laws of the Member States relating to honey.
180 Alemanno 2007, p51.
181 Council Resolution of 17 December 1973 on industrial policy.
182 EEC Treaty, Annex I, timetable for the removal of technical barriers to trade in foodstuffs.

However, harmonisation efforts were not as successful as expected for several reasons. The first difficulty resulted from the decision-making process, which required unanimity to harmonise laws at the regional level.[183] Although all Member States agreed on the desirability of a free market unimpeded by national borders, in practice the tendency remained for each country to protect its own markets and enterprises, wherever and however possible, and to trust the judgments of its own institutions. Consequently, Member States gave priority to their own laws and standards before applying the laws of the Community or other Member States.[184]

Furthermore, culinary cultures and traditions, combined with Member States' national administrative traditions, contributed to the failure of the harmonisation of laws through the traditional approach. Lastly, in the absence of Community harmonisation as regards a certain product, Member States were, in principle, at liberty to choose the level of public health protection they deemed appropriate in their own territory. As a result, several cases of trade obstacles existed within the Community, impeding the completion of the internal market and its functioning.

The European Court of Justice (ECJ) played a decisive role in the resolution of trade disputes generated by interpretation difficulties in relation to Articles 28 and 30 TEC.[185] As already stated, Article 28 prescribed the elimination of quantitative restrictions on imports and measures having equivalent effect, whereas Article 30 defined the exceptions.

As regards food law, the most noteworthy of the ECJ's rulings is the *Cassis de Dijon* ruling[186] for two main reasons. First, the *Cassis de Dijon* ruling introduced a change in the perception of the benefits of harmonisation. After this ruling, the emphasis shifted from harmonisation as a condition for the functioning of the common internal market to the need to alleviate the consequences of the common internal market.[187] In legal terms, the emphasis shifted from product-specific, vertical (recipe) legislation, to horizontal legislation, meaning general rules addressing common aspects for all foodstuffs, or at least as many foodstuffs as possible.[188]

Secondly, this ruling established the well-known principle of mutual recognition. According to the latter, goods, which are lawfully produced in one Member State, cannot be banned from sale on the territory of another

183 The first step in the Community's food law harmonisation was taken by Council Directive on the approximation of the rules of Member States concerning the colouring matters authorized for use in foodstuffs intended for human consumption.

184 Van der Meulen & van der Velde 2008, p230.

185 Now Articles 34 and 36 TFEU.

186 EC Court of Justice 20/02/1979, Case 120/78, *Rewe-Zentrale AG v Bundesmonopolverwaltung fur Brantwein (Cassis de Dijon)*, ECR 1979, p649.

187 Meulen (van der) & Velde (van der) 2008, p235.

188 Idem.

Member State, even if these goods are produced according to technical or quality specifications different from those applied to its own products.[189] Only general interest objectives, such as health or consumer protection, can limit, under strict conditions, the application of the mutual recognition principle.

In its communication on the completion of the internal market[190], the Commission confirmed the need expressed in the White Paper on the completion of the internal market to abandon its commitment to harmonise quality specifications such as rules relating to the composition or manufacture of food. Therefore, it recommended a new strategy combining the principles of mutual recognition and a more efficient mechanism for the harmonisation of laws. Community food legislation would be limited to the harmonisation of national rules justifiable on the grounds of mandatory requirements identified by the Court of Justice, such as the protection of public health and other consumer interests (information) and fair-trading practices and the necessity to implement official controls. The Commission emphasised that, through the mutual recognition principle, harmonisation could be achieved through reinforcing labelling rules to guarantee consumer information and fair-trading. Industries were encouraged to develop quality policies based on the use of voluntary instruments.

Box 3-1. Overview of the Court of Justice of the European Union

The Court of Justice of the European Union was established in 1952 as the judicial authority of the EU. In cooperation with the courts and tribunals of the Member States, the Court of Justice of the European Union ensures the uniform application and interpretation of European Union law. As such, it reviews the legality of the acts of the institutions of the European Union, ensures that the Member States comply with obligations under the Treaties, and interprets European Union law at the request of the national courts and tribunals. The Court of Justice of the European Union also settles legal disputes between EU governments and EU institutions. Individuals, companies or organisations can also bring cases before the Court if they feel their rights have been infringed by an EU institution (Articles 267–275 TFEU). Decisions of national courts cannot be appealed to the Court of Justice.

Actions brought before the Court of Justice of the European Union shall not have suspensory effect, unless otherwise decided by the Court (Article 278 TFEU). Enforcement of the Court's judgments shall be governed by the rules of civil procedure in force in the State in the territory of which it is carried out. The order for its enforcement shall be appended to the decision, without other formality than verification of the authenticity of the decision, by the national authority which the government of each Member State shall designate for this purpose and shall make known to the Commission and to the Court of Justice of the European Union. Furthermore, enforcement may be suspended only by a decision of the Court. However, the courts of the country concerned shall have jurisdiction over complaints that enforcement is being carried out in an irregular manner (Articles 280, 299 TFEU).

189 Commission of European Communities, COM(1999) 299 final.

190 Communication of the European Commission on the Completion of the internal market: Community legislation on foodstuffs (COM (85) 603 final.

3.2.3. ATTEMPTS TO ELIMINATE TRADE BARRIERS: THE NEW APPROACH TO TECHNICAL HARMONISATION AND STANDARDS

The traditional approach to harmonisation, which requires the compliance of specific products with the same technical specifications across Member States, had mixed success. The failure of this traditional approach caused the Commission to launch an innovative regulatory strategy called 'the new approach to technical harmonization and standards'.[191] The task of the Commission was no longer to define product specifications but rather to establish directives which would delineate essential requirements for foodstuffs. The related technical specifications were to be defined by European standards bodies (the European Committee for Standardization (CEN) and the European Committee for Electrotechnical Standardization (CENELEC)). These specifications, called harmonised standards, had to reflect as much as possible the compatibility of these standards with the Commission requirements. National authorities had the duty to withdraw every other legislation that could not ensure compliance with the harmonised standards. The 'new approach' constituted a first step in the involvement of market operators in the decision-making process as observed in the current EU food law.

In line with the Community's "new approach to technical harmonization and standards", the Single European Act[192] introduced the requirement for a qualified majority in the legislative process instead of unanimity, paving the way for a smoother harmonisation process.[193]

3.2.4. SPECIFIC COMMON MARKET POLICIES

A range of tools were developed to stimulate the cooperation of Member States such as the Customs Union and the Common Agricultural Policy (CAP). The place of fishery products within the common market policies was to be found in the CAP. Article 32 TEC[194] defined 'agricultural products' as products of the soil, of stock farming and of fisheries, and products of first-stage processing directly

---

191 Council Resolution 85/C 136/01 on a new approach to technical harmonization and standards.

192 The SEA followed the White Paper on the completion of the internal market, which was an attempt to solve the difficulties encountered in the effective implementation of the common market. This White Paper sets out a timetable for the measures necessary for the completion of the single market by 31/12/1992. See Completing the Internal Market: White Paper from the Commission to the European Council, COM(85) 310.

193 Alemanno 2007, p44.

194 Now Article 38 TFEU.

related to these products. The CAP then took fishery products into account before another set of policies was developed to handle the related matters.

Regulations 2141/70 and 2142/70 introduced the first specific measures related to fishery products in 1970. These regulations aimed primarily at creating a common organisation of the market in fishery products, offering structural aid for the modernisation of the sector and guaranteeing, under certain conditions, free access for fishing vessels to all Member States' waters. In 1983, Regulation 170/83 established a regime for the conservation and management of fishery resources. These instruments were not developed for safety concerns. However, measures aiming at ensuring safe fishery products were to be found through the development of the common market and related safety policies.

With regard to trade with third countries, the EU Commission promoted the adoption of a Common Customs Tariff (CCT) and the establishment of a Common Commercial Policy (CCP). As reflected in the CAP, the first commercial provisions of the CCP did not give priority to any food safety measure.

3.2.5. INTERNATIONAL DIMENSION OF THE COMMON MARKET

Regional integration cannot result in autarky with regard to the rest of the world. Aware of that factor, the founders of the EEC adopted the necessary measures to combine the smooth functioning of their internal market with taking an active part in strengthening international trade. In this respect, the Commission was the legal representative of Member States and had to negotiate agreements, on their behalf, with third countries.[195] This international cooperation aimed to ensure the common interests of the Community. Furthermore, by establishing a Customs Union, Member States would contribute to the harmonious development of world trade, the progressive abolition of restrictions on international trade and the lowering of customs barriers.[196]

The global approach of these policies paid particular attention to the specific concerns of developing countries. It thus appeared that trade relations with several Overseas Countries and Territories (OCTs) go as far back as the creation of the EEC. The establishing treaty of the Community had then considered it necessary to take into consideration the OCTs' needs by creating an 'association' with them aiming at promoting their economic and social development and establishing close economic relations between them and the Community as a whole. Such support was intended to be realised through the active participation

195 Article 216 TFEU.

196 Ex Article 131 TEC, now Article 206 TFEU.

of Members States in the investments required for the progressive development of these OCTs, to enable their progressive integration in the world's economy.[197]

In strictly commercial terms, trade relations with OCTs must benefit from the same privilege as applied between Member States. Each country or territory shall apply the same treatment to its trade with Member States and OCTs as that which it applies to the EU Member State with which it has special relations.[198] Customs duties were to be gradually abolished between the two sets of countries. However, OCTs had the possibility of departing from that obligation by levying customs duties whenever their development and industrialisation were at stake.

The relations between the Community and developing countries in Africa were essentially focused on the colonial ties or safeguarding commercial interests developed with certain countries in Europe. The Community intended to formally create a cooperation, which, far from promoting commercial links between peers, rather underlined the weakness of these African countries. Although in essence they were articulated based on free trade principles, these trade relations were mainly based upon an assistance framework directed at growth in the developing countries. The relevant part of the Treaty of Rome was rightly entitled 'Development cooperation'.

The declaration of independence of the majority of these African countries in the 1960s later resulted in extending cooperation on a contractual basis. The subsequent evolution of this cooperation could be reconsidered in the various EU-ACP conventions. The diverse ACP-EU agreements enabled the Community to grant ACP countries different trade concessions in the form of tariff preferences. The outline of these trade concessions were different, from Yaoundé to Cotonou, and even depended on the nature of the country (e.g. developing countries, Least Developed Countries).[199]

The Treaty did not lay down specific provisions as regards products coming from third countries. Therefore, one can easily infer the sovereignty of a particular Member State to decide whether a third country's product could be imported into its territory. As explained above, such an imported product must then benefit from the same privileges as a product of the Member State as regards trade advantages within the Community. As such, the EU market is potentially a very large and lucrative market for third countries. A product exported to a particular Member State's territory would then benefit from the provisions on the free movement of goods and have access to the EU market as a whole.

---

197 Ex Article 182 TEC, now Article 198 TFEU.

198 Ex Articles 183–185 TEC, now Articles 199–201 TFEU.

199 Whether granted under the Generalized System of Preferences (GSP), the Everything but Arms (EBA) initiative, or most recently the Economic Partnership Agreement (EPA), these trade concessions schemes are beyond the scope of this chapter.

3.3. GREATER FOOD SAFETY INVOLVEMENT IN POLICYMAKING

The 1990s witnessed numerous global food crises, which were inflated by the extent of the media attention and the newly-generated fear of outbreaks. Within the EU, the emergence of several food scares, most significantly the Bovine Spongiform Encephalopathy (BSE) crisis in the United Kingdom, has led to a search for a more efficient way to ensure consumer protection. As a result, consumers started to show an increased interest in food safety matters and legislation. Food safety was then propelled to the top of the political agenda, introducing several institutional as well as legal reforms.

3.3.1. GENERAL FOOD SAFETY MEASURES

In 1997, the Commission came up with a green paper on the general principles of food law in the EU.[200] This green paper underlined the general positive impact of the Community's legislative programme in the food sector. However, it also highlighted some concerns about the legislative programme that were raised over the years. First, criticism was expressed of overly detailed legislation, fragmentation, difficulties of adapting the legislation to innovation, and problems in the day-to-day functioning of the internal market. Secondly, events such as the BSE crisis "have raised doubts about the capacity of the legislation to entirely fulfil its objectives to ensure a high level of protection of public health and consumer protection".[201] Therefore, there was a need for a European food policy centred on the requirement that only foodstuffs that are safe, wholesome and fit for consumption must be placed on the market. It was thus important for the Community to align with other developed countries by transitioning from food security towards food safety. Health protection in relation to the consumption of foodstuffs was to be an absolute priority at all times and not only something to be addressed in emergency situations.[202] In this respect, the Commission intended to develop a fully-fledged food policy, which would attach fundamental importance to the protection of the consumer and his/her health.

The food safety approach defined by the Green Paper relied upon risk analysis and underlined the necessity of a regulatory framework covering the entire food chain "from farm-to-fork". The food law had to define clear responsibilities for producers, processors, distributors, retailers, and competent authorities at all stages. While food business operators would be responsible for supplying safe,

---

200 Commission Green Paper on the General Principles of Food Law in the European Union, COM (1997) 176.

201 Green Paper on the General Principles of Food Law in the European Union, p1.

202 Alemanno 2006, p11.

wholesome food fit for human consumption, of specified quality and properly identified, competent authorities had to implement adequate checks to ensure that these operators fulfil their food safety obligations. Likewise, the food law also had to lay down provisions for liability whenever there would be damage to consumer health. For that purpose, due consideration was to be given to scientific evidence and the precautionary principle had to be used in case of uncertainty.[203] Moreover, food policies should be coordinated in order to develop control measures at all critical points throughout the food chain and that should be similarly applied to EU products and imported products.

The responsibilities of the various controlling agents producers, Member States' authorities, Commission services, etc. – as well as the nature of the control – on-site inspection, audit of control systems, etc. – had to be clearly defined. Lastly, the Green Paper emphasised the need to take appropriate measures to ensure that the correct consumer information is available about the nature and content of food.

As regards imported food products, the Community reiterated its firm determination to take into account its international obligations and defined its responsibility as an 'obligation' to ensure that imported foods meet the same high standards as have been laid down for Community productions.

3.3.2. OFFICIAL CONTROL POLICIES

a. *Intra-Community controls*

To enable a better circulation of goods within its Member States, the Community established control mechanisms to guarantee that products comply with the legal provisions. In that spirit, the Community laid down general principles to control food products at all stages of the production.

Control mechanisms had to ensure that products in circulation within the Community offered the required guarantees of protection. The implementation of control policies depended on the nature of the product and the risk for human consumption. Generally speaking, the higher the risk was, the stricter the controls were.

Aware of the remaining difficulties for the completion of the internal market and faithful to its commitment to adopt measures designed to achieve that goal

---

203 The EU definition of the precautionary principle is to be found in a later regulation. The definition is given by the Article 7 of the General Food Law (Regulation 178/2002): "The precautionary principle enables the adoption of provisional risk management measures in specific circumstances where, following an assessment of available information, the possibility of harmful effects on health is identified but scientific uncertainty persists".

before the planned term[204], the Commission found it necessary to take some action aimed at the removal of trade barriers. In this regard, veterinary controls were initiated in intra-Community trade in 1989 by Directive 89/662/EEC.[205] These measures were adopted with the aim to complete the internal market and referred to animals and products of animal origin due to their sensitivity. Therefore, veterinary controls were carried out at physical borders. Confidence in the efficiency of these controls to protect public and animal health could contribute to further facilitating the free movement of goods.

The purpose of Community's checks was to ensure that veterinary checks were carried out only at the place of dispatch. Therefore, Member States were urged "to ensure that products intended for trade were obtained, checked, marked and labelled"[206] in accordance with Community rules for the intended destination. A health certificate, animal health certificate or by any other document provided for by Community veterinary rules had to accompany the products to the final consignee mentioned therein. Particular measures had to be taken to ensure the safety of the products when they had to be carried from one country to another. Even in the case of export to a third country, transport operations had to remain under the supervision of customs, up to the point of exit from the Community territory. These measures were intended to contribute to harmonisation by providing a more predictable safety system across the Member States.

It is worth underlining that responsiveness is a prerequisite for the effective implementation of regulatory measures to ensure food safety in general and particularly the safety of fishery products. This applies at the level of processing plants, at the level of competent authorities, and ultimately at the level of the Commission, which has assigned itself the role of occasionally deploying experts[207] that support national authorities through controls on production sites.

Directive 89/662/EEC established the responsibility of the competent authority of any Member State for carrying out regular checks on processing plants in order to ensure that food products intended for trade would comply with Community requirements. Measures had to be undertaken to ensure that operators comply with veterinary requirements at all stages of production, storage, marketing, and transport.[208] In the same way, in case of doubt,

---

204 The internal market must be progressively established over a period expiring on 31 December 1992.

205 Directive 89/662/EEC of 11 December 1989 concerning veterinary checks in intra-Community trade with a view to the completion of the internal market.

206 It is noteworthy to indicate that multiple community texts were adopted to regulate the issues related to food labelling. For instance, Council Directive 89/107/EEC for food additives; Council Directive 88/344/EEC for extraction solvents; and for flavourings, there are Council Directive 88/388/EEC, Council Decision 88/389/EEC, Regulation (EC) No 2232/96.

207 Directive 91/493/EEC, Article 8.

208 Directive 89/662/EEC, Article 4.

veterinary spot-checks should be performed and, if needed, the competent authority should order the consignments either to be destroyed or diverted towards other purposes in proportion with the risk detected.

b. Controls on imported products

If measures were undertaken to guarantee the circulation of safe products within the Community, it was also crucial to guarantee the same level of protection tin relation to products coming from third countries. In that respect, Member States, for which imports from certain third countries were optional, should inform the Commission and the other Member States of the existence of such imports.[209] These optional imports refer to imports of food of animal origin from certain third countries, authorised by one of the Member States.

Specific measures were established in Article 6 of Directive 89/662/EEC setting up a mandatory documentary check on imported product origins and a certification that these products were sent under customs supervision to Community's inspection posts. A distinction was introduced considering the nature of the product and different measures applied to each category. In this regard, Annex B determined a list of products which were not subject to Community harmonisation, such as fishery products intended for human consumption. Fishery products were a category of products not subject to Community harmonisation but the trade of which would be subjected to veterinary checks as established by the Directive. With the advent of Directive 91/493, the trend was reversed. Fishery products were removed from the list of products for which harmonisation was not a EU requirement and Directive 91/493 became a specific veterinary legislation.[210]

In any event, it emerged that differences could remain in Member States' legislation as regards products not subject to harmonisation. Therefore, a product imported by a Member State had to undergo an additional veterinary check before being sent to the territory of another Member in order to verify its compliance with the legislation of the Member State of destination. In such a context, the intended free movement of goods was somewhat hindered because its effectiveness depended on a wide range of requirements, which were often different from one country to another.

Generally speaking, the basic text on the controls of imported products was Directive 97/78/EC[211], adopted in 1997. Directive 97/78/EC further complemented Directive 90/675/EEC and enabled, in the interest of

209 Directive 89/662/EEC, Article 3.

210 Directive 91/493/EEC, Article 9.

211 Directive 97/78/EC of 18 December 1997 laying down the principles governing the organization of veterinary checks on products entering the Community from third countries. This Directive repealed Directive 90/675/EC, which established that veterinary checks in respect of products from third countries entering the Community shall be carried out by

transparency, the application of harmonised conditions for all products of animal origin imported from third countries. The standardisation and the transparency were made necessary by the differences existing in national legislations of Member States. In this regard, Directive 97/78/EC underlined that, in certain cases, Member States imposed additional requirements on imported products. Therefore, a single checking scheme for imported products should be applied and, when necessary, subsequent adjustments should be made.

The legal framework applicable to food products of animal origin imposed a compulsory veterinary check on all consignments of products at a border inspection post. The competent authority was expected to carry out these veterinary checks under the responsibility of the official veterinarian. Veterinary checks consisted of a documentary check, an identity check and a physical check.[212] These checks could lead to the seizure or destruction of product consignments, according to the threat to health detected, and safeguard measures could be adopted in relation to all or part of the country of origin.

In line with all these reforms, the Community established the Food and Veterinary Office (FVO) in order to achieve effective control systems in food safety and quality and to check the compliance of Member States with Community requirements. The FVO also remains responsible for carrying out inspections in third countries exporting to the EU. As such, this body plays an important role in the decision-making process.

c. *Control on fishery products*

The first specific measures dealing with the control of fishery products were established by Directives 91/492/EEC and 91/493/EEC aiming at defining the health conditions of the production and import of fishery products. The Community aimed to ensure that fishery products from third countries intended to be placed on the Community market would meet Community requirements and would not qualify for more favourable arrangements than those applied in the Community. It was therefore advisable to make sure that Community provisions would be laid down for the inspection in third countries of conditions

Member States. Directive 97/78/EC was amended by Regulation 882/2004 and Directive 2006/104/EC.

212 The definitions of these different types of controls were provided by Article 2: Documentary check means the examination of the veterinary certificate(s) or veterinary document(s), or other document(s) accompanying a consignment; identity check means a check by visual inspection to ensure that the veterinary certificate(s) or veterinary document(s) or other document(s) provided for by veterinary legislation tally with the product itself; physical check means a check on the product itself, which may include checks on packaging and temperature and also sampling and laboratory testing.

of production and placing on the market in order to enable the application of a common import system based on equivalent conditions.

In any case, the most important requirement remained that the provisions applied to imports of fishery products from third countries had to be at least equivalent to the requirements governing the production and the placing on the market of Community products.[213] However, specific conditions were to be set by the Commission after consultation with the Standing Veterinary Committee, after duly considering the health status of the third country concerned. Since this status could differ from one country to another, on-site inspections had to be conducted in third countries to verify their production and certification systems. This step would provide the information necessary to appropriately determine import conditions for products from that particular third country. Import conditions were based on the legislation in force in the third country concerned, the organisation of its competent authority and related inspection services. For this purpose, it was important to assess the ability of the competent authority to implement the necessary controls, the means available to accomplish their mission in a realistic and reliable way, and ultimately the supervision mechanisms to which they were subjected.

The competent authority was expected to provide sufficient guarantees for a number of conditions that could demonstrate the capacity of the production system to provide safe products. Therefore, the competent authority had to show evidence that inspection visits to local establishments and/or fishing vessels were performed to ensure that all necessary measures would be implemented in accordance with their activities. This implied that production establishments and fishing vessels had the required structure to accommodate significant changes in the production process. The competent authority should then be able to objectively evaluate operators and, if the conditions that led to their approval no longer existed, to withdraw their license. In addition, procedures had to exist and be implemented appropriately to carry out any organoleptic checks, any detection of parasitic or chemical contamination, and to highlight that the end product was free of contamination, either from the aquatic environment or microbiologically. Ensuring that processing establishments did comply with regulatory requirements was especially important considering that fishery products freshly caught are presumed to be free of contamination with micro-organisms, whereas contamination or decomposition may occur later as a result of unhygienic handling and treatment.[214] Lastly, the import conditions related to a particular third country product would also be motivated by the actual health conditions during the production, storage and dispatch of fishery products intended for the EU market.

213 Directive 91/493/EEC, Article 10.

214 Directive 91/493/EEC, preamble.

By virtue of Directives 91/492/EEC and 91/493/EEC, controls on third countries' products were strengthened. Other texts had also to be considered as complementing these directives. For example, Council Directive 92/48/EEC defined some hygiene rules related to fishery products. It established that compartments used on board fishing vessels for the storage of fishery products had to be designed in such a way that they could be easily cleaned and could ensure that melted water would not remain in contact with the products. They should not contain any object or product likely to transmit harmful properties or abnormal characteristics to the foodstuffs. These compartments had to be kept clean after use and especially protected from contamination by the fuel used for the propulsion of the vessel or by bilge water. Once caught, the products themselves should be protected from contamination and heat sources and should always be cleaned with fresh water or clean seawater so as to preserve their initial quality and wholesomeness. The products should be protected from bruising. Fishery products should be submitted to cold treatment or stay on board vessels no longer than eight hours after their capture. In cases of the availability of ice cubes, the ice should be made with drinking water or clean seawater. All on-board operations on fresh products such as gutting or heading should be carried out in perfect hygiene conditions, using equipment made of or coated with a waterproof material, resistant to decay, smooth and easy to clean and to disinfect. Finally, staff should be obliged to maintain the highest personal and clothes hygiene.

As a consequence of Directives 91/492/EEC and 91/493/EEC, the Commission started to draw up the lists of third countries from which Member States were authorised to import for each product or category of products. Some of these decisions fixed specific conditions applicable to some particular countries. For example, on the basis that the presence of chloramphenicol was detected in shrimps intended for human consumption and imported from China and Vietnam, and considering that the presence of chloramphenicol in food presents a potential risk for human health, the Commission decided that consignments of shrimps originating in or coming from China and Vietnam should be sampled in order to demonstrate their wholesomeness. These conditions were laid down in Decision 2001/699/EC.[215] Article 2 of this decision stated: "1- Member States shall, using appropriate sampling plans and detection methods, subject each consignment of shrimps originating or coming from China and Vietnam to a chemical test in order to ensure that the products concerned do not present a hazard to human health. This test must be carried out, in particular, with a view to detect the presence of chloramphenicol; 2–2. Member States shall inform immediately the Commission of the results of the test referred to in paragraph 1,

215 Decision 2001/699/EC of 19 September 2001 concerning certain protective measures with regard to certain fishery and aquaculture products intended for human consumption and originating in China and Vietnam.

making use of the Rapid Alert System for Food, set up by Directive 92/59/EEC". Article 6 stipulated that Decision 2001/699/EC would be reviewed on the basis of the guarantees provided by the Chinese and Vietnamese competent authorities and on the basis of the results of the tests referred to in Article 2. Likewise, Decision 95/453/EC laid down the specific conditions for imports from Korea.[216]

The categorisation of exporting third countries dated back to January 1999. The EU then designed a system for the official recognition of countries authorised to export to its territory. Third countries were then divided into two distinct groups based on their ability to comply with EU requirements. The first category of countries were granted List I status upon satisfactory assessment of their Competent Authority (CA), which certified that conditions of production and certification were at least equivalent to those of the EU. This compliance entitled such countries to export without restriction to the EU from any approved establishments. The other countries were granted List II status, which, in reality, meant that these countries were unable to comply fully with hygiene requirements. In most cases, their CA had not been inspected yet, but the CA could certify that production conditions were satisfactory. Such countries could export to the EU on the basis of bilateral agreements with Member States. In such cases, the importing Member State was responsible for ensuring that the products were safe. In any case, such consignments would go through more strict inspections at EU border posts.

Furthermore the countries' establishments authorised to export to the EU also had to be officially recognised on lists drawn up for that purpose. In this particular case, an establishment could appear on a list only if the CA of its country officially vouched for it regarding compliance with regulatory requirements and assured that there was proper monitoring by an official inspection service.

However, in specific cases, an establishment or a factory vessel might be allowed to directly export to the EU regardless of their country, when the country proved unable to provide the required guarantees. This authorisation would necessarily follow an on-the-spot inspection carried out by Commission's experts, and the decision had to clearly spell out the specific conditions surrounding such shipments. A health certificate should accompany imported fishery products, which should have an identification mark.

It is worth noting that import bans were not final, and bans had to be removed as soon as the concerned country was able to prove that adequate measures were adopted to meet the Community's requirements. Accordingly, the

216 Article 1 of Commission Decision 95/453/EC of 23 October 1995 laying down special conditions for the import of live bivalve molluscs, echinoderms, tunicates and marine gastropods originating in the Republic of Korea stated that the Ministry of Maritime Affairs and Fisheries – National Fishery Products Inspection Station (NFPIS) shall be the competent authority in the Republic of Korea for verifying and certifying compliance of fishery and aquaculture products with the requirements of Directive 91/492/EEC.

lists were reviewed on a regular basis, removing or adding countries considering the risks to health detected.

Just like other third countries, the former African colonies are also subject to Community inspection. Therefore, despite the privileged relations from ACP-EU agreements, exports to the Community market from these former colonies could also be banned when there were safety concerns. As regards food, many of these countries were authorised to export to the EU by Commission Decision 2001/635/EC. Benin was included in the list provided by Annex 2 of this Decision which listed the countries and territories meeting the terms of Article 2(2) of Council Decision 95/408/EC. Approximately 15 months later, the FVO revealed serious unsafe conditions in the whole shrimp production and certification system.

3.4. CURRENT EU FOOD REGULATORY FRAMEWORK

Despite all the precautions taken by the Community, its credibility was again seriously questioned after the Dioxin crisis in Belgium in 1999. New reforms were indispensable and the promotion of a high level of food safety became a priority. In 2000 the Commission published its White Paper on food safety, which defined a 'radical' new approach to food safety legislation throughout the food supply chain 'from the farm to the table'. The new approach aimed at implementing a coherent, comprehensive and up-to-date set of policies based on risk analysis and the precautionary principle. For that purpose, a Food Safety Authority had to be created which should provide the Commission with the scientific advice necessary to make decisions able to attain a high level of public health and consumer protection. An EU framework for the development of national control systems had to be elaborated and controls on imports should be extended to all foodstuffs. Consumers were to be informed about food safety concerns and food risks, and they should be more involved in the new food safety policy.

The White Paper did not have any binding force but it constituted the foundation of the current EU food safety law. Several safety regulations were adopted since its publication and the principles it set down provide the foundation for the regulatory framework.

3.4.1. DEFINITION AND SCOPE

The current EU food regulatory regime was established in 2002 by Regulation 178/2002, commonly called General Food Law (GFL). The GFL is a comprehensive and integrated approach to food safety, which incorporates most of the safety policies set down by the White Paper on food safety. Keeping in mind the original and still leading vision, the EU decided to couple the completion of the single market with the need to attain a high level of human life and health protection. Food safety concerns became a key priority after the unprecedented pressure during the feed and food emergencies of the 1990s and the call for action they represented for authorities – Commission, Member States and the Parliament – to reinforce, improve and further develop existing systems.[217]

As part of public health, food safety developed into a horizontal issue brought to the fore by the TFEU. Article 168 of the TFEU stipulated that "a high level of human health protection shall be ensured in the definition and implementation of all Union policies and activities".[218] Prior to the TFEU, human health protection policies were developed as part of the policies aiming at the realisation of the common market. According to the TFEU, the Union shall complement public health policies of Member States and encourage cooperation between Members to fight against major health scourges, by promoting research into their causes, their transmission and their prevention, as well as health information and education, and monitoring, early warning of and combating serious cross-border threats to health.

The GFL centralised and certified the measures previously implemented throughout the EU in order to develop a system of effective control so that products unfit for consumption would not circulate across the Member States and spread potential diseases. This law constitutes a harmonisation tool to iron out difficulties arising from substantial differences between the concepts, principles and procedures of the Member States' food laws. As such, the GFL clarified a certain number of key notions that henceforth represent the common understanding within the EU, thus levelling differences of interpretation that resulted from Member States' legislative autonomy.[219]

The GFL is the completion of a three-legged stool resting on an integrated farm-to-fork system of food safety responsibilities and enforcement, a modern system of monitoring and communication, and the protection of scientific analysis integrity on which policy decisions rely.[220] Given the position of the EU on the international market, the GFL also represents an expression of the awareness of EU decision makers that the safety and confidence of consumers are also of paramount importance beyond the EU's borders. From this perspective, the new approach incorporated an international dimension, which applied the

217 White Paper on Food Safety, p7.
218 TFEU, Article 168.
219 Alemanno 2007, p73.
220 Hoffman & Harder 2010, p24.

same coherence to food within the EU and food produced outside the EU by its trading partners.

Due to the political sensitivity of food safety, a complex regulatory structure was required to reconcile the tensions between food safety, market integration and legitimate national regulatory concerns.[221] Therefore, beyond the general framework established by the GFL, several other sets of law were later adopted to define specific rules with regard to particular areas. All these texts contribute to ensuring the safety of food products 'from farm-to-fork'. The new legislative acts dedicate an important part to operators' self-control and define the outlines of Member States' and the Commission's responsibilities as regards the food control system. Furthermore, these legislative acts established general and particular rules applicable to food import in the EU.

a. Definition of food and food law

1° Food

The starting point of the current EU food law was to clarify and develop a common basis to key concepts in safety regulation in order to eliminate interpretation differences in the Member States.

For the purposes of the GFL, 'food' means any substance or product, whether processed, partially processed or unprocessed, intended to be, or reasonably expected to be ingested by humans. 'Food' includes drink, chewing gum and any substance, including water, intentionally incorporated into the food during its manufacture, preparation or treatment. It is well acknowledged in the literature that, although the EU has been involved for a long time in food safety regulation, for the first time the GFL provided a common definition of food. That innovation is interesting in many respects: it introduces legal certainty in determining the scope of the different EU food laws and paves the way for the broad application of the new EU food regime, covering virtually the whole 'farm-to-fork' food chain.[222] However, this definition of food only applies to the context of application of the GFL and, therefore, does not apply automatically in Member States' legislation, nor does it apply in other pieces of EU law.[223]

In order to further clarify this definition, the Regulation adopted an exclusive approach by naming all substances which are not to be considered as food within the meaning of the GFL.[224] In this regard, seven categories of products were identified namely: "feed; live animal unless they are prepared for placing on the market for human consumption; plants prior to harvesting; medicinal

221 Vos & Wendler 2006, p67.
222 Alemanno 2006, p14.
223 Meulen (van der) & Velde (van der) 2008, p 254.
224 Regulation 178/2002, Article 2.

products within the meaning of Council Directives 65/65/EEC and 92/73/EEC; cosmetics within the meaning of Council Directive 89/622/EEC; tobacco and tobacco products within the meaning of Council Directive 89/622/EEC; narcotic or psychotropic substances within the meaning of the United Nations Single Convention on Narcotic Drugs, 1961, and the United Nations Convention on Psychotropic Substances, 1971; residues and contaminants.' Notwithstanding the common definition of food, a product can be considered food in one country and non-food in another country as a result of differences between national Member States' legislation. An example of such an issue is the joined cases *HLH Warenvertriebs GmbH and Orthica BV v Bundesrepublik Deutschland.* In this dispute, in which Germany categorised garlic concentrates as medicines on the grounds that garlic has beneficial effects on health, the ECJ ruled that Germany had overstepped its margin of discretion and the qualification of a food as a medicine requiring pre-market approval constituted an infringement of the free movement of goods as protected in Article 28 of the EC Treaty.[225]

The food legislation highlights a significant differentiation between products of animal origin and products of non-animal origin. This demarcation is decisive for the requirements applicable to products and operators involved in the food chain. First, food of non-animal origin includes items such as fruits, vegetables, cereals, tubers, drinks[226], food of mineral origin, spices, condiments etc. Secondly, 'food products of animal origin' cover all processed or unprocessed food derived from animals or coming from animals.

In that respect, fishery products are considered products of animal origin. This is even reflected in the definition given by the EU food law: 'Fishery products' are "all seawater or freshwater animals (except for live bivalve molluscs, live echinoderms, live tunicates and live marine gastropods, and all mammals, reptiles and frogs), whether wild or farmed and including all edible forms, parts and products of such animals".[227]

2° Food law

In EU context, 'food law' means the laws, regulations and administrative provisions governing food in general, and food safety in particular, whether at the Community or national level. Food law covers any stage of production, processing and distribution of food and also of feed produced for, or fed to, food producing animals.[228]

---

225 HLH Warenvertriebs GmbH (C-211/03) and Orthica BV (C-299/03, C-316/03, C-318/03) v Bundesrepublik Deutschland, Judgment of the Court (First Chamber) of 9 June 2005.

226 Drinks prepared from products of animal origin such as milk are not to be considered as food of non-animal origin.

227 Regulation 853/2004, Annex I, section 3.

228 Regulation 178/2002, Article 3.1.

Depending on the context and the perspective, the perception of food law can differ. Generally the term refers to any mechanisms set up to normalise processes of food production, food handling and the marketing of food. However, the FAO proceeded to a classification depending on the viewpoint. On the one hand, a narrow view would restrict food law to "the regulation of food control, food safety and food trade at national level" with a focus on laws and regulations that refer to food in general or to specific kinds of food (e.g food safety law, fish inspection law). Such a meaning grants little room for the integration of international parameters, except in relation to imports or exports. On the other hand, a broader view "would look at the wide variety of fields that must actually be regulated in order to ensure the production, trade and handling of safe food, and would take all of these into account". In such a case, every single criterion related to food is to be considered (e.g specific food law, consumer protection or fraud deterrence laws, customs laws, fish products inspection rules, etc). From this perspective, food law is an integrated discipline which addresses, beyond traditional food issues, issues related to food security while paying regard to plant protection and animal health for their correlation with food control, safety and trade.[229]

b. Scope of application

The GFL applies to all stages of the food chain, from the primary production of a food, up to and including the storage, transport and sale to the final consumer, each step having a potential impact on food safety. Primary production must be understood as the production, rearing or growing of primary products, including hunting and fishing. Moreover, the concept of food in this context is to be applied to food which is placed on the market.

'Placing on the market' means the holding of food or feed for the purpose of sale, including offering for sale or any other form of transfer, whether free of charge or not, and the sale, distribution, and other forms of transfer themselves.[230] Such a food shall necessarily be in conformity with the GFL's food safety requirements.

The GFL does not explicitly define food safety, but it states the conditions of an unsafe food. In this regard, "food shall be deemed to be unsafe if it is considered to be injurious to health or unfit for human consumption".[231] Such an evaluation must take into account the normal conditions of use of the food at each stage of production, processing and distribution and the information provided to the

229 For more details on this distinction, see Vapnek & Spreij 2005.

230 Regulation 178/2002, Article 3.8.

231 Regulation 178/2002, Article 14.2. CODEX Alimentarius adopted a relatively similar approach by defining food safety as the assurance that food will not cause harm to the consumer when it is prepared and/or eaten according to its intended use. See Recommended International Code of Practice. General Principles of Food Hygiene; CAC/RCP 1-1969, Rev. 4-2003.

consumer for its proper use. Furthermore, while assessing the safety of food, one must also consider the probable immediate or differed effects of the food on consumers and on subsequent generations, probable cumulative toxic effects and particular health sensitivities of potential consumers of a specific food.

c. General objectives of EU food law

The EU food law aims at ensuring a high level of protection of human life and health and the protection of consumers' interests, including fair practices in food trade, taking into account, where appropriate, the protection of animal health and welfare, plant health and the environment.[232] The GFL promotes the circulation within the EU of food manufactured according to its requirements. The establishment of the food regime intends to take into account existing or imminent international safety standards, as long as the latter fit with the EU's intended level of protection. The food legislation is based on requirements derived from transparency and proportionality, and, wherever applicable, on the principles of risk analysis.

3.4.2. RISK ANALYSIS

Article 6 of the GFL states that food law shall be based upon risk analysis, a process consisting of three separate but integrated components, namely risk assessment, risk management and risk communication.[233] The risk analysis scheme extends over several disciplines derived from the identification of a food safety problem that leads to a food safety objective. The effectiveness of risk analysis requires the collaboration of all stakeholders gathered around a common commitment to set up a performing food safety system.

a. Risk

The risk represents "a function of the probability of an adverse health effect and the severity of that effect, consequential to a hazard".[234] It is important to make a differentiation between the notions of 'risk' and 'hazard'. According to the GFL, a hazard means "a biological, chemical or physical agent in, or condition of, food or feed with the potential to cause an adverse health effect".[235] A risk is therefore the expression of the likelihood that a hazard could result in harm and, in such an event, the risk constitutes a way to assess the extent of potential damages.

---

232 Regulation 178/2002, Article 5.
233 Regulation 178/2002, Article 3.10.
234 Regulation 178/2002, Article 3.9.
235 Regulation 178/2002, Article 3.14.

Risk is a function of two variables: the probability of an event occurring and the magnitude or severity of the event should it occur.[236] The risk of foodborne disease is a combination of the likelihood of exposure to the pathogen, the likelihood of infection or intoxication resulting in illness and the severity of the illness.[237] Food risks, whether current or future, can derive from a scientific certainty or may just be the result of a scientific probability of potential damage from food consumption due to microbial pathogens and/or microbial toxins.

In general, safety and wholesomeness are related to a level of risk that society regards as reasonable in the context and in comparison with other risks in everyday life.[238] However, beyond subjectivity, high-risk products are products that are consumed raw without cooking because they do not undergo a processing step that would eradicate biological hazards. In contrast, products that are cooked thoroughly before final consumption are seen as being of lower risk, as such products have a heat control step that will eradicate most biological food safety hazards, except biotoxins that are heat stable.[239]

In the instance of fishery products, which are very much appreciated considering the numerous virtues[240] associated with their consumption, they can be quickly compromised because of the numerous actors intervening in the process and the probability of the product being contaminated at each step. In fact, hazards can occur at the various stages of fishing, landing, handling, processing, packaging, storage, and marketing. Hazards are related to the contamination of the environment in which fishery products grow and live, their inherent chemical composition, cross-contamination during handling and processing, and poor storage distribution and marketing practices.[241]

b. *Components of risk analysis*

1° Risk assessment

Risk assessment is a process by which scientists evaluate the potential for adverse health or environmental effects from exposure to naturally occurring or synthetic agents.[242] Risk assessment constitutes a scientifically based process consisting of four steps that are hazard identification, hazard characterisation, exposure assessment, and risk characterisation.

236 Fazil 2005, p2.
237 Fazil 2005, p1.
238 FAO/WHO 1997, p4.
239 FAO 2009, p20.
240 Fishery products provide an important source of easily digested protein, vitamins A, B12, D and E and essential amino acids, see FAO 2009, p12.
241 FAO 2009, p12.
242 Society of Toxicology 1998, p1.

Table 3.2. Steps of risk assessment as defined in "The four components of risk assessment, Communication from the Commission on the precautionary principle"[243]

Hazard identification	Hazard identification means identifying the biological, chemical or physical agents that may have adverse effects.
Hazard characterisation	Hazard characterisation consists in determining, in quantitative and/or qualitative terms, the nature and severity of the adverse effects associated with the causal agents or activity.
Appraisal of exposure	Appraisal of exposure consists in quantitatively or qualitatively evaluating the probability of exposure to the agent under study.
Risk characterisation	Risk characterisation corresponds to the qualitative and/or quantitative estimation, taking account of inherent uncertainties, of the probability, of the frequency and severity of the known or potential adverse environmental or health effects liable to occur.

Risk assessment is a process that provides an estimate of the probability and impact of foodborne disease.[244] Risk assessment is a prerequisite to risk-based standard setting, but one must acknowledge that for many food safety scenarios there is only limited quantitative information available.[245] In general terms, there are three broad categories of risk assessment. First, a qualitative risk assessment is a descriptive method consisting of establishing an estimation of risk (high, medium or low) on questions related to the severity of the hazard and the likelihood of it occurring. Secondly, a semi-quantitative risk assessment can be used to provide a numerical risk estimate based on a mixture of qualitative and quantitative data. Thirdly, a quantitative risk assessment can be performed and consists of establishing numerical expressions of risk and an indication of the attendant uncertainties.

The implementation of risk assessment is the responsibility of the European Food Safety Authority (EFSA).

Box 3-2. Role of the EFSA as established by Regulation 178/2002

The EFSA was set up in 2002 by Article 22 of the GFL to ensure a role in two complementary components. First, the EFSA must "provide scientific advice, and scientific and technical support for the Community's legislation and policies in all fields which have a direct or indirect impact on food and feed safety". Secondly, the "EFSA shall provide independent information on all matters within these fields and communicate on risks" (Article 22.2). Moreover, the EFSA "shall contribute to a high level of protection of human life and health, and in this respect take account of animal health and welfare, plant health and the environment, in the context of the operation of the internal market" (Article 22.3). Scientific risk assessment must be undertaken in an independent, objective and transparent manner based on the best available science.

243 The four components of risk assessment, Communication from the Commission on the precautionary principle, COM (2000) 1 of 02/02/2000; Annex III, p29.

244 Fazil 2005, p19.

245 Hathaway 1999, p248.

Thereby, the EFSA became the body vested with the risk assessment and should, as such, collect and analyse data that enables the better characterisation and monitoring of food safety risks (Article 22.4). This body serves as scientific support for the Commission by supplying opinions, scientific expertise and recommendations to guide decision-making with regard to the management of food safety risks. Furthermore, the EFSA must provide advice on contentious matters to properly support risk management decisions taken by the EU Commission and Member States, so as to preserve the single market from unfounded measures that could hinder trade.

As an independent European agency, the EFSA must work like a network, collaborating with the Commission, Member States and stakeholders to promote a framework for scientific cooperation, to share information and knowledge, identify common tasks, and optimise the use of resources and expertise (Regulation 2230/2004, preamble). These stakeholders, as established by the GFL, include a wide range of actors associated with the implementation of the food law, from the general public to non-governmental organisations, professional associations and also international trading partners and trade organisations.

EFSA's scientific analyses are essential for national food safety agencies throughout the EU. Similarly, the EFSA must communicate timely and reliable information to stakeholders and the public at large, provided that this risk communication is based on risk assessment and scientific expertise. Furthermore, EFSA's activities are not restricted to the EU's borders. Collaboration must be developed with third countries, which have concluded agreements with the EU stipulating the adoption and the implementation of EU legislation pursuant to the provisions of the GFL. The specifics of such collaboration, in particular its nature, extent and the manner in which third countries participate in the work of the EFSA, are to be defined by relevant provisions of the concerned agreements.

Furthermore, the EFSA may be requested by the Commission to provide scientific or technical assistance in any field within its mission (Article 31). It also plays an important role in the identification of emerging risks and may even request the Commission or Member States or other Community agencies to provide additional information in the case of a suspicion of an emerging serious risk (Article 34). It is also important to underline that the EFSA shall be the recipient of any messages forwarded via the RASFF. The EFSA shall then analyse the content of such messages with a view to providing the Commission and the Member States with any information required for the purposes of risk analysis (Article 35).

In practice, every food law is not preceded by a scientific risk assessment. In the EU context, the assertion that food law is based on science would be a 'gross overstatement' since, in fact, not one single example can be found of a regulation or directive of a general nature referring to an opinion of EFSA or another form of risk assessment that has been taken into account.[246] Therefore, contrary to conventional wisdom, there is currently no common system providing scientific advice to the EC policymakers. Scientific support is ensured through a range of different mechanisms, depending on the relevant policy area.[247] The most common sources of advice used to support EC policies, legislation and regulatory decisions are scientific committees under the control of EFSA and European Medicines Agency (EMEA), reports by advisory agencies, such as the European Environmental Agency (EEA), reports provided by external consultants (individuals, groups or companies, possibly using study contracts), national reports provided by Member States' advisory bodies, reports by ad-hoc

[246] Meulen (van der), B. & Velde (van der) 2008, p268.

[247] Alemanno, 2007b, p5.

expert groups, in-house analyses conducted by Commission officials, reports and opinions by the Joint Research Centre (JRC) and the Scientific and Technical Options Assessment group in the European Parliament (STOA).[248]

In the same way, a scientific basis is not a compulsory requirement for all food law; for instance, food law relating to consumer information or prevention of misleading practices does not require a scientific basis.[249]

The creation of a high-level and independent European Food Safety Authority is quite meaningful to provide support in principle to defend EU requirements in international fora, thanks to undisputable scientific validation.

It is worth noting that the food law provisions introduced a functional separation between the evaluation and management of risk; while risk assessment is dealt with by the EFSA, risk management is the privilege of the Commission.

2° Risk management

Risk management means the process, distinct from risk assessment, of weighing policy alternatives in consultation with interested parties, considering risk assessment and other legitimate factors, and, if need be, selecting appropriate prevention and control options.[250] This process aims at selecting the appropriate actions necessary to prevent, reduce or eliminate risks in order to ensure the high level of health protection determined as appropriate in the EU.

Risk management must be derived from risk assessment, while taking into account other factors that might be relevant for the case under consideration. Therefore, factors including societal, economic, traditional, ethical and environmental features and the feasibility of controls must be considered collectively with risk assessment. The perceived need to take 'other factors' into consideration can be seen as a way to broker divisions across Member States over controversial food safety measures.[251]

A risk management process must aim at developing standards, recommendations and guidelines appropriate to effectively control food risks. Risk management implies the observance of five compulsory criteria namely: proportionality, non-discrimination, consistency, the examination of benefits and costs of action or lack of action, and the examination of scientific developments.[252] The completion of risk management entails the integration of several elements.

---

248 Idem.

249 See European Commission, General Food Law – Principles, available at http://ec.europa.eu/food/food/foodlaw/principles/index_en.htm, visited on 08/08/10.

250 Regulation 178/2002, Article 3.12.

251 Skogstad 2001, p 491.

252 Communication from the Commission on the Precautionary principle, COM (2000) 1, 2000.

a. Risk management framework

The choice of the appropriate level of protection is a risk management privilege. This parameter constitutes the central element of risk management, given that the definition of the appropriate level of protection shapes all food law policies. Therefore, the risk management framework enables the determination of the options available to manage a risk so as to achieve the appropriate level of protection. The risk management framework comprises four different stages namely: risk evaluation, the identification and selection of risk management options, the implementation of risk management decisions, and monitoring and review.

Risk evaluation implies that the existence of an issue is an indispensable condition, without which a risk management procedure would be baseless. Therefore, any activity carried out within the framework of risk management finds its source in the preliminary identification of a food safety problem. The next step consists of profiling the risk by describing the food safety problem and its context in order to bring to light the criteria relevant for food safety standards decision making and management options. This step makes it possible to give evidence of the necessity of a risk assessment and, if necessary, to define its outlines and objectives accordingly.

The fulfilment of these various tasks has to reflect the general framework of the risk management goals by being consistent with its priorities. Analogously, they must lead to the identification of risk management priorities relevant for the case under consideration. The necessity of proceeding to a risk assessment infers the obligation of seeking the collaboration of the risk assessor in order to define a risk assessment policy. A risk assessment policy is a set of guidelines for making value judgment and policy choices, which may need to be applied at specific decision points in the risk assessment process. The definition of these guidelines falls within the realm of risk management and must be performed in advance of risk assessment. However, risk managers must collaborate in this regard with risk assessors to protect the scientific integrity of the risk assessment.[253] The Commission must then request a risk assessment, the results of which will be of guidance for its risk management decisions.

The second stage is the identification and selection of risk management options. In light of the results of the risk assessment and the criteria particular to the case, the diverse management options available are listed. The preferred option is then selected and constitutes the level of acceptable risk or the appropriate level of protection considering the result of the risk evaluation, but also all other technical, economic and societal values that might be relevant to the case. In any case, human health protection must be the decisive criterion.

---

253 FAO/WHO 2004, p4.

In the third step, the risk management decisions must be implemented. The implementation consists of setting up all mechanisms required for the proper handling of food safety matters. This could lead, as appropriate, to the adoption of control measures in order to attest to the compliance of stakeholders.

Lastly, the monitoring and review stage has a twofold purpose: firstly, it enables the assessment of the effectiveness of the risk management through the monitoring of the outcomes of implemented controls. Secondly, it makes it possible, when necessary, to review the risk management and/or assessment. Thanks to surveillance mechanisms implemented to monitor foodborne diseases and contaminants in food, this stage ensures the detection of emerging food risks and guarantees the ability to react swiftly.

It is worthwhile to underline that an efficient risk management approach must be the result of the coupled efforts of the Commission and all stakeholders. The consultative process, which ensues, is not connected to any particular stage and can intervene at any moment throughout the risk management policy formulation process.

The EU food law coordinates its policies with the view to attaining a "high level of protection". The interpretation of the meaning of a high level of protection, which is an indisputable principle of the overall food law, is nevertheless quite imprecise. In a ruling more than two decades ago, the ECJ stated that "in so far as there are scientific uncertainties at the present state of scientific research, it is for the Member States, in the absence of harmonisation, to decide what degree of protection of the health and life of humans they intend to assure, having regard however for the requirements of the free movement of goods within the Community".[254]

Box 3-3. Summary of ECJ ruling – Criminal proceedings against Sandoz BV. Case 174/82

The ruling on Criminal proceedings against Sandoz BV. Case 174/82 goes back up to July 1983. It addressed several fundamental principles of the EU food law, such as the principle of proportionality on the basis of which Member States should prohibit imports only to the extent necessary to achieve health protection. The ruling also reaffirmed the use of the precautionary principle by establishing that uncertainties inherent to scientific assessment could justify national rules which prohibit the marketing of foodstuffs on grounds of human health protection.

In this case, three questions were raised in criminal proceedings brought against SANDOZ BV based in Uden, for having sold and delivered in the Netherlands for commercial purposes and for human consumption, food and beverages to which vitamins had been added, without an authorisation from the responsible minister. These products were mostly imported from Switzerland and the Federal Republic of Germany. In fact, Article 10 of the general decree (*Algemeen Besluit*) of 1949 adopted in implementation of Articles 14 and 15 of the Dutch law on goods (*Warenwet*) of 1935 contained a clause of a ban on adding vitamins to foodstuffs and drinks without prior authorisation granted by the Minister in charge of the execution of the

254 Judgment of the Court (Fifth Chamber) of 14 July 1983. – Criminal proceedings against Sandoz BV. Case 174/82, European Court reports 1983 Page 02445, para. 16.

decree. Although the products were lawfully marketed in the Federal Republic of Germany and in Belgium, the Dutch competent authority argued first that these products should first meet a market demand and later forbade their commercialisation on the grounds that the excessive or uncontrolled consumption of vitamins A and D added to the products represented a danger to public health. The Court heard the parties on their pleas and paid regard to the scientific analysis on the effect of the consumption of different types of vitamins on the human body. The Court noticed that scientific research does not appear to be sufficiently advanced to determine with certainty the critical quantities and the precise effects of the consumption of vitamins. On these grounds, the Court ruled that:

(i) Community law permits national rules prohibiting, without prior authorisation, the marketing of foodstuffs lawfully marketed in another Member State to which vitamins have been added, provided that the marketing is authorised where the addition of vitamins meets a real need, especially a technical or nutritional one;
(ii) Community law does not permit rules which, for authorisation to put a product on the market, require the importer to prove that the product in question is not harmful to health, without prejudice to the right of the national authorities to ask the importer to submit all the information in his possession needed to assess facts;
(iii) Community law does not permit national rules, which for authorisation to put a product on the market, require the importer to prove that the marketing of the product in question meets a market demand.

This autonomy of Member States to determine the level of protection which they deem suitable was reaffirmed a few years later in another ruling of the ECJ with reference to the judgment Sandoz BV namely: Judgment of the Court of 12 March 1987 – Commission of the European Communities v Federal Republic of Germany – Case 178/84, para. 41.

B. Precautionary principle

Primarily used in environmental law, the precautionary principle has been extended to food law where the principle has henceforth occupied a pivotal place. Before the harmonisation of the precautionary principle, its use in the Member States' law was the cause of barriers to the free movement of food within the EU.[255]

The precautionary principle enables the adoption of provisional risk management measures in specific circumstances where, following an assessment of available information, the possibility of harmful effects on health is identified but scientific uncertainty persists.[256] The precautionary principle is a risk management strategy and, as such, its use implies the consideration of the general principles which refer to this discipline. Therefore, precautionary measures should not be disproportionate with regard to the risk or unnecessarily trade restrictive even when due considerations would have been granted to technical and economic feasibility and other factors regarded as legitimate for the case. Precautionary measures must not constitute an option for the pursuit of 'zero risk' which "in reality is rarely to be found".[257]

---

255 Regulation 178/2002, preamble.
256 Regulation 178/2002, Article 7.
257 Communication from the Commission on the Precautionary Principle, COM (2000) 1, 2000, p9.

To avoid subjectivity, the implementation of the precautionary principle must follow a scientific evaluation which is as complete as possible and which should determine at every stage the degree of uncertainty. Where appropriate, non-economic factors such as the protection of health must also be integrated in the scientific evaluation. While the overall cost of action or inaction must be considered in the risk mitigation options, the examination of the diverse measures available cannot be limited to an economic cost-benefit analysis. This examination must be wider in scope. Other analysis methods, such as those concerning the efficacy of possible options and their acceptability to the public may also have to be considered. A society might even be willing to bear a higher cost for an interest deemed to be a priority, such as health. In this regard, the EU Commission affirms that "requirements linked to the protection of public health should undoubtedly be given greater weight than economic considerations".[258]

The risk evaluation must highlight the potential consequences of inaction and all interested parties must be given the opportunity to study the various alternatives available, while ensuring the greatest possible transparency.[259] Precautionary measures adopted following this process are valid as long as the evolution of science does not allow complete and decisive data likely to eradicate the risk incurred by the consumer to be obtained. In light of changes caused by progress in scientific knowledge and a more comprehensive risk assessment, precautionary measures must be consequently reviewed. The application of the precautionary principle has to reflect coherence in the decision making to avoid discrimination.

3° Risk communication

Risk communication means the interactive exchange of information and opinions throughout the risk analysis process as regards hazards and risks, risk-related factors and risk perceptions, among risk assessors, risk managers, consumers, feed and food businesses, the academic community, and other interested parties, including the explanation of risk assessment findings and the basis of risk management decisions.[260] Risk communication is an integral and ongoing part of risk analysis, and is a joint responsibility of risk assessors and risk managers[261], necessitated by the involvement of all stakeholders to restore consumer confidence. An improved involvement of the general public in the decision-making process is an essential tool to achieve greater transparency

---

[258] Communication from the Commission on the precautionary principle, COM (2000) 1, 2000, p20.

[259] Communication from the Commission on the precautionary principle, COM (2000) 1, 2000, p17.

[260] Regulation 178/2002, Article 3.13.

[261] EFSA 2006, p3.

and a more effective perception of potential risks by consumers. Such a system guarantees a satisfactory level of consumer information to enable them to make informed choices. The protection of the consumer goes beyond the single requirement of providing relevant information. As stated by Article 8 of the GFL, this protection shall aim at the prevention of fraudulent or deceptive practices, the adulteration of food and any other practices that may mislead the consumer. Moreover, Article 16 provides that labelling, advertising and the presentation of food or feed such as its shape, materials used and the manner in which food is displayed shall not mislead consumers.

These provisions are part of the transparency promoted by the GFL. Risk communication at large is but one stage in the fulfilment of the transparency requirement. Transparency aims, on the one hand, to ensure an open public consultation directly or through representative bodies, during the preparation, evaluation and revision of the food law. On the other hand, transparency implies the availability of excellent public information, demanding public authorities to take appropriate steps to inform the public, where there are grounds to suspect that a food or feed may present a risk for health, of the nature of the risk and the measures which have been taken or are about to be taken to prevent, reduce or eliminate that risk.[262]

As a risk management tool, effective risk communication must aim to facilitate a higher degree of consensus and support by all interested parties for the risk management option being proposed.[263] Through the GFL, the Commission entrusted the EFSA with risk communication.

In general terms, the EFSA must develop a close cooperation with all interested parties in order to provide them with information based on a risk assessment and the scientific expertise needed to handle food safety matters properly. This could consist of publishing opinions, disseminating materials for the general public and cooperating in public information campaigns. It is worth underlining that the mission of the EFSA is not limited to the scope of food safety. The EFSA's mission also covers feed safety, nutrition, animal health and welfare, plant protection and plant health. In addition to EFSA's work, consumers' advocacy groups also have a major role in educating and informing consumers about the major safety and quality issues.[264]

---

262 Regulation 178/2002, Articles 9–10.

263 FAO/WHO 1998, p3.

264 Ababouch et al. 2005, p7.

Box 3-4. Responsibilities of the EFSA with regard to risk communication

The main responsibilities of the EFSA in the area of risk communication are spread over several Articles of the GFL. The EFSA must:

- ensure that the public and interested parties receive rapid, reliable, objective and comprehensible information in the fields within its mission (Article 23(j));
- at the request of the Commission, provide assistance concerning communication on nutritional issues within the framework of the Community health programme (Article 22(5a));
- communicate on its own initiative in the fields within its mission without prejudice to the Commission's competence to communicate its risk management decisions (Article 40(1));
- act in close collaboration with the Commission and the Member States to promote the necessary coherence in the risk communication process (Article 40(3)).

To attain its goals as regards risk communication, the EFSA has defined a strategy based on four main pillars:

- understand consumer and public perception of food, risk and risks associated with the food chain;
- bridge the gap between science and the consumer;
- harness support of key actors in order to reach consumers with pertinent and effective messages;
- promote coherent risk communications across the Risk Assessment/Risk Management interface.

Source: 'EFSA Risk Communications Strategy and Plans'.[265]

3.4.3. FOOD SAFETY RESPONSIBILITIES

The food law, which is the foundation of the free movement of goods between Member States, applies equally to all types of goods, whether these goods are produced within the EU or whether they originate in a third country. In the same way, the food law intends to ensure that unsafe food does not leave the Community or represent a vector of potential diseases for foreign countries. Food exported or re-exported from the Community must comply with the requirements of EU food law.[266] Failure to respect this rule is allowed only if the authorities of the country of destination require different criteria or if they were duly informed that the goods which they are importing do not satisfy the EU requirements. From this perspective, the definition of responsibilities falls similarly on foreign and EU food business operators, as well as national competent authorities.

265 EFSA, EFSA Risk Communications Strategy and Plans, adopted by written procedures on 8 November 2006.

266 Regulation 178/2002, Article 12.

a. *Responsibilities of food business operators*

1° Primary responsibility for food safety

Food business means "any undertaking, whether for profit or not and whether public or private, carrying out any of the activities related to any stage of production, processing and distribution of food."[267] This definition covers a wide range of actors from the producers to the preparers or servers, but also including processors and retailers. In this way, any legal or natural person whose activity is in one of the aforementioned categories has a legal duty with regard to potential consumers and the market as a whole to ensure that food placed on the market meets the requirements of food law. Whereas any individual or firm has the right to produce, process, prepare, serve, import, and export food, this right comes with the inseparable responsibility to ensure that such food is wholesome and safe and that the conduct of his business is within all applicable laws, including those regarding fraud.[268] This obligation infers that the food business operator must take, according to its particular food, all appropriate measures to produce pursuant to the GFL and to verify compliance with its requirements. Such compliance constitutes a strong incentive for food business operators, considering that a food produced according to the EU law will be deemed to be safe. The implementation of this obligation relates not only to direct or indirect production activities but its coverage extends to a commitment to ensure product traceability with the aim of collaborating with competent authorities in the preservation of a high level of protection.

2° Traceability

Food business operators are best placed to devise a safe system for supplying food and ensuring its safety. Therefore they must elaborate an integrated scheme to make available relevant information necessary for food traceability.

Traceability is the ability to trace and follow a food, feed, food-producing animal, or substance intended to be or expected to be incorporated into a food or feed, through all stages of production, processing and distribution.[269] It is well acknowledged that a good traceability system is crucial to easily define responsibilities throughout the food chain. Generally called "one step back, one step forward", traceability entails that food business operators must identify their supplier and the businesses to which their products have been supplied. Measures undertaken to enable the traceability include adequate labelling and ample documentation to facilitate the easy identification of a product.

---

267 Regulation 178/2002, Article 3.1.
268 FAO 2008, p7.
269 Regulation 178/2002, Article 3.15.

Traceability enables setting up a proactive system which, in case of risk to health, allows for a swift reaction consisting either of the withdrawal of the concerned product, wherever it is, or preventing the placing on the market of other similar products. The overall objective is to limit potential damages to consumers.

However, the need to ensure traceability does not imply that the food business operator is responsible for tracing the trajectory of the product in a third country in case of imports. The main responsibility in such a scenario is the ability of a food business operator to identify its supplier in the relevant third country and to ensure compliance with applicable requirements. In the case of import of products of animal origin, the food business operator must make sure that the products come from a third country or a part of a third country that appears on an EU list drafted for that purpose. Where applicable, the food business operator must go further and check the appearance of the establishment in an EU list. Depending on the nature of the product, the food business operator must ensure that the products carry a health or identification mark or are accompanied by a certificate issued by the representative of the competent authority of the third country. In any case, the food business operator must also cooperate with authorities by making imported products available for control at a border inspection post. In addition, all these precautions do not exempt the food business operator from carrying out any post-import operations in accordance with appropriate requirements.

The implementation of the traceability requirements implies a clear definition of tasks and responsibilities at various levels, whether in the food supply chain or in the enforcement and control of food law. In that respect, the food business operator must set up a mechanism likely to provide all the necessary information to competent authorities, to transmit that information immediately in case of risk and proceed to the removal of contaminated products from the market and the destruction of any suspect batch, lot or consignment.

Currently some traceability requirements about fishery products are defined in two main regulations, namely Council Regulation 104/2000 and Commission Regulation 2065/2001. These sets of legislation define rules that must ensure the availability of information related to the species of fishery products, catch areas, the country of origin in the case of inland waters, the production method, etc.

b. *Responsibilities of Member States*

Members States' responsibilities were established by Article 17 of the GFL which requires them to enforce food law, monitor and verify that relevant requirements are fulfilled by food and feed business operators at all stages of production, processing and distribution. Therefore, Member States must maintain in their territory a system of official controls and other activities as appropriate to the circumstances.

'Official controls' cover any form of control that the competent authority or the Community performs for the verification of compliance with feed and food law, animal health and animal welfare rules.[270] These official controls must be carried out using appropriate techniques developed for that purpose, including routine surveillance checks and more intensive controls such as inspections, verifications, audits, sampling, and the testing of samples.[271] Member States have the discretion to lay down effective, proportionate and dissuasive measures and penalties applicable to infringements in relation to the requirements of the food law.

Member States are additionally responsible for public communication on food and feed safety and risk, food and feed safety surveillance and other monitoring activities.

Provisions established by the EU Commission rely on essential principles derived from international trade rules. Therefore, non-discrimination, consistency, and transparency are guiding principles for any control completed within the framework of the EU food law.

1° Official controls

A. Control plans

Member States must designate a competent authority, which is responsible for the implementation of controls aiming at ensuring that food is safe. The competent authority must elaborate a control scheme enabling controls to be carried out regularly, on a risk basis and with appropriate frequency.[272]

In accordance with the global and uniform approach promoted by the Commission, each Member State must draw up a single integrated multi-annual national control plan. Member States' multi-annual national control plans must contain general information on the structure and organisation of their control systems. In general terms, these control plans must define strategies and responsibilities and allocate control resources, at the national, regional and local level, for emergency actions as well as training of staff. Multi-annual national control plans are to be kept up-to-date and amended in accordance with technological, environmental or scientific changes or with regard to particular factors during their implementation. Most importantly, the multi-annual national control plans must be adjusted to take account of the appearance of new hazards. Member States are requested to provide the Commission with a report on their activities within the framework of multi-annual national control plans on a yearly basis.

---

270 Regulation 882/2004, Article 2.1.

271 Regulation 882/2004, preamble, para. 12.

272 Regulation 882/2004, Article 3.

Multi-annual national control plans must be based on the broad guidelines established by the Commission for that purpose. Competent authorities must set up legal procedures to verify the effectiveness of official controls and define a statutory framework for remedial actions which they may entail. Furthermore, legal foundations must exist to define the outlines and documented procedures of official controls so as to permit a proper access to the premises and documentation of food business operators and to establish the way to perform controls.

B. The implementation of Controls

This implementation of controls must take into consideration all data pertinent for the case under consideration, including the results of previously performed controls or results of own checks of business operators based on HACCP principles. These controls must be proportionate to the risk and organised without prior warning or on an ad hoc basis at any of the stages of production, processing and distribution of feed or food and of animals and animal products. In addition, Member States are at liberty to implement additional controls, whether there is a suspicion of non-compliance or not.

In specific cases, the competent authority may delegate tasks related to official controls to one or more control bodies provided that the latter are sufficiently endowed with the required expertise and have indispensable facilities to complete that mission successfully. The delegation of tasks and power and its parameters must be notified to the Commission. However, this prerogative is restricted in some instances. Actions to be undertaken in case of non-compliance by a food business operator cannot be delegated by the competent authority.

It falls to the competent authority to circumscribe the scope of such delegated tasks and powers accurately. This collaboration must be based on the essential condition of the existence of an efficient and effective coordination between the two entities. Therefore, the control body must transmit the results of its controls to the competent authority on a regular basis, which, in turn, must organise audits and inspections of control bodies and take subsequent measures if they reveal unsatisfactory outcomes.

Depending on the case, official controls must be carried out at an appropriate place, including the point of entry of the goods, the point of release for free circulation, warehouses, the premises of the importing feed and food business operator, or other points of the feed and food chain.

Controls must take place with the same care on any product that makes up the composition of the end product regardless of their origin and their intended market, on any infrastructures of the food business, and in a general way on any element likely to influence the safety of the product, including the hygiene of the staff and the hygiene in the production premises. They must also assess all specific procedures implemented by the food business operator to reach its safety commitments, namely Good Manufacturing Practices (GMP), Good Hygiene Practices (GHP), Good Farming Practices, and HACCP.

c. Crisis management

Official controls can reveal minor irregularities, which must lead to remedial actions by the food business operator. The main concern is to ensure that the food business operator corrects the situation, but the measure imposed by the competent authority could depend on the nature of the infringement and past records of the food business operator. Considering these criteria, measures could range from the simple imposition of sanitation procedures to the suspension or withdrawal of the establishment's approval. In the case of consignments from third countries, such actions could result in the seizure of consignments followed by their destruction or re-dispatch outside the EU.

Official controls can sometimes draw attention to irregularities, which, due to their nature and their severity, represent serious risks to health. Member States must have in place operational contingency plans defining tasks and responsibilities, including those of stakeholders. This makes it possible to eliminate every risk of procrastination and to respond promptly to threats of the spreading of health risk. Contingency plans must evolve, taking into account structural changes and gained experiences.

Communication is incidentally the responsibility of national competent authorities, which must make information public on their control activities and their effectiveness.[273] In cases where a risk is identified or there are reasonable grounds to suspect a serious risk for health, national competent authorities must trace the risk as soon as possible and, if necessary, give due notice to the RASFF.[274] In addition, detailed information must be revealed to the public about the risk, its magnitude and measures taken or envisaged for its eradication.[275] This is a corollary of the obligation of transparency requested as part of their activities.[276]

---

273 Regulation 882/2004, Article 7.

274 There are two variants of Rapid Alert Systems depending on the category of the product:
(i) the Rapid Alert System for non-food consumer products (RAPEX) which was created by the General Product Safety Directive (GDSP);
(ii) the Rapid Alert System for Food and Feed (RASFF) has been legally established by the Article 50 of the GFL.

275 Regulation 178/2002, Article 10.

276 The obligation of transparency does not interfere with professional secrecy, which is an essential part of their working commitments. In the same way, professional secrecy must not serve as pretext to avoid the disclosure of crucial information to the public. In any case, information covered by professional secrecy is defined by Article 7(3) of Regulation 882/2004 and includes in particular: i) the confidentiality of preliminary investigation proceedings or of current legal proceedings; ii) personal data; iii) documents covered by an exception in Regulation 1049/2001 of the European Parliament and of the Council of 30 May 2001

2° Approval of establishments

In order to run an establishment of food of animal origin, the establishment must have the prior authorisation of the national competent authority. The national competent authority must perform an on-site control to assess all mechanisms set up to comply with the requirements of the relevant legislation. Within a period, which must not exceed six months, a conditional approval may be given to a food business operator which is able to prove an ongoing process likely to lead to imminent compliance. Numbers are assigned to approved establishments according to a system of codes which give information about the type of products of animal origin manufactured there. The essential conditions for approval are not static and the authorization can be revised, particularly on the basis of the results of the official controls. The list of authorised establishments and any related relevant information must be kept up-to-date and accessible to other Member States and the public.

In any case, the competent authority gives particular attention to the control of food of animal origin. Moreover, although it is important to make sure that implemented HACCP procedures are working properly and continuously, it is imperative to assess that such procedures enable compliance with relevant requirements on microbiological criteria, residues, contaminants, and prohibited substances, and are exempt from physical hazards.

3° Official controls on the introduction food from third countries

Recital 24 of the preamble to Regulation 882/2004 established the necessity to create uniform procedures for the control of food from third countries. This recital recalled the existence of harmonised import procedures for food of animal origin by virtue of Directive 97/78/EC and asserted that they should be maintained due to their efficiency. Given that the food law is a broad-spectrum discipline, the Commission deemed it important to supplement veterinary checks covered by this regulation with official controls on aspects such as those on additives, labelling, traceability, irradiation of food, and materials in contact with food. However, because of the lack of a dedicated import safety regime, these controls are not uniform across the sector but are instead a function of the level of risk: the higher the risk, the greater the control.[277] This differentiation appears clearly in the distinction established between products of non-animal origin and products of animal origin. From a trade liberalisation perspective,

regarding public access to European Parliament, Council and Commission documents: this refers to documents which, if divulged, would undermine public interest in general or the privacy and the integrity of the individual; iv) information protected by national and Community legislation concerning in particular professional secrecy, the confidentiality of deliberations, international relations and national defence.

277 Alemanno 2009, p13.

such a distinction becomes essential to determine conditions of access to the EU market. Therefore products of animal origin, being considered high-risk products are subject to stricter import control procedures.

The term 'import' refers to the release for free circulation of feed or food or the intention to release feed or food for free circulation.[278] "Food and feed imported into the Community for placing on the market within the Community shall comply with the relevant requirements of food law or conditions recognised by the Community to be at least equivalent thereto or, where a specific agreement exists between the Community and the exporting country, with requirements contained therein".[279] Defined as such, the disciplines on importing food into the EU imply considerable extra-territorial ambitions of the EU food law because these requirements regulate not only the conditions of the products once at the EU border, but also the way the products were handled during processing and trade.[280] Such rigorous requirements are a direct consequence of the fact that imported products, whatever their point of entry into the EU and whatever their origin, are likened to EU products and, therefore, have free access to the EU market as a whole. As a result, the EU legislator expects from its trading partners an equal commitment with regard to the protection of health and life. In this respect, the definition of responsibilities is applied similarly to foreign and EU food business operators and national competent authorities.

As regards products of animal origin, the most important import standard is the formal approval requirement of the third country or a part of the third country. In that respect, a list of authorised countries is drawn up and updated by the EU according to a wide range of criteria generally comprising the ability of the national legislation to comply with general and specific EU requirements and the financial and material capacity of competent authorities to implement, enforce and properly control rules set up by the EU legislation. The list of criteria to be considered to assess the reliability of a third-country product is as wide as diversified. These criteria refer in particular to a combination of 13 elements, which involve extensive legislation, institutions and resources.

---

278 Regulation 882/2004, Article 2.15. This definition must fit into the meaning given to the phrase 'release for free circulation' by Article 79 of Regulation 2913/92 establishing the Community Customs Code. This article stipulates specifically that "release for free circulation shall confer on non-Community goods the customs status of Community goods". Release "shall entail the application of commercial policy measures, completion of other formalities laid down in respect of the importation of goods and the charging of any duties legally due". Furthermore, 'import' in that understanding refers to an exclusive list of 15 countries defined by Annex I of Regulation 882/2004.

279 Regulation 178/2002, Article 10.

280 Meulen (van der) &, Velde (van der) 2008, p274.

Box 3-5. List of criteria to assess a third country (Article 11.4 of Regulation 854/2004)

When lists are drawn up or updated with regard to third countries and parts of third countries from which imports of specified products of animal origin are permitted, particular account shall be taken of the following criteria:

(a) the legislation of the third country on products of animal origin, the use of veterinary medicinal products, and the preparation and use of feeding stuffs;
(b) the organisation of the third countries' competent authorities, their powers and independence, the supervision to which they are subject and the authority that they have to effectively enforce the applicable legislation;
(c) the training of staff in the performance of official controls;
(d) the resources allocated to competent authorities;
(e) the existence and operation of documented control procedures and control systems based on priorities;
(f) where applicable, the situation regarding animal health and procedures for notifying the Commission and relevant international bodies of outbreaks of animal diseases;
(g) the extent and operation of official controls on imports of animals and products of animal origin;
(h) the assurances which the third country can give regarding compliance with, or equivalence to, Community requirements;
(i) the hygiene conditions of production, manufacture, handling, storage and dispatch actually applied to products of animal origin destined for the Community;
(j) any experience of marketing of the product from the third country and the results of any import controls carried out;
(k) the results of Community controls carried out in the third country, in particular the results of the assessment of the competent authorities, and the action that competent authorities have taken in the light of any recommendations addressed to them following a Community control;
(l) the existence, implementation and communication of an approved zoonoses control programme;
(m) the existence, implementation and communication of an approved residue control programme.

The ability to comply is assessed by an on-site visit to the third country by a control body of the EU, unless the risk in consideration does not require such a visit or unless other information establishes the reliability of the third country.

Moreover the same prerequisite is compulsory for establishments in third countries intending to export a product of animal origin to the EU. However, in this case, the ability of the competent authority of the considered country to provide sufficient guarantees is a precondition that determines whether the establishment could even benefit from the opportunity of a conformity assessment procedure. Due to their particular activity, some establishments do not need a prior authorisation to export to the EU. These are mainly establishments carrying out only primary production, transport operations, and the storage of products of animal origin not requiring temperature-controlled storage conditions. Moreover, some products of animal origin were not assigned any specific hygiene requirements by Regulation 853/2004. These products also do not require prior authorisation.

Furthermore, the competent authority must somehow vouch for the trustworthiness of the establishment itself, or any other establishment connected to it via the handling of raw materials of animal origin, to comply with the provisions of the national food law that are conform or equivalent to relevant EU requirements. Such a responsibility underlies the legal power of the competent authority to stop exports to the EU when an establishment is found failing to comply with essential requirements. In addition, the competent authority must establish an official inspection service in order to monitor the activities of establishments and provide the Commission with information about its supplier(s).

The competent authority of the third country must keep an updated list of authorised establishments that must be regularly communicated to the Commission. In light of relevant information, the Commission can require a modification to a list. Once informed, Member States can also raise duly justified objections against the granting of approval to an establishment.

As regards fishery products imported from a factory or freezer vessel flying the flag of a third country, a list of authorised vessels must also be drawn up and updated on a regular basis.

The general implementation of provisions of the food legislation does not prevent the adoption of particular measures in specific conditions. Therefore, specific import conditions may be adopted for a single product or group of products of animal origin, applicable to a single third country, regions of a third country or a group of third countries. Those measures are dependent on the nature of the risk associated with these products and are the results of the information provided by EU controls in the third country (ies).

In a more general framework, official controls on products of animal origin are considered by category and depend on the precise activities connected to their production. In such a way, the EU Commission established specific rules referring to controls on meat, live bivalve molluscs or fishery products.

4° Official controls on the production and placing on the market of fishery products

Official controls on the production and placing on the market of fishery products are to include, in particular, regular checks on the hygiene conditions of landing and first sale, inspections at regular intervals of vessels and establishments on land, including fish auctions and wholesale markets and checks on storage and transport conditions.[281]

With regard to fresh fishery products landed in the EU directly from a fishing vessel, a mission of inspection must take place on all vessels entering into the territorial waters of the EU, irrespective of the flag. Furthermore, particular

281 Regulation 854/2004, Annex III.

rules govern official controls on fishery products and must refer to the control of certain elements that are decisive in ensuring the safety of these products.

Official fishery products controls must include organoleptic examinations, freshness indicators, histamine, residues and contaminants, microbiological checks, parasites, and checks on poisons. Excessive levels of residues and contaminants, the non-compliance with relevant legislation on organoleptic, chemical, physical, or microbiological elements, the presence of poisons are all sufficient grounds to declare a fishery product unfit for human consumption. Furthermore, such a statement could come from the competent authority when it considers that fishery products may constitute a risk to public or animal health or are for any other reason not suitable for human consumption.

c. *Responsibilities of the Commission*

A high level of human health protection corresponds to one of the fundamental criteria, which the EU must take into consideration in defining and implementing its policies and activities.[282] This condition is further strengthened by the requirement to give due consideration to consumer protection requirements in defining and implementing other EU policies and activities.[283] Therefore, the extent of EU Commission's prerogatives, far from resulting from the food law itself, is the reflection of the trend established by the TFEU. The TFEU conferred exclusive or shared competence on the Commission, depending on the area and its importance within the overall policy of the Union. This delimitation is also the result of implications or structures required for the specific implementation of a particular set of laws.

For food safety matters, a shared competence between the EU Commission and Member States applies in the area of consumer protection and common safety concerns in public health matters.[284]

The Commission, in addition to establishing the appropriate legislation, must guarantee the coordination of actions undertaken by diverse Member States and ensure the swift circulation of information received through the RASFF. In cases where a serious risk is revealed through that channel, and Member States failed to take adequate measures, the responsibility falls on the Commission to undertake immediately, on its own initiative or at the request of a Member State, measures compatible with the gravity of the situation. In general terms, measures adopted in such situations are the result of the work of the Standing Committee on the Food Chain and Animal Health (SCFCAH). Nevertheless, in cases of emergency, the Commission may take provisional actions, provided, within a period of ten working days, these measures are confirmed, amended,

282 TFEU, Article 9.
283 TFEU, Article 12.
284 TFEU, Article 4 (f) and (k).

revoked, or extended in the context of the SCFCAH. In another scenario, when the Commission, duly informed about the existence of a serious risk, fails to take consequent actions, the Member State at the origin of the transmission of data relative to the risk is allowed to take interim protective measures. These national measures are also subjected to the SCFCAH according to the same deadlines and the SCFCAH can also adopt actions aiming to confirm, amend or revoke the national measures. Whether the risk results from an EU product or an imported one, the purpose of such measures has to be the prevention of the product being placed on the market.

1° Official controls

The Commission must delegate experts to perform inspections in Member States in order to verify the effectiveness of national strategies derived from the multi-annual control plans. These controls must also assess the functioning and organisation of competent authorities, investigate important or recurring problems in Member States, and examine emergency situations, emerging problems or new developments in Member States.[285] These general and specific audits are carried out in Member States by experts of the Food and Veterinary Office (FVO), which can be assisted by experts from Member States appointed by the Commission.

Official controls must also be performed in third countries to assess the conformity or equivalence of their legislation with EU requirements. Controls in third countries have a wider scope than the mere traceability check and are the grounds of numerous decisions on import conditions within the EU. The frequency of such controls depends on several variables covering three major dimensions. First, controls in third countries depend on information about the third country in question, such as the volume and nature of its exported products or the arising of emergency situations that require investigation or contingency measures. Second, the Commission bases its decision on controls in third countries on data emanating from its own system, such as a risk assessment of products exported to the EU, provisions of EU food law, results of former controls, or information from the EFSA or similar bodies. Third, the Commission refers to information transmitted by internationally recognised bodies such as the World Health Organization (WHO), the Codex Alimentarius Commission (CAC), and the World Organization for Animal Health (OIE) or from other sources.

2° Assessment of equivalence

As the risks are diverse, the mechanisms set up by countries for their regulation are different. These variations in approaches to food safety regulation can result

---

285 Regulation 882/2004, Article 45.2.

in substantial disparities that could constitute barriers to trade. The recognition of the equivalence of legislation established by the EU is not defined in the GFL but rather in the Regulation 852/2004 on the hygiene of foodstuffs. 'Equivalent' standards are standards, which "in respect of different systems" are "capable of meeting the same objective".[286] It follows that different measures can be adequate to overcome the same risk and therefore achieve the same level of protection. The recognition of equivalence is of interest in ensuring that health protection is maintained while providing the greatest quantity and variety of safe foodstuffs for consumers, the best availability of safe inputs for producers, and healthy economic competition.[287] Considering that the prevalence of risks could differ considerably across countries, the recognition of equivalence is of great importance in so far as equivalence enables countries to adopt measures appropriate to their particular features or environment, thereby facilitating their proper implementation and enforcement.

The recognition of equivalence requires the evaluation of the overall performance of a system, rather than a focus on individual measures, given that its ultimate goal is to weigh up the resulting level of protection. In this regard, the implementation of equivalence may require an on-the-spot visit to verify different aspects of a system such as legal basis, general objectives and infrastructures. In such a way, the equivalence implies the development of a highly efficient control system so as to consistently certify compliance of different set of laws.

In reality, equivalence requires difficult scientific assessments of the effectiveness of other countries' standards and entails extensive resources.[288] Despite the intensity of its involvement in food safety regulation, the EU itself has developed about ten equivalency agreements so far.

With regard to fishery products, the EU has applied a one-way assessment of equivalence that enabled many countries, including developing countries, to gain access to its market. This approach has enabled the EU to decide on its own initiative to evaluate the food safety laws and systems of third countries that intend to export to the EU. In this regard, on-spot missions in the third country concerned enable an assessment of the ability of its competent authority to inspect and certify establishments and/or fishing vessels in a way that is at least equivalent to relevant EU requirements. Following such controls, a country whose laws and systems of inspection and certification are conform or deemed equivalent to EU requirements obtains an approval to export fishery products to the EU.[289]

It is worth mentioning that, as regards the concept of 'equivalence', in circumstances where a country lacks its own facilities, the EU authorities may

286 Regulation 852/2004, Article 2 (e).
287 Weidong 2006, p739.
288 CTA 2003, p5.
289 The EU approach to equivalence is further explained in chapter VIII.

accept as 'equivalent' health certificates issued by acceptable bodies in another country. The most quoted cases are Namibia, whose establishments can be certified by South Africa health certification bodies, and New Zealand, which can certify establishments in certain Pacific Islands.[290]

3.4.4. HYGIENE OF FOODSTUFFS

The innovative approach introduced by the White Paper on Food Safety was extended to the area of the hygiene of foodstuffs. Embracing a coordinated and holistic approach, the Commission cleared the way for the simplification and the merger of multiple hygiene requirements stipulated in several directives. Spread out over time, these directives constituted responses to specific issues and referred to a wide range of products. The first such directive dates back to 1964 and referred to the hygiene of fresh meat. For many years the rules were developed with regard to meat and its by-products such as eggs and milk (Directive 64/433/EEC). Afterwards, over 20 directives were adopted. A general observation shows that all of the directives were linked to products likely to be easily contaminated. This trend was extended to fishery products in 1991 by Directives 91/492/EEC and 91/493/EEC. Specific hygiene rules related to fishery products were established the following year by Directive 92/48/EEC, setting up minimum hygiene rules applicable to fishery products caught and brought on board certain vessels in accordance with its Article 3 (1)(a)(i).

In 1993, the first harmonised hygiene rules were adopted through Directive 93/43/EEC that defined a general framework for the implementation of rules on the hygiene of foodstuffs and procedures for the verification of compliance with them.

Before the harmonisation of the legal framework of hygiene, and apart from existing specific measures, the main hygiene rules adopted by Directive 93/43/EEC had already established some basic common principles, which were also integrated in subsequent laws. These principles referred, for instance, to the introduction of HACCP principles, which should be applied by all food business operators other than those engaged in primary production. Directive 93/43/EEC also established the complementary responsibility of competent authorities for carrying out ex-post controls aiming at ensuring proper rules on implementation, including a general assessment of potential food safety hazards related to the food business operators' activities.[291]

As regards third countries, any hygiene issue likely to represent a serious risk to human health should lead the Commission to take consistent action, either on its own initiative or at the request of a Member State. These measures have to

[290] Ababouch et al. 2005, p9.

[291] Council Directive 93/43/EEC, Article 8.2.

be commensurate with the risk involved, translated either into the suspension of imports or the setting of special conditions for foodstuffs from all or part of the third country concerned. If required, application of the suspension of imports could be extended to the transit third country.[292]

In 2004, a set of regulations was adopted, commonly referred to as "food hygiene package". The 'Hygiene Package' must be implemented in a transparent fashion as a common framework for the hygienic production of all food and applies subsequently to all food business operators throughout the food chain. In addition, this set of laws includes differentiation between products of non-animal and of animal.

The 'Hygiene Package' comprises three basic Regulations, namely 852/2004, 853/2004 and 854/2004, along with Regulation 882/2004 on official controls addressed to competent authorities. The rules defined in these regulations have been clarified by several implementing directives and guidance documents that have no legal value.

Regulation 852/2004 is the cornerstone of the current EU food hygiene framework. This regulation sets up basic rules and principles. Regulation 853/2004 supplements Regulation 852/2004 and defines specific hygiene rules applicable to food of animal origin. Regulation 854/2004 is specifically devoted to national authorities and sets rules for the control and enforcement of food hygiene policies.

The food hygiene framework has established the importance of preserving the valuable and irreplaceable traditions of Member States. With this in mind, the Member States must take action at the national level to adapt hygiene requirements in the light of traditional methods that have proven safe by virtue of their long application, even though they do not entirely satisfy the Community hygiene requirements. National measures should also take into account specificities of establishments facing particular constraints due to their geographical location.

The Hygiene Package based food safety monitoring on three basic principles, including minimum hygiene requirements, official controls to check compliance of food business operators, and the establishment and operation by food business operators of food safety programmes and procedures based on HACCP principles.[293]

a. *Definition and scope*

While it was defined in 1993 as "all measures necessary to ensure the safety and wholesomeness of foodstuffs"[294], food hygiene was more clearly explained in 2004

---

292 Council Directive 93/43/EEC, Article 10.1.
293 Regulation 852/2004, preamble, para. 12.
294 Directive 93/43/EEC, Article 2.

as "measures and conditions necessary to control hazards and to ensure fitness for human consumption of a foodstuff taking into account its intended use".[295]

This definition introduced two major differences. Firstly, a goal-oriented factor which implies that measures are not merely taken to comply with standards deemed objective by food business operators, but all disciplines must be designed to converge towards the achievement of an effective hazards control during production. Secondly, the new definition implies an additional responsibility, meaning that food hazards control is itself designed with respect to the destination of the final product. This precision is very important in determining the measures to be considered for example to ensure that the product released onto the market later meets food additives or contaminants requirements.

As is customary since the entry into force of the GFL, the primary responsibility for compliance with relevant hygiene requirements rests on food business operators. To this end, the legislation laid down measures applicable to all operators regardless of their activity or the size of their business. The only differentiation lies in the flexibility allowed to operators involved in primary production.

b. Prerequisite requirements

Prerequisite requirements are a set of measures representing the foundation of any hygiene procedure. Generally speaking, these requirements stipulate key rules relating to the premises, staff and more commonly to any infrastructure likely to influence or alter food products.

Premises and installations therein must be erected so as to enable a good carrying out of activities of maintenance, cleaning and disinfection, and avoid the accumulation of potential harmful substances that could nest on walls or hidden recesses. These infrastructures must be suitable to complete good hygiene practices and, if necessary, be perfectly adaptable to maintain the required temperature according to the type of products. In this regard, where appropriate, the cold chain must not be interrupted. Moreover, only the use of potable water is permitted in all premises. This requirement is challenging for rural fishing communities in some developing countries like Benin, where the access to potable water is still an issue in many areas.

The staff must apply the strictest rules of personal hygiene and avoid, in the event of disease, being active in food-processing areas in order to prevent cross-contamination.

In addition, food business operators are expected to comply with microbiological criteria testing to avert hazards and implement adequate hazard control mechanisms. Regulation 2073/2005 on microbiological criteria for foodstuffs defines 'microbiological criterion' as "a criterion defining the

---

[295] Regulation 852/2004, Article 2 (a).

acceptability of a product, a batch of foodstuffs or a process, based on the absence, presence or number of micro-organisms[296], and/or on the quantity of their toxins metabolites, per unit(s) of mass, volume, area or batch".[297]

Microbiological criteria give guidance on the acceptability of foodstuffs and their manufacturing, handling and distribution processes and must be an integral part of the implementation of HACCP-based procedures and other hygiene control measures.[298] Food safety microbiological criteria are used to define thresholds for acceptable contamination limits for the relevant microorganisms.[299]

The EU food law established, according to the food category, the micro-organisms for which tests should be performed by operators, their sampling-plan, limits, analytical reference method, and the stage where the criterion applies.[300]

Regulating microbiological criteria is essential for food hygiene compliance because the criteria can be used as a yardstick to validate and verify the proper implementation of good hygiene practices and HACCP principles.

c. *Hygiene requirements for food business operators*

1° General obligations

Food business operators must verify that food hygiene requirements are correctly applied and make sure that their systems and procedures are properly implemented to ensure compliance. These procedures must specifically target compliance with microbiological criteria and temperature control requirements, the maintenance of the cold chain and the realisation of relevant sampling and analysis.

In the case that the production process involves several different actors, the actor responsible for the supply of raw materials has a higher responsibility in the sense that he must make sure that "raw materials" are free from germs likely to corrupt the end product. "A food business operator is not to accept raw materials or ingredients, other than live animals, or any other material used in processing products, if they are known to be, or might reasonably be expected to be, contaminated with parasites, pathogenic microorganisms or toxic, decomposed or foreign substances to such an extent that, even after the food business operator had hygienically applied normal sorting and/or preparatory or processing procedures, the final product would be unfit for human consumption".[301]

---

296 Directive 2073/2005 also defines 'micro-organisms' as bacteria, viruses, yeasts, moulds, algae, parasitic protozoa, microscopic parasitic helminths, and their toxins and metabolites.

297 Regulation 2073/2005, Article 2(b).

298 Regulation 2073/2005, preamble.

299 Idem.

300 Fishery products must be tested for the level of the micro-organism histamine during their shelf-life when the products are placed on the market. As for shelled and shucked products of cooked crustaceans and molluscan shellfish, they must be tested for E.coli and Coagulase-positive staphylococci at the end of manufacturing process.

301 Regulation 852/2004, Annex II, Chapter IX (1).

In this context, the issue arises as to the meaning to be given to the expression "might reasonably be expected to be contaminated". Such a stipulation puts an additional burden on a food business operator, which might be confused with the alternative to rely on discernible product characteristics or to carry out further sample tests to estimate a product's safety. It is easier to trust a usual partner in relation to whom one can presume their credibility with regard to implementing essential measures to protect their products from contamination. However the food business operator must avoid that this vote of confidence jeopardises its own reliability. In any case, it falls on the food business operator to strike a balance between the preservation of trade relations, the tendency to trust the routine, and the permanent commitment to do his utmost to get supplies of safe products.

2° HACCP requirements

The major component of the EU food hygiene legislation has been the reiteration of the implementation by operators of a method based on the identification and control of potential hazards in food through the so-called Hazard Analysis and Critical Control Point (HACCP) system. HACCP is a control technique based on total quality management principles.[302] HACCP focuses on measureable indicators and may thus offer a cheaper and more timely way of controlling food safety than standard product sampling and testing.[303]

The HACCP requirement, which is compulsory for all food business operators involved in the food chain after the threshold of the primary production, entails the set up, implementation and maintenance of a permanent procedure or procedures based on HACCP principles.[304] The wording "permanent" does not constitute a mere qualifier because it underlies the idea of an evolutionary system able to be adjusted and applied in all circumstances. Moreover HACCP-based procedures are expected to have an international connotation due to the explicit recommendation of the Commission that such requirements take account of Codex Alimentarius principles.[305]

HACCP is a systematic and science-based approach that enables the detection of potential food safety hazards in order to take preventive measures accordingly. HACCP does not represent a simple execution of a linear activity, which applies indiscriminately to any activities throughout the food chain. Far from that, the requirement should be adapted to each specific operation and is to be applied separately. The HACCP procedure must pay regard to several criteria such as the impact of raw materials, the likely-use of the end product or consumer categories.

302 Bernauer & Caduff 2006, p86.

303 Idem.

304 Regulation 852/2004, Article 5.1.

305 Hitherto, the relevant CODEX standards are contained in the CODEX document CAC/RCP 1-1996, rev.4-2003.

The adoption of a HACCP procedure consists of identifying the essential food safety stages along the processes of preparation, processing and distribution. Called Critical Control Points (CCP), these stages are the basis for the detection of potential hazards in foodstuffs and represent the way forward to the setting down of the most adequate system for their prevention, elimination or reduction to acceptable levels.

Table 3.3. Seven principles of a HACCP system

Principles	Tasks
Conducting a hazard analysis	Since the HACCP is a multidisciplinary system, its elaboration requires a team with the appropriate skills, considering the technicality of products and manufacturing processes. The intended use of the final product and the potential related food hazards must also be of guidance in the gathering of experts endowed with the suitable knowledge. The implementation of hygiene requirements, specifically procedures based on the HACCP principles, requires the full cooperation and commitment of food business employees. In this respect, food business operators must ensure that their personnel get the adequate training. Furthermore, food business operators must do their utmost to associate external workforce at any time they lack appropriate internal human resources. This step requires a clear definition of the HACCP scope through the delineation of the relevant food chain segment and the type of related hazards. Whether these hazards are biological, chemical or physical depend on the particular product characteristics, taking into account the specific vulnerability of its potential consumers. A flow diagram of each sequence of the process must be designed, providing sufficient technical data and including the margins of delay. The operational effectiveness of this diagram should be verified on-site during operating hours in order to make necessary amendments for its accuracy. This process is completed only when a proper analysis of identified risks is made and measures are planned to eliminate or reduce the risks that are likely to adversely affect health to acceptable levels.
Identification of CCPs	The identification of CCPs must be performed at the step or steps at which control is essential to eliminate potential harmful effects. A CCP is "a step at which control can be applied and is essential to prevent or eliminate a food safety hazard or reduce it to an acceptable level".[306] Therefore, the identification of CCPs is a very sensitive task that requires the utmost rigour. This identification must be done throughout the whole manufacturing process and lead to the establishment and implementation of a monitoring system at each critical point. The recommendation to perform these tasks through the use of measurable indicators provides a more cost-effective approach to control than product sampling and testing, which is more expensive and may not provide timely results.[307]

306 Codex 1969, p21.
307 Unnevehr & Jensen 1999, p627.

Principles	Tasks
Establishment of critical limits at CCPs	Critical limits correspond to the extreme values acceptable for food safety. Therefore, previously established control measures must result in critical limits in order to separate acceptability from unacceptability. These critical limits are established for tangible parameters such as temperature, additives, preservatives, or time.
Establishment and implementation of effective monitoring procedures at CCPs	This phase encompasses a set of observations or measurements performed at each critical point in order to make information available with regard to a specified critical limit. These tasks would enable necessary corrective actions to ensure compliance. The frequency of such observations, whether continuous or intermittent, is left to the discretion of the food business operator as long as the selected method is satisfactory to prevent nonconformities.
Establishment of corrective actions	The HACCP system must be reactive enough to enable an immediate implementation of corrective actions. It ensues that the entire outlines of such a system must be clearly defined beforehand, highlighting not only the actions to be undertaken but also the persons in charge of their execution. It is noteworthy to underline that such a schematisation would not be complete unless there is a description of additional measures with regard to products manufactured during the period when the process was out of control.
Establishment of verification procedures	Specific parameters for the business must guide in the design and implementation of check procedures to assess the performance of the overall HACCP system. This entails random sampling and analysis that are to be reinforced at selected critical points. The proper repartition of tasks is rather important due to the requirement to insert a functional separation between persons in charge of the monitoring and corrective actions, and those responsible for verification procedures.
Organisation of documentation and record keeping	Any action planned or executed within the framework of the HACCP system must result in accurate records and archiving. Correctly performed, this function includes a double advantage: on the one hand, this principle enables a conscientious follow-up of the system to guarantee its efficiency and, on the other hand, the principle is a key asset to fulfil the obligation to make data available for competent authorities in case of audit.

d. HACCP Flexibility

In view of the complexity of the HACCP system, the food law authorises a certain level of flexibility with regard to its implementation. The HACCP system should in no case constitute a burden, which obliges food business operators to implement requirements that do not correspond to the nature of their activity. Food business operators are merely requested to use guides to good hygiene practices developed at various levels as an example to develop their own methods, taking particular account of the essential characteristics of their production system.

More generally, HACCP flexibility refers to the primary production[308] of foodstuffs. Primary production must be understood as the production, rearing or growing of primary products including harvesting, milking and farmed animal production prior to slaughter. Primary production also includes hunting and fishing and the harvesting of wild products. For this purpose, fishery products remain primary products even after slaughter, bleeding, decapitation, gutting, removing fins, refrigeration, and placing in containers for transport at the level of primary production. The products resulting from further handling such as filleting or vacuum packaging are not primary products.

The flexibility provided is underlined in recital 15 of Regulation 852/2004, which covers three distinct aspects. First "the HACCP must provide sufficient flexibility to be applicable in all situations", especially when the nature of the business does not enable an identification of critical control points. Second, "the requirement of establishing 'critical limits' does not imply the necessity to fix a numerical limit in every case". Third, "the requirement of retaining documents needs to be flexible in order to avoid undue burdens for very small businesses". Therefore, all primary production activities and related operations benefit from less stringent hygiene rules.

In general, all activities that do not alter the nature of the primary product, such as transport, handling and storage at the place of production, are considered primary production activities. The same applies to transport operations from the place of production to an establishment to deliver primary products such as fishery products. The main hygiene rules in such instances simply entail taking care to avoid product contamination, whether with elements resulting from nature such as air, soil and water, or deriving from human practices such as chemical contaminants.

Food business operators at the primary production level can either base their hazard control mechanisms on traditional agricultural practices or have recourse to guides to good practices. However, they are still bound by the rigorous archiving rules as to the use of veterinary medicinal products or pesticides in order to make their documents available upon the request of competent authorities.

Food business operators must apply for the registration of their establishment and units under their control. To that end, they must cooperate with national control authorities by providing the latter with all the information required to ensure the registration of establishments. In the same vein, any significant change or closure should be notified in a timely manner. Finally, Food business operators shall operate only after the approval of their establishment, following after at least one on-site visit of the CA that has checked compliance with hygiene

308 European Commission/Directorate-General for Health and Consumers, Guidance document on the implementation of certain provisions of Regulation (EC) No 852/2004 on the Hygiene of Foodstuffs, SANCO/1731/2008 Rev.6, 2009), p11.

rules of Regulation 852/2004 or the rules adopted at the national level and with decisions duly adopted by the Commission. Such an obligation compels the food operators not to put on the market products that were in one way or another related to or made by a non-registered establishment.[309] National authorities determine the rules that determine the approval of establishments, as well as the procedures to be followed to obtain approval.[310]

According to the nature of the food business or the nature of the food handled, several scenarios can appear in the management of food hazards. On the one hand, owing to particular characteristics, the mere implementation of the prerequisite requirements could be satisfactory to control potential food hazards. This refers in general to food establishments which do not need any food preparation, manufacturing or processing. In such cases, the prerequisite requirements could be assimilated to the first step of the HACCP procedure, namely the hazard analysis. Similarly, in other businesses, the hazard analysis could reveal that all food hazards could be controlled via the implementation of the prerequisite requirements.

As for critical limits, when monitoring procedures are based on visual observation, such as faecal contamination of carcases in a slaughterhouse or the boiling temperature of liquid food, there is no need to fix a numerical value. In the same vein, food business operators may not set up monitoring procedures, specifically in cases where this step is based on visual observation similar to the previous examples. In other cases, the preparation is made by means of standard processes, using calibrated equipment. In this instance, an adequate exploitation of the features of the equipment is completely analogous to HACCP monitoring procedures.

The simplification permitted by the ease of the manufacturing process can result consistently in a lowering of record-keeping obligations. Thus, the use of good practice or generic HACCP can substitute individual documentation on HACCP-based procedures. In the same way, when the monitoring is based on visual observations, the establishment of a record is compulsory only when the system does not function properly. This enables keeping track of occurrences of non-compliance and subsequent corrective measures.

e. *Hygiene rules for fishery products*

Food business operators must carry out a visual inspection on a representative number of samples to detect visible parasites present on fishery products. This is especially appropriate since these parasites are in essence clearly distinguishable from fish tissues due to their dimension, colour or texture. Visual inspection is

309 Regulation 853/2004, Article 4.2.

310 Regulation 882/2204, Article 31.1.a.

defined as a "non-destructive examination of fish or fishery products with or without optical means of magnifying and under good light conditions for human vision, including, if necessary, candling".[311] The frequency and the scale of visual inspections must be determined according to the type of fishery products, their geographical origin and their use. In cases of evisceration, qualified persons must carry out the inspection on the abdominal cavity, livers and roes intended for human consumption.

If the implementation of visual inspection raises concerns about the freshness of the fish, the chemical checks could help determine whether the fish is unfit for consumption, especially when the Total Volatile Basic Nitrogen (TVB-N) limits are exceeded.

f. Hygiene of imported food

The rules on imported food hygiene must meet the requirements of Articles 3 to 6 of Regulation 852/2004 in accordance with the basic rules set forth in particular in Article 11 of the GFL. This article is at the origin of the basic rule that imported products must meet standards conform with or recognised to be at least equivalent to those of the EU.

In the case under consideration in this study, imported food hygiene rules must satisfy obligations concerning operators as detailed above in terms of responsibility, respect of specific rules of hygiene, implementation of HACCP, and cooperation with authorities, in particular regarding the disclosure of relevant information and the approval of establishments.

The rules on imported products also involve the responsibility of food business operators since they must ensure that the establishment they intend to get supplies from is recognised by one of the lists drawn up for this purpose by the EU Commission. It goes without saying that the country of origin must also have official recognition by the EU as a reliable source for the export of the products concerned to the Community market.

Over time, FVO missions enabled the assessment of the implementation of the food hygiene framework. Despite its apparent complexity, the implementation of the hygiene package did not raise major difficulties for food business operators and competent authorities, except for some small establishments and to varying extents.[312] The findings of the relevant FVO missions were relayed by the Commission in its compulsory report on the application of the food hygiene regulation. Among others, some small businesses were sometimes obliged to

---

311 Regulation 2074/2005, Annex II.

312 See European Commission/Directorate-General for Health and Consumers, Report from the Commission to the Council and to the European Parliament on the experience gained from the Implementation of the Hygiene Regulations (EC) No 852/2004, (EC) No 853/2004 and (EC) No 854/2004 of the European Parliament and of the Council of 29 April 2004, European Communities 2009, p5.

use external consultancy, which were in some cases not relevant for the reality of the establishment, resulting in more documentation and records than was mandatory. In addition, external consultancies were not efficient and were overly expensive for these small businesses.[313] Some minor problems were raised about the difficulties in satisfying the record-keeping requirement, which is seen as an administrative burden for small businesses. At the same time, the guides to good practice were appreciated for their valuable input for primary producers.

According to the findings of the FVO, the competent authorities had difficulties to properly assess HACCP-based procedures, which were slightly improved later. Moreover, some Member States reported difficulties with regard to the vague nature of certain objectives set down in Regulation 852/2004 and the lack of clear guidance for primary producers.[314] Lastly, it is worth underlining that microbiological criteria were rarely taken into account by food business operators in their procedures and were even quite often not addressed by the CA's official supervision.

However, the situation is not so simple in developing countries. In Benin, for example, until 2002, even though the companies had HACCP plans, they did not reflect their activity, were outdated and were not applied. Implementing HACCP principles proved an arduous task for processing plants due to the technicality of the method. This situation was later resolved only through significant investments in staff training and restructuring within the processing plants.

3.5. ENFORCEMENT OF EU REQUIREMENTS TOWARDS THIRD COUNTRIES

For the implementation of its measures concerning third countries, the EU has several organs that enable the carrying out of appropriate controls and whose work can help provide justifications for the measures taken. These organs are essentially the Food and Veterinary Office (FVO) and the Border Inspection Posts (BIPs). In addition, to allow an efficient food risk communication, key information is transmitted through the RASFF.

3.5.1. IMPLEMENTATION OF CONTROLS THROUGH THE FVO

After the BSE crisis and the redefinition of the food safety policy it required, the Commission initiated its Communication "Commission's green paper on food law" that propelled the creation of the FVO in 1997. The FVO became the organ

---

313 Idem.

314 Idem.

par excellence for the implementation of EU control policies that should lead to the official approval of third countries exporting fishery products to the EU. In the early days, given the number of Member States to inspect, the multiplicity of third countries and the small staff resources of the FVO, controls were sometimes limited to a mere documentary assessment. Documentary assessment refers to a desk analysis of information provided by third countries on their legal and institutional framework as regards the conditions of production and control of fishery product safety, as well as a report on the overall health status in the country. For instance, in 1998, documentary assessments led to the temporary authorisation of 37 countries, while the 35 others were asked to provide more information and guarantees since the first guarantees they provided were insufficient.

However, increasingly, on-site visits are conducted by FVO agents to assess the actual conditions under which involved stakeholders operate. Later on, priority was given to third countries with past records of health issues and to those with a large volume of trade with the EU. FVO missions can also answer the request for approval addressed to the EU by a third country or in response to disease outbreaks. Additionally, the FVO uses the information transmitted through the RASFF to identify the priorities for its programme.

FVO missions were classified into two categories: the first missions to audit the CAs are called "evaluation missions", while "inspections" are carried out for the follow-up to the evaluations. When the results of a follow-up inspection reveal that satisfactory measures had been undertaken, the report is closed. Otherwise, the report is referred to the Commission Services to consider the most appropriate course of action to be taken.[315]

The FVO checks compliance with EU food safety and quality requirements at both processing plants and CAs. To ensure transparency, results of the inspection missions are made available promptly to enable the inspected country to respond about the observations made and, if necessary, to take necessary measures in due course.

FVO missions have a clear impact on the development of food policies and can help redesign control procedures. Their recommendations to the Commission are of crucial importance, since there are strong presumptions that inspectors, having been on the sites, could actually measure the magnitude of risks and are best suited to recommend appropriate solutions to prevent or minimise any risk.

Missions in third countries in the early days allowed for the adoption of policies to monitor production standards for fishery products and to decide on emergency restrictions when essential improvements were needed.[316] In general,

[315] European Commission, FVO annual report 2001.

[316] European Commission, FVO annual report April 1998- March 1999.

inspection results can be used to refuse, withdraw or modify export approvals to the EU.

3.5.2. IMPLEMENTATION OF VETERINARY CONTROLS

Despite all the precautions surrounding the import of products and even though all requirements would be respected on both sides, products from third countries must inevitably undergo veterinary controls before being released on the territory of the Union. This obligation makes it possible to further safeguard supplies and ensure market stability by instituting a legal framework for veterinary checks on all consignments of products from third countries through Directive 97/78/EC. Based on the characteristics of the products involved, veterinary controls apply differently, being most of the time commensurate with the potential risk.

Products of animal origin are regarded as those with the highest risk due to their ability to transmit serious diseases. Therefore, a consignment of products of animal origin must satisfactorily undergo specific checks leading to the issuance of a Common Veterinary Entry Document (CVED) before they are released for entry into the EU.

Veterinary checks have initially been developed with regard to the completion of the internal market and referred to physical checks and/or administrative formalities intended for the protection, direct or otherwise, of public or animal health.[317] In the beginning, imported products were subject to a documentary check on the origin of the products before being shipped under customs supervision to inspection posts to undergo veterinary checks.[318] For this purpose, a differentiation should be made. First, products such as fresh meat and some of its by-products or heat-treated milk should not be given customs clearance unless the veterinary checks have shown compliance with the rules harmonised at Community level. Second, products not subject to Community harmonisation, such as fish products, after entering the territory of the EU, should not be re-dispatched unless veterinary checks show that they are in compliance with the rules of the Member State of destination. Alternatively, after a visual check to ensure that products conform to accompanying certificates, products are deployed to the country of destination, which will carry out the veterinary controls.

In general terms, Directive 97/78/EC sets up conditions to implement documentary, identity and physical checks to be carried out at Border Inspection Posts (BIPs), provided that consignments are introduced into the

---

317 Council Directive 89/662/EEC. The same definition was later taken up by the Council Directive 90/425/EEC.

318 Directive 89/662/EEC, Article 6.

EU only via one such post of a Member State. This step essentially enables the verification of the accuracy of data relative to the products passed on beforehand, as well as the information mentioned on accompanying documents and certificates. Such requirements may be flexible depending on the assurance that a third country can give with regard to products subject to harmonised import conditions.

The Commission can decide, on its own initiative or at the request of a Member State, to reduce the frequency of veterinary checks on products from a particular third country or some parts of that country, considering satisfactory health guarantees offered by the third country with regard to products subject to harmonised import conditions or results of previous checks. It is nevertheless advisable to underline that not less than ten criteria are to be considered to decide on such derogations. From this perspective, the Commission must establish a file referring to each of these criteria to be submitted to the Standing Veterinary Committee. Generally speaking, they refer to particular sanitary data of the country, implemented veterinarian and hygiene measures, the nature of the product and the related risk, and the outcome of on-site visits or import checks. However, there is still a possibility for a third country to negotiate on a reciprocal basis the reduction of checks on the grounds of a veterinary equivalence agreement concluded with the Union.

The detection of potential risks in a third country must result in immediate action by the Commission. The consequent measures depend on the gravity of the case under consideration and could consist of the suspension of imports from all or part of the third country, the implementation of special conditions with regard to its products or the adoption of particular control measures. When the detection of risks refers to a consignment, the consignment must be seized and destroyed and all relevant information must be transmitted to other BIPs and the Commission. In the same logic, special measures must be taken with regard to consignments from the same origin.

Causes resulting in consignments being rejected at EU borders are diverse. Generally they result from bad or insufficient controls in countries of origin resulting in the presence of undesirable substances or germs in the end products. Some rejections of consignments are based on mere organoleptic aspects, while some cases might refer to the failure to comply with presentation and labelling requirements such as packaging defects. It should nevertheless be noted that the actual cause of rejection for some consignments are not properly transmitted via the RASFF and are gathered under the category "not determined/other".

From all border rejections of consignments of food of animal origin, fishery products often make up the greatest share. Overall parasitic infestation, heavy metals, bad hygienic state, and veterinary drug residues are essentially the reasons that trigger the rejection of fishery product consignments.

In any case, a consignment, which is introduced in the EU without having undergone the required veterinary checks, must be seized by the CA and destroyed if the products do not comply with relevant import conditions or their checks reveal some irregularities. When the checks do not reveal potential dangers related to their consumption, the products could be re-dispatched outside the EU.

Although it could be taken with reservations, the importance of border rejections of consignments could reflect the weakness of the control systems of the countries of origin of the rejected goods. If one assumes that products shipped to the EU follow the same rules or conform to strict rules to ensure the level of protection determined by the EU, this would simply have two implications. On the one hand, processing plants would have applied strict hygiene rules implementing the HACCP system and implemented the required own-checks. On the other hand, competent authorities would have carried out official controls, and, in the case of products of animal origin, the appropriate certificates would have been issued on the basis of the appropriate analyses. In such a case, why are so many consignments of products from third countries rejected? Before jumping to hasty conclusions, one should certainly keep in mind that many alerts also relate to EU products. Therefore, common sense suggests that conclusions are drawn upon a comparison between the volume traded and the number of alerts for each entity.

3.5.3. MARKET SURVEILLANCE THROUGH THE RASFF

The logic of the common market raises the challenge to develop an integrated system likely to curb the risks related to the removal of physical barriers between the EU Member States. Such a system implies a shared commitment by each participant to maintain an adequate level of communication and responsiveness to ensure two essential objectives for consumer protection. First, the system must prevent the marketing of unsafe products. Second, such a system must ensure that, when unsafe products are already on the market, adequate logistics exist for their withdrawal as soon as the danger or the susceptibility to cause harm is discovered.

To achieve this challenge, the EU designed and created a the Rapid Alert System for Food and Feed (RASFF) that was developed and strengthened according to the experiences and needs identified over the years to ensure its efficiency.

Box 3-6. Origin and development of the rapid alert system

The origin of the rapid alert system can be traced back to 1978. An extremist group calling itself the Arab Revolutionary Army-Palestine Command injected mercury in oranges from Israel to disrupt Israel's economy. The first infected fruit was discovered in Maastricht (the Netherlands) and the Dutch authorities then initiated a nationwide search that led to the identification of 25 contaminated oranges, while many others were found in nine cities in the then West Germany. This situation resulted in a food safety panic and the suspension of the sale of oranges. At the time Germany used to import 140 million tons of citrus fruits from Israel. Then, the Member States' food control authorities came up with the idea of a rapid alert system aiming at keeping each other informed in cases of a food-related risk to human health. Belgium, Denmark, France, Germany, Ireland, Italy, Luxembourg, the Netherlands, and the United Kingdom came to a 'gentlemen's agreement' to set up a system while awaiting formal legislation.[319]

The very first legal basis for such a rapid alert system was laid down in 1979 by a proposal that established the exchange of information relating to actions taken or about to be taken as regards products presenting a danger to consumers.[320] The proposal then took into account the product, extensively defined, including not only food products but also, among others, household appliances or pharmaceutical products not intended for professional use. This step was followed by an amended proposal[321] and, two years later, Council Decision 84/133/EEC. The latter confirmed once again the basic principle and also urged Member States' competent authorities to exchange information on all measures they have taken following the receipt of initial information on a product risk. Meanwhile, the Rapid Alert System for non-food products (RAPEX) split and developed. It was only in 1992 that some procedural aspects were set up to operate the rapid alert system for food products. The RASFF was formally created by Article 8 of Directive 92/59/EEC which established a procedure to inform both EU Member States and EFTA/EEA countries whenever a product presents a serious risk for the health and safety of consumers.

The legal basis of the RASFF system has been clearly laid down in the integrated approach introduced by Regulation 178/2002, which stipulates the actors, their responsibilities and the functioning of the system. Thus, the RASFF is set up as a network for the notification of direct or indirect risk to human health deriving from food or feed, which connects contact points respectively designated by Member States, the Commission and the EFSA, provided that the management of the network is led by the Commission.[322] The importance of involving the EFSA in this network is that by virtue of its role in risk assessment, it can add value to the information with scientific or technical knowledge that can facilitate a prompt and appropriate action of Member States about the risk identified.

319 European Commission 2009b, p11.

320 Proposal for Council Decision introducing a Community system for the rapid exchange of information on dangers arising from the use of consumer products, COM (79) 725 final.

321 Amended Proposal for a Council Decision introducing a Community system for the rapid exchange of information on consumer products, COM(82) 837 final, 16/12/1982, O.J. C 321, 22.12.1979.

322 Regulation 178/2002, Article 50.1.

This contributes to its role in monitoring health and nutritional food risks as effectively as possible by providing information needed for risk analysis.[323]

Information transmitted through the RASFF is based on a whole range of causes ranging from consumer complaints or an establishment's own checks on food poisoning and official market controls. These procedures are gathered under the heading market control. A second category of controls refers to products originating in third countries and is called border controls. In general, border controls are made on each product consignment from third countries, by carrying out sample checks.

One refers to "border control – consignment released" in cases where a sample is taken for analysis but the consignment is released onto the market pending the results. But in other cases, where the presence of an outbreak was reported or there are strong suspicions as to a human health risk with respect to a third country or an establishment of a third country, the consignment may be blocked by the customs control until laboratory testing is performed and the results are known.

Consequently, all information related to a risk identified in food or food contact materials, the products concerned, their traceability and the measures taken shall be communicated immediately by Member States to the Commission, which in turn will immediately relay the information to other network members. This process applies equally to EU products and risks related to third countries products that are detected at an EU point of entry or a border post.

Measures taken by Member States to deal with emergency situations that have established the need for swift action must be notified to the Commission. This is the case when, because of a risk to human health, measures are taken to restrict the placing on the market, by forcing the withdrawal of the product from the market or a food recall. The same rule applies to food consignments or cargos rejected by a CA at an EU border post to deal with a direct or indirect risk to human health. In either case, the information is transmitted by the EU Commission to other Member States and, when relevant, to all other border posts and to third countries of origin.

When changes occur with regard to the initial information transmitted, especially in cases of modifications or withdrawal of the measures concerned, the Member shall also notify the Commission.[324] In a more general framework, Member States shall immediately inform the Commission of the actions implemented or measures taken following the receipt of notifications and supplementary information transmitted under the RASFF.[325]

323 Regulation 178/2002, Article 35.
324 Regulation 178/2002, Article 50.3.
325 Regulation 178/2002, Article 50.5.

The RASFF system gained dynamism over the years and the classification of information transmitted through the network was more precisely defined and enriched. In this respect, given the severity and seriousness of the risk detected, the contact point of the Commission would forward the information by categorising it either as an alert, information or a border rejection notification.

Table 3.4. Type of notification forwarded through the RASFF

Type of information	Definitions
'Alert notification' or 'alert'	An alert refers to information sent when a food, feed or food contact material presenting a serious risk is on the market and when rapid action is or might be required in another country than the notifying country.[326] In general, an alert refers to a product already or about to be withdrawn from the market. An alert is transmitted through the RASFF network to enable Member States to verify the presence of the implicated product on their market and, if necessary, take appropriate actions.
Information notification	An information notification relates to a product with respect to which the risk identification does not require any rapid action because the product has never reached the market or is already withdrawn from it.
Border rejection notification	A border rejection notification is mentioned whenever a consignment is refused entry to the Community market due to the identification of a risk to human health. In certain cases, samples are taken for organoleptic investigation or for laboratory analysis, while the consignment is released. These cases are referred to as 'border control – consignment released'.
RASFF news	RASFF news cannot be classified under any of the above denominations, but it is relayed simply because it is valuable for control authorities in the Member States. These cases mostly indicate that information was picked up in the media or forwarded by colleagues in food or feed authorities in third countries, EC delegations or international organisations, after having been verified with the Member States concerned.[327]

Whether alerts or information notifications, one can distinguish between two main types of RASFF notifications: the information transmitted about a new case related to one or more consignments called "original notification" and the information provided complementarily to previously relayed information called 'follow-up notification'.

326 European Commission 2011, RASFF annual report 2010, p12.
327 European Commission 2011, annual report 2010, p13.

Figure 3.1. Functioning of the RASFF

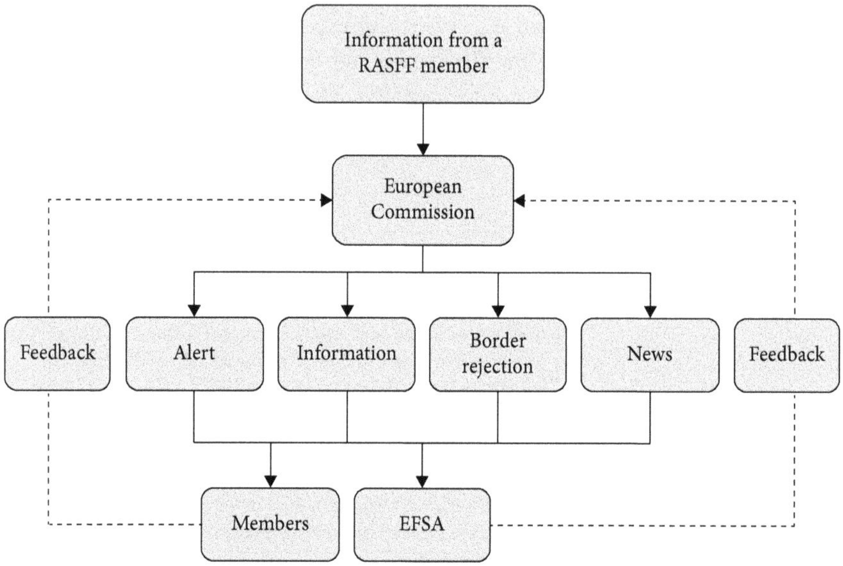

Source: RASFF leaflet

The RASFF system works through determined rules and criteria and some information provided by Member States can be removed by the Commission upon their agreement if it emerges that the criteria required for the notification are not met or when the information is deemed insufficient. Where appropriate, the initiating country could be asked to provide additional information to enable the Commission to reconsider the rejection. Beyond matters of form, some notifications are also removed from the system if the data that motivated them were not valid from the beginning or when the transmission of information was made erroneously.

In a similar vein, given the gravity of additional information, the classification of a report can be changed. Notification information can be upgraded to an alert notification, while an information notification can simply be withdrawn.

Since 2009, an alert may equally come from a third country and be the source of the notification. Called an "official control in non-member country", such an alert refers to cases where a third country informs an EU Member State of the possible presence on the Member State's market of a product found potentially dangerous during official controls. This information must be transmitted to the EU Commission and other Member States following the usual procedure. Switzerland has been the source of most of these cases in 2009, next to the United States of America and Canada.

Following the recurrence of certain problems about a given third country, it may be decided to strengthen the controls on its products. For instance, after Commission Decision 2006/236/EC urged Member States to check every consignment of fish from Indonesia for heavy metals, the number of mercury notifications for that country increased coincidentally from 4 in 2005 to 18 in 2006, making that country with the most notifications in 2006 with regard to mercury in fishery products.[328]

Moreover, adjustments are made not only in relation to the definition of limits of certain substances in food products, but changes are also introduced in response to the reality that some standards were too strict. This was the case for example when it was established that the cooking of crustaceans does not reduce the presence of sulphites, as it was expected. Council Directive 2006/52/EC was then adopted to reduce limit levels. As a result, notifications regarding excessive rates of sulphites in crustaceans began to decline the same year even if they remained substantial. 80 notifications relating to high levels of sulphites were recorded in 2006 instead of 101 in 2005, including 45 referring to crustaceans compared to 63 in 2005.

Substances commonly detected in the products are not the same and often depend on the nature of the product and its mode of production. In general, as regards fishery products, RASFF notifications are related to residues of veterinary medicinal products, or mercury.[329] Other unauthorized substances have also been detected repeatedly in fishery products, such as the fungicidal dye malachite green, which was the most detected unauthorised substance in 2005, resulting in 50 notifications. Antibiotics like the fluorquinolones ciprofloxaxin and enrofloxacin were also notified. Specifically with regard to crustaceans, one can quote the detection of nitrofuran metabolites. The presence of such substances is prohibited for reasons ranging from fear of antibiotic resistance to that of the spread of resistant pathogenic bacteria. In other cases, consequences can be observed faster like in the event of food poisoning, which, depending on its severity, can lead to serious damage and even death. Therefore, the legislator defines the acceptable limits in foodstuffs for most of these substances.[330]

The RASFF has grown significantly since its establishment with regard to both procedures and the range of information exchanged through the network. The number of information exchange instances rose from 698 in 1999, 823

---

328 European Commission 2007, RASFF annual report 2006, p29.

329 Fish and seafood contain mercury as a result of its natural presence in the environment and from pollution. Mercury exists in several variants but generally methyl mercury, the organic and most toxic form of mercury, can make up more than 90% of the total mercury in fish and seafood. Large predatory fish, such as swordfish, shark and tuna, accumulate higher levels of mercury through intake over a long lifetime. See European Commission, RASFF annual report 2006.

330 To name a few examples, Maximum levels of Polycyclic Aromatic Hydrocarbons (PAH) in several foodstuffs including fishery products are set since 1 April 2005 in Commission Regulation (EC) No. 208/2005 amending Commission Regulation (EC) No. 466/2001. Maximum levels of mercury in fishery products are set in Commission Regulation No 466/2001 depending on the species of the fish and whether the fish is fresh or processed.

in 2000, and 1,567 in 2001 to 3,024 in 2002. In 1992, there were only 10 alert notifications, and the number did not change significantly until 1997 when it rose to 67 before growing to 133 in 2000, 302 in 2001, and finally 434 in 2002. With regard to information notifications, there was only one in 1992. These notifications began to grow in importance, reaching 16 in 1997. The following year, 156 information notifications were transmitted and the growth was then constant until 2001 (406). In 2002, more than the double the number of notifications was relayed and amounted to 1,092 information notifications. Over the years notifications have related to some products more notified than the others. In general, products of animal origin have the highest proportion, with fish and crustaceans ranking in the top three.

The following table summarises third countries' share in all notifications by the origin of the products.

Table 3.5. Notifications by the origin of the product (share of third countries in percentage)

Categories	2003	2004	2005	2006	2007	2008
Alerts	28	33	36	35	32	36
Information	77	79	78	75	73	44

Source: Own compilation from RASFF annual reports

For food of animal origin, border rejections of consignments most often concern fishery products due to heavy metals, veterinary drug residues, bad hygienic state, or parasitic infestation. The management of food additives can prove to be very delicate in some cases. A distinction must be made, for example, when one is confronted with a case of undeclared sulphite not mentioned on the label or with a case where sulphite is used as a food additive but turns out to be unauthorised or its content is too high. It is noteworthy that only "undeclared sulphite" is considered an allergen-type problem.[331]

The following table shows an overview of the share of fish and fishery products in percentage among all products categories.

Table 3.6. Notifications by categories of products (share of fishery products in percentage)

Categories	2002	2003	2004	2005	2006	2007	2008
Alerts	26	21	24	20	20	21	20
Information	35	24	20	16	18	18	16

Source: Own compilation from RASFF annual reports

331 European Commission 2010, RASFF annual report 2009, p19.

Some countries, such as China, Thailand and Turkey, are found very often in the forefront of the statistics, ranking as the countries with the most notifications. In 2002, African countries accounted for only 6% of the total alerts, which was equivalent to 90 alerts for 22 countries. Countries like Morocco and South Africa could be clearly distinguished from the rest with regard to the number of notifications they accumulated on their own. Morocco and Namibia were even listed in 2002 among the ten most reported third countries.

However, these figures should be viewed with great reservations when one wants to draw conclusions about a country or a group of countries because they do not necessarily reflect the food safety state in one of these countries or another. On the one hand, a high number of notifications may simply indicate that a greater number of food checks are carried out or it can simply translate the efficiency of communication systems in the country.[332] This might also merely be a function of the overall share of these countries in the total trade for the period considered. One could not reasonably establish a correlation, whether positive or negative, by considering a set of countries in which one exports a few tons of shrimp annually while the other exports twice the same quantity monthly. The likelihood that the latter country would be found far more frequently among the reported countries is clear and undeniable.

On the other hand, it is necessary to make a distinction between notifications regarding Member States and notifications referring to third countries. While for third countries controls are only carried out on products at border inspection posts upon their entry into the Community, with regard to Member States controls are operated throughout the entire production chain, making the detection of hazards possible at any stage of production. Therefore, for all risks identified during the production, there is no RASFF notification since the products had not yet reached the market.[333] Basing the RASFF system on whether the product has reached the market or not has shown its limitations since a classification as alerts should normally result from an appreciation of the degree of risk relating to the case under consideration. However the urgency required in most cases makes it difficult to apply a quick and consistent risk assessment to a RASFF notification even though the risk factor could give more value to the classification.[334]

The RASFF system works smoothly in most cases, but there have been occasional errors which reflect deeper dysfunctions challenging its credibility. For example, honey and royal jelly, which are more considered to be grocery products than products of animal origin, are not always submitted to the rigour required for the traceability of animal products. In 2005, Switzerland was mentioned in five notifications as the country of origin although it does not

---

332 European Commission 2011, RASFF annual report 2010, p25.

333 European Commission 2011, RASFF annual report 2010, p24.

334 European Commission 2007, RASFF annual report 2006, p49.

produce royal jelly. This country is most likely a trading focal point where honey and honey products are imported from third countries and re-exported to the EU.[335]

Some RASFF notifications again raised issues about the very functioning of the single market because all standards are not harmonised at the Community level. For example, a court decision ruled that carbon monoxide fish could not be banned from the Dutch market. Although this law is national in scope, the Dutch authorities took no action to prevent such fish imported into their country from being redistributed to other EU Member States, eventually resulting in notifications on carbon monoxide treated tuna that was imported through The Netherlands.[336]

In general, the Commission must inform third countries exporting to the EU whenever their products are notified via the RASFF to enable them to take appropriate actions. To support this objective, it is worth mentioning that, along with the RASFF, a web-based veterinarian certification tool called TRACES has been created since 2009 to control the import and export of live animals and products of animal origin to and from the EU. Exporting countries are given access to TRACES and, in that respect, they are trained by the Commission through the "Better Training for Safer Food (BTSF) programme". TRACES has further improved controls on relevant products. For instance, in 2009, TRACES enabled the collection of more notifications on bad hygiene and temperature.[337]

In addition, with a view to strengthening cooperation with third countries, the EU Commission established a new tool called RASFF Window in 2008, aiming at speeding up the transmission of information with third countries by organising their direct access to notifications. Thanks to that technology, third countries' authorities have direct access to relevant notifications through their nominated contact points. The third country's embassy in Brussels, the EU delegation in that country, and desk officers responsible for that third country at the EU Commission are also given access to notifications. For this purpose, notifications are, in principle, uploaded within 24 working hours from being issued in the RASFF and are immediately available to be checked online in the RASFF Window. The concerned countries, which are regular members of the system, receive automatic e-mails informing them about new notifications or follow-up notifications of interest for their country in the RASFF Window. In this respect, a third country is a regular member of the RASFF system when this country submitted a request accordingly and designated a contact point that had received the necessary credentials to log into the RASFF.

335 European Commission 2006, RASFF annual report 2005, p16.

336 European Commission 2006, RASFF annual report 2005, p19.

337 European Commission 2010, RASFF annual report 2009, p34.

3.6. CONCLUDING REMARKS

The completion of the single market in the EU led to diverse policies to achieve regulatory harmonisation. Despite several strategies implemented to achieve harmonisation, there remained barriers to trade arising from differences in national regulations, the absence of relevant legislation in some EU countries, differences in the interpretation of EU legislation, late transposition, or lack of enforcement.[338] In this context, food safety regulation was merely incidental, being specific responses to issues related to the realisation of the common market. In the wake of the food scares in the 1990s, food safety regulation was given greater importance. The protection of life and health became a priority and a fully-fledged food safety law was developed. Following the White Paper on Food Safety in 2000, Regulation 178/2002 was adopted in 2002 as a framework to control and monitor the production, prevention and management of risks.

Specific and more stringent provisions are adopted for high-risk food such as fishery products. Already in 1991, Directive 91/493/EC was adopted to lay down requirements not only for EU products but also for fishery products originating in third countries. The implementation of these requirements caused trade disruptions and concerns for many third countries exporting fishery products to the EU.

From an EU perspective, control measures helped to improve food safety in the EU in various ways. With the strengthening of controls, some risks that were not commonly detected could be highlighted and subsequent measures could be taken to overcome related threats. For example, prior to 2001, heavy metals, mercury and cadmium, were the main risk agents, and accounted for nearly 70% of the cases. With the reinforcement of controls, two other chemical agents, namely chloramphenicol[339] and nitrofuran, were revealed to entail higher risks. These substances appeared dramatically in border cases in 2001 and 2002. In fact, these two chemicals accounted for 65% of border cases, while heavy metals accounted for only 14% of border cases. The increase in the detection of these two veterinary drugs is due to rigorous testing regimes imposed in 2001 and 2002 on shrimp (and other food) imports from various Southeast Asian countries by the EU.[340] Likewise, in the case of Benin for instance, EU border controls were strengthened on all consignments due to the deficiencies reported in the domestic production and certification systems, as well as alerts raised on Benin's shrimps by Spain and Italy. These cases are obvious examples that the increased stringency in controls results in the detection of new parameters that affect the safety of food products.

---

338 Guimarães 2012, p21.

339 This antibiotic has been reported to cause fatal leukaemia and anaemia in human beings.

340 Ababouch et al. 2005, p31.

Clearly, many products would previously cross borders unimpeded by physical controls despite high levels of certain substances currently considered harmful. But in reality, despite the fact that these apparently non-compliant products used to make their way to the EU market, the high levels of these chemicals were never the subject of health crises. However, it would be erroneous to conclude that these substances are therefore harmless to consumers. Such an example adds substance to the debate on the long-term consequences of certain substances on the human body, highlighting the complexity of decision making in relation to food risks.

The implementation of the EU food law affected third countries in various ways. For example, South Africa did not experience too many problems with regard to its exports to the EU. During the early 1990s, Italy banned imports from one or two South African suppliers due to mercury problems, and Spain rejected a few consignments of South African white fish because of a so-called parasite infestation in 2001. But the French ban in 1994 was certainly the most important. It was alleged that French authorities literally implemented Directive 91/493/EC overnight because they were trying to appease their fishermen who had gone on a rampage in Brittany to protest difficult economic conditions and cheaper imports.[341] This was clearly an abuse that could happen only because fish and fishery products were in the so-called "non-harmonised products" category that allowed Member States to apply national rules along with the Directive. In this case, most Member States applied an adaptation time to exporting countries, unlike France. That problem could be solved only after four months of "diplomatic bargaining" followed by the "provision of every conceivable guarantee"[342] that ultimately led France to put South Africa on its list of authorised exporting countries.

In another case, the European Commission (EC) banned shrimp imports from Bangladesh from August to December 1997, because the processing plants in that country could not meet EC standards. It is estimated that this ban, after considering shipments diverted to other countries, cost US$14.7 million to the Bangladesh frozen shrimp processing industry.[343]

Another notable example was the series of bans and lifting of bans with regard to the import of Nile Perch caught in Lake Victoria. This series of events had affected the countries involved, Uganda, Tanzania, Mozambique, and particularly Kenya, during the period 1997–1999. The causes of these import restrictions ranged from salmonella contamination in Nile Perch from Kenya, to pesticide contamination of fish from Lake Victoria, and a cholera epidemic in East Africa in December 1997.[344]

---

341 Jooste et al. 2003, p265.

342 Idem.

343 Ababouch et al. 2005, p66.

344 These cases are discussed in more detail in chapter VIII of this book.

In the same way, the EU has allegedly pushed some third countries like Benin and Togo to voluntarily decide on a suspension of their exports to the EU, presenting that measure as the only alternative to an official EU ban that would have more disastrous consequences.

At first glance, the application of EU law took a decisive turn since the BSE crisis. Prior to that scare, the EU was less strict and used to grant third countries a phase-in period. The subsequent shift can be analysed as a political strategy aiming at appeasing the collective consciousness of EU consumers. This process was caricatured as a performance ritual to show EU consumers that "everything is fine in the system" by allowing only a limited number of upgraded sites in third countries to handle all fish for export.[345] This is especially true considering that most EU restrictions result from dysfunctions of the system of production and certification rather than from verified evidence of health risks.

However, it is important to emphasise that there were undoubtedly shortcomings in the food legislation of these third countries and questionable practices in the enforcement of existing laws. Obviously, threats of export bans led a lot of them to upgrade their legislation and build institutional capacity to ensure better handling of food production and certification. This can positively impact the competitive position of these countries and their industrial firms.[346] However, these adjustments are time-consuming and costly and, in the short or medium term, it is not evident that they are actually beneficial for all these developing countries.

Moreover, implementation and enforcement issues are also not non-existent within the EU internal market. For example, in 2000, FVO inspections in Ireland and Austria revealed that Community veterinary legislation concerning the production of fishery products was not properly and uniformly implemented. These Member States lacked inspection procedures, their documentation of supervision was insufficient and the enforcement of corrective actions was ineffective.[347] Yet, they did not face export restrictions, as would have been the case for a third country.

In 2004 and 2005, some "horizontal problems" were found and "concerned insufficient capacities of CAs, inadequate supervision of establishments and fishing vessels, and deficiencies in both establishments and vessels".[348] Even in Border Inspection Posts, major non-conformities were reported in 2001 mostly with regard to hygiene.[349]

In a similar vein, measures towards third countries were not always consistent. In some cases, there was no ban despite obvious fundamental non-compliance. In Mauritius, for instance, an inspection in 2004 revealed

345 Ponte 2007, p64.
346 Nyangito et al. 2003, p1.
347 European Commission 2001, FVO annual report 2000.
348 European Commission 2006, FVO annual report 2005.
349 European Commission 2002, FVO annual report 2001.

clear shortcomings that led to a two-year moratorium by the EU. In 2006, the follow-up inspection showed that there was still no adequate legal text and control staff were not only involved in too many other tasks in different departments but they even had limited awareness of the EU requirements. Yet, no import ban was implemented.

Furthermore, there is a claim that fish consignments are rarely, if ever, recalled, and most of the time problems are settled with a price arrangement between the parties, which leads to the fact that sub-standard fish is sold on the EU market anyway.[350] Furthermore, quality problems identified by European operators are often resolved through private negotiations or arbitration[351] and no information is transmitted about this in the RASFF network.

While some of these issues could raise suspicions, many cases were also based on actual dysfunctions in the production and certification systems in third countries. However, differences in treatment cannot immediately be seen as discrimination at face value. In this regard, WTO rules, in particular the provisions of the SPS and TBT Agreements must be explored to seek answers to the trade concerns of third countries.

350 Ponte 2007, p64.
351 Idem.

CHAPTER IV
FOOD SAFETY REGULATION IN BENIN

4.1. INTRODUCTION

Despite the serious shortcomings revealed by the first FVO mission in Benin, the regulation of the fisheries sector and the protection of consumers and their health have not always been absent from the agenda of policymakers. In fact, many texts were inherited from the colonial era, especially in the fishing sector to address issues such as sustainability. Afterward the colonial era, Benin attempted to develop supplementary texts to respond to concerns arising from particular contingencies. With regard to health protection, the most important of these texts was certainly Law 84–009 on the control of foodstuffs adopted in 1984. However, the implementation of this law was to be defined by subsequent decrees of application that were mostly never adopted. The fact remains that the poor implementation and enforcement of existing texts led to the severe weaknesses pointed out in 2002 by the first FVO mission.

This chapter intends to give some insights into the protection of health and the safety of food in Benin. It focuses particularly on the regulation of the fishery sector and its incidental coverage of safety issues.

The second section (4.2) outlines the importance given by Benin to food safety in its development projects. The third section (4.3) then explains the main requirements laid down by the texts before 2002. The fourth section (4.4) dwells upon the upgrading of the legal framework in the aftermath of the first FVO mission in 2002. The last section (4.5) concludes.

4.2. IMPORTANCE OF FOOD SAFETY IN DEVELOPMENT PROJECTS

The fight against poverty and food insecurity has become returning objectives in all development projects in many developing countries. Over time, more than the quantity, the concept of "adequate food" also gained importance in light of the evolving character of concepts at the international level. In this regard, an elite group of consumers in developing countries, particularly within urban populations, is increasingly concerned about food safety and quality rather than mere food availability and sufficiency.

In Benin, such an evolution appeared at the governmental level through the development goals established during the previous decade. Thus, in its rural development strategy, the Beninese government recognised that contributing to the improvement of the population's standard of living, amounts to increasing producers' purchasing power, fighting against poverty and controlling food quality and safety.[352] To achieve these goals, the rural development strategy further defined as strategic orientations the implementation of a fearless policy for the quality control of import and export products and the sanitary product controls, in particular animal and fishery products.[353] This required the updating of all laws governing rural structures and the definition and implementation of specific actions relating to the establishment of an adequate legal framework likely to ensure the quality of both products of plant and animal origin, to ensure best public health conditions.[354]

At the constitutional level, food safety has not been clearly established as a right for people or a sovereign governmental function. However, the African Charter of human and peoples' rights, to which Benin subscribed in its constitution, recognises in Article 16 that everyone has the right to the highest attainable standard of physical and mental ability. This definition could be related to the extensive definition of health provided by the World Health Organization (WHO). In reality, the WHO defined health in 1946 in the preamble to its Constitution as "a state of complete physical, mental and social well-being" that "is not merely the absence of disease or infirmity." Established as one of the fundamental rights of every human being, health seen from this perspective cannot ignore sanitary and nutritional aspects related to the ingestion of food. It goes without saying that countries logically strive at all times to ensure that people can not only have access to satisfactory health care, but also that they have the adequate food, which contributes to the satisfaction of their sanitary needs. Thanks to its accuracy, this definition of health remained unchanged until the modern era.

4.3. FOOD SAFETY REGULATION BEFORE THE CRISIS

Contrary to the right to a sound environment, the protection of consumers' life and health was not explicitly recognised as a constitutional right in Benin. Article 27 of Law 90–32 laying down the Constitution of the Republic of

352 République du Bénin/Ministère du Développement Rural 2000, p10.
353 République du Bénin/Ministère du Développement Rural 2000, p20.
354 République du Bénin/Ministère du Développement Rural 2000, p22.

Benin stated: "Every person is entitled to a sound, satisfying and sustainable environment and has the duty to defend it. The State shall ensure the protection of the environment". Article 7 however stipulated that the "human person is sacred and inviolable" and, as such, the State shall, among other duties, ensure to its citizens "equal access to health". Although this article may be interpreted very extensively, no food safety or consumer protection law ever referred to it.

However, well before the adoption of the current constitution in 1990, Article 42 of Law 87–015 on the Code of Public Hygiene prohibited the production or marketing of spoiled food or food containing toxic substances that can harm human health. Furthermore, in 1990, Article 30 of Law 90–005 setting the terms for the exercise of commercial activities in the Republic of Benin acknowledged that trade restrictions might be allowed for health protection. While recognising that the importation of goods coming from EEC countries in the XOF franc zone and the ACP is free with or without the transfer of foreign currency, this article, however, set a restriction as follows: "these provisions do not preclude prohibitions or restrictions on imports, exports or goods in transit justified on grounds of public morality, protection of health and life of human, animal or plant life or health [...]".

4.3.1. GENERAL FOOD SAFETY FRAMEWORK

Consumer health protection texts were not always specific texts adopted to ensure food safety and quality. These texts were often of general scope, regulating various aspects of human life or activities, but they mostly focused on one main topic such as hygiene.

In reality, the structure of the economy determined the priority areas that were regulated in Benin. Thus, agriculture, livestock, hunting, and fishing benefited from the work of the legislature, already from the colonial period. This trend was reinforced under the socialist, Marxist-Leninist regime, from 1972 to 1989, which gave priority to freeing the peasantry from exploitation, by giving real and effective value to agricultural products and encouraging an increase in production in order to achieve food self-sufficiency in Benin.[355]

The decisive step in protecting consumers from food risks was undoubtedly made in 1984 by the adoption of Law 84–009 on the control of food. This law through its Article 28 repealed all earlier texts that contained provisions for the same purpose or opposite dispositions. Law 84–009 aimed mainly at protecting consumers against any risk related to deception and falsifications in relation to food by all actors involved in the production, marketing and advertising of food.

---

355 Lawogni & De Sadeleer 2002, p5.

While defining some key concepts connected to food control[356], Law 84-009 laid down the basic food control principles and paved the way for the organisation of such controls and penalties for offenders.

Several sectoral laws were adopted over time by reference to Law 84-009. These laws covered various aspects of life and economic activity, but they also referred incidentally to consumer health protection. Beyond the agricultural sector, one can cite, for instance, Interministerial Decree No. 106/MCT/MS/MF/MDR/MIPME/CAB/DCE/SRE regulating the importation and marketing of iodised salt in Benin, which declared in its first article the aim of regulating the importation and marketing of iodised salt in the fight against disorders caused by iodine deficiency and promoting the health of the population in the Republic of Benin. This decree conveyed the idea that only iodised salt could be consumed in Benin and banned the import of any other salt. The decree further asserted that even the salt produced by a local craft or industrial process must be iodised according to relevant standards before it was placed on the local market. To this end, the decree defined the standards of iodised salt and even fixed conditions for its labelling, packaging and storage. In the same vein, in order to protect consumers, Decree 550 MDR/DCAB/CC/CP, prohibiting the slaughter of animals in the slaughterhouse of Bohicon, banned all slaughtering activities in the city of Bohicon, due to notoriously unsanitary conditions in 1994.

4.3.2. PROTECTION OF CONSUMERS AGAINST FRAUDULENT PRACTICES

The premise of consumer protection against abuses by traders was laid down in Article 3 of Law 84-009. This article mainly prohibited any advertising containing allegations or false statements or presentations likely to mislead consumers. The prohibition covered in particular product identification aspects such as species or origin, characteristics related to a product's composition, aspects related to the actual or the intended use of the product. Labelling was to be considered as an integral part of the packaging. In this regard, all

[356] Here are a few important definitions within the context of that moment. Most of these definitions have been revised or enriched in the current legislation. Food means any substance, whether processed, partially processed or raw for human consumption and includes drink, chewing gum, and all substances used in the manufacture, preparation and processing of food, excluding those used only as drugs or cosmetics. Production includes all operations consisting of farming, harvesting, gathering, fishing, slaughtering, manufacturing, processing and packaging of goods, including storage during manufacture and before the first marketing. As for the marketing, it includes all operations that involve the bulk storage or semi-wholesale, transportation, possession for sale, offering for sale, displaying for sale, sale or transfer for free of all goods, including import and export. Finally, Handling means any action applied to a food, from the stage of its production to its delivery to the consumer.

products had to be labelled in French regardless of the product's origin. In this regard, the indication of all products' ingredients became mandatory so as to warn consumers against potential risks of allergies that might result from consumption. This information obligation could be seen as highlighting the notion of the shared responsibility of both producers and consumers with regard to food safety and quality. While producers must inform, the consumers must be aware and use the products accordingly. However, the import of goods not compliant with the rules governing food labelling and presentation might in some cases be authorised. This derives from Article 13 of Decree 85–242, which stated that the importation of consignments of food which did not comply with rules on labelling and presentation of foodstuffs could be considered to address an urgent and clearly defined need, and the products could be placed on the local market. However, this derogation is subject to the joint authorisation of the relevant ministry and the ministry of rural development. In addition, the domestic operator had to fulfil its obligation with regard to labelling. In case of perishable goods, such labelling had to cover the food's microbiology, which means that the expiry date and appropriate storage conditions had to be mentioned on the products.

Law 84–009 also established the first provisions on traceability by requiring to connect the product to each person or entity that intervened during the production process at any stage of manufacturing, packaging or marketing.

4.3.3. RESPONSIBILITY OF FOOD OPERATORS

Articles 5 and 7 of Law 84–009 placed a responsibility on food operators by prohibiting them from offering for sale, or even from having in their possession without legitimate grounds, in any place of production or marketing, food they knew to be corrupt, toxic or not having the required level of microbiological or hygienic quality. The implementation of these provisions relies mainly on operators' awareness of the potentially dangerous nature of the food. In this respect, the absence of apparent defects on food would favour operators because their bad faith could not be presumed. It was therefore of utmost importance that adequate legal instruments existed to monitor every step of the manufacture and handling of fishery products effectively so as to ensure that the finished product was actually safe for consumption.

Food business operators are also responsible for implementing hygiene requirements throughout the production process, both in respect of their establishment and their staff. On the one hand, operators had to comply with requirements laid down by Decree 85–243 on the hygiene of the production and marketing of food. Strict hygiene conditions were adopted with regard to conditions of handling premises, equipment and food contact material to avoid the contamination of fresh fishery products. Moreover, operators had to comply with rules on microbiological, hygienic, physicochemical and organoleptic food characteristics. On the other hand, staff had to follow strict hygiene standards and companies' leaders had to make available the relevant and necessary facilities. This provision was reaffirmed by Article 36 of Law 87–015 on the Code of Public Hygiene, which compelled staff in contact with food to commit to "greater personal cleanliness and clothing under the responsibility of the employer". In addition, Article 44 of the same law stated that staff had to be free of diseases that can contaminate food and they should be subjected to periodic medical examinations and vaccinations.

Non-compliance with the food-related provisions was punishable by payment of various kinds of penalties or fines, which could be reinforced by a prison sentence depending on the infringements. In this regard, the law made a distinction in the amount of fines or the duration of the sentence based on the conscious character of the offense or the fact that the offense was only the result of professional negligence. In addition, the court could order that all or part of the sentence be published or displayed in newspapers or in some premises according to conditions determined by the court judgment.[357]

4.3.4. SPECIFIC MEASURES FOR FISHERY PRODUCTS

The field of fishery products did not remain unregulated throughout Benin's history. As a matter of fact, Benin was involved in the regulation of fishing activities for quite a long time. The first initiatives in this area were primarily the preservation of species and the protection of aquatic ecosystems. Benin inherited several texts from the colonial period. These texts include: 1) Order of 1 March 1907 regulating river fishing in the waters of the Colony, which defined the various types of mesh to be used for river fishing depending on the species concerned; 2) Decree of 15 May 1914 in French West Africa promulgating Decree of 12 April 1914 regulating the fishing and industrial exploitation of whale in French colonies; 3) Decree of 29 July 1924 prohibiting fishing in French West Africa performed using explosives, poisons or other drugs, 4) Decree No. 207 of 30 January 1950 banning the use of firearms or explosives as a means of fishing, which also prohibited the use of any substance or drug that may poison or kill fish and crustaceans.

In addition to these texts, Benin started adopting its own texts in various fields of fishery products soon after its independence in 1960.

In 1964, Article 1 of Decree 204 establishing a control of fishery products and the conditions of their marketing, instituted measures "in the interest of public health to ensure the safety and quality". This decree's provisions required a mandatory control of all fishing vessels authorised to unload their

---

357 Law 84–009, Article 21.

products in Benin and any plant for the conservation, sale or processing of fishery products. The control of any fishery product, regardless of its state and whether it was stored on a fishing vessel or in an establishment on land, was also made mandatory. This rule applied both for products intended for immediate consumption or for further processing.

Following Decree 204, there was a shift towards an emphasis on sustainability. Subsequent regulations focused on the protection of fishery products, the delimitation of fishing zones and the implementation of fishing activities with adequate means so as to protect species and prevent the degradation of the aquatic environment. For example, in 1965, Law 65-10 banned trawling, and generally the practice of any fishing using towed gears within Benin's territorial waters. Towed gears are gears that include a combination of some or all elements mechanically pulled: a) funes or towing attached to one or more vessels, and used to move the craft on the seabed; b) panels or other devices placed at the end of the fune and used to maintain the distance between the net; c) net formed by the wings and a floated pocket or not at the top and weighted at the bottom. These items were considered to destroy the seabed and the offender was charged with the payment of a fine proportionate to the seriousness of the offense committed. The fine could vary from around 155 euro to 750 euro. Likewise, in 1966, Decree 183/PR/MDRC laid down the general regulation of fishing in Benin's inland waters. This decree banned the use of fishing tools bearing snoods of less than 50 inches equipped with hooks used without bait. It also defined the conditions that would allow the use of sedentary fishery as a means of fishing.

The first specific step towards the regulation of shrimp fishing was made in 1974 through the interministerial Decree 5/MDRC/MEF that defined the means to be used and the sizes of shrimp allowed for fishing, in particular to protect the stock of *Penaeus duorarum*. In addition, to avoid adverse consequences of an excessively intense fishing effort, an annual export quota of 700 tons of shrimps was granted to companies exporting lagoon shrimps. This decree also created a mandatory selling area for the sale of lagoon and lake shrimps intended for marketing or processing purposes.

a. Product requirements

Fresh fishery products should have certain attributes for the catches to be unloaded in the territory of Benin. In this regard, the freshness of the product is an essential aspect of their fitness for consumption. Already in 1964, Articles 2 and 3 of Decree 204 establishing a control of fishery products and the conditions of marketing for these products established that fishery products had to be preserved cold less than an hour after their capture, according to a refrigeration system fitting with the features of the device used.[358] A number of qualities related to odour and general aspects (the rigidity of the body, skin tone, brightness of eyes, and colour of the gills…) attest to the freshness. These attributes were referred to as organoleptic characteristics by Article 2 of Decree 98–215, as the "physical freshness state of fishery products using sight, smell, touch, in short, all sense organs to determine the degree of product freshness".

In the case of fishery products already frozen on board a fishing vessel, different organoleptic criteria would apply. For instance, the anal orifice had to be closed and the flesh had to be of the hardness of wood. Furthermore, after thawing, the skin should be bright in colour and the abdominal wall should be without greenish appearances.

Possibly, especially in the case of a disagreement between the operator and control agents, additional freshness characteristics could be checked or biological and chemical analysis could be performed on a sample. A favourable review resulted in a certificate being issued. Otherwise, the competent authorities had to proceed to seizure, followed by destruction or the diversion of the product to another use[359], such as delivery to a waste treatment establishment under the supervision of the control agent.

Beyond these aspects related to the intrinsic nature of the product, the use of additives during the production process was also regulated. To this end, the use of a particular additive was approved only if the latter was subjected to appropriate toxicological testing and evaluation. In addition, the use of the additive had to be necessary and aim at reaching defined objectives. In general, food additives should contribute to the preservation of the nutritional quality of the product, meet nutritional needs of specific consumer groups, increase the conservation or the stability of a food or improve its organoleptic properties. Moreover the additive should be of substantial importance for one step in the production process. Lastly, Article 4 of Decree 85–241 stipulated that food additives should not be used to mask quality and safety defects.

b. Granting and withdrawal of approval

The requirements for granting and the withdrawal of approval applied both to the fishing activity itself but also to the production and marketing of fishery products.

On the one hand, the necessity to request a fishing license was not a requirement that responded to the need to monitor the sector with the view of ensuring safety or quality. In fact, the right to fish was considered to belong to the State, which could grant this right to individuals and communities that are customary users of fishing waters. Order 20/PR/MDRC/SP, laying down

358 Decree 204, Articles 2 and 3.

359 Law 84–009, Article 23.

the general regulation of fishing in inland waters of Dahomey, adopted in 1966, stipulated in its Article 3 that the fishing communities had to possess an administrative authorisation granting the right to fish in inland waters.

In 1989, Order 0056/MET/DGM/DEP/DMM/SRD laying down the terms and conditions for the registration of canoes and trawlers in the Republic of Benin established a legal obligation to register canoes and fishing vessels. This registration had to be carried out by the Directorate of Merchant Marine after the collection of a fee in accordance with the Code of the Merchant Marine. This code referred essentially to vessels for sea fishing. Failure of fishing vessels in complying with hygiene rules could then constitute grounds for a ban on landing and a suspension or withdrawal of approval to carry out fishing activities.[360]

On the other hand, Article 4 of Decree 85-233 stated that the production and marketing fishery products, whether intended for the local or export market, required a license issued by the Minister of Rural Development[361], which is nowadays called the Ministry of Agriculture, Livestock and Fisheries. This provision is in line with Law 84-009, in which Article 9 stipulated that the production and marketing of food might in certain instances be subjected to a declaration or a prior authorisation of the administrative authority after inspection. In this regard, the authorisation to produce fishery products should be delivered only if the applying processing plant fulfilled hygiene provisions relevant to its activity and other conditions relating to premises, equipment, staff, and if necessary with adequate internal controls.[362] The maintenance of an authorisation might be subject to periodic or systematic inspection by competent agents[363], and the authorisation might be withdrawn by the competent authority if the conditions that gave rise to it being granted or its maintenance were no longer existing.[364]

More generally, severe cases of violations of food-related requirements could result in a temporary or permanent closure of an establishment or a permanent ban on the exercise of any profession related to the production or marketing of the same or similar products.[365]

c. *Protection of the natural environment*

Preserving the natural environment is very important as regards fishery products and this cannot be separated from measures put in place to ensure their control, because the quality of the finished product will depend crucially on the

360 Decree 204, Article 10.
361 Decree 85-233, Article 4.
362 Decree 85-233, Article 7.
363 Decree 85-233, Article 8.
364 Decree 85-233, Article 9; this provision was also laid down by Article 26 of Law 84-009 with regard to food in general.
365 Law 84-009, Article 22.

quality of the freshly caught fish. Water resources in Benin are threatened by the lack of wastewater collection and treatment, poorly maintained septic tanks, runoff from solid waste dumps, and industrial wastewater.[366]

To ensure the protection of the natural environment of shrimps, regulatory work mainly focused on water conservation, in particular through Law 87-015 on the Code of Public Hygiene. This law was considered one of the first general sources of environmental law in Benin and the most detailed about the various environmental issues to which the Code relates.[367]

But before this important step, the preservation of the natural environment of shrimps had been addressed since 1970 through Decree 152 MDRC/S.P. pursuant to which the State caused the withdrawal of traditional fishing methods called "*acadja*" for their adverse effects on water quality.

Conditions appropriate to the protection of the natural environment of shrimps fall under the responsibility of municipalities instead of the Central Administration since the adoption of Law 97-029 laying down the organisation of municipalities in the Republic of Benin. While the first local elections were organised in 2002, municipalities in general still lack autonomy, and the full transfer of competences and resources advocated by the law to insure their effective functioning has not been achieved. Only about 4.5% of the country's tax revenues, or an equivalent of 0.7% of the GDP, represented the communes' resources in 2010, with serious imbalances: "the resources of the ten poorest communes represent 5% of the resources of the richest ones".[368]

It is worthwhile to tackle recurring problems that have plagued the fishing industry and could, in the long run, constitute substantial issues with regard safety and quality. First of all, the water quality is uncontrolled. This is likely to increase the progressive change of the rate of salinity of main rivers, which is an essential criterion in the development and survival of shrimp. Another problem arises from the absence of an effective system for the treatment of household waste, which result in it being used as material to fill swamps or it is dumped along river shores. This situation can even raise concerns about the introduction of residual insecticides or herbicides in waters. Moreover, the misuse of inappropriate methods and fishing equipment contributes to the increased degradation of aquatic ecosystems.

d. *Quality assurance of fishery products*

Specific measures for fishery products were adopted in 1998 through the application of Law 84-009 through Decree 98-215 on quality assurance of fishery products in Benin. Quality assurance is defined as a strategic function

366 Dominguez & Foster 2011, p20.
367 Lawogni & De Sadeleer 2002, p17.
368 Caldeira et al. 2010, p11.

that sets the policies, adapts the programmes to the objectives, and ensures that the measures adopted are effectively implemented. Decree 98–215 is a bit unusual because it brought together in one format all health rules in relation to fishery products, which were adopted in a scattered manner over time. The decree also specified in an exhaustive manner different terminologies referring to food in general and particularly to the control of fishery products. The advantage of a clear definition of a framework and specific objectives was to allow Decree 98–215 essentially to depart from the usual pattern of defining laws of general application and subjecting their implementation to subsequent decrees. This method proved to be unsuccessful because it rarely led to effective implementation and enforcement.

In the light of this brief history, one can realise that measures existed for a long time aiming at ensuring the safety and quality of food products in Benin. But, over time, despite the established rules and responsibilities, as well as the sanctions that were laid down, implementing decrees were not adopted and laws remained simple goals. However, apart from the lack of decrees of application, it was a problem that these laws, which often had become obsolete, were sometimes inherited from the colonial period and no longer fit the socio-economic realities. In addition, many shortcomings of the administrative and institutional frameworks created a situation that made it difficult to implement and enforce the laws.

Moreover, because of a general lack of resources, there was virtually no capacity for monitoring and controlling, and capacities for analysis were rather limited. It is also worth mentioning that the law did not reflect the conditions of the marketing of fishery products on the domestic market. The absence of a strong demand for food safety on the domestic market never created a real need to implement the laws in force. This situation led to numerous shortcomings revealed in the production and certification system.

4.3.5. INSTITUTIONAL FRAMEWORK

a. *Authorities responsible for the control of offences*

The definition of the institutions responsible for food control followed a very heterogeneous dynamic. Over the years, and in accordance with the reasons for a specific legislation, the agents or departments in charge of controls could be quite different.

In 1964, Decree 204 empowered officers of fishery departments with all controls on fishing activities. To this end, these officers were allowed to carry out inspections of equipment and storage conditions, storage and processing of fishery products, and, as such, they had free access to ships and establishments on land involved in any one of these activities.[369]

In 1966, Order 20/PR/MDRC/SP took over the rules laid down by Decree 207 E.F./A.P.A of 30/01/1950 banning the use of firearms or explosives as a means of fishing. This order defined fishing as the capture of any fish or crustaceans with the exception of aquatic reptiles and mammals.[370] It prohibited the use of any drug, substance, herb, fruit, root, leaf or bark intended to kill, put to sleep or make fish drunk. The formal ban by the same law on discharging any of these substances in water, regardless of the reason, attested to the desire to preserve the natural development of aquatic fauna. The implementing decree of this order stipulated that police officers, sworn agents of the Fisheries Department and departments of the Ministry of Rural Development and Cooperation were authorised to report infringements to fisheries regulations.[371] However, the decree was silent on the scope of the responsibilities of each body and the interactions that should exist between them.

Much later, Law 84–009 also stipulated that control agents had the right to enter any place where food is manipulated in order to make necessary controls and take any measure that would be useful such as sampling, seizure or the destruction of all suspect or non-compliant food. However, this law failed to specify the officers that should be considered control agents.

Several texts were adopted pursuant to Law 84–009 and defined the duties and responsibilities of stakeholders in the food production process better. In this regard, Decree 85–238 defined the list of persons entitled to control and investigate breaches of the law on the control of foodstuffs. Specifically, agents of the Directorate of Fisheries were qualified to carry out the control of fishery products. If necessary, officers of the judicial police could also carry out the same controls, but the latter were obliged to collaborate with the relevant technical directions.

Later, the Code of Public Hygiene took over some provisions of the former texts, namely the rules on hygiene and staff and rules with regard to premises, facilities and equipment. To avoid redundancy, the Code of Public Hygiene repealed all conflicting provisions. However, while in Law 84–009, the control of infringements was the role of agents of some directorates and their relevant departments, the Code of Public Hygiene rather empowered police officers. Health brigades also had the authority to visit production facilities in order to determine breaches of the Code of Public Hygiene. In addition, while the former control departments were under the supervision of their respective directorate or ministry, the ministry of public health was mandated for the hierarchical supervision of the health brigades.

---

369 Decree 204, Article 4.

370 Order 20/PR/MDRC/SP, Article 2.

371 Decree 183/PR/MDRC/SP, Article 15.

Through these different laws, one can easily infer that procedures were progressively organised to ensure transparency and impartiality in the control. Even sampling and subsequent analyses were designed to obtain results that reflected the reality as much as possible and under conditions that ensure sufficient anonymity to eliminate the risk of biased results. It appeared that control procedures were supposed to be based on scientific evidence in order to eliminate subjectivity in the control of food regulation. In addition, the controlled actor had the possibility to request a second analysis of the test results that concluded that his products were not inconformity. In such a case, the actor could choose his preferred laboratory from the list of approved laboratories.

b. Other institutions

Article 12 of Law 84–009 set the rules for the creation of an inter-ministerial and multi-disciplinary organ whose attributions were subsequently identified by Decree 85–239. Called a Technical Committee for the Control of Foodstuffs, this body was responsible for coordinating the activities of services or directorates qualified to intervene in food control. This body could make suggestions and give useful advice for the application of the law on food control. The body was supposed to initiate the food control legislation proposals that are necessary to respond to market trends.

The Technical Committee for the Control of Foodstuffs was composed of officials from all directorates and services authorised to carry out checks on food. The aim of that broad integration was to offer a niche for these various actors to coordinate their individual actions when necessary. In addition this collaboration could enable every stakeholder to benefit from control experiences of his peers in order to make adjustments at his own level to increase efficiency. In the same vein, the cooperation set the stage to develop a constructive debate on texts to be adopted within the framework of controls so as to ensure that legal texts are not disconnected from local circumstances, leading to poor implementation and enforcement.

However, Law 84–009 also allowed flexibility to services and departments within their field of responsibility to decide on the administrative sanctions they deemed necessary, after consulting the Technical Committee for the Control of Foodstuffs. Given the divergences that could already exist at the simple level of collaboration between departments within the same directorate, this rule certainly called for a degree of cooperation and interconnection sufficiently strong to transcend the bureaucracy in public administrations. In doing so, Law 84–009 seemed just to describe the ideal towards which the control must strive without actually binding public departments at various levels. As the provisions stipulated, control departments were not sufficiently liable. The lack of binding effect of the results could not induce or compel public departments to respond promptly to ensure the proper implementation of their responsibilities, even if the implementing decrees would not be adopted in a timely manner.

It is worth noting that, before giving any advice, the Technical Committee for the Control of Foodstuffs had to consult the Codex Alimentarius National Committee. The latter is responsible for giving the government all useful advice about the discussion and implementation of international standards developed by the Codex Alimentarius Commission and the adoption of national regulations on food quality and their application in Benin. The Codex Alimentarius National Committee is a multidisciplinary body that brings together all governmental departments involved in activities related to one of the stages of food production.

There is a multitude of institutions whose activities are not directly relevant to fishing activities. However, it is worth mentioning the existence of a National Committee of Fisheries since 1976, created by Ordinance No. 76–49 establishing the National Committee of Fisheries. This Committee is responsible for developing national fisheries policy and proposing programmes for the development of maritime and continental fishing. Chaired by the ministry in charge of rural development, the National Committee of Fisheries is supposed to provide a framework for consultation, gathering a wide range of stakeholders, such as relevant public authorities or the fishing industry, to discuss issues relating to fishing.

4.4. UPGRADING THE LEGAL FRAMEWORK

4.4.1. CONTEXT

In response to FVO's recommendations, Benin's authorities immediately initiated an action plan in November 2002, which was annexed to the FVO's report. This action plan defined the actors responsible for the realisation of each action and included timelines that were to serve as guarantees. In this context, draft texts already under consideration were complemented by four other texts in order to take into consideration the lacking maximum limits pointed out by FVO experts. The adoption and the publication of these texts were expected no later than 25 February 2003.

To support these reforms, Benin also immediately initiated a request for funding. The application for funding covered some targeted corrective measures of the action plan and was sent to the EU Commission.

A few months later, the suspension of exports also called for action in view of the social unrest that resulted from the interruption of the activities of processing plants. Therefore immediate action was especially needed as part of Benin's commitment not only towards its citizens, but also towards the EU as a trading partner.

The challenges were then to be able to legislate in light of the domestic legislative and regulatory context, as well as the administrative framework, while aiming at reaching the level of protection of the EU. Striking a balance between these two sets of legislation would guarantee an applicable and sustainable system that at the same time would enable shrimp exports to be revived.

Beninese authorities then realised that it was no longer possible to adopt texts that would remain dead letters, but legal reforms had to be accompanied by the required administrative and institutional changes. To be effective, the food safety legal, institutional and administrative framework had to integrate many factors related to the laws and regulations in force in Benin, but also in relation to the EU normative framework, considering that Benin's shrimps targeted the EU market exclusively. In terms of food safety, specifically for food intended to be part of international trade, it is no longer possible to ignore the regional and international trends with regard to risk regulation.

Taking into consideration initiatives at the regional level essentially requires Benin to refer to the regulatory framework developed by the UEMOA. As regards the international framework, the issue is more complex. Ensuring compliance then aims to integrate and comply with WTO requirements, especially those arising from the SPS and TBT agreements. However, complying with EU requirements represented an even more pressing challenge for market access.

Government actions built on the rules embodied since 1984 by Law 84-009. However the provisions had become obsolete in light of changes in risk perception, production methods and commercial practices, which resulted in the need to review relevant control systems to ensure the safety of fishery products. In this regard, Decree 114 on the quality assurance of fishery products was adopted to implement Law 84-009. But in contrast to the latter the scope of which extended to foodstuffs in general, Decree 114 intended to establish specific rules to be applied merely to fishery products. This decree defined the health rules regime for fishery products, their conditions of processing, preservation, and marketing, as well as the related tax system.[372] Furthermore, rules were also established regarding the import of fishery products in Benin. For example, these measures required importers to submit to control any imported fishery products and their coating materials. This would result in a health certificate being delivered in advance of placing the product on the market (Articles 19-21). Similarly, the importation and even possession of fishery products had to be subject to the authorisation of the CA (Article 10).[373]

As such, Decree 114 began to lay the foundations for a more appropriate implementation of safety rules. The decree merely laid down general principles leading to the safety of fishery products, while defining responsibilities for

[372] Decree 114, Article 1.

[373] Although these measures, which relate specifically to imports, are very few, this analysis will not dwell too long on them, for reasons of consistency.

monitoring to achieve these goals. For an effective implementation, the decree refers to the adoption, when necessary, of implementing orders that shall extensively specify hygiene conditions in establishments on land and vessels.[374]

Furthermore, a set of seven orders were adopted at a time in relation to fishery products in rather diverse areas related to establishments, hygiene, good laboratory practices, and limits of certain substances in fishery products.

Table 4.1. List of texts adopted to comply with EU requirements in the fishing sector

Date of adoption	Title	Date of publication
07/04/2003	Order 418/MAEP/D-CAB/SGM/DA/DP/CSRH/SA carrying verification of good practices of laboratory of fishery products	OJ No 20 of 15/10/2003
07/04/2003	Order 419/MAEP/D-CAB/SGM/DA/DP/CSRH/SA laying down limit values of total volatile basic nitrogen, trimethylamine and histamine in fishery products	OJ No 20 of 15/10/2003
07/04/2003	Order 421/MAEP/D-CAB/SGM/DA/DP/CSRH/SA laying down the conditions for granting licenses and approval for establishments on land, vessels and isothermal facilities for fishery products	OJ No 20 of 15/10/2003
07/04/2003	Order 425/MAEP/D-CAB/SGM/DA/DP/CSRH/SA defining the hygiene conditions in establishments on land	OJ No 20 of 15/10/2003
07/04/2003	Order 425/MAEP/D-CAB/SGM/DA/DP/CSRH/SA laying down the limit values of lead, mercury and cadmium in fishery products	OJ No 20 of 15/10/2003
07/04/2003	Order 426/MAEP/D-CAB/SGM/DA/DP/CSRH/SA defining hygiene conditions on board fishing vessels and factory vessels	OJ No 20 of 15/10/2003
07/04/2003	Order 427/MAEP/D-CAB/SGM/DA/DP/CSRH/SA setting out the quality of waters used in establishments on land for the treatment of fishery products	OJ No 20 of 15/10/2003
09/04/2003	Decree 114 laying down the quality assurance of fishery products in the Republic of Benin	OJ No 20 of 15/10/2003

Benin's authorities continued to carry out reforms both in terms of the adoption of legal texts and subsequent measures to ensure the proper implementation of the texts adopted. In 2005, a certain level of completion and the promise to continue reforms according to the action plan were considered sufficient guarantees to allow fishery products from Benin to have access to the EU market once again.

374 Decree 114, Article 36.

Benin had then studied and adopted its own texts, even if they took into account the deficiencies detected in comparison with the EU food law each time. However, after the EU Hygiene Package came into force, the need of compliance arose one more time. This resulted in a radical change of the situation that gave rise to the literal replication of the EU food law into the Benin legal order.

4.4.2. FIRST ATTEMPTS OF REGULATION

The control of the food chain involves the definition of various levels of responsibilities and a mixture of recommendations and procedural rules that are reflected in the orders adopted in Benin. These orders cover all conditions leading to the obtaining of a safe product and are elaborated by the Directorate of Fisheries. Essentially, the orders monitor compliance with installation and approval conditions of establishments, hygiene and own checks implemented by operators, conditions for the acceptability of products with reference to national and international standards, the treatment of various products, traceability, and even the presentation of products.

a. Definition and responsibilities

Decree 114 was adopted to lay down specific rules for fishery products pursuant to Law 84–009 on the control of foodstuffs. As such, the Decree defines the regime of safety requirements and the conditions for the processing, preservation and marketing of fishery products as well as related taxes.[375]

Quality assurance is a strategic function that is the basis of any safety-oriented system in the sense that it sets the policies, adopts the programmes according to the established objectives, and ensures that these measures are effectively implemented.

While quality assurance ensures a strategic role, quality control is a technical function that includes all technical and operational activities implemented to meet product quality requirements.[376] The two functions are complementary because quality control eventually enables the implementation of the activities defined in advance by quality assurance. Ultimately, quality assurance is the interactive process that allows the convergence of all actions of diverse stakeholders to reach food safety objectives. The implementation of quality assurance requirements falls mainly on the CA and food business operators. Moreover, the work of the CA's inspectors must be supported by proper analyses.

The effectiveness of the entire certification system relies on the CA and the results obtained depend on the commitment of actors. Therefore, the CA

375 Decree 114, Article 1.
376 Decree 114, Article 2.

must engage in a process of continuous improvement of the system by setting up an internal quality assurance system and a mechanism for the autonomous management of the material and financial resources of the control services. According to the EU law, the CA is the interlocutor confirming the effective implementation of the control system over the entire food chain and certifying products conform to relevant requirements.

In Benin, quality assurance is delegated to a CA established as the Directorate of Fisheries[377], provided that the latter may delegate some of its powers to any entity deemed appropriate.[378] As such, the CA is rightly referred to in Article 2 of Decree 114 as the administration of fisheries in charge of quality assurance and quality control of fishery products. As such, the CA must deploy the necessary logistics for the effective implementation of the tasks embodied in the texts. Apart from the obvious responsibilities of coordination and making available necessary resources, the Directorate of Fisheries must provide periodic training and guarantee the integrity of control agents. In this case, the CA must organise for its agents to take an oath. Within the same logic, the CA should develop material, financial and moral incentives[379] aiming at avoiding corruption among its officers. The introduction of these provisions is very significant given suspicions previously raised by operators about the implementation of controls based on friendly relations and the issuing of undeserved certificates. Even though these provisions cannot guarantee the integrity and ethics of control agents, their proper implementation should make it possible to offer at least a presumption of transparency and impartiality. These assets should *a priori* ensure the credibility of the control system until it is questioned by laboratory tests. In this respect, the Directorate of Fisheries should also establish an internal system of quality assurance. A good system should always be able to evaluate itself in order to diagnose its deficiencies and curb internal dissent that could hinder its performance and efficiency in a timely manner.

The Directorate of Fisheries is also qualified to investigate and detect violations of quality assurance measures and to carry out inspections of counter-inspections of fishery products.[380] For this purpose, food control inspectors are responsible for checking hygiene and health conditions, ensuring good conditions of landing, transport and the storage of fishery products, monitoring conditions of good practices of manufacturing in establishments on land, and carrying out products quality control. For this purpose, all fishery products intended for human consumption are to be presented to inspectors so as to enable them to carry out organoleptic checks and to organise microbiological and chemical analyses. An effective control of fishery products must be evidenced

377 Decree 114, Article 4.
378 Decree 114, Article 3.
379 Order 2008-086, Article 18.
380 Decree 114, Article 34.

by the issuance of a health certificate, which must necessarily come from a food control inspector. This document represents the validation of compliance with safety requirements. In case of doubt about the quality, any authorised fishery officer may intercept fishery products pending the implementation of the required procedure by the food control inspector. If it turns out that the products are clearly unfit for human consumption, these products must be subject to seizure and destruction at the owner's expense, under the supervision of an authorised food control inspector. In this regard, the assistance of other public officials may be required. Accordingly, any police officer, gendarme, customs or law-enforcement officer may assist the food control inspector in the exercise of his functions.[381]

When these agents determine a violation of quality assurance measures of fishery products, the offense is punishable according to Law 84–009 on the control of foodstuffs.[382] Sanctions are the payment of a fine and/or a custodial sentence, depending on the misconduct. The sanction can be strengthened and the fine increased if the offense is accompanied by fraudulent practices or has had the consequence to putting human health at risk. The consequence of paying a fine or imprisonment may also be the result of operators' practices to prevent relevant officers from fulfilling their functions with regard to research and the detection of infringements of safety requirements. In the same logic, retention or dissimulation of administrative, accounting, technical or commercial documents or messages contained in commercials, and the disclosure of false or misleading information also give rise to the same type of sanctions according to their gravity. Sanctions must also apply when the operator takes the liberty, without prior authorisation, to make use of goods that were blocked or seized by qualified authorities or when the operator diverts such goods from the intended destination.[383]

While certification relies mainly on the CA, the implementation of safety requirements surrounding the production process falls on food business operators. First, the creation or the operation of any establishment on land[384], factory vessel, fishing vessel or isothermal installation is conditional upon obtaining an approval or authorisation upon request of the food business operator.[385] The authorisation granted to fishing vessels must be issued after the signing of a fishing agreement between the CA and the applicant. This authorisation, which is subject to the payment of the fees applicable, shall be renewed annually after technical and health inspections of the CA.[386] The

381 Decree 114, Article 26.
382 Decree 114, Article 30.
383 Law 84–009, Article 20.
384 An establishment on land is any premises where fishery products are prepared, processed, chilled, frozen, packaged, or stored (Decree 114, Article 1; Order 422, Article 1).
385 Decree 114, Article 8.
386 Order 421, Articles 4–6.

apparent degradation of facilities and a breach of the fishing contract and safety requirements should lead to a suspension of the approval until corrective actions are undertaken.[387]

However, this obligation does not extend to fishermen's wives and retailers. The latter can conduct their processing, preservation and marketing activities upon identification and training by the services of the CA. In practice, this training is not carried out since such activities are often the privilege of those within the informal sector who are difficult to identify and control. In any case, these activities refer primarily to traditional processing methods for the production of smoked products for the local or regional market.

With regard to analyses, the CA must approve laboratories that have sufficient capacity and materials and equipment to carry out reliable tests on fishery products. To reinforce this reliability, the CA must verify the respect of good laboratory practices in all approved laboratories.[388] This verification refers to the mode of organisation and conditions of planning, execution, recording, and the dissemination of laboratory tests results on fishery products, as well as water, ice and other additives and ingredients used in the preparation of fishery products.[389] For example, the CA and/or State-approved laboratories must perform analyses of the water on the basis of the monitoring plan established by the CA.[390] A microbiological analysis of water is essential because the quality of fishery products is related to that of the water in which they were caught. Therefore, analyses must be performed on a regular basis to search for contaminants present in the aquatic environment

To carry out good laboratory practices, the minister in charge of fisheries establishes a multidisciplinary team annually on the basis of proposals by the Directorate of Fisheries. To be effective, the resulting plan must be established by a protocol agreement. Cases of non-compliance must be punished by a withdrawal of authorisation.

b. Product requirements

In order to be recognised as fit for human consumption and certified accordingly, fishery products must meet certain requirements. However, it is virtually impossible to find clearly the criteria that determine the safety of a fishery product through the legislation. It follows that, to understand the characteristics of a safe product, one must follow a deductive logic since the texts extensively define the criteria that make a product unfit for consumption and therefore unacceptable.

---

387 Order 421, Article 7.
388 Order 418, Article 2.
389 Order 418, Article 1.
390 Decree 114, Article 7.

These criteria refer both to limits for the presence of environmental contaminants in finished products and limits for additives used during the production process. For instance, Article 4 of Order 425 requires the processing plants comply with heavy metal standards to ensure the protection of public health. Article 2 indeed stated that fishery products whose chemical analysis indicates levels of lead, mercury and cadmium above the norms established are considered unfit for human consumption. The maximum levels are then clearly defined by the text for each category of heavy metals according to the type of product. These norms frequently refer to the causal link between the consumption and its potential consequences on the human body. Thus, the determination of the limits may specify, as in Article 3 of Order 425, that the presence of heavy metals in fishery products should not be in such quantities that the calculated dietary intake exceeds the acceptable daily human intake. That being said, Order 425 limits itself to such a statement without going into depth about what would be considered appropriate. Evidently, such a limit involves a variety of parameters such as the characteristics of the consumers involved or appropriate scientific analyses of the effects of one substance or another on the human body.

Following the same logic, Article 2 of Order 419 provides that "are considered unfit for human consumption, fishery products whose organoleptic analysis reveals a lack of freshness, and whose microbiological control indicates that the rate of TVB-N, trimethylamine and histamine are above the limits required". The limit values of TVB-N, of trimethylamine and histamine in fishery products are defined according to the type of fish, whether it is a bony or cartilaginous fish, a crustacean or cephalopods (Order 419, Article 2). The limit values for lead, mercury and cadmium (contaminants of the aquatic environment) in fishery products are fixed by Order 425. These limits relate to the muscle meat of fish, crustaceans except brown crab meat, bivalve molluscs and cephalopods without viscera. These criteria respond to the need to maintain a balance between the purely visual observations and analyses of samples to be sure of achieving the appropriate level of safety. The control of these diverse substances is done by the CA according to monitoring and sampling plans that depend on the nature of the products and the minimum number of samples required per batch for each product category. The CA shall define the procedures regarding changes to reference methods of analysis found to be necessary in light of scientific and technical progress.

c. *Hygiene requirements*

1° Hygiene requirements in establishments on land

Hygiene conditions in establishments on land basically relate to premises, equipment, to products themselves, and staff working in these establishments.

Hygiene conditions for premises are divided into two complementary components. The first requirements refer to the construction of premises and equipment. Essentially, establishments on land must contain workplaces of a sufficient size that are arranged and fitted so as to avoid any warming, pollution of the product or contamination from the outside. The lighting must be adequate and the infrastructure as a whole, including the equipment must be easy to clean and disinfect.[391] There must be safety devices against insects and animals, and suitable arrangements to avoid that products are in contact with the floor, walls or ceilings.[392] Vehicles used to transport products must be isotherm and must have no negative impact on products.[393] For example, Article 5 of Order 422 stipulated that the access to establishments must be prohibited for vehicles that emit potentially harmful exhaust fumes.

The second requirements relate to the handling and storage of fishery products. In this regard, packaging and materials in contact with fishery products must be free of contamination and comply with the regulation in force. In the same way, products must be handled under strict conditions of cleanliness and at a proper temperature, and protected from contamination from toxic chemicals such as detergents or abrasives.

Any operation performed on fishery products, whether they are fresh, frozen, thawed, or processed must follow perfect hygiene conditions. The maintenance of the cold chain so as to preserve products' freshness is compulsory.

In the specific case of crustaceans and molluscs, cooking must take place within a particular site or, otherwise, in a site sufficiently isolated. Rapid cooling carried out in appropriate hygiene conditions must immediately follow the cooking.[394] Operations such as shelling or shucking must be carried out under required hygiene and sanitation conditions, while the finished product should be kept or stored at temperatures appropriate to avoid the development of germs.[395]

Lastly, the staff responsible for the handling of products must be adequately qualified to apply good manufacturing practices and be subjected to the observance of good hygiene behaviour at the site of production. The health status of the staff must be medically checked and lead to the issuance of certificate.

2° Hygiene requirements on board factory vessels and fishing boats

Hygiene requirements on board factory vessels can be summarised as the need for operators to have a HACCP plan[396] and to observe the hygiene rules in force.

---

391 Order 422, Articles 1–5.
392 Order 422, Article 8.
393 Order 422, Article 10.
394 Order 422, Article 39.
395 Order 422, Article 40.
396 Order 426, Article 11.

These rules could be compared to the requirements that apply to establishments on land.

With regard to fishing boats, these rules do not apply in a similar way, because their activities are mostly artisanal. Article 1 of Order 3477 defines the fishing boat as any boat propelled by paddle or outboard motor to perform the fishing or to ensure the collection of fishery products. As is customary in terms of hygiene conditions, requirements for fishing boats are related to the boat itself and the materials intended to come into contact with products. The structure of this equipment should be such as to enable easy maintenance and cleaning. Subsequently, given the relatively small size of these boats and their catches, additional requirements have been adopted to maintain a high level of product freshness. For example, ice flakes made with potable water must be used to chill products at an ideal temperature between 0 and 5 degrees Celsius.

In addition, fishermen and other middlemen should commit themselves to good personal hygiene and avoid carrying out acts around the products that could be a source of contamination, such as smoking. Order 3477 went even a step further by establishing that any collector of fishery products must have a medical certificate issued by a registered medical practitioner.[397]

Lastly, in response to the risks of contamination from the wooden walls of canoes mentioned by FVO inspectors, all boats must be equipped with a device such as cold storage insulated bodies or coolers to help keep fishery products at the level of freshness required.[398]

Unloading and landing must be carried out promptly using appropriate and properly cleaned materials to avoid the deterioration of edible parts or cross-contamination and to ensure the maintenance of the cold chain.

d. Requirement to use potable water for processing

Article 1 of Order 427 requires the use of potable water for all activities related to the processing of fishery products. Potable water is defined as water with no odour or unpleasant taste intended for human consumption, which meets standards of physical, chemical or microbiological requirements.[399] If the potable water is obtained through a treatment by chlorination, the establishment's manager must take the necessary steps to check the level of chlorine several times a day and to ensure the proper use of the chlorine.

Laying down this principle was very important because the use of chlorine was a major issue for shrimp processing plants in Benin. In the absence of legal standards, processing plants were accustomed to the excessive use of chlorine to disinfect products. This led the FVO to report unacceptable practices in 2002,

---

[397] Order 3477, Article 6.
[398] Order 3477, Article 5.
[399] Order 427, Article 2.

namely the use of chlorine not intended for food use and the use of chlorine and additives without proper knowledge of their dosage, the frequency of baths and methods of control. Establishments claimed that they acted in good faith, which could certainly be presumed until proven otherwise, given the lack of legal norms.

Moreover, establishing a mandatory use of potable water was also important since fishermen must use ice to maintain a good state of freshness of the catch. Because fishermen represent small units of operation, they may simply purchase the ice in their neighbourhood, while it is commonly known that access to potable water is limited in fishing communities. Therefore, it becomes difficult to guarantee the use of drinking water – according to the definition of Order 427– for cooling products on board fishing boats. In this regard, a mandatory requirement of compliance induces the cooperation and collaboration of each actor in the food chain.

e. *Complementary texts*

After the first texts were adopted, regulatory work focused on more specific requirements focusing on products allowed in establishments and limits of additives. This second series of legislation covered the period 2004 to 2008.

Table 4.2. List of complementary texts in the fishing sector from 2004 to 2008

Date of adoption	Title	Date of publication
22/01/2004	Order 2004–087/MAEP/D-CAB/SGM/DRH/DP/SA listing cleaning and disinfection products authorized in establishments on land, ships and isothermal installations of fishery products	OJ No. 22 of 15/11/2004
03/08/2004	Order 2004–1101/MAEP/D-CAB/SGM/DRH/DP/SA laying down limit values of additives authorized in the processing of fishery products	OJ No. 22 of 15/11/2004
02/11/2005	Order 2005–3068/MAEP/D-CAB/SGM/DRH/DP/S concerning materials and objects intended to come into contact with fishery products	OJ No. 11 of 01/06/2005
02/11/2005	Order 2005–3069/MAEP/D-CAB/SGM/DRH/DP/SA setting the limits of organohalogen substances and other molecules of pesticides in fishery products	OJ No. 11 of 06/01/2006
22/11/2005	Order 2005–3477/MAEP/D-CAB/SGM/DRH/DP/SA defining hygiene conditions on board fishing boats	OJ No. 11 of 06/01/2006
30/12/2005	Interministerial Order 1683/MFE/MAEP/D-CAB/D-CAB/DRF/DP/SA implementing fees of control and monitoring of products and fishing facilities	OJ No. 11 of 06/01/2006

Date of adoption	Title	Date of publication
11/10/2007	Order 0334/MAEP/D-CAB/SGM/DRH/DP/SA establishing conditions for export, import and distribution of fishery products in the Republic of Benin	OJ No. 9 of 01/05/ 2008
30/10/2007	Order 0362/MAEP/D-CAB/SGM/DRH/DP/SA laying down maximum levels for certain contaminants in foodstuffs in the Republic of Benin	OJ No. 9 of 01/05/2008
18/03/2008	Order 2008-086/MAEP/D-CAB/SGM/DRH/DP/SA laying down organization rules, procedures for quality control, safety and traceability of fishery products	OJ No. 9 of 01/05/ 2008

While most of these complementary texts also referred to fishery products, a broader scope was introduced from 2007 to extend safety regulation to all food in general. This resulted in the adoption of Order 2007-0362 laying down maximum levels for certain contaminants in foodstuffs. This Order provided a number of definitions of concepts such as risk, risk analysis and risk assessment. However, the clarification of these notions was of no importance for the purpose of the Order and no use was made of these notions throughout its provisions. In fact, these definitions were merely aimed at aligning with similar notions contained in EU food law. Just like Regulation (EC) 178/2002, Order 2007-0362 defines food as any food substance or product, whether processed, partially processed or unprocessed, intended or reasonably expected to be ingested by human beings, including substances to be assimilated to food such as drinks and chewing gum.

As a result, the definition also includes water intentionally incorporated into food during its manufacture, preparation or treatment. But, quite surprisingly, the definition of Order 2007-0362 specified that food includes "water at the point of compliance defined in Article 6 of Directive 98/83/EC and without prejudice to the requirements of Directives 80/778/EEC and 98/83/EC". The reference to the EU standards for drinking water is literally inserted in Benin's law irrespective of the existence of Benin's own standard of drinking water since 2001 as laid down by Decree 2001-094. Since the EU Directives referred to were never taken over by Benin's national legal system, it would have been more suitable if this EU standard had been at least clarified in Order 2007-0362. However this was done neither in the Order itself, nor in its appendix.

This section further underlines the requirements for materials and objects and provisions on the organisation and traceability of fishery product controls.

1° Requirements for materials and objects

Requirements referring to materials and objects used in the production and final presentation of fishery products are also of paramount interest in protecting the consumer. In fact, Order 2005/3068 dedicated the proper management of materials and objects used in the production and final presentation of fishery products as the "basis to ensure a high level of protection of human health and consumer interests."

Article 1 of Order 2005/3068 lays down the principle that "all materials and articles intended to come directly or indirectly into contact with foodstuffs must be sufficiently inert so as not to transmit components in a quantity likely to endanger human health, cause an unacceptable change in the composition of food, or impair organoleptic characteristics of food". In the present case, "materials and objects" are those which, at the stage of finished product, are already or are intended to be in contact with foodstuffs and those which may reasonably be expected to be brought into contact with food or to transfer their constituents to food under normal or foreseeable conditions of use.[400]

It is appropriate to clarify that "material and objects" include two categories of materials intended to come into contact with foodstuffs. First, the "active materials and articles" are intended to extend the shelf life or maintain or improve the condition of packaged foodstuffs. Second, "intelligent materials and articles" control the state of packaged foodstuffs or the environment of food. Coating materials such as coverings that form a part of cheese and are likely to be consumed with it are not to be classified in either category.

In any case, food and food contact materials must be manufactured according to Good Manufacturing Practices (GMP) so that, under normal or foreseeable conditions of use, they do not transfer constituents to foodstuffs in quantities which could either present a health hazard or cause an unacceptable change in the food composition or bring about a deterioration in the organoleptic characteristics thereof.[401]

The regime applicable to materials and food contact objects are also largely connected to the protection of consumers against misleading and deceitful practices. The relevant provisions prohibit all practices intended to abuse the consumer through means of labelling, advertising, the presentation of a material or object, and information mentioned on products.[402] Lastly, materials and objects must be labelled so as to enable consumers to distinguish the edible parts and make a clear distinction according to whether the materials are active or intelligent.

---

400 Order 2005/3068, Article 2.

401 Order 2005/3068, Article 5. The same Order establishes that active materials and objects may change the composition or the organoleptic characteristics of foods in cases where they comply with the provisions applicable to foodstuffs, among other provisions of Order 1101.

402 Order 2005/3068, Articles 6 and 10.

A new perspective was introduced with Order 0334 adopted in 2007. At first sight, this order seems to constitute an essential part in the regulation of fishery products because for the first time its provisions gave a legal definition of a number of concepts often used in diverse legal texts but which were never actually and explicitly defined.[403] But, contrary to expectations, it made no use of the concepts clarified and, according to its title, merely laid down a few requirements as regards the importation, export and marketing of fishery products.

With respect to exports, the most important requirement was set out in Article 2 submitting the detention or export for sale purposes to safety requirements related to storage and marketing, prescribed by national control regulations. Therefore, any export of fishery products is subject to prior the registration of the establishments and/or suitable arrangements aiming at keeping products at the required temperature conditions. The head persons of these facilities must proceed to carry out regular checks throughout the production chain to ensure good product traceability. Similarly, any application for an export certificate requires official control procedures to certify the products' analyses performed by the operator.[404]

2° Organisation of the controls of fishery products

Operational criteria for the control of fishery products were established only in 2008 through Decree 2008-086. As specified in Article 1 of this Decree, these criteria refer to the procedures, organisation methods, inspections, sampling, analysis, and certification of fishery products and the quality assurance measures in all places of handling. Decree 2008-086 established a distinction between the control of fishery products and fishing police, which mostly targets fraudulent practices likely to threaten sustainability.

The control of fishery products is organised according to a hierarchy of tasks based on the quality of the involved officers. Official control means "any form of control under the responsibility of the CA for verifying compliance with the legislation relating to the production, export and import of fishery products". In general, the officers of the CA are responsible for all activities related to the production and placing on the market of fishery products, ranging from primary production to industrial processing. Article 2 of Order 2008-086 defines an officer of the CA as a person who is authorised to carry out the control of fishery products as inspector, controller or technician and who operates under the responsibility of the CA. Therefore, the coverage of these officers extends to production facilities

403 It defined for example concepts such as "fishery products", equivalence, inspection, audit, control system, etc. For all practical purposes, it defines a fishery product as any halieutic product or aquaculture fish, including eggs and roes, excluding aquatic mammals and frogs.

404 Order 0334, Articles 5-7.

which, due to the nature of their activities, intervene incidentally in the fishery food chain. This could refer for instance to institutions such as ice plants, landing sites, or cold storage warehouses, as well as the recently built bases of compulsory control and platforms for the transfer of fishery products.

The implementation of audits and inspections include the collection of samples and required analyses according to the product under consideration. Where applicable, these operations should result in the certification of safe products and the withdrawal from the market of suspicious products or products unfit for consumption. Furthermore, the CA's officers shall ensure the implementation and monitoring of all corrective measures imposed or recommended following an inspection. Ultimately, CA's officers are responsible for the management of safety risks in relation to fishery products.[405] This raises concerns of legitimacy since risk management is meant to be a strategic function as regards food safety decision making. In this respect, given what is at stake, such an important function should not be entrusted randomly to any agent. It is worth mentioning that risk management is defined in Order 2007–0362 in conformity with the definition provided in Article 3.12 of EU Regulation 178/2002.

With regard to the practical distribution of control tasks, the most important functions are conferred on the quality control inspector and s/he even ask the government to temporarily block the import of fishery products. By contrast, measures taken by the controller shall not extend beyond the provisional seizure or blocking of fishery products. Control inspectors can then decide on the mere destruction or decide to divert the products to more secure purposes other than human consumption. Lastly, the control technician has the authority to apply a temporary blocking measure or issue a basic health certificate. The latter is a document prepared by the technician or controller of fishery products during the checks carried out at the Base of Compulsory Control or Platforms of Transfer of fishery products or any other especially deigned location authorised by the CA.

For transparency purposes, control of fishery products must be exercised in accordance with documented procedures contained in a regularly updated practical manual of inspection and quality assurance of fishery products in Benin.[406] In addition, the control agent must be autonomous in the conduct of operations and in reporting its results.

However, whether the inspection is complete, periodic or random, control agents must demonstrate technical abilities, probity and professional rigour. This requirement highlights the importance of giving appropriate training to these officers and adopting adequate measures to prevent them from giving in to corruption.

---

405 Order 2008–086, Article 4.

406 Order 2008–086, Article 10.

Control agents must be aware of the extent of their powers and responsibilities in order not to exceed their authority. These agents must immediately report their measures to their manager who is competent in the concerned territorial jurisdiction and must draw the attention of the latter to the findings that might necessitate other measures outside the agent's mandate.[407]

3° Traceability of fishery products

The concept of traceability emerged for the first time in Benin's food safety law in 2005 in Article 4 of Order 2005-3068 concerning materials and objects intended to come into contact with fishery products. A mere definition was then given, without any reference to the concept in the provisions of the order, whether in regard to its interest in food safety matters or any requirements that it might imply. Similarly, traceability was again defined in the same way in Article 1 of Order 2007-0362. These facts betray a somewhat staggered development of the law.

Traceability is the ability to trace the path of a material or object through all stages of production, processing and distribution.[408] As a performance measurement tool, traceability shall be used for fishery products, as well as any material incorporated, expected to be incorporated, or intended to come into contact with these products. Traceability must extend to all stages of storage and export.[409]

To facilitate the attainment of traceability objectives, the CA must take into consideration the large number of actors involved in the fishery products food chain. Therefore, an approval system is set up for establishments on land, and fishermen, collectors, wholesalers, carriers and bodies of water involved in the export-oriented food chain of fishery products must be registered.[410] However, the main responsibility towards traceability relies upon the food establishments, which must implement a clearly documented traceability system, so as to enable control agents to verify the effectiveness and efficiency of that system.[411]

f. Relations with the Food Safety Authority

Within the framework of its activities, the CA must take steps to participate in food safety programmes so as to use the results of risk assessment, monitoring and evaluation of control performance. These additional responsibilities were laid down in Order 2008-086 stipulating organisation rules, procedures for quality control, safety and the traceability of fishery products. As stated

407 Order 2008-086, Article 8.
408 Order 2005-3068, Article 4(a).
409 Order 2008-086, Article 14.
410 Order 2008-086, Article 15.
411 Idem.

by Article 21 of this order, food safety programmes could enable not only efficient risk management, but also the participation in training networks and information exchange on risks associated with fishery products. As it will be shown later, the Food Safety Authority is an interministerial body and, as such, it will certainly offer a forum for exchanging experiences and ideas on how to better address the management of food safety risks. The competent authority must be part of the monitoring, alert and crisis management system, and must constantly check the functionality of the system of notification, withdrawal or recall of products.[412] The purpose of this cooperation is to ensure good responsiveness to the detection of food risks.

4.4.3. SECOND GENERATION: THE TRANSPOSITION OF EU TEXTS

In 2009, within the space of two months, five new orders were adopted with regard to food safety in Benin. At first glance, two important observations emerge. First, these texts form part of a broader framework: unlike their predecessors essentially devoted to fishery products, they refer to food in general, with specific requirements for food of animal origin. Secondly, these texts correspond exactly to the texts that constitute the legal food safety framework in force within the EU. As a matter of fact, this constitutes merely an open secret since Benin's stakeholders use the legal transplant and even translate the different counterparts into their official documents. Unsurprisingly, one could easily read in official documents statements such as "Decree 075 corresponding to Regulation EU 178/2002" to highlight the compatibility between Benin and EU food laws. This is so exaggerated that many agents of the Directorate of Fisheries recite more spontaneously the corresponding EU regulations than the national law. The same trend is even observed in the texts put online in the context of the "information systems on sanitary and phytosanitary measures" in Benin.

Table 4.3. List of laws transplanted by Benin to comply with EU food law

Date of adoption	Title	Corresponding EU law
26/02/2009	Order 074/MAEP/D-CAB/SGM/DRH/DP/DE/SA laying down specific rules for the organization of official controls on products of animal origin intended for human consumption	Regulation 854/2004
26/02/2009	Order 075/MAEP/D-CAB/SGM/DRH/DP/DE/SA laying down general principles and requirements of food law, of food security, and laying down procedures in matters of food safety	Regulation 178/2002

412 Order 2008-086, Article 22.

Date of adoption	Title	Corresponding EU law
23/03/2009	Order 122/MAEP/D-CAB/SGM/DRH/DP/DE/SA laying down hygiene of foodstuffs	Regulation 852/2004
23/03/2009	Order 123/MAEP/D-CAB/SGM/DRH/DP/DE/SA laying down specific hygiene rules for food of animal origin	Regulation 853/2004
23/03/2009	Order 133/MAEP/D-CAB/SGM/DRH/DP/DE/SA laying down rules for official controls to verify compliance of the legislation on animal feed and foodstuffs with the provisions on animal health and welfare	Regulation 882/2004

Given that these texts are essentially the same as those in force in the EU that were already addressed in chapter 2, this section focuses only on the major changes they brought with respect to all the texts already adopted by Benin since the beginning of legal reforms in 2003. This will help to identify whether the legal transplant was really necessary to achieve the food safety objectives equivalent to the EU level of protection.

a. Definition of concepts

The new orders were particularly rich in defining concepts related to food safety that were being used for a long time without being legally clarified. Some of them were also established in previous orders while their definitions were somewhat irrelevant at the time. This refers, for example, to the definitions of concepts such as risk analysis, risk management, risk assessment, and traceability included in Order 2007-0362.

Among these definitions, some deserve attention. Order 2009-075 provides a new definition of food. As stated previously in Order 2007-0362, the definition of food includes water intentionally incorporated into the food during its manufacture, preparation or treatment. However, the new definition takes care this time not to refer in the definition of water to that of the EU Directive 98/83/EC, as was previously done so aberrantly in Order 2007-0362. Furthermore, the definition of drinking water was clarified better later by Article 3 of Order 2009-122, which states that drinking water is "water meeting the minimum requirements set by Decree 2001-094 establishing standards of quality of drinking water in the Republic of Benin". It is worth noting that the new definition of foods is also more complete since it gives a explicit list of the substances which under no circumstances should be considered as foodstuffs.

b. Principles of food law

1° General requirements

Adopting a copy of the EU texts at least has the merit of defining in a more visible manner the principles that must be the base of food law. Like in the EU law, the food legislation must be based on risk analysis, the use if necessary of the precautionary principle, and the protection of consumer interests. This requirement had previously never emerged under Beninese law and it gives a new dimension to the management of food risks. Within the current framework, it is necessary to keep in mind that for a policy to succeed, it has to have resources. In line with this new dynamic, Benin has been attempting, at least in the fishing sector, to implement the law with the assistance of many donors.

The option to base all food safety measures on sound scientific risk analysis complies with international standards and implies a dynamic and responsive institutional support that Benin did not have at the time and which is still lacking to a certain extent. Building an institutional support that would facilitate a risk-based food risk management was to be supported by the creation of a Food Safety Authority in Benin. However, while this body was finally set up in 2012, it is not yet fully operational.

The new set of laws also refers to the principle of transparency from a different perspective. Transparency in this respect was to be implemented far beyond the mere scope of control. The current challenge is to extend transparency to the communication of risk to the public. In this regard, responsiveness becomes very important because authorities can properly communicate to the public about food risks only if they were able or are in the process of taking adequate measures immediately when health issues arise. The lack of a proper balance between risk communication and responsiveness of the overall food safety system would raise trust issues that could undermine the credibility of the system.

2° Primary responsibility of food business operators

A significant change in the transplanted law is the institution of the primary responsibility of food business operators with regard to the safety of their products. This provision makes it possible to dilute the CA's accountability for the attainment of food safety objectives. This requirement could constitute a ground for a mandatory duty of care for operators because it makes them more aware of the greater risks they incur in the event of failure to comply with food safety requirements.

The primary responsibility comes concomitantly with traceability obligations schematised as "one step back, one step forward". This process is the essential support to easily and swiftly locate hazardous products before they can cause harm to consumers. Moreover, traceability is an asset to clear the food chain of dishonest or careless actors who would be often singled out for safety reasons related to their products. Traceability in the fishery sector in Benin is essential because of the multiplicity of actors involved, especially the fishermen that work on a very small scale. The requirements of labelling are also defined more precisely to serve the requirements of traceability.[413]

Similarly, operators are responsible for activating the process of removing hazardous or potentially hazardous products from the market. This requirement is compatible with the ongoing self-checks process operators must implement and completes their primary responsibility. The previous system refers more to arranging the withdrawal of products from the market when, during its inspections, the CA discovers some potential risks. In this particular case, it would mean that if controls were not made with the expected frequency or the required probity, there would be higher risks that unsafe products would circulate on the market. Clearly, if the law were to be respected to the letter, such dysfunctions would not be found by the CA. However, for the sake of caution, it is always appropriate to have several alternatives in case one option would not work out. Past poor implementation issues in Benin call for this kind of caution. In any case, the implementation of *ex post* controls by CA's officers already existed in national law. But the new system is more reactive because it involves close collaboration and communication between operators and the CA, especially when a risk to human health is detected in connection with a product that has already reached the market and therefore requires an immediate response.

In order to strengthen their primary responsibility, food business operators are also expected to proceed to a widespread application of procedures based on HACCP principles, together with the implementation of Good Hygiene Practices (GHP).[414] Formerly, this requirement was exclusively addressed to factory vessels. But its extension to all operators other than those of primary production is noteworthy because it injects dynamism into the production process. In fact, considered as such, HACCP management becomes like a roadmap, which calls for greater responsiveness.

To facilitate the HACCP implementation, food business operators can develop and disseminate guides to GHP and the application of HACCP principles under the aegis of a national standards body or another structure competent in the field.[415] Beninese authorities encourage the dissemination and use of these guides, provided that food business operators may use them on a voluntary basis.[416]

---

413 Order 2009-075, Article 31.

414 Order 2009-122, Article 1.

415 Order 2099-122, Article 11.

416 Order 2009-122, Article 20.

An evolutionary dimension was added to the implementation of food safety requirements. This translates into general hygiene provisions being updated to reflect experiences gained in the implementation of HACCP-based systems, technological change and its practical consequences, consumer expectations regarding food composition, scientific opinions, and microbiological and temperature criteria for foodstuffs.

3° Crisis management and emergency situations

A reference was made to crisis management in national law, but the characteristics of such a system and its functioning were not clarified. In this respect, Order 2009-075 is quite innovative because it organises the notification of direct or indirect risks to human health through the creation of a rapid alert system. The effectiveness of the rapid alert system depends on the CA's ability to supplement the information transmitted with any other scientific or technical evidence that could facilitate decision making. Furthermore, the alert network strengthens and facilitates the duty of risk communication falling on the CA. Last, a rapid alert system connects, for the first time in a tangible way, communications between control agents and border post agents and considers potential collaboration with third countries or international organisations.

A. Crisis management plan

Order 2009-075 requires Beninese authorities to have a general plan for the management of a crisis related to food and feed safety. The plan must be sufficiently clear to specify "the types of situation involving direct or indirect risks to human health related to food or feed that are not likely to be prevented, eliminated or reduced to acceptable levels by existing provisions, or cannot be managed appropriately by the mere application" of recommended emergency measures.[417] The general plan must also specify the necessary practical arrangements for crisis management, including transparency principles, and communication strategy.[418]

For the purpose of applying the general plan for crisis management, there are operational contingency plans setting out measures to be implemented in case of serious risks. These plans shall specify the requirements for administrative authorities to intervene, their powers and responsibilities, and the ways and procedures for the exchange of information among stakeholders.[419]

---

[417] Order 2009-075, Article 49.

[418] Order 2009-075, Article 51.

[419] Order 2009-133, Article 36.

B. The Crisis Unit

When a crisis situation requires action that cannot be properly handled by emergency measures identified by the legislation, the CA must immediately notify Beninese authorities. The authorities must in turn immediately establish a crisis unit, to which the CA participates and provides all needed scientific and technical support.[420]

4° Approval or suspension of establishments

Order 2009–074 further defines the outlines for the approval of establishments and procedural details relating to the granting and withdrawal of approval. This order subjects the granting of an approval to the respect for requirements with regard to infrastructure and equipment and defines the conditions for conditional approval if it can be expected that the establishment can quickly comply with relevant requirements. However, if this conditional approval is renewed, it should not apply beyond six months, or twelve months in the case of factory vessels or freezer vessels flying the flag of Benin.

In case of breaches of the legislation, decisions must be taken considering not only the nature of the identified deficiencies but also the history of the establishment in question.[421] If the history shows repeated offenses vis-à-vis food law, it will be accordingly punished more severely. Measures range from the simple imposition of sanitary measures to the suspension of the activity of the establishment.[422]

5° Preservation of traditional methods

Order 2009–074 leaves room in its Article 38 for national measures intended to enable the continued use of traditional methods at any stage of the production, processing or distribution of food. Long-standing traditional practices in the particular case of Benin, and specifically with regard to fishery products are related to artisanal processes such as smoking or drying, carried out under questionable hygiene conditions, and following standards left at the discretionary assessment of operators in the informal sector. However, the fact that these practices have never raised major health concerns gives them the benefit of a simple presumption of safety that might suggest that the desire to preserve these traditional methods is legitimate. In any event, it would still be necessary to be able to translate the methods into documented procedures.

---

420 Order 2009–075, Articles 51 and 52.
421 Order 2009–074, Article 28.
422 Order 2009–074, Article 29.

6° Competent Authority and official controls

Order 2009-133 provides more details about the appointment of the members of the CA. Article 10 states that it is the responsibility of the Minister to appoint members of the CA who are responsible for defined objectives and official controls. However, it would be important to keep in mind that the choice shall be made by mutual agreement with the Directorate of Fisheries, since the latter is more likely to provide relevant information about the qualifications and abilities of its agents.

Regarding the delegation of tasks, Order 2009-133 clarifies in its Article 16 that, most importantly, the control body must work and be accredited according to the European standard EN 45004 "General criteria for the functioning of various types of bodies performing inspection" and/or other standards that would be considered more relevant to the tasks. However the organisations designated through this process are not responsible for decision making. As such, if testing results show or lead to a suspicion of failure, the delegated body shall immediately inform the CA. In any case, the CA must conduct audits or inspections of these bodies and withdraw the delegation of power if they fail to conduct their tasks properly or to implement corrective measures. At the internal level, the CA should ensure the formation and upgrading of its agents and make sure that the agents have the aptitude for multidisciplinary cooperation.

The scope of application of official controls is also broadened. The control is now aimed at verifying compliance with the legislation, in particular to prevent or eliminate risks that may arise, either directly or through the environment, in humans and animals, or to reduce these risks to an acceptable level. The integration of new parameters such as environmental considerations gives more latitude in terms of decision making. These parameters are also useful to ensure fair practices with regard trade in feed and food and the protection of consumers' interests, including labelling and other forms of consumer information.[423]

7° Sampling and analysis

Order 2009-133 gives more details on the setting of procedural rules for the application of sampling and analysis methods. Article 32 requires that samples are handled and labelled so as to guarantee both their legal and analytical validity. Furthermore, Article 28 states that sampling and analysis methods used in the context of official controls shall comply with applicable regulations or rules or protocols recognised internationally, in the event of a lack of such rules at the national level. The lack of international standards is, in turn, compensated by any other methods fit for the intended purpose or developed in accordance with scientific protocols. In so doing, Order 2009-133 gives more latitude to take

[423] Order 2009-133, Article 1.

advantage of international instruments to fill the gaps of domestic law. Finally, the order sets criteria for characterising methods of analysis such as accuracy, applicability, reproducibility, or linearity.

Furthermore, Article 31 of Order 2009-133 provides that business operators must be able to obtain samples in sufficient numbers for a supplementary expert opinion, unless this is impossible in the case of highly perishable products or very low amount of substance. This requirement provides more opportunities for transparency and more guarantees of impartiality. Operators are no longer just subjected to controls, but they can be part of the control process. Moreover, the multiplicity of stakeholders and the separation between them offer a broader guarantee of reliability of the results. In addition this factor could also reduce the risk of corruption.

4.5. CONCLUSION

The former legal framework of fishery products does not seem *a priori* to be completely failing to address the challenges of food production and certification. The laws defined procedures, actors responsible for their implementation, and even determined penalties for breaches. It is therefore legitimate to ask how, after nearly half a century of regulatory work, EU inspectors identified such important failures in the production and certification system. From catching the fresh shrimps to the finished product, there was not a single area that was not found deficient in one way or another. In this regard, the insufficiency of implementing decrees, the scattered provisions resulting in a lack of accountability and the absence of incentives to implement food safety requirements for the domestic market are major issues that contributed to the inexistence of an effective food safety system in Benin.

The inconsistency between the provisions of laws and their implementing decrees was blamed as the main weakness of the food safety law in Benin.[424] Looking through the texts, it was easy to notice redundancies and incoherencies. Laws with a similar objective were adopted and the most recent laws would simply repeal all earlier contrary provisions. However, many of these provisions were scattered through several different laws which remained in force even though some of their requirements would then become unenforceable. This could result in overlapping mandates or conversely create a situation where no authority would actually be responsible for food controls.

Furthermore, the shared responsibility promoted in most food-related texts created obvious conflicts of jurisdiction between different actors in different departments and ministries. This is likely to dilute the accountability of authorities empowered to investigate and record violations of requirements.

424 Amaskane 2010, p21.

All these irregularities led to the severe shortcomings revealed by the first FVO mission in 2002. This situation and the desire to sustain the shrimp export sector were catalysts for major reforms both at the legislative and infrastructural levels. With regard to regulatory activity, EU law was the main reference for Benin's policymakers. First, Directive 91/493 was essentially used to adopt a series of texts to ensure the safety of fish and fish products. Subsequently, the EU Hygiene Package was literally transplanted in Benin. These efforts led to some recognition of compliance during the second FVO mission in 2009. The process is still ongoing but the recovery of the sector has not kept pace. As far as international food trade is concerned, the ability to meet food safety and quality requirements seems to continue to determine the market players.

CHAPTER V

IMPROVING COMPLIANCE TO ACCESS THE EU FISHERY PRODUCTS MARKET

5.1. INTRODUCTION

The FVO mission in Benin in 2002 and the voluntary moratorium on shrimp exports in 2003 were undoubtedly major issues and a catalyst for a series of reforms at various levels. Well before the suspension, it was the FVO report that triggered the mechanism to overcome the legal lethargy that characterised food risk regulation in Benin.

Benin had been registered for the export of fishery products to the EU since 30 June 1998 in the part II of the list annexed to Decision 97/296/EC, following a documentary assessment of the approval file sent to the EU Commission. After carrying out their inspection and pursuant to their negative observations, FVO inspectors urged Benin authorities to implement several remedial measures, most importantly the updating of the food legislation. Obsolete legislation amounted to the lack of a legal basis for Benin's CA to set up a control system aiming to ensure and certify exported fishery products in conformity with EU requirements. After initiating an action plan for the implementation of compliance measures, Benin submitted an application for EU funding and engaged in an upgrading process.

This chapter intends to assess the effectiveness of the food law development in Benin in improving the production and certification system. The second section (5.2) describes the process of legal transplant that led to the food law currently in force in Benin. Then the strategic approach to comply with the EU law is explained (5.3), including the search for alternative solutions (5.4). The fifth section (5.6) focused on the steps to build capacity in the shrimp export sector. The following sections assess technical assistance in the sector (5.6) and the interactions between the EU and Benin (5.7). The last section (5.8) concludes.

5.2. LEGAL TRANSPLANT

Regulatory autonomy is of paramount importance for sovereign countries. But in some cases, this autonomy may prove constrained by factors beyond their control. In the area of food regulation, upgrading reactively always limits the regulatory autonomy of the country concerned. In Benin, the exclusive dependence on the EU market for shrimp exports is a major constraining factor that results in immediate pressure to seek ways to comply with the EU requirements whenever there is a threat that market access might be denied.

In the light of the obvious non-conformities of Benin's law with EU requirements, Beninese authorities had to make a strategic choice if they wanted to maintain their access to the EU food market. The EU law is rather clear in its principle as established by Article 11 of Regulation 178/2002 (GFL) that "food imported into the Community for placing on the market within the Community shall comply with relevant requirements of food law or conditions recognised by the Community to be at least equivalent thereto".

The first efforts of compliance resulted in the development of a food law at the national level for fishery products. Thanks to that initiative, Benin regained EU approval after 18 months of a voluntary export suspension. However, at the advent of the GFL and the hygiene package in the EU, the need to comply with this holistic approach arose and called for other steps to ensure compliance. In this instance, Benin decided to become a 'standards taker' rather than to engage in a whole new legislative process. 'Standards takers' are "groups of interest with less bargaining strength that are unable to participate in the rule-making process, having then no other choice than to adjust to the standards of others".[425] In the case of Benin, the current EU food law was literally transplanted in Benin's legal system. In reality, the legal transplant decision was seen as a response to the need to ensure compliance with the EU food law so as to maintain access to the EU market, with the view of sustaining the economic opportunity provided by the shrimp export sector. Sovereign countries always make sovereign decisions as regards their legal system. This legal transplant option in this case could appear odd, but it is important to underline that French law has been a system of reference for Benin law for a long time, in an old habit of some African countries of importing the law of their former colonisers.

Nevertheless, other factors also played a role in the choice of the compliance strategy adopted by Benin. First, Benin has concluded a tacit agreement with the EU by developing and committing to implement an action plan that summarised the corrective actions required after the FVO mission. Considering that the failure to fulfil the contract could lead to an EU protective measure, Benin was compelled to actually undertake regulatory reforms quite urgently. Secondly, the threat of an EU import ban and the limited national capacities and financial resources confined Benin to the adoption of a reactive approach that left little room for coordinated self-conceived strategies that could be more appropriate to the domestic needs.

425 Wilson and Abiola 2003, pxxix.

The legislation of the EU was complex and it would take resources and expertise for Benin to design a whole new framework that would comply with EU requirements. Furthermore, engaging in such a process entails the risk that the legislation is ultimately found by the EU to be non-compliant. Moreover, according to the SPS Agreement, the burden of proof in demonstrating the equivalence between importer and exporter's legislation rests on the importing country.[426] In this regard, the lack of expertise is again a major challenge. Lastly, it is important to mention that the approval given to Benin in 2005 was based on the former 'list I- list II' scheme. Benin was then still authorised to export to the EU through bilateral agreements. With the advent of the GFL, that scheme of approval was meant to disappear. Therefore, Benin was also under pressure to undertake the required reforms as fast as possible to gain 'full approval' from the EU as a 'safe source' for fishery products. Copying EU law therefore appeared to be the easiest option to ensure compliance.

But some parameters in the transplanted law suggest that Beninese authorities did not have a full grasp of the EU texts, because some errors suggest gaps with regard to the true meaning and spirit of the texts of the EU law. As an example, one might point out articles where references are wrongly made. This is the case for Articles 50 and 51 of Order 2009–075, which provides crisis management measures to supplement the requirements set by Article 47, if complying with the requirements of Article 47 proves inadequate to ensure an efficient management of food risks. While in the EU GFL, this reference relates to emergency measures for imported products, the correlation is established under Beninese law with regard to professional secrecy. Article 50 provides that a general plan must be established to clarify the practical modalities for managing a crisis for which risks cannot be effectively prevented, eliminated or reduced to an acceptable level by the provisions of Article 47. Similarly, Article 51 refers to the same Article 47 and requires the competent authority to inform Beninese authorities whenever measures of Article 47 are not sufficient for an efficient management of risks involved. However, contrary to expectations, the Article 47 referred to in both cases does not provide any measure of food risk management. Article 47 states that "the protection of professional secrecy shall not prevent the dissemination to the competent authorities of information relevant to the functioning of market surveillance and enforcement in the field of food and feed. The authorities receiving information covered by professional secrecy shall ensure its protection in accordance with Article 46". Those contradictions are likely to compromise the implementation of the laws.

Similarly, one could point out the non-coordinated efforts to comply at all costs with EU law. For example, certain concepts, such as risk analysis, that were never mentioned in Benin law, and were largely unknown in Benin, were suddenly introduced and defined in certain orders, while they did not have the

426 This issue will be addressed in chapter VIII.

slightest interest for the orders in question and none of the provisions of these orders referred to them.

The choice of the legal transplant may prove interesting because it enables Benin to have a food legislation that is compatible with the requirements currently preponderant in the international market. This implies that Benin through its food business operators is now potentially competitive in the international arena. However, if having the adequate law is an important step, the ability to implement this law is equally important and might even represent a bigger challenge. The history of Benin is plagued with poor implementation and enforcement issues. The same difficulties related to the lack of material, human and financial resources applied also in the case of the first texts adopted immediately after the first FVO mission. The failure to apply these texts properly suggests that the transplanted measures would even have a harder time finding a way through the administrative and legal structures in Benin. The effectiveness of such a transplanted law relies heavily on its ability to be meaningful in the domestic context so as to provide an incentive to citizens to use it and to demand that institutions work to enforce and develop the law.[427] In effect, legality is a function of the demand for law and only a high demand can create high voluntary compliance, leading a society to invest in legal institutions necessary for upholding the legal order.[428] Legality is determined by the ability of a country to give meaning to the transplanted formal legal order and to apply it within the context of its own socioeconomic conditions.[429] In Benin, the demand for a complex legislation for the domestic fishery market was practically non-existent. The entire process of law updating merely responds to the need to comply with EU requirements to avoid trade restrictions from the EU.

5.3. COPING WITH THE LEGAL TRANSPLANT

The lack of domestic demand for a high-quality food legislation led to a complex situation at the national level. *De facto*, there is a parallel existence of two domestic shrimp supply chains. First, despite the legal transplant, the first supply chain intended for the domestic market is still subject to the 'old non-compliant' system with all its related shortcomings. Secondly, the other supply chain is exclusively intended for export to the EU market and is therefore obliged to comply with the requirements of the transplanted law. The fact remains that these two supply chains are still interconnected because the same small-scale actors – fishermen, fishmongers – are still supplying the fresh shrimps to the domestic market and the processing plants for exports to the EU. It is difficult

427 Berkowitz et al. 2003a, p167.
428 Berkowitz et al. 2003a, p189.
429 Berkowitz et al. 2003a, p167.

to imagine that some of the fishermen consent to subject themselves to strict hygiene rules, even for higher selling prices, while the remaining fishermen may cheerfully continue with the old routine in a 'no-rule scheme'. Despite the higher prices offered by the collectors of processing plants, the latter fear that the overemphasis on hygiene measures and related constraints would in the long run become a disincentive for fishermen, resulting in their preference for supplying the more flexible local and regional markets. While the fishermen supplying the shrimp processing plants seemed to enjoy a better quality of life before the export suspension, it is not possible to draw definitive conclusions as to their willingness and their ability to comply with even stricter rules deriving from the current Benin food law. After the shrimp export suspension in 2003 and the subsequent regulatory reforms, Benin's processing plants have practically exported no shrimps to the EU. It is therefore difficult to measure the impact of the more stringent requirements on the fishermen and their behaviour once confronted with compliance issues arising from the current food law.

Furthermore, the fresh shrimps rejected by the plants' collectors are neither destroyed nor seized and may have unimpeded access to the local market. This reveals that the lack of awareness of food safety risks is still a major inhibiting factor for the sustainability of the efforts in capacity building in the fishing sector, especially due to these grassroots actors. A recent survey revealed that the awareness of the fishing community of the compliance issue is still relatively low.[430] This fact alone constitutes a significant stumbling block, considering that the quality of the finished product is closely linked to the quality of the raw material. Therefore, if a substantial raising of awareness combined with training is not undertaken with regard to the entire population of fishermen, the very foundations of an effective food safety system will be undermined.

In addition, as long as the institutional environment is not also readapted to create the conditions necessary for the implementation of the law, it is still doubtful that an improved law alone would lead to safe products as required by the EU. For example, after the first upgrading measures and the authorisation to resume exports that ensued in February 2005, Benin was mentioned four times in the EU Rapid Alert System (RASFF), even though the exported quantities substantially decreased. These notifications are evidence that, despite the improvement in the regulatory framework, some more steps as regards implementation were still necessary to reach an actually improved quality of Benin's shrimps. This argument is further confirmed by the FVO report in 2009, which revealed that the production and certification system was still not reliable, even after the legal transplant and the subsequent capacity building.

430 Houssa & Verpoorten 2013, p21.

5.4. SEEKING ALTERNATIVE SOLUTIONS

The very logic of trade implies that when a market niche closes for some reason, alternative ways are sought to keep the business activity alive and even flourishing. It is obvious that the first question that comes to mind in the case of the shrimp processing plants in Benin is why the possibility of exporting to other countries was not considered as an alternative to the measure of the government to suspend shrimp exports to the EU. This question is even more relevant considering that, after more than a year of inactivity, both processing plants and governments agreed to destroy the processing plants' old shrimp stocks so as to be allowed to export again to the EU.

In fact, the financial capacity of a company is determinative of its autonomy with regard to decision making. Seeking alternative ways also requires investment and is sometimes a time-consuming process. In the case under consideration, most processing plants were for a large part financially dependent either on the banks or on their own customers. For example, one shrimp processing plant revealed that it used to benefit from a prefunding from its main customer right at the beginning of the shrimp season.[431] This constitutes an undeniable advantage because it gives enormous financial flexibility and also facilitates banking transactions. However, in case the processing plant would fail to deliver all or parts of the goods agreed upon, it must reimburse its customers for the corresponding amounts.

Under these circumstances, a sudden ban on exports put the shrimp processing plants in a complex situation in which they are no longer able to meet their financial commitments. Therefore, it undermines their credibility with regard to financial institutions that are reluctant to inject more funds, especially if this relates to mere exploratory or marketing strategies whose outcome is rather uncertain.

Overall, the financial statement review of the processing plants shows negative own funds, important short and long-term debts, lack of real guarantees to offer and a low debt capacity.[432] Furthermore, entering new markets is made more challenging due to the shadow cast on the credibility of the Benin's shrimp production and certification system by the shortcomings revealed by the first FVO inspection, as well as the subsequent governmental suspension, which somehow confirmed that reasonable doubts are permitted about the safety of Benin's shrimps.

In any event, the processing plants deemed that diversification must go along with the increase of their volume of activity, which implies an increase in their production capacity. The funding needed for the diversification and consolidation are summarised in the following table:

431 Interview in Cotonou, Benin, March 2011.
432 PASP 2007b, p17.

Table 5.1. Investments planned by processing plants for diversification and consolidation (million XOF)

	2007	2008	2009	2010	2011	2012	Total
CRUSTAMER	0	460	56	111	6	3	636
FSG	32	20	103	55	5	5	220
SOBEP	0	0	0	0	0	0	0
DIAX	0	26	46	60	12	10	154
Total	32	506	205	226	23	18	1010

Source: PASP, 2007b

Given the importance of the resources necessitated and the financial difficulties, the corresponding plans for diversification and consolidation were never carried out in any of the processing plants.

5.5. BUILDING CAPACITY FROM 'FARM-TO-FORK'

Following the difficulties of the shrimp export sector in Benin to comply with EU food safety requirements, many reforms were undertaken to provide the institutional framework necessary for carrying out a proper implementation of the newly adopted laws. Due to the difficulties of the government to cope with the heavy investments required, many external donors committed to providing assistance in diverse fields of the sector. Main donors include the Belgian Technical Cooperation (BTC), the Japanese Cooperation (JICA), the Millennium Challenge Account – Benin (MCA – Benin), and the EU.

The assistance of the BTC covered two components. The first component relates to the project of "Support for the Development of the Fishery Sector of Benin" (ADEFIH), which started in 2008 for a period of 3 years. The project ADEFIH aimed to improve the artisanal fishing around Lake Ahémé to improve the income level of artisanal fishermen while preserving the environment and resources of the lake. With regard to food safety, the project intended to contribute to the compliance with national and international requirements of activities related to the collection, storage and transportation of fishery products. The project enabled the construction of two control units (Bases of Compulsory Check- BOCs), twelve Platforms of Transfer (PFTs), and latrines along Lake Ahémé, the strengthening of the capacities of the competent authority for the food safety control of fishery products, as well as the training of grassroots stakeholders. Secondly, the Support Program for Expertise of the government of Benin (PAEX) provided technical assistance to create an umbrella structure of the competent authority comprising the different sectors of the Ministry of Agriculture, Livestock and Fisheries.

The JICA helped to build a new artisanal fishing port in Cotonou that fulfils the conditions required for export. This new infrastructure was inaugurated in November 2005.

The MCA – Benin is more focused on industrial fishing. Nevertheless it has invested in the realisation of a feasibility study for the construction of a BOC at the Autonomous Port of Cotonou.

The European Union intervened through the Project of Support to the Private Sector (PASP), which aims at harmonising and improving the coordination of actions with a view to resuming export to the EU. Other EU programmes such as Strengthening Fishery Products Health Conditions in ACP/OCT Countries (SFP) and Better Training for Safer Food (BTSF) are also providing support to many African countries including Benin.

It is worth mentioning that the UEMOA Quality Program and the Special Regional Program for Food Security (PSRSA), which are executed at the regional level, also supported the capacity building in Benin.

5.5.1. QUALITY OF WATER

The pollution level at the site of capture is an important factor in the deterioration and the freshness of shrimps.[433] The level of water pollution affects the sensory quality of shrimps.[434] Ensuring the microbiological and physico-chemical quality of water in lakes and lagoons is a major challenge for Benin. Several factors affect the quality of these waters, which is crucial for the caught shrimps.

In general, the problems are related to organic waste resulting from the population density on the shores, the accumulation of other waste associated with human activities, chemical pollution (heavy metals, organohalogen substances, organophosphorus compounds, etc.), shoreline erosion, deforestation, the proliferation of water hyacinths, and the proliferation of prohibited fishing methods likely to reduce the oxygen in the water.[435] Of all

433 In fact, according Sèdogbo (2004) the deterioration and the freshness of the shrimps depend on many factors including the gender, age, size, species, and the level of pollution of the place of capture. For example, female shrimps, which are generally larger, contain more water and rot faster than male shrimps. Likewise, small shrimps rot more slowly than larger ones, and immature shrimps begin to rot at a slower pace than mature shrimps. According to sensory analyses reported by Dossou et al. (2010), *penaeus monodon*, which are large shrimp species, were the first to rot from the head in batches of shrimps inspected. (The decomposition of fresh shrimps always begins from the head and can be noticed by an alteration of the natural colour, mostly resulting in 'red heads' of the shrimps).

434 Dossou et al. 2010, p128.

435 PASP 2007. It is worth mentioning that the organic pollution is very strong for Lake Nokoué. The pollution on this lake is exacerbated by the practice of fish traps traditional known as 'Acadja', which is an important source of organic waste, the poor solid waste management in Cotonou (30%), the illicit trade in petroleum products using the water bodies that bind the

the samples inspected, shrimps harvested near major population centres with high anthropogenic activities – and therefore more polluted – decomposed faster than shrimps fished further away from the shores.[436] Furthermore, the sanitation problem is a factor aggravating the issues related to the management of water quality in Benin. Some survey results revealed that 90% of the waterside communities interviewed do not have latrines, 72% defecate in the lake or on the shore and 67% of existing latrines, whose walls and sides are not fully waterproof, are very close to the lakes.[437]

All these factors require an adequate monitoring of the microbiological quality of lake water, which is the natural environment of shrimps. However, none of the technical assistance projects actually addressed this issue. As circumvention to the problem, these projects rather insisted on adequate control of freshly caught shrimps before the processing plants' collectors are allowed to proceed to their collection. It is within this scheme that the construction of BOCs and PFTs along Lake Ahémé finds its justification.

5.5.2. HYGIENE AND SAFETY OF FRESH SHRIMPS

The storage of fresh shrimps at the bottom of the canoes was underlined during the FVO mission in 2002 as a major issue due to the possibility of contamination from the wooden walls of the canoes. A rather simple solution was considered to overcome this weakness. This consists of providing all fishermen with isothermal boxes in which the shrimps are stored with ice cubes until they are delivered to the processing plants' collectors. Apparently simple, this solution becomes more complex when it is considered that the ice to be used must be made with potable water. Most fishermen live along lakes and lagoons and have limited access to public drinking water. Consequently, many people, including in 'big' cities, often consume water from wells routinely. The well water is made safe for drinking through traditional methods. Even though this kind of 'potable' water does not constitute any real danger for local populations, it fails to meet the definition of 'drinking water' as required by Article 3 of Order 2009-122.

In any event, this issue had been overlooked and, owing to technical assistance programmes, the provision of isothermal boxes to fishermen was started. However, this activity could not be completed because it was connected to the identification and registration of all fishermen involved in the shrimp export sector, which was also uncompleted. Alternatively, the fishermen would be provided with clean trays and ice produced in the BOCs.

Lake Nokoué to the lagoon of Porto – Novo and leading to Nigeria, and the high population pressure on these water bodies (lacustrine villages of Ganvié, Sô Ava, etc.) and their surroundings.

436 Dossou et al. 2010, p128.

437 Dossou et al. 2010, p127.

To address the quality issues related to fresh shrimps, a quite innovative idea was implemented by the ADEFIH project thanks to funding from the BTC. This initiative, which is one component of the ADEFIH project, intends to replace the previously used fishing ports where the hygiene and landing conditions were considered unsuitable. The initiative aims at improving the sanitary conditions of production, collection and transport of fishery products on Lake Ahémé, through the construction of two types of landing infrastructure called Platform of Transfer (PFT) and Base of Compulsory Check (BOC). Twelve PFTs and two BOCs were built along Lake Ahémé. The ADEFIH project also enables the construction of forty toilets to solve the sanitation problems of local populations. In addition, the construction of 3 PFT was started along Lake Nokoué, while two PFT were started along the lagoon of Porto Novo. The completion of these works was planned by December 2010.

The PFTs are simple infrastructures made of a thickly paved area covered with a roof on which fishermen and collectors would exchange clean isothermal boxes containing chilled shrimps, dirty trays and ice. The objective is to receive, sort and rinse fresh shrimps with potable water before placing them in isothermal boxes by collectors.

BOCs are improved versions of PFTs, including an ice factory. Most importantly, BOCs allow for the conduct of random sampling for organoleptic controls on freshly caught fishery products.

Next to these initiatives, the investment needed to improve the handling, hygiene and compliance with the cold chain onboard canoes, fishing boats and shrimp collection vehicles for the shrimp export sector were as follows:

Table 5.2. Investments planned to improve hygiene and the cold chain: fishing and collection (million XOF)

Type	Unit cost	Number	Total cost
Fishing canoes	100	1,700	170,000
Coolers for canoes	4	16,000	64,000
Isothermal boxes (for collectors)	145	750	108,750
Total amount			342,750,000 ≈ 522,600€

Source: Blanc 2003, p 78

It is worth mentioning that these figures are based on the construction of 13 PFT, 4 BOCs, 4 ice factories (10t/day/unit) and a certain number of boats for shrimp collection.

5.5.3. ENSURING TRACEABILITY ALONG THE FOOD CHAIN

The main difficulty with regard to traceability lies in the multiplicity of fishermen involved in the supply chain. Therefore, the competent authority undertook to identify and register all fishermen to facilitate the monitoring of supplies of fresh shrimps. This is important to determine responsibilities in the case of health issues and, if necessary, take action against fishermen who regularly violate hygiene rules. However, this activity could not be successfully completed due to the important number of fishermen and the resources necessitated. To remedy this, an alternative solution was to empower the collectors in order to avoid the need for processing plants to engage in the tedious work of ensuring the traceability up to the fishermen. For this purpose, about 125 collectors were trained and are responsible for all the supplies to processing plants. Therefore, the traceability system relies on the credibility of collectors.

However, such a system does not leave processing plants powerless because in case of repeated safety issues related to a particular collector, plants still have the possibility to remove the liable collector from the list of approved collectors to safeguard their own integrity.

5.5.4. ENSURING COMPLIANCE OF PROCESSING PLANTS

Compliance with requirements deriving from EU food law meant substantial investments for the processing plants. In addition to the diverse training received through technical assistance programmes to acquire sufficient expertise, it was necessary to undertake works aiming at upgrading their premises, particularly in terms of layout. Such reforms are also essential to implement HACCP requirements.

The processing plants considered it necessary to make upgrading investments as summarised in the following table.

Table 5.3. Investments planned by processing plants to comply with EU requirements (million XOF)

	2007	2008	2009	2010	2011	2012	Total
CRUSTAMER	0	26	13	13	15	14	81
FSG	23	23	34	13	13	13	119
SOBEP	0	500	50	50	50	50	700
DIAX	0	133	28	25	30	22	238
Total	23	682	125	101	108	99	1,138

Source: PASP 2007b

The destruction of old shrimp stocks could also be considered as costs incurred to ensure compliance with EU requirements.

5.5.5. IMPROVING RISK MANAGEMENT AND COMMUNICATION

The improvement of food risk management and communication has included the establishment of a body in Benin taking the example of and replicating the European Food Safety Authority (EFSA). Called the Beninese Food safety Authority (BFSA), this agency was created in 2012 and is responsible for ensuring the quality of foodstuffs from farm-to-fork. The BFSA was supported in its creation, implementation and sustainability by two BTC projects, the Project of Institutional Support to the Ministry of Agriculture, Livestock and Fisheries (AIMAEP), and the Project for the Improvement of the Sanitary and Phytosanitary Quality of Agricultural and Food Products (ASPS). The latter benefitted from EU funding.

The BFSA is responsible for surveillance, alerts and information, and for ensuring the respect of the transparency obligations with regard to food safety, with the understanding that its activity must in principle cover both the domestic and the international markets. To perform its functions, the BFSA must collaborate with the Central Laboratory for Food Safety (LCSSA), which is the reference laboratory for carrying out food risk assessment.

5.5.6. BUILDING ANALYTICAL CAPACITY

Analytical capacity is very important because only test results provide conclusive evidence of a product's safety at the end of the production and in support of the certification process. Deriving from the food legislation, it is crucial for the laboratories to have sufficient analytical capacity. For example, based on Decision 2455/2001/EEC, a good laboratory should be able to conduct analysis for the detection of certain priority substances in relation to water such as: the detection of heavy metals (lead, cadmium, mercury), detection of hydrocarbons (Polycyclic Aromatic Hydrocarbons (PAHs)), detection of halogenated compounds (polychlorinated biphenyls, organochlorine, organophosphorus).

The choice of the laboratories to be supported through technical assistance programmes was made after proper consideration of various factors. In fact, the programme for "the development of an accreditation, standardization and quality promotion system within the UEMOA" delegated two expert missions to detect the laboratories in Benin that are capable of conducting microbiological and physico-chemical analyses as required for the implementation of HACCP principles in the shrimp export sector.[438] These experts identified two laboratories operating in different areas. First, the National Laboratory of Public Health (LNSP), through its Section Hygiene, Waters and Food (SHEA), could be supported for microbiological analyses. Secondly, the Laboratory of Soil, Water and Environment Sciences (LSSEE) could benefit from assistance to enhance its capacity for chemical analyses, specifically analyses related to heavy metals, TVB, TMA, and histamine. However, the experts rejected the laboratory of the Directorate of Food and Applied Nutrition (DANA) despite the approval the latter received from the competent authority. The DANA is the reference authority in Benin for the inspection of food products. Therefore a product certified by DANA benefits generally from consumers' confidence with regard to its safety. Yet, the experts found it would be inappropriate to fund the DANA laboratory because it lacks financial and human resources to carry out its mission, leading to its inability to ensure the proper operation and maintenance of its equipment.[439]

In any event, it was later held that because of their fragmentation into several structures, the potential of the existing laboratories was not properly exploited. Therefore, the authorities decided to bring together the strengths and equipment of diverse laboratories in a central laboratory, called Central Laboratory of Food Safety. Within this framework, the Project of Support to the Private Sector (PASP) gave support to three laboratories, the SHEA, the LSSEE and the laboratory of the DANA. While the SHEA depends on the Ministry of Public Health, the LSSEE and the DANA are under the MAEP. The private laboratory IRGIB and public laboratories DANA, LSSEE, and SHEA are part of international networks of laboratory inter-comparison.[440]

The implementation of this technical assistance can be seen as a continuation of the assistance provided from the regional level to support the LNSP and the LSSEE. But if that first assistance aims to enable these laboratories to get accreditation on an individual basis, this second component at the national level is considering a merger into a single body. This would make it possible to circumvent the fragmentation of resources arising from the dispersion of these laboratories, which, in reality, are not sufficiently equipped to carry out all the required analyses at their respective levels. It follows that if such a vision had been envisaged from the outset, the resources could have been better used to address the issue of laboratories.

Yet, despite the assistance of the regional programme for "the development of an accreditation, standardization and quality promotion system within the UEMOA", the LSSEE and the LNSP were not deemed sufficiently equipped to engage in the process of accreditation. Therefore, if the results were left at

438 Blanc 2003, p12.
439 Blanc 2003, p12.
440 Mialet 2010, p25.

that stage of achievement, it appears that this technical assistance would not have been very beneficial. Given the interests at stake, the rules governing the obtainment of accreditation are quite strict and cannot be bypassed. Firstly, to obtain accreditation, a laboratory must effectively demonstrate competence and have the equipment necessary to conduct the tests required by international standards. Secondly, the French Accreditation Committee (COFRAC) only certifies the laboratories whose activities are sufficient to maintain their competences.[441] In this regard, the reduced number of the total absence of analyses for each laboratory unit is incompatible with the objectives of the accreditation.

The initiative of a central laboratory is therefore an ideal solution to take advantage of the scattered competences of these diverse laboratories. To obtain accreditation according to the requirements of standard ISO 17025, the LCSSA benefits from support in expertise provided by the Belgian Federal Agency for the Safety of the Food Chain (AFSCA).

5.6. ASSESSING CAPACITY BUILDING IN THE SHRIMP EXPORT SECTOR

Many projects began to build capacity in Benin in the fishery sector to enable shrimp processing plants to resume export to the EU. It is undeniable that technical assistance programmes have contributed in many ways to capacity building in Benin and have raised Benin's potential to comply with international food safety requirements, especially the EU requirements. From farm-to-fork, every area of the production and certification system benefited in one way or another from the diverse programmes developed in the sector. But, given the current status of Benin whose operators can no longer export despite the approval granted by the EU, judging the effectiveness of technical assistance projects calls for a little caution. Capacity building is not a goal in itself, but the capacity should be strengthened to achieve a higher goal, in this case, ensuring compliance with food safety requirements to gain, improve and sustain market access. But while the law has been upgraded and the corresponding institutional framework built step-by-step, the ultimate goal of market access has not been achieved and Benin is experiencing a major setback as regards its 'initial' situation in 2002.

After a decade, the fact remains that many of these technical assistance projects are uncompleted. Several factors have influenced the development of these projects. On the one hand, the multiplicity of technical assistance programmes can be pointed out as a factor contributing to the dispersion

441 Gavard 2006, p13.

of resources. The abundance of resources is in itself a positive asset because it allows more room to engage in ambitious capacity building programmes as required by the situation in Benin. The diversity of donors is also intrinsically beneficial because it made it possible to allocate given resources to particular sections or issues so as to concentrate efforts better to achieve an improved support with regard to the areas identified. However, the results achieved might have been more substantial if a better coordination of certain programmes had been developed. This is the case for example for building analytical capacities and providing support to accompany laboratories towards accreditation.

On the other hand, a better definition of the initial objectives of technical assistance programmes is a prerequisite for their ultimate success. For example, the exhaustive census of fishermen was seen as a prerequisite for the effective implementation of traceability. Later, this option was abandoned for an alternative solution because the implementation of the census proved tedious and its relevance for the purpose of traceability was moreover questioned. The need for a better definition applies also to the strategic choices of technical assistance programmes. For example, it was decided that the first PFTs and BOCs must be built along Lake Ahémé due to the better quality of its water compared to Lake Nokoué and the lagoon of Porto Novo. However, Lake Ahémé provides merely one third of the total shrimp production. In addition, this lake is located more than one-hour drive from the processing plants, which are all in Cotonou, and are then closer to Lake Nokoué, the richest lake in fresh resources. Since these infrastructures were a requirement of the EU, it appears that as long as other programmes are not finalised and executed to build the same facilities for the other bodies of water, the production capacity of the processing plants would be rather limited.

Furthermore, because of this multiplicity of technical assistance programmes, certain actions may prove redundant. For example, with regard to the support to the System of Sanitary Control of Fishery Product (SYCOPAS), the SFP programme and the programme for the "Establishment of a system of accreditation, standardization and quality promotion within the UEMOA" have similar objectives.[442] Such a situation may lead to a waste of technical assistance resources.

Nevertheless, taken individually, the individual objectives of several projects were attained. Officials of the competent authority and processing plants even argue that Benin is now better equipped than many other countries of the West African region to meet the challenge of compliance to food safety standards.[443]

---

442 Blanc 2003, p30.

443 Interviews with a quality manager of a processing plant and officers of the Directorate of Fisheries, Benin, 2011.

5.6.1. POOR GOVERNMENTAL COMMITMENT

The completion of some projects could not be achieved because the Beninese government failed to invest its share of the budget within the agreed timeframe. This is the case for example for the construction of the BOCs and PFTs along Lake Ahémé. Similarly, the share of the budget that was to be provided by Benin with regard to the equipment of the central laboratory was not made available, thereby jeopardising the success of the technical assistance.

The lack of resources is the main argument provided to support the non-fulfilment of financial commitments. Yet, even in the case budget lines were not originally planned at the start of the shrimp export issue, one cannot lose sight of the fact that the situation has continued for a decade. Therefore, even if the political will was not initially strong enough, ways and means could have been found in the meantime to include food safety as a priority in the development of State programmes so as to release the funds required to support this goal.

In any event, it appears that, beyond the case of public infrastructure, the government also fails to meet its commitment with regard to the private sector. In order to compensate the processing plants for the losses incurred due to the export suspension and the destruction of their old stocks, in July 2008 at the Council of Ministers, the government committed to guarantee bank loans for processing plants. However this commitment never became a reality. Even though the reasons for this governmental failure are unclear, it is argued that the earlier failure of the processing plants to justify the use of a soft loan of 500 million XOF (about 763000 euro) granted by the government in 2007–2008 to help them make the investments required for compliance with EU standards is a pending issue.[444]

The challenge herein is significant because donors do not generally support private sector initiatives, even though processing plant workers have benefited from training programmes funded by technical assistance projects. Therefore, in the absence of the promised State subsidy and/or other solutions to deal with the insolvency of the processing plants, the substantial investments required to comply with food law requirements could prevent the plants from resuming their activities.

However, in this specific case, strengthening public control and certification capacities is not really useful if the private sector, which is the driving force of the industry, no longer exists. The existence of efficient laboratories, of an agency of risk management and communication and inspectors well equipped to monitor and certify fishery products is certainly a necessary condition, but it not sufficient to activate the expansion of the sector. Without a competent authority meeting EU standards, processing plants cannot export. But without

[444] Houssa & Verpoorten 2013, p14.

the processing plants to give life to the industry, the competent authority loses its raison d'être.

5.6.2. SUSTAINABILITY OF THE CONTROL AND CERTIFICATION SYSTEM

The major problem with some technical assistance programmes is that they leave works in the state that could be achieved through the duration of their implementation. Therefore, whether completed or not, infrastructures are delivered once the term of the programmes is up or once the resources allocated for their implementation are exhausted. It is therefore up to the recipient government to take responsibility to follow up and ensure the sustainability of the infrastructure delivered.

Under the current circumstances, whether Benin is capable of achieving this result remains rather uncertain. First, considering the past failures of the government to meet its financial commitments, there are reasonable doubts that the political will is strong enough to ensure that public policies will definitely support the investment necessary to complete and maintain the works, especially in the current state of inactivity in the sector. Secondly, despite heavy investments in the training of stakeholders, there are still concerns that the expertise is lacking to ensure the functioning and the maintenance of some infrastructures such as the PFTs and BOCs.[445] Likewise, it is reported that the lack of experience is an obstacle to finalising protocols in laboratories.[446] Thirdly, the persistence of certain structural problems in Benin is likely to jeopardise the functioning of infrastructures. These issues must first and foremost be addressed to truly give meaning to technical assistance programmes. For this purpose, public policies must find ways and means to solve for example the problem of access to potable water or the sanitation issue of the local population.

In addition, the personnel and organisational concerns related to public administrations must also be resolved. It is important to promote the concept of the right skills in the right positions to provide adequate expertise for the implementation of the technical aspects concerning the implementation of control and certification procedures. Some officials of the competent authority, for example, were trained within the framework of technical assistance programmes, but their initial educational background is still a problem for the proper use of the new knowledge acquired.

---

445 BTC, Appui au Développement des Filières Halieutiques du Bénin, BEN0601311, Rapport Final, 2011.

446 Gavard 2006, p20.

5.6.3. WASTED RESOURCES?

The collapse of the shrimp export industry results in a pessimistic view of the technical assistance programmes. Currently, because of the inactivity of the processing plants, many fishermen trained in good hygiene practices have been diverted to local and regional markets and no longer respect hygiene rules. Likewise, many trained collectors and processing plant workers are currently unemployed. The situation with regard to processing plants is even more dramatic because of their heavy investments in terms of layout and restructuring. Moreover, the control units of Lake Ahémé are also unexploited. Because this infrastructure was specifically designed for the improvement in the shrimp sector, they cannot be used for any other purposes. The most unfortunate point is that, given the current state of food safety at the domestic level, considering using these infrastructures for the domestic shrimp market is not even a reasonable option due to the operational costs involved.

The situation with regard to laboratories is somewhat more encouraging. Analytical capacities can already serve products other than shrimps. The process towards accreditation could also be continued provided that the required resources are available for this purpose. Similarly, the creation of the BFSA could become meaningful if the necessary dynamism is given to this body to enable it to start playing a role with regard to food safety, at least in the field of risk communication. Much will depend on the food safety objectives established for other food areas, since all the recent initiatives were focused on the shrimp export sector.

With regard to the law, Benin has certainly moved from one unsuitable food law to another. The first one was too outdated to comply with international standards. The second one is elaborate enough to comply with international and EU standards. But both laws did not take sufficiently the needs and the realities of the domestic market into account. While institutional reforms have been undertaken to enable all the same the implementation of the current law, doubts remain as to the ability of Benin to implement this law and ensure its effectiveness.[447]

5.6.4. INTERACTIONS AMONG STAKEHOLDERS

Studies revealed that business settings in many African countries do not leave room for mutual confidence between buyers and salesmen with regard to the quality of traded products.[448] But, in the context of the new vision

447 On the issue of the effectiveness of transplanted law, see chapter VIII of this research.

448 According to Fafchamps & Gabre-Madhin (2001) in their paper on non-standardised products in Benin and Malawi, 10 out of more than 2,000 traders declare relying on the their

in the field of food safety, relations of trust and cooperation are henceforth essential. Relationships between actors along the food chain must shift from being purely transactional to becoming more co-operative because they are inter-dependent managers of the quality of the same final product.[449] Yet, a lack of communication and the mistrust seems to prevail in the shrimp sector. For example, despite the lengthy ban and its effects on the actors, only 33% of fishermen knew about the ban and the reasons for it. Likewise, the fishing community is fragmented between different ethnic groups and inter-group trust is very low.[450]

Furthermore, the issue of mistrust also appears at the higher level of the chain. Mistrust is illustrated by the reluctance of the government to continue to support processing plants following allegations of their misuse of a soft government loan.[451] The failure of the government to give this loan is considered one of the greater reasons for the non-resumption of activities of the processing plants.

5.6.5. ADDRESSING THE CHALLENGE OF DAILY RISK MANAGEMENT

The problem of health risk management is rather complex in the context of fishery products in Benin. The challenge is that the sector of industrial processing is exclusively oriented towards export to the EU. It follows that all the efforts that converged in the upgrading of the legislation and the strengthening of institutional capacity only responded to the necessity to regain or maintain access to the EU market. Such a situation implies that the initial demand for high-quality legislation was non-existent for the needs of the local fishery market. This lack of domestic demand is likely to undermine the effective implementation of the regulatory requirements adopted to comply with the EU food law.

The actual implementation will therefore depend to a large extent on the interests of stakeholders that would then mobilise the will and resources to raise a 'spontaneous' compliance with standards. Under normal circumstances, the risk of being excluded again from the EU market at any time for failure to comply with its requirements is in itself a sufficiently motivating factor – or perhaps a sufficiently constraining factor – to ensure the implementation and the enforcement of the legislation. However, in the case of Benin, the collapse

suppliers to identify the variety and assess the quality. In that respect, buyers have to resort to the direct inspection of their purchase and this process could prove quite time-consuming and burdensome.

449 Houssa & Verpoorten 2013, p25.

450 Houssa & Verpoorten 2013, p26.

451 Houssa & Verpoorten 2013, p25.

of the shrimp export industry could lead to the opposite result. In fact, not only the processing plants have not exported for a couple of years but also, and most importantly, processing plants are not in a financial position that predicts an imminent resumption of their activities, unless a spectacular reversal of the situation occurs in the form of an injection of funds by the government and/or donors, or loans granted by the banks regardless of their current losses. This means that, in the short term, there seems to be no factor likely to inject new dynamism into the shrimp export industry. Therefore, considering that the demand for such a high-quality law did not arise domestically, Benin might fall back into the previous situation of poor implementation and enforcement with regard to its food law, even though its law currently meets international standards and the institutional framework exists for its implementation.

Another major risk is that the lack of a real demand for a high-quality food law would result in the fact that crisis management and rapid alert would be unnecessary at the national level, leading to poor implementation of a monitoring safety system. The absence of the formalisation of such a system involves an inability to prevent, respond or limit the impacts of food safety crises.[452] A study revealed that public action upon the occurrence of a sanitary event with a potential or proven impact on the health of the population is organised on a "case-by-case" basis in Benin.[453]

In any case, despite the importance of a crisis management system, its relevance for Benin under the current circumstances is still up for debate. Creating a Beninese rapid alert system to the image of the EU RASFF requires the sufficient involvement of all stakeholders involved in the production and certification system and their commitment to communicate in a timely manner about the risks detected. In this regard, it would certainly be important to tackle the issues of the availability of proper means of communication. To date, there is still the problem of access to Internet, which could constitute an obstacle for the establishment of a well-functioning rapid alert system. The latter also implies that food business operators in general are willing to put consumers' safety at a higher level than their commercial interests and therefore agree to run the risk of the withdrawal of their products from the market and incur the resulting potential losses.

This analysis becomes even more relevant with respect to the Beninese shrimp export industry. Considering that the product is exclusively intended for the EU market, it would be unlikely that the problems related to exported finished products would be reported in a rapid alert system in Benin. Border rejections of consignments or other safety issues discovered after the products were released for export to the EU market would be reported in the EU RASFF and possibly communicated to Benin, the exporting country. It appears that, in

452 Mialet 2010, p6.
453 Mialet 2010, p15.

this scheme, a rapid alert system in Benin is not very relevant for managing food safety risks related to processed shrimps.

Likewise, if safety issues appear upstream of the export, they would be either at the level of fishermen or collectors and would be detected in the batches delivered to processing plants. In these cases, processing plants can, with an adequate traceability system, take subsequent actions including the withdrawal of the approval of the liable collector, without necessarily resorting to a rapid alert system. Furthermore, if the safety issue is detected with regard to the finished product, it is up to the competent authority not to proceed to the product certification, thereby preventing the export of the unsafe products.

In light of this analysis, one can infer that, with respect to shrimps export, there is no urgent need to set up a rapid alert system in the image of the system in the EU. However, given the need to embrace a more holistic vision, it would be appropriate to introduce such a system for the monitoring of food safety in general. These foundations are required to contribute gradually to an increase in the safety level in the country and to enable stakeholders to build and enrich their experiences with regard to food safety management.

5.7. INTERACTIONS BETWEEN EU AND BENIN

5.7.1. INFLUENCE OF THE EU POLICY

The current situation of the shrimp sector in Benin is certainly an unexpected outcome for Benin and the EU alike. For Benin, the process was merely a question of undertaking some reforms to continue to export to the EU. In this respect, benefiting from the EU's assistance could even appear as a factor that would greatly simplify the entire process. For the EU, the situation amounted to providing assistance to a non-compliant country so that the latter could secure its access to the EU market. After the voluntary suspension, decided by Benin, DG-SANCO even proposed to consider the possibility of allowing exports of whole raw shrimps. However, even though this exemption was granted, the losses would remain very important because processed products represent about 85% in value of exports, worth 3.25 billion XOF (about 5 million euro).[454] In any case, this EU proposal responds to its commitment with regard to trade facilitation. The EU is indeed determined to play an assertive role in promoting trade openness to benefit from its triple benefit, namely more growth, jobs and lower consumer prices.[455] Such a vision translated in the implication of the EU in a range of trade agreements, revealing sometimes a 'carefully differentiated approach depending on the level of development' of its trading partners.

454 Blanc 2003, p10.

455 European Commission 2010, p4.

The implementation of such a policy aimed, for an important part, to help emerging economies alleviate poverty and benefit more substantially from trade liberalisation. Trade openness in this context encompasses two variants. On the one hand, the EU offered unilateral trade preferences through mechanisms such as the General System of Preferences (GSP) for exports from developing countries. On the other hand, the EU granted Aid-for-Trade to poorest countries for capacity building. ACP countries were the main beneficiaries of these EU expansionist policies mostly oriented towards the elimination of tariff barriers to trade due to the reciprocal significance these two markets represent for each other.

With regard to Benin, the collapse of the shrimp industry was not included in any of the scenarios that could be envisaged. In most countries, EU food safety policies could impact the trade flow temporarily. The actual costs of compliance and duration of possible trade restrictions would often depend on the ability of the country to react rapidly by undertaking upgrading measures. In some cases, some processing plants would not be able to regain their approval, even if the competent authority of their country managed to provide sufficient guarantees to the EU.

Leaning on the case of four countries in West Africa, it appears that the size of the industry and hence the traded volume is crucial to the country's ability to undertake reforms more or less quickly or successfully when non-compliance issues are detected.

With regard to traded volume, Senegal and Ivory Coast exported respectively 43,000 and 25,000 tons of fishery products in 2011.[456] Before the voluntary export suspensions, Benin, in its best year in 2002, exported only about 700 tons, while neighbouring Togo exported 1,500 tons in 2001.[457] Similarly, while Senegal and Ivory Coast could ensure an acceptable level of compliance with food requirements, in Benin and Togo mere basic hygiene requirements were not met.

As regards the size of the industry, in Senegal more than 140 processing plants have received EU approval, and Ivory Coast accounts for 11 approved processing plants. At the same time, in Benin and Togo, the whole industry rests respectively on merely 3 and 2 approved processing plants. These figures seem to suggest a correlation between the size of the industry and the capacity of reactivity of the country concerned. While in all these four countries, the FVO detected significant shortcomings at some point, Senegal and Ivory Coast have had a better reactivity, while Togo and Benin were slower in undertaking reforms.

---

456 Ivory Coast also exported about 100,000 tons through direct transshipment in the EU from freezer vessels flying the flag of either a third country or an EU Member. See respectively Commission Européenne 2013a, p2 & Commission Européenne 2013b, p2.

457 Another 1000 tons were transshipped in the EU. See Commission Européenne 2002, p4.

Already in 1997, the food safety systems in Senegal and Ivory Coast were found compliant with that of the EU. Although compliance issues were later reported by the FVO, both countries managed to take the necessary steps to upgrade to a satisfactory level.[458] In contrast, the deficiencies in Benin and Togo were much harder to overcome. Both countries decided to suspend their shrimp exports to the EU in 2003 and to apply for EU funding to undertake regulatory and institutional reforms. Despite the EU's assistance, the outcome of the upgrading process is not very positive. While the shrimp export sector in Benin has practically disappeared, Togo is facing an official EU ban for fishery products except live lobsters.

These examples point out that many factors can influence an upgrading process. When the stakes are high, the reactivity and the commitment of domestic stakeholders also tend to be higher, resulting in a better outcome. High-quality food safety standards then become catalysts, contributing to building capacity to ensure higher safety of fishery products for the export food chain, which might later result in positive spillovers on the domestic market. But standards will act as barriers for smaller industries, especially when they rely heavily on only one outlet market.

Another important factor is the mobilisation of resources for the process of upgrading. Exclusive reliance on external aid to undertake reforms casts some doubts as regards the viability and the sustainability of the improved food safety system. Technical assistance in Benin and Togo has led to better laws but not to more effective food production and certification systems.

One should not lose sight that law is not an end in itself but is always a means to other ends.[459] In Benin, the aim was to at least formally have the law required by the EU and, ironically in a way, they succeeded in that. Keeping pace with regulatory changes of the trading partner is another issue. Will Benin change its law whenever new parameters are incorporated into the EU food legislation? Is it possible for Benin to reach a 'real' regulatory autonomy with regard to food risks management in the future? There are probably no straightforward answers to these questions. The future of the food production and certification systems in Benin will depend on the steps taken in the near future to make the management of food risks a reality. This implies that despite the collapse of the shrimp export industry, the Beninese government remains in the current dynamic of building a food safety framework in the country.

It is important to realise that if the shrimp export industry does not resume its activity, the true motivations for the recent reforms in the field of food safety collapse. But, if regardless of this factor, the government makes it a commitment

---

458 However, it should be noted that the FVO reported in 2013 that doubts remain about the reliability of laboratory analysis results in Ivory Coast. Likewise, some shortcomings were pointed out in the control system and some recommendations from earlier FVO reports were yet to be applied.

459 Watson 2001, p198.

to pursue the work in progress, especially with the BFSA, this would certainly bring a whole new perspective. Making such a body active would mean gathering the expertise, monitoring, and actually communicating about food risks at the domestic level. Ultimately, this will result in progressively integrating food safety as part of domestic food trade rather than a policy objective for accessing export markets.

5.7.2. EFFECTIVENESS OF THE BENIN APPROACH

The enforcement of the EU food safety policy has placed Benin in the shoes of most developing countries that become "standard-takers"[460] for the sake of their commercial interests. In so doing, some of them expect to be able to reach the same institutional and operational level as the EU from scratch. Implementing such a high-quality food law has proved to be very difficult for Benin, given the existing administrative and institutional gaps. In fact, building an effective food safety framework is always a gradual process.

Even within the EU, the implementation of the food law is not without risks or potential flaws. The current EU legislation was the outcome of a long process that made it possible to capitalise on experiences and mistakes in order to realise over time the adjustments necessitated by either structural constraints or scientific contingencies. Health crises such as BSE and the dioxin crisis testify that despite the progressive tightening of EU measures after the green paper on food safety, the implementation system was far from being perfect. But this gradual hardening is useful and even necessary because it enables operators to evolve step-by-step and prepares them to be more readily able to update when slightly more stringent measures are introduced. In this respect, the adoption of the hygiene package did not bring about major implementation issues for FBOs and CAs in the EU.

However, reforms are often challenging when the companies are operating on a relatively smaller scale like in Benin. This has also proven true for small establishments in the EU that found it rather cumbersome to implement the hygiene package.[461]

The institutional support was progressively enhanced at national and EU levels to cope with changes in adopted legal requirements. For instance, the EFSA was created and the RASFF acquired a new dynamism. This demonstrates that an evolving synergy that enables continuing feedback and remedial measures throughout the production and control chain is a prerequisite for the effective implementation of a high-quality food safety law.

460 Ponte 2007, p70.
461 European Commission 2009b, p5.

However, the fact remains that while the rules were being strengthened for EU Member States and their operators, they were equally strengthened for third countries, especially with the advent of the conformity or equivalence requirement. Even though in the field of fisheries products Directive 91/493 established the principle of prior approval before a country can export to the EU, it is obvious that the law and institutions in exporting countries would not evolve with the same pace as the EU. This is particularly true considering that the old approval system of the EU relies in many cases on a mere documentary assessment. The case of Benin perfectly illustrates the shortcomings of this system, showing that after Benin was approved in June 1998 by Decision 97/296/CE, based on a documentary assessment, this country had virtually no proper law and therefore no consequent institution in 2002. Furthermore, by transplanting the stringent requirements of the EU food law in 2009, Benin ignored the gradual process necessary for a proper development of the law. Although assisted by many donors, Benin was not yet able in 2009 to implement the first measures adopted in 2003 properly to comply with EU law in the fishery sector. Under these conditions, it is predictable that Benin could not directly rise to the level of the EU with regard to food safety risk management. This is supported by the deficiencies still in existence in the production and certification system even after a decade of reforms.

5.7.3. EFFECTIVENESS OF THE EU APPROACH

At first glance, the approach of the EU seems perfectly equipped to monitor food risks both with regard to EU products and products originating in third countries. In this regard, the FVO plays an important role in the implementation of the EU policy concerning third countries. Yet, despite the serious shortcomings revealed by the FVO inspection in Benin in 2002 and the subsequent recommendation to take protective measures against Benin, the EU did not officially take any action. Therefore Benin remained on the list of countries that were authorized to export to the EU. This implies that, even though Benin decided to implement a voluntary export suspension, Benin was still considered a potentially 'safe source' of fishery products with regard to EU law.

The next EU step consisted of 'lifting' the ban on shrimp exports decided by Benin by confirming Benin's status as a safe source through Regulation 2076/2005/EC, allowing Benin to export to the EU through bilateral agreements. The legitimacy of this step can be questioned because it did not follow a new inspection in Benin, as previously planned, to check the actual improvement that had occurred. Given the serious shortcomings still revealed in 2009, one could assume that the food safety law and system in Benin in 2005 would not be any different. The adoption by Benin of new legislation was no guarantee of a better enforcement that would lead to safer products. In this regard, giving approval on the basis of written guarantees provided by Benin is again a return to the documentary assessment approval system with its inherent flaws.

In another step, the EU granted 'List I status' to Benin after the FVO inspection of 2009, simply on the basis of the equivalence established between Benin and EU laws, even though the inspection also revealed significant shortcomings in the entire implementation system. This second approval not only confirmed Benin as a safe source of fishery products, but it also 'promoted' it for its efforts to comply with EU law. This process does not take into consideration two essential aspects. First, the past records of weak enforcement plaguing Benin's history, combined with the poor performance resulting from nearly a decade of reforms, reasonably suggest that food safety is still and might continue to be an issue in Benin in the short-term. Secondly, Benin's government had not shown a real commitment in the upgrading process. All major reforms and needed expertise were subject to the assistance of donors, while Benin neglected its share. This dependence on external aid to reach the food safety objectives set by a legislation that is too stringent to be feasible considering Benin's specific circumstances is also an indication that the food safety level might stagnate or even regress in the near future. This is already evidenced by many unfinished works such as the platforms of transfer or the equipment of laboratories. The lack of properly functioning laboratories in Benin entails a lack of accreditation, which in turn implies that the EU cannot – or should not –trust the test results and certification from Benin fully. Therefore, the CA in Benin cannot provide assurance that the inspection of shrimps was performed in an equivalent way to that of the EU.

Seen in this light, if the shrimp export sector was still functional, the EU's approval would allow a loophole in its own system that could result in potentially harmful products on its market. Therefore, the legitimacy of the EU approach in ensuring proper controls in the food safety system of third countries is undermined by the inconsistencies between the results reported by FVO's inspectors and the actions taken by the Commission. This kind of process has been labelled 'white-coat machinery' to reassure insecure European regulators and consumers.[462] Genuine health concerns should not be compromised prior to the availability of evidence of the unreliability of a food safety system of a given third country. Thus, equivalence must not be granted on dubious grounds,

462 Ponte 2007, p2. This white-coat machinery consists of "fixing the system of regulations and inspection by performing the ritual of laboratory testing for all exports consignments". The phrasing was specifically used to qualify a similar situation of alternative bans and lifts of bans that occurred in Uganda at the end of the 1990s. More generally, the EU import bans had then affected the countries that export Nile Perch to the EU that are captured in Lake Victoria. Various reasons motivated these bans, such as a cholera outbreak in the region, alleged poisoning of the lake from the use of pesticides as means of capture and deficiencies in the regulatory and control systems.

because it might take away the very benefits of the establishment of equivalence, such as the elimination of duplicative testing procedures.

5.8. CONCLUSION

Stakeholders often blamed the inconsistencies in the law and decrees as a reason for the weak implementation of the law. However, inconsistencies in regulation are probably not the only reason for unsuccessful food safety law. Despite efforts made to improve both the legislative and institutional frameworks, the lack of appropriate capacity in terms of inspection, monitoring and analysis, the fragmentation of stakeholders' responsibilities and recurrent financial and technical problems are still major impediments to the proper implementation of the food law in Benin. Furthermore, due to the exclusive reliance on donors for upgrading and the small size of the shrimp export industry coupled with its exclusive dependence on the EU market, it is quite unlikely to attract the adequate commitment from the government and local financial institutions.

To some extent paradoxically the chaotic situation both in formal regulation and in practice is partially the result of eager efforts of Benin to comply with the relevant provisions of EU law. It should be noted that the reforms undertaken were intended solely for the export-oriented industry so as to regain and secure their market share. As a result, even the implementation efforts are only oriented towards that sector. It follows that the collapse of the shrimp export sector leads to the absence of internal demand that could induce additional implementation efforts. The lethargy is likely to persist, as society seems to have a remarkably high tolerance for unsuitable law.[463] Considering all these factors, it can be inferred that the demands of the EU were mostly a triggering factor leading to the collapse of the shrimp export industry in Benin.

However, the fact remains that, despite persistent inconsistencies with regard to the institutional framework and the conditions of production, the EU has given its approval to Benin on the basis of the "compliant" legislation and the guarantees to further pursue the capacity building process. This shows some more general weaknesses concerning the control and approval procedures in force within the EU. An excessive focus on the equivalence of the legislation seems to pay little regard to actual compliance with respect to implementation and enforcement. This formal control suggests that some potentially harmful products may still find their way onto the EU market.[464] This can be evidenced

[463] Not only in Benin, but also more generally, see Wise 1990, p3.

[464] EU food law provides for a system of traceability that enables the recall of products for which doubts exist as to their safety for consumption. In the same way, consignments that are found failing to meet the requirements must be seized or destroyed according to the seriousness of the risk. However this does not happen in practice. Problems are solved contractually among the parties, usually with a price discount. (See Ponte 2007).

by the numerous notifications through the RASFF. Not only can this policy be inefficient in protecting EU consumers, it may also be problematic from a development perspective.

Could one then conclude that Africa, and in this particular case Benin, and the EU remain worlds apart? As this case showed, the EU imposes its food safety requirements on exporting countries, while some African States seem (given economic pressure) to be willing to cooperate. Both Benin and the EU seem to see eye to eye as to the results of a proper food safety law, but their challenges and local contingencies are fundamentally in conflict.

CHAPTER VI

FOOD SAFETY AT THE REGIONAL LEVEL

6.1. INTRODUCTION

The West African Economic and Monetary Union (UEMOA) is considered a model of economic integration in West Africa. One of the goals of this organisation is to achieve a common market to further facilitate trade among its Member States and enhance their access to the international market. In this regard, the UEMOA became involved in the process of updating of laws and institutions necessary in its Member States, following a logical harmonisation of legislation. Regional programmes funded by external actors, such as the EU and the Food and Agriculture Organization (FAO), largely supported the implementation of the necessary reforms.

This chapter explains how this regional cooperation has been implemented. It specifically focuses on the way in which this cooperation contributes to the development of the national food legislation of the Member States and to capacity building both at the national and regional levels.

After a short presentation of the UEMOA and its legal regime (6.2), this chapter presents the characteristics of the food safety legal frameworks of UEMOA countries (6.3). The chapter then gives an overview of the common market as laid down by the law of the UEMOA (6.4). The fifth section (6.5) explains the process for building a regulatory food safety framework within the UEMOA. The next sections present the legal food safety framework within the UEMOA (6.6), the institutional framework (6.7), the harmonisation scheme of activities of accreditation, certification, standardisation and metrology within the UEMOA (6.8) and the challenges of food safety within the UEMOA (6.9). The last section (6.10) concludes.

6.2. PRESENTATION AND LEGAL REGIME OF THE UEMOA

Created in 1994 by the Treaty signed in Dakar on 10 January 1994, in the beginning the UEMOA brought together the seven countries of West Africa which shared the use of the CFA franc, namely Benin, Burkina Faso, Ivory Coast, Mali, Niger, Senegal and Togo. The treaty entered into force on 1 August 1994 after ratification by the Member States. The circle was extended three years later, on 2 May 1997, to Guinea Bissau after its accession to the monetary system of the CFA franc. The UEMOA was born from the need to extend to the economic sphere, the community that bound its Member States at the monetary level, through their common membership in the West African Monetary Union (UMOA).[465]

The objectives of the union are set out in Article 4 of the UEMOA Treaty and include the objectives to: (a) enhance the economic and financial competitiveness of Member States; (b) achieve economic performance and policy convergence among Member States through the institution of a multilateral monitoring procedure; (c) create among the Member States a common market based on the free movement of persons, goods, services, capital, and the right of establishment; (d) coordinate national sectoral policies in such areas as human resources, physical planning, transport, telecommunications, environment, agriculture, energy, industry, and mining; e) harmonize, to the extent necessary for the proper functioning of the common market, the laws of the Member States, and in particular the tax system.

The realisation of these objectives should contribute to the economic and social development of Member States. Socially, UEMOA's actions must essentially converge towards the respect of the fundamental rights set forth in the Universal Declaration of Human Rights of 1948 and the African Charter on Human and Peoples' rights of 1981.[466]

The UEMOA relies on a number of organs to attain its objectives.

Table 6.1. Organs of the UEMOA (pursuant to the UEMOA Treaty)

Executive organs	
Conference of Heads of State and Government	The Conference of Heads of State and Government meets at least once a year to define the general guidelines of the UEMOA. Where appropriate, this organ takes additional acts to the UEMOA. These acts are annexed to the Treaty, which they complement without modifying it. UEMOA's organs and Member States must comply with the additional acts (Articles 17,18).

465 The original UMOA treaty was signed by Benin (then Dahomey), Burkina Faso (ex-Haute-Volta), Ivory Coast, Niger, and Senegal. Togo joined the UMOA in 1963 while Mali joined only in 1984.

466 UEMOA Treaty, Article 3.

Council of Ministers	The Council of Ministers meets at least twice a year. This organ ensures the implementation of the general guidelines established by the Conference of Heads of State and Government. Whenever the UEMOA Treaty provides for the adoption of a legal act of the Council of Ministers on the basis of a proposal from the Commission, the Council can make amendments to the proposal only upon a unanimous decision of its members (Articles 20, 22).
Commission	The Commission is composed of members called commissioners, who are nationals of the Member States. The Conference of Heads of State and Government appoint these commissioners on the basis of criteria of competence and moral integrity. A commissioner's mandate shall be four (4) years, renewable. The commissioner's term is irrevocable, except in case of serious misconduct or incapacity. However, the Conference of Heads of State and Government may ask the Commission to submit its resignation, as a result of a vote of a motion of censure by the Parliament. Member States are required to respect the commissioners' independence. The Commission shall exercise the powers conferred by the UEMOA Treaty for the proper functioning and the general interest of the Union. To this end, the Commission shall: (a) transmit to the Conference and the Council recommendations and opinions it deems appropriate to the preservation and development of the Union; (b) Exercise the power to perform the acts it takes, by delegation of the Council and under its control; (c) implement the budget of the Union; (d) collect all information relevant to the fulfilment of its mission; (e) establish a general annual report on the functioning and development of the Union that is communicated by its Chairperson to the Parliament and the legislative bodies of Member States; (f) develop an action plan that is submitted by the Chairperson at the regular session of Parliament following its appointment; (g) shall publish the Official Journal of the Union. The deliberations of the Commission shall be reached by a simple majority of its members. In case of a tie, the Chairman has the casting vote (Articles 26–34).
Parliament	Democratic control of the organs of the Union is provided by a parliament created by a specific treaty. The Parliament takes part in the decision-making process and integration efforts of the Union in the areas covered by the UEMOA Treaty. The Parliament meets in two ordinary sessions a year, convened by its President. The second regular session is a budget session. The Parliament may also meet in extraordinary session on a specific agenda. Its Rules of Procedure are adopted at its inaugural session (Articles 35–37).
Advisory bodies	
BCEAO BOAD	Advisory bodies comprise the Central Bank of West African States (BCEAO) and the West African Development Bank (BOAD). They are autonomous specialised institutions that contribute independently to the achievement of the objectives of the UEMOA Treaty (Article 41). The Governor of the BCEAO or its representative takes part in an advisory capacity, in the meetings of the Commission and may request the inclusion of an item on the agenda or suggest that the Council invite the Commission to take an initiative in the framework of its mission (Article 31).

Judicial control organs (as established by Additional Protocol No. 1)	
Court of Justice	The Court of Justice monitors compliance with its law as to the interpretation and application of the Treaty of Union. The Court of Justice decides on Members' breaches of their obligations under the UEMOA Treaty, brought before it by the Commission or any Member State. Members must implement the judgments of the Court. In case of a failure of a Member to comply, the Commission may refer to the Conference of Heads of States and Government to urge the Member to comply. On appeal by a Member State, the Council or the Commission, the Court of Justice rule on the legality of regulations, directives and decisions. Recourse to the Court for the assessment of the legality of any act of an organ of the Union causing adverse effects is open to any affected natural or legal person. The interpretations of the Court of Justice as part of proceedings are binding on all administrative and judicial authorities in all Member States. Failure to comply with these rulings can lead to infringement proceedings (Articles 1–22 Additional Protocol No.1).
Court of Auditors	The Court of Auditors ensures control of accounts of all organs of the Union, including the regularity and efficiency of the use of their resources. The Court of Auditors is composed of three advisers appointed by the Conference of Heads of State and Government, from nominations proposed by the Council and offering all the guarantees of competence and independence required. The appointment covers 6 years and is renewable one time. Advisers may be assisted by collaborators and can have recourse to an external audit system. The control procedures are adopted by the Council, acting by a majority of two-thirds (2/3) of its members on the recommendation of the advisers (Articles 23–26 Additional Protocol No.1).

Article 6 of the UEMOA Treaty stipulated that "acts adopted by the organs of the Union for the objectives of this Treaty, and in accordance with rules and procedures established by the latter, are applied in each Member notwithstanding any contrary, anterior or posterior national legislation". This article implies that two basic principles apply for the implementation of UEMOA's legal instruments. First, the principle of immediate and direct applicability applies pursuant to which Community legislation is incorporated in domestic legislation as soon as it is published, without requiring supplementary domestic legislation, and can be invoked directly by individuals. Second, the principle of primacy of community law over domestic law also applies, which entails that, in the event of a conflict between the two, the former takes precedence over the latter.[467] These two principles confer on the UEMOA a 'supranational' character according to which Member States surrender part of their sovereignty to the regional organisation, entailing a differentiation of the UEMOA from a simple regional cooperation organisation.[468]

467 UNCTAD 2007, p4.

468 Idem.

To reach its goals, the UEMOA has several legal instruments. To have legal force, the acts taken by the UEMOA must emanate from the bodies that have express competence for their adoption and meet the formal provisions provided for that purpose.

A certain hierarchy can be observed between these texts that include additional acts, regulations, directives, decisions, recommendations and opinions, and parliament acts. First, the additional texts shall be annexed to the Treaty that they complement without changing it. Adopted by the Ministerial Conference, the additional acts are binding on the authorities of Member States. Second, regulations have a general scope, are binding in their entirety and are directly applicable in all Member States. Regulations can originate from the Council or the UEMOA Commission, which can issue regulation for the implementation of the acts of the Council. Third, directives are binding on all Members States as to the results to be achieved. Directives can be issued by the Council. Fourth, decisions are binding in their entirety on the recipients they designate. Decisions can be issued by the Council or the Commission. Fifth, recommendations and opinions have no binding force and can be issued either by the Commission or the Council. Finally, the Parliament takes acts whose legal status is determined by the Treaty establishing that organ.

It should be mentioned that additional acts, regulations, directives and decisions are published in the Official Bulletin of the UEMOA and only come into force after their publication at the date they specified. Decisions must be notified to their addressees and become effective from the date of notification. Decisions of the Council or the UEMOA Commission are not adopted only with regard to States. In case such decision refers to a person and comprises a monetary obligation, Article 46 of the UEMOA Treaty stipulates that these decisions are directly enforceable. The enforcement must be governed by the rules of civil procedure of the enforcing country. The enforcement order is affixed, without other formality other than the verification of the authenticity of the decision by the national authority designated for this purpose by the each Member. The enforcement may be suspended only by a decision of the Court of Justice of the UEMOA. However, the control of the regularity of enforcement measures falls within the jurisdiction of national courts.

6.3. THE COMMON MARKET

Article 76 of the UEMOA Treaty stipulates that the completion of the common market amounts to the progressive realisation of several objectives, *inter alia* the elimination between Member States of customs duties, quantitative restrictions on entry and exit, taxes having equivalent effect, and all other measures having equivalent effect which might affect intra-regional trade.[469] To this end, Member States shall abstain from introducing any new customs duties on imports and exports and any taxes having equivalent effect and increase the charges they apply in their mutual trade relations. Secondly, they must avoid introducing between themselves any new quantitative restrictions on exports or imports or measures having equivalent effect and abstain from making more restrictive quotas, standards and other provisions of equivalent effect.

However, "subject to the measures to harmonize national legislations implemented by the Union, Member States preserve the right to maintain and enact prohibitions or restrictions on imports, exports and transit justified on the grounds of public morality, public order, public security, protection of health or life of people and animals, environmental conservation, protection of national treasures of artistic, historic or archaeological value, and protection of industrial and commercial property".[470] Such measures shall not constitute a means of arbitrary discrimination or a disguised restriction on trade between Member States. Furthermore, these measures must be notified to the Commission which performs an annual review in order to propose their harmonisation or their progressive elimination.

The realisation of the common market should aim *inter alia* at the implementation of the principles of free movement of persons, establishment and services as well as that of the free of movement of capital required for the development of the regional financial market. The common market also relies on the harmonisation and the mutual recognition of technical standards and accreditation procedures and the certification of the monitoring of their compliance.

Achieving the common market also requires strengthening the competitiveness of financial and economic activities so as to provide a wide range of products to UEMOA consumers. This is a key component of a broader objective of achieving the free movement of goods, services, persons, and capital. The free movement of goods must be achieved in conjunction with the establishment of a common external tariff and a common commercial policy.

With these goals in mind, several sectoral policies were identified. These sectoral policies are set out and defined in the Additional Protocol No II[471], which is an integral part of the UEMOA Treaty. Sectoral policies include the Common Industrial Policy (CIP) and the Agricultural Policy of the Union.

On the one hand, the Common Industrial Policy was established along with the mining policy by Article 21 of the Additional Protocol No. 2 on sectoral policies of UEMOA. The Industrial and Mining Policy aims essentially at the emergence of successful and competitive companies both at the national

469 Regulation 007/2007, Article 76-a.
470 Regulation 007/2007, Article 79.
471 Additional Protocol No. 2 on Sectoral policies of UEMOA.

and Community level, able to meet domestic demand, face international competition, and promote social progress. The Industrial and Mining Policy must be oriented towards a balanced regional economic development and the harmonisation of regulatory frameworks for industrial and mining activities, including the development of a community investment code. The specific provisions related to the industrial policy were subsequently clarified by Additional Act 05/99 adopting the Common Industrial Policy of the UEMOA. In addition the general objectives previously defined, this additional act also focuses on increasing the growth of agricultural, livestock, fisheries, and mining resources of Member States of the UEMOA. Article 2 of the Additional Act 05/99 emphasises the specific purpose of preservation and development of Member States' export capacities, under the new realities of global trade. It is within this context that Article 4 identifies, among other programmes to be implemented, the development of structures and programmes to promote quality, investment and exports.

On the other hand, the Agricultural Policy of the Union covers all the activities of agriculture, forestry, livestock and fisheries. Agricultural products are broadly defined to also cover products resulting from agriculture but having undergone a transformation necessary for first use. It is worth noting that the fishing sector is not considered part of the five agricultural priority sectors selected within the UEMOA, namely the rice, corn, livestock/meat, poultry, and cotton sectors.[472] However, the strategic importance of the fishing sector was recognised and a triennial programme was adopted in March 2003 to ensure the development of fisheries within the UEMOA.

Adopted in December 2001, the Agricultural Policy of the Union intends to implement the principles of subsidiarity and complementarity of the economies and agriculture of the Member States to take into account the comparative advantages of different production areas of the UEMOA. This would help target the areas of intervention for optimal use of available resources and thus avoid the fragmentation of efforts.[473]

While the Agricultural Policy of the Union is primarily based on the development of agricultural sectors, the CIP focuses on developing the competitiveness of the companies of the Union in order to meet consumers' demand and equip them properly enough to compete at the international level. It emerges that food security falls within the Agricultural Policy of the Union as defined by Article 14-a of the Additional Protocol No. 2. However, this food security refers certainly more to quantitative aspects, because the same article further underlines the importance of achieving an adequate degree of self-sufficiency within the UEMOA, taking into account complementarities

472 Regulation 06/2007/CM/UEMOA, Article 2.

473 Commission de l'UEMOA, Compétitivité des filières agricoles dans l'espace UEMOA, Plan directeur des filières prioritaires, 2007.

between Member States and their respective comparative advantages. Tackling safety and quality issues within the framework of the Agricultural Policy of the Union would only be incidental. However, Article 3 of Additional Protocol No. 2 provides that "the Union shall implement, in cooperation with specialized international or regional organizations, joint actions to improve the health status of populations".

In any case, the place of food safety is found in the CIP. To this end, programmes such as the "promotion of investment and exports" and the "development of structures and programs to promote quality" play a key role. Through the promotion of quality, the UEMOA and its Member States intend to emphasise their awareness that the integration in international trade involves the ability to manufacture products that meet international standards and to acquire labels. A full understanding of standardisation issues is also a contributing factor for the elimination of technical barriers to intra-Community trade and the protection of local production, health and consumer safety. Lastly, quality control systems provide the additional benefit of serving as a source of competitive advantages to reduce the costs related to manufacturing defects. However, given the significant changes they induce, the strengthening of institutions responsible for quality and their accompaniment to accreditation must be regarded as a process revolving around two poles. First, the wide diffusion to the whole industrial network of the "UEMOA quality culture" will enable the effective dissemination of standards and certification. Secondly, the certification of companies must be promoted to help ensure in the short term, to defend, conquer, and consolidate export positions by the most competitive ones. It should be emphasised that most of the actions to be undertaken are the responsibility of the Member States. The UEMOA Commission only provides a framework for sharing experiences, while creating a UEMOA quality Oscar, intended to serve as incentive. As for Member States, they should start the certification process through the "quality audit" of companies. Most of the actions were planned to begin in January 2000 and only the quality audit was expected to be completed by 31 December 2000.

6.4. CHARACTERISTICS OF FOOD SAFETY LEGAL FRAMEWORKS OF UEMOA MEMBERS

Many similarities can be observed in the legal and administrative frameworks of UEMOA countries. This trend can be explained by the fact that these frameworks are generally based on the same foundations. Within this logic, the same imperfections also seem to materialise in the administrative systems of the countries, thus generating similar results with regard to the implementation of laws.

The laws of UEMOA countries are derived from the legacy of French or Portuguese colonisation. Therefore, the legal system falls in general within the Romano-Germanic system, while food safety programmes are mainly integrated in "French public law", with some elements of private company law and the progressive inclusion of principles derived from international law.[474] This system places the law and central State administrations at the base of food law, which is primarily defined as a special police activity of State services, encompassing a set of administrative control powers, regulation, prohibition, and sanctions whose legitimacy is the protection of public health and economic order.[475] A major feature is that the powers related to inspection or control are scattered and dissolved through many ministries or ministerial departments, raising important accountability issues. In general, these powers are spread through health ministries and agricultural ministries, involving medical practitioners, government officers, decentralised officers, border police, and even environmental police. These factors generate overlap and can make the legal structure confusing for the enforcement agents, producers and distributors, resulting in a duplication of efforts and gaps in enforcement.[476]

The situation of food safety and conformity assessment was impaired by several shortcomings which could suggest that a high level of safety protection in the region would be hardly attainable. One could *inter alia* refer to the virtual inexistence of national quality infrastructure in most countries, the lack of national or regional accreditation bodies, the absence of well-defined product or process standards, and a limited number of certified enterprises. Moreover, a National Standards Body (NSB) was non-existent in two countries, while in most of the other six countries, the NSBs were non-operational due to a lack of human and material resources. Most NSBs were not members of the International Organisation for Standardization (ISO), leading to the lack of international standards. Only one NSB operated a product certification body and granted merely a few certifications.[477] Furthermore, only around 30 enterprises were certified ISO 9001 in all eight UEMOA countries while local consultancy support to enterprises was available in merely two countries.[478]

The obsolescence of the legal framework depicted in the case of Benin appears to be a general phenomenon in UEMOA countries. Existing laws are also very poorly implemented and enforced and do not sufficiently involve the judicial system to ensure the legitimacy of the actions undertaken. In these systems of law, the judge is considered to guarantee the rule of law. However, in UEMOA countries, up until 2004, judicial intervention was never indicated either in the form of jurisprudence or as a control of legality or in the form of

474 Féral & Coulibaly 2004, p19.
475 Idem.
476 Smith DeWaal & Robert 2005, p27.
477 Kaeser & Bau 2007, p4.
478 Idem.

penal sanctions.[479] This situation suggests that from a strictly legal point of view, all the laws and regulations related to food safety in all countries were never properly applied.[480]

The inapplicability of laws are explained mainly by the fact that the food safety regulations resulted from the colonial era or laws were adopted through a process of transplantation that does not fit properly to the local social, economic, scientific, and legal realities of the countries. In fact, most UEMOA countries had no legislation covering standards and conformity assessment issues and, despite the provisions for the mutual recognition of conformity assessment procedures in the UEMOA Treaty, there were no arrangements to ensure the implementation.[481] In most countries, there was no national quality policy to encourage and assist private and public sector enterprises to implement standards or quality tools in their processes. As was the case in Benin, it is important to underline that across UEMOA countries there was in general little demand for standards and conformity assessment services by industry, consumers and other major players.[482] In this regard, EU requirements with regard to fishing sectors have been a catalyst for major reforms in countries like Benin, Ivory Coast, Togo, and Senegal.

Beyond all these deficiencies, it is important to underline the issue of laboratories, because ultimately, and even in a system that emphasises control at all stages through a farm-to-fork approach, laboratories remain essential tools for the establishment of efficient control systems. Within the UEMOA, there is a general lack of modern laboratory testing equipment. Most laboratories did not work according to the accreditation standard ISO/IEC 17025.[483] Moreover, analytical, testing and calibration laboratories of UEMOA countries have serious difficulties. The main difficulties are the failure to comply with the standards of laboratory installations and Good Laboratory Practices (GLP), the poor knowledge of the ISO 17025 reference standard by all laboratory personnel, the lack of familiarity with the documentary system, the lack of internal auditors in laboratories, the absence of appropriate service companies in most countries, the low level of professionalism in suppliers of consumables, the high cost of consumables and the weakness of inter-laboratories comparison.[484] Furthermore, in the West African region in general, most of the public health laboratories lack the capacity to test for chemical contaminants and naturally-occurring toxins, and there is often a lack of systematic monitoring for food contaminants because sampling is usually performed only for enforcement

---

479 Féral & Coulibaly 2004, p23.
480 Féral & Coulibaly 2004, p23.
481 Kaeser & Bau 2007, p4.
482 Idem.
483 See Kaeser & Bau 2007, p4.
484 Bayili 2003, p6.

purposes.[485] Sampling is also often disorganised due to the improper coordination between food laboratories, surveillance and food inspection services.[486]

It is also important to underline the deficiencies related to the systems of surveillance. Few UEMOA countries have surveillance systems sensitive enough to identify common agents of foodborne diseases and surveillance data is often patchy and unreliable. Furthermore, inadequate record-keeping is likely to create a vicious cycle resulting in the absence of information to serve as a basis for local decision making, regulations and food standards[487], sustaining the gaps in regulatory frameworks.

6.5. BUILDING A REGULATORY FOOD SAFETY FRAMEWORK WITHIN THE UEMOA

The UEMOA has adopted an ambitious set of objectives in the field of standardisation, certification and quality promotion for its members. The achievement of these objectives, supported by the development of a legislative and regulatory framework has been largely done through the UEMOA Quality Program and the Regional Special Program for Food Security (PSRSA).

On the one hand, the execution of the Quality Program is the most important agenda item of the Common Industrial Policy. The UEMOA Quality Program was initiated in 2002 for the establishment of a system of accreditation, standardisation and quality promotion in order to increase the volume of regional and international trade. The first component of the programme was executed by UNIDO with EU funding amounting to 12.5 million euro for a period of three years. The implementation of the Quality Program resulted in the adoption in 2005 of Regulation 01/2005/CM/UEMOA, establishing a scheme for the harmonisation of accreditation, certification, standardisation, and metrology activities within the UEMOA. The second phase of the Quality Program was launched in 2008 and also included the countries of West Africa, which are not members of the UEMOA. The EU funded this phase with 14 million euro. The UEMOA component aims to consolidate the achievements of Phase 1 by helping the UEMOA to implement its Community safety legislation and use the tools previously developed to remove safety-related barriers encountered in the marketing of priority products on Community and export markets.[488]

On the other hand, the PSRSA is a cooperation agreement between the FAO and the UEMOA that incorporates a twofold objective. First, it aims

485 Smith DeWaal & Robert 2005, p28.

486 Idem.

487 Idem.

488 UEMOA 2008, p1.

at the establishment of a legislative and regulatory framework as well as the institutions for the implementation in the animal health, phytosanitary and food safety sectors. Second, the programme focuses on the strengthening of national food security special programmes. As far as food safety is concerned, the PSRSA, which started in August 2002, adopted an approach aimed at assessing the legal and institutional frameworks of Member States so as to evaluate the role of institutions, identify gaps and weaknesses, and identify synergies and complementarities. This process must lead to recommendations to strengthen the official control systems that could promote an integrated approach to safety issues and the harmonisation of legislative and regulatory texts. In this respect, identifying the weaknesses in the existing systems is a core objective insofar as it helps to pinpoint the needs accurately.

The implementation of the programme was carried out through extensive surveys of the legislative and institutional framework of Member States, their monitoring, control and analytical capacities. In this regard, the recommendations were more rooted in local specificities, while establishing a better linkage between diverse national regulations and international requirements.

The PSRSA enabled the development of draft regulations and directives for the UEMOA. These drafts comprised a regulation of the UEMOA Council of Ministers on food safety, an implementing regulation laying down the responsibilities, organisation and functioning of the sanitary committees of the Union, and some directives for the control of food safety within the UEMOA. These diverse drafts were adopted in 2006 during a regional validation workshop, subject to minor amendments.

It is noticeable that, contrary to legislative developments observed in Benin, the UEMOA regulatory framework does not focus on the law of any importing trading partner in particular, but rather puts more emphasis on the compliance of its texts with WTO international agreements, specifically the SPS Agreement. This appears distinctly in the first title of the draft regulation of the UEMOA Council of Ministers, which incorporates the requirements of the SPS Agreement.

6.6. LEGAL FOOD SAFETY FRAMEWORK WITHIN THE UEMOA

The UEMOA has adopted a set of legislation that is intended to inspire the development of national food safety provisions and which must ultimately facilitate the harmonisation of food legislation at the Community level. The most important in this set of legislation is Regulation 007/2007 on the Safety of Plants, Animals and Food in the UEMOA, which is often referred to in Member

States' laws. The protection of consumers' health, the prevention of the spread of diseases and the enforcement of food trade procedures are all acknowledged as a "fundamental necessity" in the preamble to Regulation 007/2007. This Regulation intends to provide a basic framework for all UEMOA countries as regards their national food safety rules, as well as the proper implementation of provisions at the regional level in order to ensure the same compliance with safety standards.

Regulation 007/2007 aims to establish the general principles, provisions and organisational procedures to ensure the safety of plants, animals and food, at the Community and national level.[489] Regulation 007/2007 applies to all aspects of safety, including products resulting from modern biotechnologies.[490] The UEMOA establishes the structures and mechanisms for cooperation in safety matters within the Union, provided that its provisions apply to all stages of production, processing and distribution.

An efficient implementation of its provisions is based on the agreement upon a number of principles.

6.6.1. PRINCIPLES OF THE FOOD LAW AT UEMOA LEVEL

a. *Principle of free movement of goods and equivalence*

The principle of free movement intends to establish the unrestricted marketing on the common market of products originating in one Member State in accordance with the quality and safety standards in force in UEMOA countries. In that respect, each Member State must accept on its territory food products conform to technical and health standards adopted by another Member State.[491]

In case of compliance with the technical requirements, regulations and safety measures in force, imported food benefits from the principle of free movement within the Union. In this case, the burden of proof of compliance rests with the importing operator.

---

489 Regulation 007/2007, Article 2.

490 Regulation 007/2007, Article 3.

491 Regulation 007/2007, Article 10. The production and marketing of novel foods are subject to prior authorisation by the National food Safety Authority, at the request of the person responsible for their preparation, their cultivation or their first placing on the market. Such an authorisation must comply with the precautionary principle and be duly justified by the opinion of the Advisory Council for risk analysis. The authorisation may be given on a provisional basis, for a specified period. It can also be revoked at any time or be limited in scope regarding the conditions of production, marketing or consumption. Moreover, novel foods are subject to mandatory enhanced consumer information. Informative labelling must accompany them, mentioning in particular the presence of GMOs or other treatment received, and informing the consumer about the precautions for proper use of the novel food.

Subject to reciprocity and unless otherwise provided, food recognised as complying with the safety and quality regulations of the exporting country may freely circulate within the territory of the UEMOA.

Under the principle of equivalence and national treatment, each Member State shall accept on its territory any product or service that responds to a technical rule or a procedure for evaluating the compliance adopted by another Member State and considered equivalent to its own, when the exporting Member State, in collaboration with the importing Member State, proves that the product is legally manufactured or marketed on its territory. Instances of non-acceptance of norms and standards must be duly motivated and be brought to the knowledge of the exporting country in writing upon its request. In case of divergences, Member States must undertake discussions to assess the trade barrier so as to prepare and ultimately proceed to harmonisation in the field under consideration.

In most of the measures it promotes, the UEMOA places a strong emphasis on international agreements and institutions. For example, the UEMOA encourages Member States to make their notifications of sanitary measures in accordance with the procedure provided by the SPS Agreement.[492] Similarly, in cases of proven health crises, the UEMOA urges countries to adopt safeguard sanitary measures in accordance with the requirements of the SPS agreement.[493] Even to ensure the free movement within the Union and to facilitate the integration of Member States into international trade, Member States should base their sanitary measures on international standards, guidelines and other recommendations including those of the Codex Alimentarius, the WTO (SPS and TBT), the International Plant Protection Convention (IPPC), and the OIE. They must also assist the safety structures of the Union in assessing the appropriateness and extent of the adoption of international standards.[494]

b. Principle of mutual recognition

Within the framework of the realisation of a common market, UEMOA Member States must mutually recognise their laws, while additionally ensuring a "coherent combination between harmonized legislation, standards and instruments of compliance verification".[495] Mutual recognition within the UEMOA is enshrined as a flexible and gradual implementation of arrangements for the free movement of goods and services and the elimination of trade barriers.

---

492 Regulation 007/2007, Article 21.
493 Regulation 007/2007, Article 34.
494 Regulation 007/2007, Article 5.
495 Regulation 01/2005, Article 9.

Mutual recognition within the UEMOA is assessed at three levels, namely the recognition of technical regulations, standards and specifications, the recognition of conformity assessment procedures and the recognition of the results of those assessments.[496] Article 31 of Regulation 007/2007 lists extensively that mutual recognition encompasses technical regulations and prescriptions, sanitary measures, procedures of control, sampling and verification by analysis, and finally the methods of sampling and analysis, and systems for the interpretation of test results. It falls on the exporting country to demonstrate that the products under consideration are lawfully produced and marketed in its territory, and that they comply with relevant guidelines deriving from Regulation 01/2005/CM/UEMOA.

c. Level of protection and risk evaluation

It falls on each Member State to determine the level of protection it deems appropriate in its territory, while complying with international standards and avoiding arbitrary or unjustifiable distinctions. This determination must be made "in close collaboration with the UEMOA Commission", through the structures of safety established at the regional level.[497] However, a conclusive determination of the level of protection should be based on a coherent and non-arbitrary approach, resulting from an appropriate health risk assessment based on scientific data. This step goes along with the adoption and the implementation of subsequent risk management measures, necessary and proportionate to the risk incurred, following the same pattern of removal of unnecessary obstacles to trade, subject to the limitations expressly permitted under Article 79 of the UEMOA Treaty. Pursuant to this article, Member States retain the right to maintain and enact prohibitions or restrictions on imports, exports and transit justified on diverse grounds including among others the protection or the health and life of human and animals.

The UEMOA seems to promote the sovereignty of its Members with regard to food safety risk management. But the disparities in the national levels of protection can work against the coordination of collective actions that could be undertaken at the regional level. This task amounts to ensuring cooperation for carrying out common actions to achieve the appropriate levels of protection of eight different countries. Within the EU, institutions like the FVO work well because the food safety objectives are generally the same across the countries and this facilitates the decision-making process.

Seeking harmonisation seems to be a good alternative to reduce the difficulties that might arise from such a system. It clearly appears that there is no requirement to harmonise the level of protection within the UEMOA

496 Regulation 01/2005, Article 10.
497 Regulation 07/2007, Article 6.

and disparities between Member States are authorised as long as they do not introduce any discrimination. Generally speaking, the harmonisation of Member States' legislation to the extent necessary for the proper functioning of the common market is one of the objectives set in the UEMOA treaty.[498] In relation to food safety, the UEMOA committed itself to contribute to the harmonisation of safety policies and actions.[499] This implies the establishment of a common strategy for food safety aiming at strengthening existing infrastructure and rationalising their utilisation. Moreover, the UEMOA coordinates the rapprochement of Member States' actions and sanitary standards by administering notification procedures for Member States, proposing technical regulations for the harmonisation and the adoption of common UEMOA standards, and coordinating Member States' positions in the relevant international and regional organisations. Notwithstanding these rules, the harmonisation of levels of protection is highly desirable on the medium or long run to facilitate a better convergence at the regional level.

It is worth mentioning that although the determination of levels of protection falls under the sovereignty of Member States, in the context of the implementation of precautionary measures, Regulation 07/2007 establishes in its Article 7 that "measures taken by Member States should be proportionate and should not be more trade restrictive than is required to achieve the high level of health protection chosen by the UEMOA, taking into account technical and economic capacities". This article creates confusion as regards the responsibility for the determination of the levels of protection as established by Article 7. Evidently, if each Member State determines its own level of protection, a level of protection determined at the regional cannot possibly exist independently as it could be in conflict with Member States' levels of protection.

d. Risk analysis and Precautionary principle

Within the framework of the Common Market and the implementation of the Agricultural Policy of the Union, the UEMOA must resort to risk analysis as an objective and justifiable method for evaluating and managing health risks and to ensure communication on these risks throughout the decision-making process.[500] Therefore, the management of food risks involves taking into consideration scientific data. According to the principle of risk evaluation, each Member State may conduct a risk assessment and, according to its legitimate objectives, decide to maintain or adopt restrictions that impede the free movement of goods and services. Member States must make available the relevant documentation on the procedures for risk assessment used in

498 UEMOA Treaty, Article 4.e.
499 Regulation 007/2007, Article 8.
500 Regulation 007/2007, Article 9.

determining the level of protection that justifies the measures of prohibition or restriction under consideration.

However, the lack of full scientific certainty should not be an excuse for postponing the adoption of effective risk prevention measures. In such particular instances, when the risk of adverse effects on health is established, Member States must adopt, according to their capacity, provisional measures consistent with their level of protection.[501] Subjecting the adoption of measures to the ability of each Member State highlights an important observation: it implies that a Member State may abstain from taking any action, even when risks are accurately put forward, and may simply argue the lack of relevant capacity to react. This very fact underpins profound disparities as regards the management of potential risks and, not only induces uncertainty about maintaining an appropriate level of protection at the regional level, but also questions the regional trade balance advocated by the common market. Whereas the porosity of borders is a fundamental feature in the region, efficient health risks management should not simply rely on rules based on the good faith of Member States to take appropriate action when necessary. This amounts to implicitly validate the movement of products of questionable health status, while hiding behind the banner of provisions intentionally left insufficiently coercive. One cannot lose sight of the fact that, given the economic and institutional constraints and the importance of socio-economic challenges prevailing in most Member States, rules that are too flexible would simply act as mere recommendations without actually resulting in action, as it should.

In cases of proven health risks, the UEMOA Commission must ensure that sanitary safeguards and other precautionary measures are taken by Member States. Article 37 of Regulation 007/2007 stated that failure by one or more Member States involved in the health crisis to take the appropriate measures must lead to an emergency meeting at the initiative of the Commission or national competent bodies in order to mutually agree on injunction or substitution measures required by the situation at hand. However, this article remains silent on how to apply that provision in practice. Do the measures amount to the suspension of intra-regional exports? Do they relate to measures of recall or withdrawal of products from the market? How would such actions be funded? The lack of precision in this respect is detrimental to the implementation of this measure, since the adoption of national measures is subject to the capabilities of the Member State concerned. An element of response to the question of funding emergency measures was given by the UEMOA Commission, which encourages Member States, through Article 38 of Regulation 007/2007, to put in place a national health emergency fund to which the Commission is also expected to contribute through its Regional Fund for Agricultural Development.

501 Regulation 007/2007, Article 7.

e. Communication and popularisation

The UEMOA, along with its Member States, has a duty of information towards the Union's citizens and relevant partners about their activities with regard to food safety. The implementation of that obligation amounts to the organisation of sensitisation seminars, advertisement or the publication of reports and opinions. These activities aim to contribute to the promotion of a participatory dynamic of citizens in the detection, assessment, prevention, and management of health risks within the UEMOA.[502] This seems rather important to compensate for information gaps among citizens and to raise awareness about the vital nature of food safety. Improved risk communication could lead to inducing a demand for standards from the consumers themselves so as to compel the public authorities to act and to help avoid that standards are adopted and applied only with respect to products intended for export markets.

6.6.2. SECTORAL FOOD SAFETY RULES

Beyond the general rules applicable to all areas of safety, sectoral rules have also been determined to accommodate the peculiarities of each sector. As regards food, they refer essentially to the obligations of actors, the requirements related to control and inspection, and the rules governing the movement of food.

a. Obligations of food safety stakeholders

The main responsibilities with regard to food safety rely upon Member States, food business operators and the Food Safety Authority.

On the one hand, Member States shall prohibit within the UEMOA the release for consumption of any food or foodstuffs injurious to health and unfit for human consumption.[503] For this purpose, they must comply with the sanitary principles and measures enacted by the UEMOA, by organising the safety conditions with regard to both production and intra-community trade, defining the measures of the verification of conformity accordingly and identifying the obligations of security and loyalty of operators. This last component also aims to clarify the precautions jointly applicable to the safety and health of humans and animals and the prevention of environmental risks. In addition, Member States should establish national structures and schemes conducive to their participation in the mechanisms of cooperation and expertise as regards food safety at regional level. This implies the definition of experts or representatives involved in the network of expertise and laboratories or which

502 Regulation 007/2007, Article 36.
503 Regulation 007/2007, Article 78.

could serve in the Regional Committee for Food Safety. Member States must also set the parameters of their participation in the alert network and the procedures necessary to ensure the proper supply of information to the databases of the regional observatory.

On the other hand, Regulation 007/2007 lays the primary responsibility of Food Business Operators (FBOs) regarding the sanitary quality of food they place on the market. FBOs must ensure that their products satisfy food law requirements from farm-to-fork. In performing their activities, FBOs must conform to three types of obligations. First, the obligation to monitor urges operators to stay informed about the risks related to their products and to take substantial measures to avoid them. It should be pointed out that, with regard to imports, self-control is the responsibility of the importer that relies on objective and verifiable guarantees offered by the exporting country. The operator must be able to provide the necessary justifications to demonstrate the proper implementation of the own-checks requirements. Second, the obligation of prudence requires the operator to inform the competent authorities whenever he has reasons to suspect the prejudicial nature of the products he placed on the market and to take all measures necessary to prevent injury to consumers. Thirdly, the obligation of security obliges the operator to comply with certain rules defined with respect to features, characteristics and known effects of the product, its packaging, labelling and the consumer groups for which it is intended.

It is the responsibility of the Member States to evaluate and adopt concrete measures to implement these requirements so as to fulfil the obligations of self-control, security and monitoring, given the nature of the product, its conditions of production, marketing or consumption. These measures should be defined based on appropriate scientific advice collected from the Scientific Authority and regional bodies of cooperation and expertise.

Furthermore, the UEMOA established a safety authority at the regional level that must be supported by Member States. The latter are required to set up an Advisory Council for risk analysis which will assist the ministerial authority in deciding all or part of the measures necessary for risk analysis and prevention. In addition to playing a role in representing the various stakeholders, the Advisory Council ensures cooperation with the bodies of the Union, in particular to define the national policy of precaution necessary for the safety and health of people and the protection of the environment.

b. Control and inspection of food

Verifications of compliance must be implemented to help ensure that FBOs have diligently met their obligations to prevent harmful products from being placed on the market and to ensure that appropriate information is provided to consumers. When products satisfactorily undergo official controls, they are presumed compliant with the requirements of the food law. Moreover, verifications of compliance also aim to ensure that products on the market do meet the code of ethics of international trade in food of the Codex Alimentarius Commission. The UEMOA Commission may in special cases decide to alleviate *ex post* verification for certain FBOs whose list must be duly established.

Products originating in Member States and those accompanied by a certificate of compliance issued by the official authorities of the exporting country and meeting the requirements of its regulation are also considered compliant with UEMOA's requirements. Therefore, these products are granted official recognition of conformity and can benefit from all related advantages.

In the event of serious or immediate danger to human health, the national food safety body implements measures of police. These measures could be the suspension of production or even export, the withdrawal of products in all places, or the destruction of unsafe products.

Local authorities have the discretion to implement emergency measures provided they inform the national food safety authority within 24 hours. However, measures taken through this procedure should cease to apply after one month, unless the central authority notifies other special provisions. This procedure is certainly a good way to meet emergency obligations that can sometimes arise, while submitting their application in the long run for the central authority's approval in order to prevent or limit abuses. In any event, measures of police shall cease to apply as soon as it is proven that the food is no longer in violation of safety requirements.

6.7. INSTITUTIONAL FRAMEWORK

At the institutional level, the programme of restructuring and upgrading the industries of UEMOA Member States was adopted according to the modalities of the annex to Decision 12/2006.[504] This programme supports the capacity building process within the UEMOA. Five key components were identified: a) sub-regional and national Institutional Capacity Building in the area of restructuring and upgrading; b) support to the design and implementation of funding mechanisms for the restructuring and upgrading, at sub-regional and national levels; c) establishment or capacity building of technical agro-industrial centres; d) a pilot programme to support the restructuring of agro-industrial companies; e) a pilot programme to support the upgrading and improvement of the competitiveness of agribusiness firms. The upgrading aims to improve the production system in order to meet technological and quality international standards.

504 Decision 12/2006, Article 1.

The UEMOA Commission should subsequently define the procedures relating to the implementation of the programme while ensuring that it provides the necessary flexibility.[505] The effective implementation falls on both the UEMOA Commission and Member States, which must deploy the necessary efforts to obtain funding from development partners.[506] One study, for example, has highlighted that the accreditation process in Senegal, like in all UEMOA countries, is carried out under pressure from the demands of donors, European reference regulation, instead of at the instigation of national coordination.[507] This analysis is not applicable merely to the process of accreditation and it holds true for the upgrading of the food safety infrastructure as a whole. This observation is certainly at the heart of the uncoordinated efforts observed in the adoption and implementation of Community food safety legislation. Many texts adopted were never followed by the appropriate decrees of implementation and some institutions established through regulations were never really set up. Food safety itself is taken into consideration by several different programmes. By way of example, the cooperation agreement that links the UEMOA to the FAO for the implementation of the PSRSA devotes its first component to the "Establishment of a legislative and regulatory framework, and the institutions for the implementation in animal health, phytosanitary and food safety sectors". In the meantime, the UEMOA quality program, funded by the EU and implemented by the United Nations Industrial Development Organization (UNIDO) was devoted to the achievement of the same task. In the field of quality, the Metrology programme funded by the German Government and implemented by the PTB (German Metrology Organization) was also executed.

One should not lose sight of all the programmes executed at the national level. Only in Benin, in addition to the UEMOA quality program, the CTB was also involved in capacity building in the field of fisheries. National bodies also developed several other projects.

In any event, for the effective implementation of the safety principles established, Regulation 007/2007 has set an important institutional framework that brings together various regional and national structures.

6.7.1. REGIONAL COMMITTEE OF SAFETY OF PLANTS, ANIMALS AND FOOD

A regional organ is created to act as a technical and advisory structure with regard to all health related matters in the sense of Articles 5 to 8 of Regulation 01/2005. Placed under the authority of the UEMOA Commission, the

505 Decision 12/2006, Article 2.
506 Decision 12/2006, Article 3.
507 Bayili 2003, p11.

Regional Committee of Safety of Plants, Animals and Food is responsible for assisting the UEMOA Commission in the organisation of health cooperation between Member States and contributing to the coherence of a safety policy by providing the appropriate technical advice. This committee plays a supporting role for both the Commission and Member States in relation to international trade negotiations as regards the SPS Agreement. As such, the Regional Committee of Safety of Plants, Animals and Food must coordinate Member States' positions in order to facilitate their representation in relevant international organisations.[508]

To carry out its activities properly, the Regional Committee of Safety of Plants, Animals and Food is subdivided into three subcommittees, each of which is specialised in one aspect of safety namely food, plants or animals. The committee also relies upon the expertise and cooperation mechanisms based on networks and observatories. In principle, in each area there must be a set of networks including a network of experts, a network of laboratories, an alert network, a network of national organisations, and a network of training institutions.[509] Observatories are responsible for creating and managing databases necessary for health cooperation and establishing an inventory of international safety texts and agreements binding Member States.[510]

Table 6.2. Missions of network created in support of the Regional Committee of Safety of Plants, Animals and Food (Article 18 Regulation 007/2007)

Network of experts	The network of experts supports regional safety structures of safety, on their request, by providing scientific advice, particularly during health crises.
Network of laboratories	The regional network of analytical laboratories brings together public and private laboratories in Members that may constitute reference institutions for analyses.
Alert network	The regional alert system is responsible for monitoring and immediate transmission of information on health risks to relevant structures.
Network of national organisations	The regional network of national safety agencies reinforces health cooperation between Members and ensures the circulation of information in the areas of health policy of the Union.
Network of training institutions	The regional network of training institutions contributes to improving training within the UEMOA.

508 Regulation 007/2007, Articles 13–14.
509 Regulation 007/2007, Article 18.
510 Regulation 007/2007, Article 19.

The institutional provisions of Regulation 007/2000 could be schematised as follows:

Figure 6-1. Institutional safety framework of the UEMOA

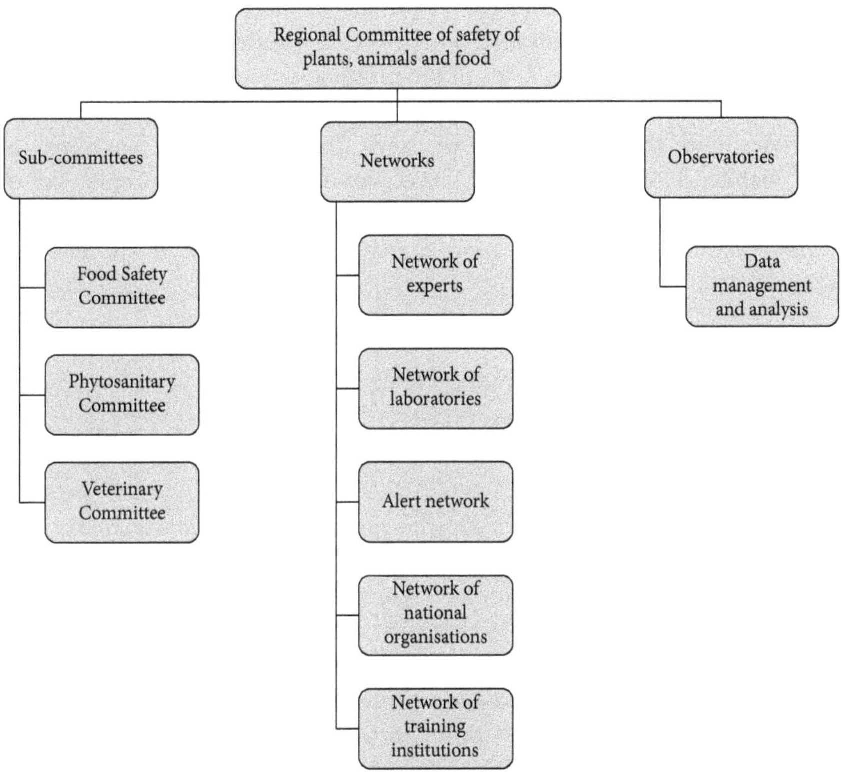

The UEMOA must contribute to bringing together the policies and actions of its members in the field of safety.[511] For this purpose, the Regional Committee of Safety of Plants, Animals and Food must provide the UEMOA Commission with the information needed to conduct the annual review of safety regulations having a direct or indirect effect on regional trade, in the view of their harmonisation or progressive elimination.[512]

The harmonisation of legislation depends to a large extent on the willingness of Member States to achieve its completion. For instance, Member States must develop technical and legal capabilities to enable the implementation of effective and rational cooperation. In a similar vein, they must create or align the structures and practices of their national safety bodies.[513]

511 Regulation 007/2007, Article 8.
512 Regulation 007/2007, Article 22.
513 Regulation 007/2007, Article 24.

6.7.2. VETERINARY COMMITTEE

Article 1 of Regulation 01/2006 created a technical consultative committee called the Veterinary Committee of UEMOA. Placed under the authority of the UEMOA Commission, the Veterinary Committee is responsible for providing technical consultative advice on all questions and measures of Community interest in the fields of the health and well-being of aquatic and terrestrial animals, the safety of food of animal origin, veterinary pharmacy, zoonoses and the veterinary profession. The Veterinary Committee is also mandated to assist the UEMOA Commission, by the formulation of opinions and technical recommendations, during the drafting of Community legislation and the harmonisation of national legislation in all relevant areas.[514]

6.7.3. CONSULTATIVE COMMITTEE ON THE HARMONIZATION OF POLICIES AND LAWS OF UEMOA MEMBER STATES

Pursuant to the provisions of Articles 10 and 14 of Additional Act No. 03/2001, adopting the Agricultural Policy of the Union (PAU), Regulation 04/2007 establishes a Consultative Committee on the Harmonization of Policies and Laws of UEMOA Member States, relating to fisheries and aquaculture.[515] The Committee's mission is to provide technical advice on the coordination and harmonisation of national laws and policies relating to fisheries and aquaculture within the UEMOA.[516] In trade matters, the Committee advises the UEMOA Commission on issues relating to relevant international standards, the improvement of product quality throughout the food chain and the contribution of fisheries to food safety and food quality.[517] The Committee also advises on stakeholders' capacity building in the field of trade, sustainable fisheries management, as well as health standards for the fishery sector.[518]

---

514 Regulation 01/2006, Article 2.
515 Regulation 04/2007, Article 1.
516 Regulation 04/2007, Article 2.
517 Regulation 04/2007, Article 4.3.
518 Regulation 04/2007, Article 4.7.

6.8. HARMONIZATION SCHEME OF ACTIVITIES OF ACCREDITATION, CERTIFICATION, STANDARDIZATION AND METROLOGY WITHIN THE UEMOA

While the measures defined by Regulation 07/2007 are focused on food safety issues, quality aspects are addressed by Regulation 01/2005 establishing a scheme for the harmonization of accreditation, certification, standardization and metrology activities within the UEMOA. The implementation of this scheme essentially aims to promote the free movement of goods and services at Community and international levels through a progressive elimination of inappropriate or unnecessary barriers to trade. The scheme intends to achieve the mutual recognition of national regulations and standards within a Community framework while strengthening the capacities of Member States in developing and enforcing texts relating to accreditation, certification, standardisation, and metrology in order to promote quality. Such an initiative should help Member States to benefit from their rights and respect their obligations under WTO Agreements and other cooperative agreements.[519]

For this purpose, Regulation 03/2010 laying down the harmonization scheme of activities of accreditation, certification, standardization and metrology in the UEMOA repeals and replaces Regulation 01/2005. Therefore, the former covers technical activities to ensure the quality of products and services, in particular standards, technical regulations, procedures for conformity assessment, accreditation and authorisation procedures, as well as metrology within the UEMOA.[520] However, Regulation 03/2010 does not lay down its own standards and merely urges Member States to implement the international guidelines on Technical Barriers to Trade enacted under WTO Agreements.[521] At the same time, the development and monitoring of the policy of the Union and the Community legislation in the field of quality is delegated to the UEMOA Commission. The settlement of disputes between Member States with regard to quality also falls within the competence of the UEMOA Commission.[522]

Regulation 03/2010 in Article 6 establishes three technical structures of quality namely: a regional accreditation organisation called West African System of Accreditation (SOAC); a Regional Secretariat of Standardization, Certification and Quality Promotion called NORMCERQ; and a regional metrology organisation called the West African System of Metrology (SOAMET). These regional bodies are responsible for ensuring coherence of the quality policies of Member States with the international context.

519 Regulation 03/2010, Article 2.
520 Regulation 03/2010, Article 3.
521 Regulation 03/2010, Article 4.
522 Regulation 03/2010, Article 5.

Moreover, Article 7 of Regulation 03/2010 creates a Regional Committee for Quality (CREQ) whose mission is to assist the UEMOA Commission in the implementation of Community policy as regards quality. The CREQ must coordinate the activities of regional technical institutions and formulate, where appropriate, recommendations and opinions.

In general, the regional technical institutions and the CREQ have the mandate to achieve the harmonisation and mutual recognition of technical standards, as well as approval and certification procedures in force in the Member States under the UEMOA Treaty. However, the organisational and functioning modalities of these institutions are not defined and are left to implementing regulations, which had to be subsequently taken by the UEMOA Commission.

Table 6.3. Technical quality institutions (Articles 6–7 Regulation 03/2010)

West African System of Accreditation (SOAC)	The SOAC is responsible for accreditation activities within the UEMOA and ensures their compliance with requirements of international institutions. The board of SOAC must promote accreditation in the UEMOA and set directions and priorities for accreditation.
Regional Secretariat of Standardization, Certification and Quality Promotion (NORMCERQ)	The NORMCERQ must collect Member States' national standards, receive their annual standardisation programmes and ensure their management. It must coordinate the transmission of standards-related information between Member States and the process of mutual recognition. Standards that are the subject of consensus are proposed for Community accreditation.
West African System of Metrology (SOAMET)	The SOAMET must contribute to the definition and implementation of the Community policy on metrology. It must ensure the development of metrology in the UEMOA and the establishment of an infrastructure that meets international standards, through the coordination of metrology's activities.
Regional Committee for Quality (CREQ)	The CREQ must assist the Commission in the implementation of the Community policy in terms of quality.

Member States must recognise as equivalent to their own evaluation, conformity assessment bodies of other Member States, provided that the latter offer sufficient guarantees, especially after a certification by the SOAC or by an organisation approved by the SOAC. National and regional bodies must refer to the guidelines and standards of international standardisation bodies. Moreover, Member States must ensure that their organisations adhere to the standards of internationally recognised standards organisations. The latter refer in particular to the African Regional Organization for Standardization (ORAN), the African Electrotechnical Standardization Commission (AFSEC), the International Standardization Organization (ISO), and the International Electrotechnical Commission (IEC).

The positions of national organisations are supposed to be harmonised within NORMCERQ, which ensures their representation within regional and international organisations where such representation is consistent with the statutes of the host organisation.

6.9. FOOD SAFETY CHALLENGES IN THE UEMOA

Although most UEMOA Member States have similar levels of development, the fact remains that disparities appear in the levels of protection that each of them is able to provide. For example, while Senegal and Ivory Coast managed to upgrade their regulatory and institutional frameworks to a level deemed satisfactory by the EU, Benin and Togo undertook the upgrading process at a slower pace, leading them to the suspension of the export of their fishery products to the EU. In this regard, the development of a regional framework is beneficial, as it could provide countries like Benin with a model to draw upon to undertake important reforms. Moreover, the existence of a regional framework that complies with international requirements relieves the burden from individual countries, which would no longer necessarily need to invest time and resources to design their own laws in their entirety. This would solve, at least partially, the issue related to the lack of resources and expertise to upgrade their outdated and inadequate national legal frameworks in a timely and consistent manner. In this regard, the development of accompaniment programmes has helped to achieve many improvements in diverse food safety related areas.

The assistance provided to the national laboratories to achieve accreditation is important for the credibility of conformity assessment bodies in the UEMOA. This was enabled through technical assistance programmes operated at the regional level to assist laboratories in terms of equipment and acquiring appropriate expertise. But most importantly, it provided the framework for the networking of laboratories that can facilitate the harmonisation of test methods for food products so as to enable laboratory comparisons. Such a synergy is valuable for the international recognition of the laboratories involved. Moreover, setting common criteria for the certification of products is useful to facilitate intra-regional trade.

The establishment of a regional system of standardisation created a ripple effect in the UEMOA region to strengthen national capacities. For example, through the development of a regional framework, NSBs may be established in Niger and Guinea-Bissau, while existing NSBs in other countries could be strengthened.

With regard to fisheries sectors, the UEMOA organised assistance for countries in which the need arose, namely in Togo and Benin, which were facing problems of non-compliance identified by the EU. Through the UEMOA Quality Program, the training of industry personnel and managers from regulatory authorities was carried out in these two countries and technical assistance was provided to some of their laboratories. Moreover, exporting plants benefited from technical assistance in the form of training in relation to HACCP principles. The implementation of the Quality Program in this regard contributed largely to the authorisation granted by the EU to Benin in 2005 to resume its shrimp exports to the EU. In the meantime, laboratory equipment was provided to Ivory Coast to enable the performance of histamine analysis in fishery products, while Guinea-Bissau benefited from support to ensure its compliance with regulatory requirements.

Furthermore, even if the results remain limited in terms of market access – particularly in the cases of Benin and Togo – the development of a food safety framework at the regional level could launch the debate on food safety, which provides a framework for outreach and awareness of food risks, and the need for actually implemented and enforced appropriate legislation. Therefore, a regional framework revives and sustains the pursuit of food safety objectives and may have a ripple effect on countries for the improvement of their national food laws and implementing institutions.

From the perspective of intra-UEMOA trade, whether disparities between countries' levels of protection will result in trade obstacles is still debatable. This is certainly exacerbated by the porosity of borders that makes it difficult to monitor the movement of goods between Member States properly and to have reliable statistics. For example, substantial quantities of Benin shrimps are sold on the regional market and it is not possible to determine the actual importance of this trade. If it is virtually impossible to monitor the flow of goods across countries, it means that not only the traded quantities are beyond the control of public authorities, but it implies that the quality and the safety status of food products escape their vigilance as well. This situation impedes the implementation of certain provisions of the regional legislation. In general, pursuant to Article 10 of Regulation 007/2007, products lawfully produced in one Member State must be accepted in the territory of other Member States. However, under the current circumstances, even the food products that do not conform to the national regulations of Member States can 'easily' find their way onto the regional market. This raises a fundamental question: to what extent is the development of the regional food safety framework consistent with the intrinsic realities of the Member States? The trend being the absence of control over the domestic markets, it is difficult to realistically consider a rapid and drastic upgrade that can comply with a high-quality food law, especially in contexts where minimum hygiene rules are often lacking. Moreover, the failure of the former system based on sanitary police and fraud prevention is by no means a technical problem or a problem of material means; it is primarily a problem of method, administration and legal linkages.[523]

6.9.1. ISSUES RELATED TO THE SMALL SIZE OF INTRA-UEMOA TRADE

Trade between UEMOA countries is rather limited. It is reported that, on average, only about 10 to 12% of African trade takes place among African nations, and it remains more onerous, costly and time-consuming to export and import in Africa than in all other regions.[524] These figures are partly attributed to the slow implementation of regional integration agreements designed to eliminate tariff and non-tariff barriers.[525] Exports within the UEMOA represent 13% of total exports.[526] But if regional trade is not sufficiently developed, the motivations for the development of a regional framework for food safety are minimal. Benin, just like Togo, exports most of their fishery products to the EU. It follows that the issue of the demand for a high-quality food safety legislation that arose in Benin may also arise at the regional level. Does this then imply that the level of protection provided by the UEMOA would simply be a reflection of the actual levels of protection in the Member States? It stands to reason that the food safety regional framework is dependent upon the commitment of Member States to cooperate for its effective implementation. Member States must therefore be willing to fulfil the core functions that come with State sovereignty. It is the responsibility of Member States to develop analysis and consultation processes to achieve the improvement or restructuring necessary for the effectiveness and efficiency of their control systems.[527] These refer for example to the establishment of food safety policy and objectives, the definition of the organisation and responsibilities of food control services, the organisation of a proper connection between control services and laboratories, etc. If some countries do not take the necessary measures, it can have the result that they remain lagging behind despite the opportunity provided by the regional framework. In Togo, for example, despite the ongoing development at the UEMOA level and the assistance of the EU, the food safety level could not be

523 Féral & Coulibaly 2004, p35.
524 Hartzenberg 2011, p11&16.
525 Economic Commission for Africa 2010, p10.
526 African Development Bank Group, UEMOA urged to boost its impact on inter-regional trade, 2013.
527 Banque Mondiale 2006, p84.

raised sufficiently to gain approval for the export of fishery products to the EU, except for live lobsters.

Lastly, the development and strengthening of food safety institutions only for exported food product channels does not promote a broader vision that enables attaining seek food safety from a more general perspective. In Benin, despite the recent leap forward, structural and financial problems are still impediments to the effectiveness of the implementation of food safety law in the fishery sector. Furthermore, the symmetrical development of two food safety systems, one system for the domestic market and the other for the export market, is still and will continue to be a major bottleneck for an effective synergy of food safety schemes on the domestic markets.

Yet, integrating food safety into national policies is a precondition for the success of any initiative aiming at its achievement. For example, already in 2003, it was reported that in the eight UEMOA Member States there was no national policy on the implementation and development of an accreditation system or to encourage the implementation of the accreditation process. This obviously resulted in the absence of laws and regulations and the lack of legal framework for accreditation systems.[528] The lack of awareness of decision-makers, lack of material, financial and qualified human resources, low consideration of accreditation by research laboratories or the lack of qualified laboratory auditors reinforce legal difficulties.

The implementation of the accreditation process in UEMOA Members is done under pressure from donors' demands and EU regulation, rather than being the result of national coordination.[529] In Benin, before the beginning of the reforms to comply with EU law, there existed a department of accreditation in the flowchart of the Beninese Centre for Standardization and Quality Management (CEBENOR). But this department did not carry out any activities. The laboratories selected and assisted for the purpose of accreditation are still not accredited, although they were predicted to be able to obtain the accreditation in 2007 and later in 2009.

However, the absence or underdevelopment of national frameworks for food safety does not automatically predict the failure of the regional framework. Developing institutions such as a regional accredited laboratory or a regional accreditation body could be very helpful to solve some of the problems encountered by Member States to create such infrastructure at the national level. Furthermore these types of initiatives can provide experiences and collaboration schemes upon which Member States can capitalise to develop these institutions at the national level, thereby progressively improving the supporting institutional environment, which will eventually lead to the emergence of an actual food safety management system.

528 Bayili 2003, p11.
529 Idem.

But, for this to be a reality, two conditions are essential. First, the commitment issue must once again be underlined. Even though the regional programmes are carried out with the agreement of Member States through their funding and the expression of their technical objectives, there was no involvement of national political authorities in response to the programmes.[530] In this regard, these programmes do not sufficiently bind governmental authorities in their commitments and obligations or establish the prior conditionality that they would ensure the sustainability of results achieved through their adhesion to the programmes.[531] Secondly, the effectiveness of the regional framework will depend on the extent of powers and legitimacy conferred to the UEMOA Commission. In principle, pursuant to the principle of subsidiarity, the UEMOA Commission has the power to ensure the drafting and promulgation of technical specifications that could support Member States' national laws.

Yet, while UEMOA's regulations are binding and directly applicable in Member States, it can be observed that this does not effectively take place. Benin, for example, merely referred to the UEMOA Regulation 007/2007 in the preamble to its general food law. This is not in itself very detrimental because many principles are shared by these two laws, such as the primary responsibility of food business operators for the safety of food, the principle of risk analysis, etc. Nevertheless, adopting national laws independently from regional regulations undermines the legitimacy of the Union, calling into question the fundamental principles underlying the legal cooperation between Member States through the Union. Moreover, this practice erodes the benefits of the convergence in terms of a more efficient management of national resources devoted to food safety. It is therefore important to ensure that the adoption of different national legislation *a posteriori*, regardless of the regional legislation, does not work against the objective of harmonisation and does not constitute one more obstacle to intra-regional convergence and trade.

6.9.2. REGIONAL INTEGRATION CROSS-CUTTING ISSUES

Since their independence, African States have embraced regional integration as an important component of their development strategies.[532] A large number of Regional Integration Arrangements (RIAs) exist on the African continent and are usually neighbourhood arrangements with significant membership overlap. In general, the African paradigm is that of linear market integration, following stepwise integration of goods, labour, and capital markets, and eventually monetary and fiscal integration. This type of integration starts usually as a

530 Banque Mondiale 2006, p87.
531 Idem.
532 Hartzenberg 2011, p2.

free trade area, followed by a customs union, a common market and then the integration of monetary and fiscal matters to establish an economic Union.[533] The regional arrangements within African States resulted however in a limited number of success stories, because they are generally ambitious schemes with unrealistic timeframes towards deeper integration.[534] This rather discouraging picture may foreshadow insurmountable difficulties for the successful implementation of an effective high-quality food law within the UEMOA. In this respect, one of the major challenges is the lack of resources for capacity building, as well as ensuring sustainability in the long run. The observation in Benin that the food safety-related reforms have almost entirely been undertaken thanks to donors' assistance is also extended to the regional level. The lack of resources is a recurring issue in most UEMOA countries. This was at the basis of many implementation issues of their former food safety schemes, and it still remains a challenge for the sustainability of the infrastructure acquired through technical assistance programmes. Even the design of the Community legislation was the result of several surveys carried out in Member States by international experts funded by technical assistance projects. It is clear that even though these experts conduct their missions in collaboration with resource persons at national levels, some important daily realities or issues can always escape their attention, because of the general stereotypes generally related to patterns in developing countries.

In any case, acknowledging the lack of resources is only one step in the process of changes. It is currently important to move beyond this hurdle so that countries can start to actually seek ways to provide the means for their policies. Furthermore, poor implementation and enforcement seem to be even bigger issues than the simple lack of resources, be it financial, human or material. The adoption of texts conform to international standards has no value if the implementation does not follow. In this regard, the first step towards the success of the regional cooperation is for the Member States to solve the issues of overlapping jurisdictions and responsibilities plaguing their public administrations. Defining the responsibilities and linking them to precise functions would pave the way towards a dynamic that could trigger the search for strategies to improve the execution of the tasks assigned. Making Member States accountable for the implementation is certainly equally important. Rules that are too flexible provide Member States with the possibility to avoid the implementation of the food law. Mandatory provisions must be considered to compel Member States to implement basic control measures and give dynamism to their quality infrastructure, even with regard to food chains intended for domestic markets. A lack of resources should not be used as an excuse for Member States to avoid their responsibility with regard to food

533 Idem.

534 Idem.

safety regulations. It is essential to clarify that the UEMOA will not replace the Member States for the effective implementation of their food legislation. The UEMOA, at the current stage, must remain a support for its members whenever the need arises to combine efforts to facilitate the implementation of food laws. Member States could thus reap greater benefits from networks of laboratories, alerts or experts set up at the regional level.

6.10. CONCLUSION

The challenges in matters of food safety are currently very important and cannot continue to be ignored by UEMOA countries. The systems of risk management are developed and perfected on a daily basis in developed countries and, like it or not, they are binding on the UEMOA countries which often depend exclusively on markets such as the EU to sell their products, since intra-region trade is still embryonic and too exposed to internal constraints. Only a clear definition of food safety objectives that includes a development on the domestic markets is likely to create the impulse necessary for an efficient and sustainable development of food safety frameworks. In their endeavour, Member States must take into account that microbiological risks associated with the hygiene standards of preparation, transport, packaging and placing on the market of products remain major food risks in most UEMOA countries. Aiming for basic hygiene must therefore be a priority that will be associated with the physico-chemical risks related to the food industry.[535]

Furthermore, the development of food safety for export markets with the vision that this strategy will have spillover effects on domestic markets will remain an illusion for a long time, because domestic markets are still confronted with too many primary issues. The street food is still a preponderant phenomenon and official controls are rare or non-existent. Raising sufficient awareness and letting the demand for food law and controls grow domestically is a *sine qua non* condition for the development of food safety on the internal markets. The coexistence of two food safety systems on the same market, one for the domestic market and one for the export market, is no longer an option, especially with regard to fishery products where actors are interconnected and mingled. Moreover, integrating domestic markets in the strategies of compliance will better reflect the socio-economic and legal realities and will lead to the adoption of more realistic standards which would then be easier to apply.

It is important to underline that the public-private partnership is not currently efficient within the UEMOA. The regulation of food risks by public authorities is not sufficiently considerate of the needs of the private sector. There is a huge gap between the food safety systems in most countries and the food

---

535 Féral & Coulibaly 2004, p13.

safety objectives targeted by the regional food safety framework. This makes the upgrading process more challenging for the private sector, which experiences the lack of resources more severely because technical assistance projects are generally not focused *per se* on the strengthening of the private sector. In this regard, UEMOA Member States must seek smarter ways of regulation to better accommodate the socio-economic development of their private sectors and domestic markets.

In recent years, many donors invested in several national programmes for updating and capacity building to help UEMOA countries comply with international standards. In this context, it is important to ensure that technical assistance programmes developed at the regional level are not redundant next to national programmes. When necessary, complementarity must be sought between these programmes and that could even facilitate their implementation.

CHAPTER VII

ASSESSING THE IMPLEMENTATION OF THE SPS AND TBT AGREEMENTS

7.1. INTRODUCTION

The evolution of science, the structure of markets and consumer awareness are the source of the emergence of new approaches to food regulation in industrialised countries, making public health the primary goal of food safety regulation.[536] This revolution has followed some common patterns worldwide, highlighting several trends, such as the increased use of risk analysis or HACCP principles[537], the emphasis on a farm-to-fork approach, or the improvement of market performance through the provision of information.[538]

Increasing food safety standards in developed countries' markets has become a significant challenge for many exporting developing countries. The ability to meet import requirements is a decisive criterion for access to major markets that depends on the trust and confidence of importers and consumers in the integrity of exporters' food systems.[539] Detention and rejection of consignments, explicit bans on imports, and the costs of compliance with stringent requirements adversely affect export competitiveness, translating into impediments to trade, especially for higher-value foods such as fish.[540] Food safety and quality requirements are under the spotlight because of their extraterritorial effect and the difficulties to duly assess their effects on third countries' economies. As food trade evolves, it appears crucial to ensure that these requirements are based on genuine concerns and do not become a convenient excuse to justify trade barriers.[541]

---

536 Roberts & Unnevehr 2005, p472.

537 According to Caswell & Hooker (1996, p778), chemical and microbiological hazards are the food safety concerns that have fueled the increased use of HACCP-based regimes.

538 Roberts & Unnevehr 2005, p472. The provision of information translates into the use of voluntary guidelines or standards, provision of third-party certification, provision of information through labelling, establishing legal liability for food safety, and establishing voluntary or mandatory systems for traceability (See Roberts & Unnevehr 2005, p475).

539 FAO 2009, p4.

540 Jaffee & Henson 2004, p1.

541 Calvin & Krissoff 1998, p352. Jaffee & Henson (2004, p2) underline that there is a presumption that food safety and agricultural health measures can help provide 'scientific' justifications

Developing countries argue that food safety measures are abused for protectionist purposes by developed countries, resulting in diverse trade restrictions that negatively influence their economy.[542] Furthermore, due to the stringency of the measures of their developed trading partners, compliance costs for developing countries are excessively high and may thus reduce their competitiveness.[543] Also, the loss of markets results in unemployment, loss of foreign exchange and incidental harm of developing countries' reputation.

Considering the foregoing points, mixed feelings exist, after several years of implementation, about the effectiveness of the SPS and TBT Agreements to truly ensure a non-abusive use of sanitary and quality measures. There are suspicions for example that the SPS Agreement does little to address the new challenges arising from international trade, and "merely represents a method by which nations can create exemptions to each other's food safety laws to advance trade".[544]

Based on the shrimp export trade from Benin to the EU, this chapter intends to examine from a practical perspective to what extent the SPS and TBT Agreements are suitable to ensure the 'protection' of Benin from adverse trade impacts of the food safety regulation in the EU. In other words, considering that Benin is impaired by a *bona fide* food safety regulatory delay, could the SPS or TBT Agreements then provide mechanisms to circumvent genuinely justified or disguised protectionist EU measures? Similarly how could the EU ensure the attainment of its appropriate level of protection or regulatory objectives while still fulfilling its obligation with regard to the SPS and TBT Agreements?

The second section (7.2) provides an overview of the SPS and TBT Agreements. The third section (7.3) examines the levelling of differences through regulatory cooperation. The fourth section (7.4) gives an insight into non-discrimination. The next sections examine the disciplines on food risk assessment (7.5) and on the choice of measures (7.6). The seventh section (7.7) assesses the implementation of EU requirements with regard to the SPS and the TBT Agreements. The provisions on transparency (7.8), developing countries concerns (7.9) and on dispute settlement (7.10) are further examined. The next section (7.11) assesses the compliance of Benin's approach with WTO law. The last section (7.12) concludes.

---

for import prohibitions or discrimination resulting from higher standards or more rigorous regulatory oversight on imported products.

542 Jayasuriya 2006, p2.

543 Henson 2003, IFPRI Focus 10, Brief 5.

544 Silverglade 2000, p517.

7.2. OVERVIEW OF THE SPS AND TBT AGREEMENTS

7.2.1. FOOD SAFETY IN THE SPS AGREEMENT

a. *Definition and scope*

The approach of the SPS Agreement is intended to promote the adoption of measures that could depart from the fundamental principle of the WTO to promote trade liberalisation among its Members, provided these measures are meant to protect human, animal or plant life or health. In its eighth recital, the SPS Agreement affirms the desire of Members to elaborate rules for the application of the provisions of the General Agreement on Tariffs and Trade (GATT) 1994 relating to the use of sanitary or phytosanitary measures, in particular the provisions of Article XX(b). This relationship between the GATT and the SPS Agreement was clarified by the Panel in EC-Hormones (Canada). In this regard, the Panel acknowledged that "some provisions of the SPS Agreement elaborate on provisions already contained in GATT, in particular Article XX(b), for example the basic rights and obligations in Article 2 of the SPS Agreement".[545] However, this is not conclusive evidence that, on this basis, the SPS Agreement would apply only if a prior violation of a GATT provision has been established. In the Panel's view, the desire to improve the human health, animal health and phytosanitary situation in all Members and to further the use of harmonised sanitary and phytosanitary measures between Members, as contained in the second and the sixth recitals of the preamble to the SPS Agreement, impose 'substantive' obligations which go significantly beyond and are additional to the requirements for invoking Article XX(b) of the GATT.[546] Therefore, while Article XX(b) provides for a general exception which can be invoked to justify any violation of another GATT provision, the SPS Agreement provides for specific obligations to be met in order for a Member to enact or maintain specific types of measures, namely sanitary and phytosanitary measures.[547]

Through the regime of the SPS Agreement, WTO Members may adopt and enforce measures necessary to protect human, animal or plant life or health, provided that such measures do not comprise arbitrary or unjustifiable discrimination and do not constitute a disguised restriction on international trade. Therefore, while offering the liberty to implement the sovereign right of WTO Members to adopt health measures within their territory, the SPS Agreement aims concomitantly to set some boundaries to avoid the improper use of its provisions that could lead to trade distortions.

[545] Panel Report, EC-Hormones (Canada), para. 8–41.
[546] Idem.
[547] Panel Report, EC-Hormones (Canada), para. 8–42.

However, rather than creating specific SPS standards, the SPS Agreement lays down general rules for governments to follow when establishing SPS measures.[548] Obviously, such flexibility was necessary to accommodate differences resulting from climate, culture, levels of development, and subsequent regulatory needs. In the same way, differences arising from risk perceptions, available market information, the incidence of production risks, and traditional methods of food processing and preparation may all contribute to disparities in food safety outcomes among countries and result in significant differences with regard to the costs of compliance.[549] These factors create room for diversity in legislative processes among countries that might lead to conflicts or tensions. In this context, the SPS Agreement is a response to the necessity of dealing with complex and conflicting regulatory requirements in different jurisdictions.[550]

The definition of SPS measures in annex A(1)(a) through (d) of the SPS Agreement delimits its coverage. As far as the scope is concerned, one could distinguish the substantive scope, the temporal scope, the institutional coverage and the relationship of the SPS agreement with other WTO Agreements.

Substantively, Article 1.1 provides that the SPS Agreement "applies to all sanitary and phytosanitary measures which may, directly or indirectly, affect international trade. Such measures shall be developed and applied in accordance with the provisions of this Agreement". Drawing on this article, the Panel in EC-Hormones identified two requirements that are essential for a measure to fall within the realm of the SPS Agreement: the measure in dispute must be a sanitary or phytosanitary measure and this measure must have the potential to affect international trade, either directly or indirectly.[551]

The Agreement defines an SPS measure as any "measure applied to protect animal or plant life or health within the territory of the Member from risks arising from the entry, establishment or spread of pests, diseases, disease-carrying organisms or disease-causing organisms; protect human or animal life or health within the territory of the Member from risks arising from additives, contaminants, toxins or disease-causing organisms in foods, beverages or feedstuffs; protect human life or health within the territory of the Member from risks arising from diseases carried by animals, plants or products thereof, or from the entry, establishment or spread of pests; or prevent or limit other damage within the territory of the Member from the entry, establishment or spread of pests".

The relationship between the SPS measure and one of these three objectives "must be manifest in the measure itself or otherwise evident from the

548 Stewart & Johanson 1999, p56.

549 Roberts & Unnevehr 2005, p492.

550 Zleptnig 2010, p118.

551 Agreement on the Application of Sanitary and Phytosanitary Measures, Article 1; see also Panel report EC-Hormones (Canada) para. 8.39.

circumstances related to the application of the measure".[552] Annex A(1) further states in its second part that "SPS measures include all relevant laws, decrees, regulations, requirements and procedures including, *inter alia*, end product criteria; processes and production methods; testing, inspection, certification and approval procedures; quarantine treatments including relevant requirements associated with the transport of animals or plants, or with the materials necessary for their survival during transport; provisions on relevant statistical methods, sampling procedures and methods of risk assessment; and packaging and labelling requirements directly related to food safety."

The definition of SPS measures relies on the regulatory goal of a measure, rather than the policy instrument itself.[553] In this respect, "a measure is an SPS measure if it is applied 'to protect' life or health from certain enumerated risks, or if it is applied 'to prevent or limit' certain other damage."[554] In the EC-Biotech dispute, the Panel stated that, in determining whether a measure is or not an SPS measure, one must regard the purpose of the measure, its legal form and its nature.[555] The Panel in US Poultry indicated that the qualification of an SPS measure was not required to be a rigid three-part test. For the Panel, the nature of a measure is an intrinsic element of its form and, "reading the second part of Annex A(1) as a whole, means that an examination of whether a measure is of the type set forth in Annex A(1) will encompass a holistic examination of the measure, including, both its form and nature".[556] In this regard, the analysis should then consider whether the measure at issue serves one of the purposes set forth in Annex A(1)(a) through (d) and whether the measure is of the type listed in the second part of Annex A.[557] Considering A(1)(a) through (d) as the list of specific purposes that are the defining characteristic of every SPS measure, the Appellate Body in Australia-Apples noted the importance of relating this list to the second part of Annex A(1) to impart the full meaning to words such as 'relevant', 'include' and 'all'. In fact, "the words 'include' and 'all', which also introduce the list of instruments, suggest that the list is both illustrative and expansive. Taken together, the words 'include' and 'all relevant' therefore suggest that measures of a type not expressly listed may nevertheless constitute SPS measures when they are 'relevant', that is, when they are 'applied' for a purpose that corresponds to one of those listed in subparagraphs (a) through (d)".[558] Furthermore, for one of the examples of measures – such as laws, decrees, regulations, requirements – listed in the second part of Annex A to actually

552 Appellate Body Report, Australia-Apples, para. 172.
553 Roberts 1998, p382.
554 Panel Report, EC – Approval and Marketing of Biotech Products, paras. 7.196, 7.207 and. 7.2555.
555 Panel Report, EC-Approval and Marketing of Biotech Products, para. 7.149.
556 Panel Report, US-Poultry, para. 7.101.
557 Panel Report, US-Poultry, para. 7.102.
558 Appellate Body Report, Australia-Apples, para. 175.

qualify as an SPS measure, this example of measure must manifest a clear and objective relationship with at least one of the purposes set out in subparagraphs (a) through (d).[559]

However, falling within the definition of an SPS measure is a necessary but not a sufficient condition for a measure to be covered by the SPS Agreement. In this regard, the Panel in US-Poultry (China) emphasised that "even if a measure falls within the definition of an SPS measure in Annex A(1) of the SPS Agreement, further to Article 1.1 of the SPS Agreement, such a measure still needs to be a measure that directly or indirectly affect[s] international trade to be covered by the disciplines of the SPS Agreement".[560] It is worth noting that, under no circumstances, the trade effect of a given measure shall be considered to determine whether that measure qualifies or not as an SPS measure.[561]

The SPS Agreement is designed so as to include negative inducements (sticks) and positive incentives (carrots).[562] These negative inducements aimed at dissuading the use of SPS measures for protectionist purposes and prohibitions on non-scientific measures and the positive incentives rely upon the confidence in credible commitments provided by the new regime. They include the creation of the SPS Committee, the notification obligation, the opportunity to challenge other countries' regulations, and the establishment of a source of information for exporters on importer SPS regulations.[563]

With regard to the temporal scope of application, the Appellate Body in EC-Hormones held that the SPS Agreement would apply to situations or measures that had not ceased to exist, unless the SPS Agreement revealed a contrary intention. The Appellate Body then stated that "the SPS Agreement does not contain any provision limiting the temporal application of the SPS Agreement, or of any provision thereof, to SPS measures adopted after 1 January 1995".[564] The same ruling also underlined that "other provisions of the SPS Agreement, such as Articles 2.2, 2.3, 3.3 and 5.6, expressly contemplate applicability to SPS measures that already existed on 1 January 1995".[565]

As far as institutional scope is concerned, Article 13 of the SPS Agreement states that Members are fully responsible for the observance of all obligations of the Agreement. In this respect, Members must formulate and implement positive measures and mechanisms to ensure compliance with the obligations contained in the SPS Agreement by bodies other than central government bodies. Furthermore, Members must take reasonable measures to ensure that non-governmental entities within their territories, as well as regional bodies in

559 Appellate Body Report, Australia-Apples, para. 176.
560 Panel Report, US-Poultry (China), para. 7.87.
561 Panel Report, Japan-Apples, para. 8.24.
562 Josling et al. 2004, p4.
563 Josling et al. 2004, p5.
564 Appellate Body Report, EC-Hormones, para. 128.
565 Idem.

which relevant entities within their territories are members, comply with the relevant provisions of the SPS Agreement. Furthermore, Members must not take measures that require or encourage, directly or indirectly, one of these bodies to act in a manner that is inconsistent with the provisions of the SPS Agreement. Lastly, Members may rely on the services of non-governmental entities for implementing SPS measures only if these entities comply with the provisions of the SPS Agreement.

In defining the coverage of the SPS Agreement, it is important to examine its relationship with other Agreements, in particular the TBT Agreement and the GATT. As regards the relationship between the SPS and the TBT Agreements, Article 1.4 of the SPS Agreement states that nothing in the SPS Agreement shall affect the rights of Members under the TBT Agreement with respect to measures not falling within the scope of the SPS Agreement. Article 1.5 of the TBT Agreement provides that the provisions of the TBT Agreement do not apply to SPS measures as defined in Annex A of the SPS Agreement. Read together, these two articles thus determine that the SPS Agreement and the TBT Agreement are mutually exclusive. This means that once a measure qualifies as an SPS measure, it is subject to the SPS Agreement to the exclusion of the TBT Agreement, even if this measure is also a technical regulation or standard within the meaning of the TBT Agreement.

As explained earlier, the SPS Agreement is a self-standing agreement and there is no need to establish a violation of the GATT for the applicability of the SPS Agreement. Also, no provision makes the SPS Agreement and the GATT mutually exclusive and both the SPS Agreement and the GATT may simultaneously cover a measure. While compliance with the SPS Agreement entails a presumption of compliance with the GATT, the Panel in EC-Hormones stated that "nowhere is consistency with GATT presumed to be consistency with the SPS Agreement".[566]

b. Basic rights and obligations

Article 2 of the SPS Agreement sets out the basic rights and obligations under the Agreement. Under Article 2.1, Members are conferred the right to take SPS measures necessary for the protection of human, animal or plant life or health, provided that such measures are not inconsistent with the provisions of the SPS Agreement. The Panel in US-Poultry (China) stipulated that the 'overarching and encompassing' title of Article 2, namely "Basic Rights and Obligations" leads the Panel to conclude that the obligations in Article 2 inform all of the SPS Agreement.[567] As such, and as observable in the case law, the rights and obligations developed in Article 2 are further elaborated on in subsequent

566 Panel Report, EC-Hormones (US), para. 8.42.
567 Panel Report, US Poultry-China, para. 7.142.

articles and sometimes need to be read in conjunction with some subsequent articles in order to have their full meaning.

The right for Members to take necessary SPS measures is circumscribed by a few conditions. Article 2.2 states that measures shall be based on scientific principles and must not be maintained without sufficient scientific evidence, except in cases where relevant scientific evidence is insufficient as provided for in Article 5.7. The evaluation of this principle is rather delicate. In order to understand the extent of the word 'sufficient' or the expression 'maintained without sufficient scientific evidence' in Article 2.2, it is important to read that article in combination with several other articles of the SPS Agreement.[568] This implies that the notion of sufficiency is not straightforward and must always be explained within a specific context. Linking Article 2.2 to Article 5.1 for instance would require analysing 'sufficiency' with regard to the risk assessment carried out to support the measure, keeping in mind the particular circumstances at hand. In any case, the evaluation of such concepts is quite sensitive. As the Appellate Body put it in EC-Hormones, a panel, while examining the sufficiency of scientific evidence may and should "bear in mind that responsible, representative governments commonly act from perspectives of prudence and precaution where risks of irreversible, e.g. life-terminating, damage to human health are concerned."[569]

The Appellate Body established a constant connection between Articles 2.2 and 5.1 of the SPS Agreement, as it considered that the former imparts meaning to the latter.[570] From this perspective, a violation of Article 5.1 entails a presumption of non-compliance with Article 2.2. Therefore, a measure not based on a risk assessment is presumed not to be based on scientific principles or to be maintained without sufficient scientific evidence within the meaning of Article 2.2.[571] The opposite is not necessarily true. Since Article 2.2 has a more general character, not all violations of the requirement to base SPS measures on scientific principles are covered by Articles 5.1 and 5.2[572] that stipulate respectively that measures should be based on a risk assessment and the particulars of such an assessment of risk.

WTO case law qualified 'sufficiency' as a relational concept, which substantially requires the existence of a sufficient or adequate rational or objective relationship between the SPS measure and the scientific evidence.[573] In that respect, "the scientific evidence must also be sufficient to demonstrate the

568 In the Japan-Agricultural Products II case, the Appellate Body highlighted essentially Articles 5.1, 3.3 and 5.7 of the SPS Agreement. See Appellate Body Report, Japan-Agricultural Products II, para. 74.

569 Appellate Body Report, EC-Hormones, para. 124.

570 Appellate Body Report, EC – Hormones, para. 180.

571 Appellate Body Report, Australia – Salmon, para. 138.

572 Appellate Body Report, Australia – Salmon, para. 137.

573 Appellate Body Report, Japan-Agricultural Products II, para. 73.

existence of the risk which the measure is supposed to address".[574] Such evidence may include evidence that a particular risk may occur or that a particular requirement may reduce or eliminate that risk. However the requirement that the evidence must be collected through scientific methods implies that the scope of the provision in Article 2.2 excludes insufficiently substantiated information or a non-demonstrated hypothesis.[575] Yet, to support their measures, Members might equally have recourse to direct or indirect evidence. The rational or objective relationship that links the measure and the scientific evidence is to be determined on a case-by-case basis considering the particular circumstances of the case.[576] "A measure as a whole should be considered to be maintained 'without sufficient scientific evidence' if one or more of its elements are not justified by the relevant scientific evidence addressing the risk at issue."

Article 2.3 lays down another limitation on the right of Members to impose SPS measures by stipulating that "Members shall ensure that their sanitary and phytosanitary measures do not arbitrarily or unjustifiably discriminate between Members where identical or similar conditions prevail, including between their own territory and that of other Members. Sanitary and phytosanitary measures shall not be applied in a manner which would constitute a disguised restriction on international trade". In Australia-Salmon (Canada), the Panel identified three elements, cumulative in nature, that are necessary to find a violation of the first sentence of Article 2.3. First, the measure discriminates between the territories of Members other than the Member imposing the measure or between the territory of the Member imposing the measure and that of another Member. Secondly, the discrimination is arbitrary or unjustifiable. Thirdly, identical or similar conditions prevail in the territory of the Members compared.[577] The discrimination mentioned in Article 2.3 is not restricted to similar products, but it could also extend to different products. As a way of example, the Panel in the Australia-Salmon case suggested that one could refer not only to discrimination between Canadian salmon and New Zealand salmon or to Canadian salmon and Australian salmon but also to discrimination between Canadian salmon and Australian fish including non-salmonids.[578] Analysing Article 5.5, which deals with arbitrary or unjustifiable distinctions in the levels of protection imposed by one WTO Member for different situations, the Panel in Australia-Salmon concluded that a finding of violation of the more specific Article 5.5 could be presumed to imply a violation of the more general Article 2.3.[579] However, the converse is not true. The Panel further underlined that "given the more

574 Panel report Japan-apples, para. 8.45.
575 Panel report Japan-apples, para. 8.179, 8.180, 8.182, 8.192.
576 Appellate Body Report, Japan – Agricultural Products II, para. 84.
577 Panel Report, Australia-Salmon (Article 21.5 – Canada), para. 7.111.
578 Panel Report, Australia – Salmon, para. 7.112.
579 Panel Report, Australia-Salmon, para. 8.109 and Appellate Body Report, Australia-Salmon, para. 252. The conditions for a violation of Article 5.5 are discussed in section 7.5 below.

general character of Article 2.3, not all violations of Article 2.3 are covered by Article 5.5".[580]

Lastly, and pursuant to Article 2.4 of the SPS Agreement, the conformity of SPS measures with relevant provisions of the SPS Agreement "shall be presumed to be in accordance with the obligations of the Members under the provisions of the GATT 1994 which relate to the use of sanitary or phytosanitary measures, in particular the provisions of Article XX(b)".

7.2.2. OVERVIEW OF THE TBT AGREEMENT

a. *Definition and scope*

TBT rules are established on the basis of the acknowledgement of the important contribution of international standards and conformity assessment systems to the improvement of the efficiency of production, the transfer of technology from developed to developing countries and the facilitation of international trade.[581] Just like in the case of SPS measures, WTO scrutiny is essential to eliminate arbitrary or unjustifiable discrimination between countries and avert disguised restrictions on international trade. The rules of the TBT Agreement govern WTO Members' technical regulations, standards and conformity assessment systems, while aiming at a twofold objective. In this regard, the TBT Agreement intends to preserve the right of WTO Members to take measures to protect certain legitimate interests, while ensuring that Members' TBT measures do not result in unnecessary obstacles to trade.

The Panel in EC-Asbestos held that some similarities were noted in Article 2.2 of the TBT Agreement and Article XX of the GATT 1994 as regards the criteria on the preparation, adoption or application of technical regulations. Likewise, the Panel pointed out that the preamble to the TBT Agreement was found to repeat some of the wording of Article XX of the GATT.[582] In any event, the purpose of adopting the TBT Agreement was the control of the development and application of standards that involve situations in which protectionist aims can be better disguised and for which the existing disciplines within the GATT appeared to be inadequate.[583]

The TBT Agreement operates through a specialised legal regime that applies solely to a limited class of measures, by imposing obligations on Members that seem to be different from, and additional to, the obligations imposed on Members under the GATT 1994.[584] In fact, three different types of scope of

580 Panel Report, Australia-Salmon, para. 8.109.
581 TBT Agreement, Preamble, 3rd and 8th recitals.
582 Panel Report, EC-Asbestos, para. 8.55.
583 Panel Report, EC-Asbestos, para. 8.49.
584 Appellate Body Report, EC-Asbestos, para. 80.

application can be distinguished in the TBT Agreement: the substantive scope, the personal scope and the temporal scope.[585]

As regards the substantive scope, Annex I sets out that the TBT Agreement applies to technical regulations, standards and conformity assessment procedures. Annex I provides specific definitions for these terms and several other terms. Article 1.1 of the TBT Agreement stipulates that general terms for standardisation and procedures for the assessment of conformity defined in the Agreement shall normally have the meaning given to them by the definitions adopted within the United Nations system and by international standardising bodies, taking into account their context and in the light of the object and purpose of the Agreement. Referring to the Chapeau of Annex 1, the Appellate Body in EC-Sardines stated that "the terms defined in Annex 1 apply for the purposes of the TBT Agreement only if their definitions depart from the ones in the ISO/IEC Guide 2: 1991 (the 'ISO/IEC Guide')".[586] In other words, in the absence of a specific definition in Annex 1 of the TBT Agreement, the definition in the ISO/IEC Guide applies.[587]

A technical regulation is defined as a "document which lays down product characteristics or their related processes and production methods, including the applicable administrative provisions, with which compliance is mandatory. It may also include or deal exclusively with terminology, symbols, packaging, marking or labelling requirements as they apply to a product, process or production method".[588] In interpreting this definition, the Appellate Body sets out three criteria that a document must meet to qualify as a technical regulation within the meaning of the TBT Agreement.[589] First, the document must apply to an identifiable product or group of products.[590] Second, the document must lay down one or more characteristics of the product, which can be intrinsic or may simply be related to the product.

In the EC-Asbestos case, the Appellate Body stated that the 'characteristics' of a product include any objectively definable 'features', 'qualities', 'attributes', or other 'distinguishing mark' of a product. These might relate *inter alia*, to a product's composition, size, shape, colour, texture, hardness, tensile strength, flammability, conductivity, density, or viscosity. Moreover, 'product

585 Bossche (van den) et al. 2005, p5.

586 Appellate Body Report, EC-Sardines, para. 224.

587 Panel Report, US-Tuna II (Mexico), para. 7.663.

588 TBT Agreement, Annex 1.1.

589 Appellate Body Report, EC-Sardines, para. 176 and Appellate Body Report, EC-Asbestos, paras. 66–70.

590 In EC-Asbestos, the Appellate Body stated that this requirement does not mean that the products referred to must be expressly identified in a technical regulation; that is there must not be actually named, identified or specified in the regulation. In this respect, there may be sound administrative reasons to simply make the products identifiable – for instance, through the 'characteristic' that is the subject of a regulation. (See Appellate Body Report, EC-Asbestos, para. 70).

characteristics' include, not only features and qualities intrinsic to the product itself, but also related 'characteristics', such as the means of identification, the presentation and the appearance of a product.[591] The characteristics may be prescribed or imposed in either a positive or a negative form, that is to say that the document can provide that products must possess certain 'characteristics' or it may require, negatively, that products must not possess certain 'characteristics'.[592] Analysing the definition of a technical regulation in Annex 1.1 of the TBT Agreement, the Appellate Body in EC-Seal Products held that "it is 'compliance' with the content of the document laying down product characteristics or their related PPMs that must be found to be 'mandatory'. Accordingly, the scope of Annex 1.1 appears to be limited to those documents that establish or prescribe something and thus have a certain normative content".[593] Furthermore, "the subject matter of a technical regulation may consist of a process or production method that is related to product characteristics. In order to determine whether a measure lays down related PPMs, a panel thus will have to examine whether the processes and production methods prescribed by the measure have a sufficient nexus to the characteristics of a product in order to be considered related to those characteristics".[594] Furthermore, in case a mandatory document laying down product characteristics or their related processes and production methods also contains related "administrative provisions", "those administrative provisions are to be considered as an integral part of the technical regulation and are thus subject to the substantive provisions of the TBT Agreement".[595] Therefore, in the context of Annex 1.1, the appositive clause "including the applicable administrative provisions" refers to provisions to be applied by virtue of a governmental mandate in relation to either product characteristics or their related processes and production methods.[596]

The third criterion stipulates that compliance with the product characteristics must be mandatory. In such a way, a technical regulation must regulate the characteristics of products in a binding or compulsory fashion, having the effect of prescribing or imposing one or more characteristics.[597]

A standard is defined as a "Document approved by a recognized body, that provides, for common and repeated use, rules, guidelines or characteristics for products or related processes and production methods, with which compliance is not mandatory. It may also include or deal exclusively with terminology,

591 Appellate Body Report, EC-Asbestos, para. 67.
592 Appellate Body Report, EC-Asbestos, para. 69.
593 Appellate Body Report, EC-Seal Products, para. 5.10.
594 Appellate Body Report, EC- Seal Products, para. 5.12.
595 Appellate Body Report, EC- Seal Products, para. 5.13.
596 Idem.
597 Appellate Body Report, EC-Asbestos, para. 68.

symbols, packaging, marking or labelling requirements as they apply to a product, process or production method".[598]

Standardisation has proven to play an important role in industrial development, trade facilitation and improving market access.[599] Moreover, standards have the potential to increase efficiency, thereby boosting economic growth.[600]

Lastly, a conformity assessment procedure is "any procedure used, directly or indirectly, to determine that relevant requirements in technical regulations or standards are fulfilled".[601] In this respect, conformity assessment procedures include, *inter alia*, procedures for sampling, testing and inspection; evaluation, verification and assurance of conformity; registration, accreditation and approval as well as their combinations. Conformity assessment activities can be carried out at three different levels, namely assessment or evaluation, accreditation and recognition.[602]

Assessment involves comparing a product or process to a given technical regulation, either by producers, laboratories or certifiers. A good example is the Suppliers Declaration of Conformity (SDoC), which is a procedure by which a supplier provides assurance of conformity to the specified requirements. The TBT Committee asserts that, when used in appropriate circumstances, the SDoC could be a means of facilitating trade without prejudice to the fulfilment of legitimate public policy objectives, through flexibility and the reduction of the cost of conformity assessment.[603] The TBT Committee underlined that SDoC can improve market access for developing country exporters in case of their acceptance by the importing Member. However the value of this procedure should not be over-estimated. To be effective, SDoC must be product and sector-specific and should be combined with a number of tools, such as effective product liability laws, well-developed market surveillance system, penalties for false or misleading declarations, or appropriate incentives to encourage compliance.[604]

Accreditation as identified in Article 6.1.1 is a tool for Members to verify the technical competence of conformity assessment bodies (testing, certification and inspection bodies) in exporting country Members. This procedure enables the determination of whether a particular body has the required personnel qualifications, equipment and the ability to perform specified tests, inspections or certifications.[605] As such, accreditation is a mechanism that could promote confidence when operated according to relevant international standards, guides

598 TBT Agreement, Annex I.2.
599 ISO/UNIDO 2008, p8.
600 Charnovitz 2002, p1.
601 TBT Agreement, Annex I.3.
602 Akyoo & Lazazo 2008, p9.
603 Committee on Technical Barriers to Trade 2003, para. 33.
604 Committee on Technical Barriers to Trade 2003, paras. 34–35.
605 Akyoo & Lazazo 2008, p9.

and recommendations[606], since accreditation enables conformity assessment bodies to demonstrate their competence[607] and underpins the integrity, transparency and consistency of their work.[608]

The whole mechanism relies upon the acceptance by governmental regulatory authorities of the results of accreditation bodies. Through Article 6.1.3, the TBT Agreement foresaw Mutual Recognition Agreements (MRAs) as one of the approaches to facilitate the acceptance of conformity assessment results. In fact, accreditation bodies are third party conformity assessment providers that deliver unbiased and factual assurance to both parties to a transaction. They, in turn, need to attain recognition to demonstrate their impartiality and competence through peer review and international recognition using ISO/IEC standards on conformity assessment. They are often established as national or regional entities that take part in mutual recognition arrangements or are Members of relevant international bodies.[609] In this regard the West African Accreditation System (SOAC) developed by the UEMOA is a good example of regulatory cooperation related to accreditation.

From a more general perspective, the TBT Committee elaborated an indicative list of approaches to facilitate the acceptance of conformity assessment results. Next to MRA's, this list includes co-operative voluntary agreements between domestic and foreign conformity assessment bodies, the use of accreditation to qualify conformity assessment bodies, government designation, the unilateral recognition of results of foreign conformity assessment and manufacturer's/supplier's declarations. Voluntary agreements between domestic and foreign conformity assessment bodies include arrangements among accreditation bodies, as well as arrangements between individual laboratories, certification bodies and inspection bodies.[610] The use of accreditation to qualify conformity assessment bodies consists of the development of global networks that take the form of multilateral recognition agreements or arrangements (MLAs), whereby each participant undertakes to recognise the accreditation granted or certificates issued by any other party to the agreement or arrangement as being equivalent to that which it granted and to promote that equivalence throughout its territory of operation.[611] Government designations are arrangements through which governments designate specific conformity assessment bodies, including bodies located outside their territories, to undertake conformity assessment.[612]

The effective functioning of such a system relies upon adequate market surveillance, substantial penalties for false or misleading declarations, an

606 Committee on Technical Barriers to Trade, 2003, para. 37.
607 ISO/UNIDO 2008, p7.
608 ISO/UNIDO 2008, Appendix 2, p175.
609 ISO/UNIDO 2008, p7 & 18.
610 Committee on Technical Barriers to Trade, 2000, Annex 4.
611 Idem.
612 Idem.

appropriate regulatory environment, and an appropriate product liability regime.[613] In any event, the choice of the approach depends on the situation of Members and the specific sectors involved. The application of one or more approaches within or across sectors results from the consideration of variations in procedures in different Members and perceived risk levels in the acceptance of results in different sectors[614], provided that these approaches offer sufficient transparency, are non-discriminatory and do not create unnecessary obstacles to trade.[615]

It is worth noting that, although a single measure can combine both a technical regulation and a procedure to assess conformity with that technical regulation, the Panel in EC – Trademarks and Geographical Indications stated that, by definition, technical regulation and conformity assessment procedures are mutually exclusive. Therefore, under no circumstances could a conformity assessment procedure also fall within the definition of a technical regulation.[616]

Irrespective of the form, a single measure can have several objectives. In this regard, the Panel in EC-Biotech stated that "to the extent the requirement in the consolidated law is applied for one of the purposes enumerated in Annex A(1), it may be properly viewed as a measure which falls to be assessed under the SPS Agreement; to the extent it is applied for a purpose which is not covered by Annex A(1), it may be viewed as a separate measure which falls to be assessed under a WTO Agreement other than the SPS Agreement".[617] The Panel's "view is premised on the circumstance that the requirement at issue could be split up into two separate requirements which would be identical to the requirement at issue, and which would have an autonomous raison d'être, *i.e.*, a different purpose which would provide an independent basis for imposing the requirement". It follows that some objectives of a measure can fall within the definition of the SPS, while others fall within the TBT Agreement (and the GATT).

However, a requirement that is found to comply with the definition of an SPS measure is automatically excluded from the scope of the TBT Agreement.[618] Lastly, the provisions of the TBT Agreement apply to all products, including industrial and agricultural products.[619] While there is no explicit product limitation in the SPS Agreement, the latter has in principle a narrower coverage than the TBT Agreement, with the understanding however that the objective of the measure is a decisive criterion in its qualification as an SPS measure.

As far as the personal scope is concerned, although WTO Agreements are fundamentally binding for government bodies, the TBT Agreement

---

613 Idem.

614 Committee on Technical Barriers to Trade 2000, para. 27.

615 Committee on Technical Barriers to Trade 2000, para. 28.

616 Panel Report, EC- Trademarks and Geographical Indications (Australia), para. 7.512–7.513.

617 Panel Report, EC-Biotech, para. 7.165.

618 TBT Agreement, Article 1.5.

619 TBT Agreement, Article 1.3.

acknowledges the role of local government bodies and non-governmental bodies in the preparation, adoption and application of technical regulations and standards. With regard to technical regulations, Members are responsible for ensuring that local government bodies and non-governmental bodies comply with the general obligations of the TBT Agreement, with the exception of rules on notification. For this purpose, WTO Members shall formulate and implement positive measures and mechanisms in favour of compliance and must avoid taking measures that would require or encourage local government bodies and non-governmental bodies to act inconsistently with the TBT Agreement.[620]

As regards standards, WTO Members must ensure acceptance and compliance by their central government standardising body with the Code of Good Practice for the Preparation, Adoption and Application of Standards laid down in Annex 3 to the TBT Agreement. Acceptance and compliance must also be ensured in case one or more bodies within the territory of a WTO Member are also members of national local government and non-governmental standardising bodies or regional standardising bodies.[621]

WTO Members' responsibilities for the implementation of the TBT Agreement are also extended by Articles 7 and 8 to local government bodies and non-governmental bodies within their territories. This implies that WTO Members must adopt policies that would ensure or support the observance of conformity assessment procedures by these bodies other than central government bodies. WTO Members must also refrain from adopting policies that would require or encourage local government bodies and non-governmental bodies to act inconsistently with Members' obligations vis-à-vis conformity with technical regulations and standards. As regards conformity assessment procedures, central government bodies shall rely on the assessment procedures operated by non-governmental bodies only if there is assurance that the latter satisfy relevant provisions of the TBT Agreement.

Lastly, the TBT temporal application issue was settled in the EC-Sardines case. In this regard, the Panel held that Article 2.4 "applies to measures that were adopted before 1 January 1995 but which have not ceased to exist".[622] Following the same logic, the Appellate Body held that excluding existing technical regulations from the obligations set out in Article 2.4 would undermine the important role of international standards in furthering the objectives of the

620 TBT Agreement, Articles 3.4 and 3.5. It is worth mentioning that the trade issues related to private standards will not be addressed in this research due to a lack of reliance on these standards in Benin's shrimp sector.

621 It is worth noting that the non-acceptance of the Code of Good Practice by a standardising body does not exonerate a Member State from its obligation to aim at the compliance of the standardising body with the Code of Good Practice (Article 4.1). Furthermore, when a standardising body accepts and complies with the Code of Good Practice, it must be considered as complying with the principles of the TBT Agreement (Article 4.2).

622 Panel Report, EC-Sardines, para. 7.60.

TBT Agreement related to harmonisation, trade facilitation and improvement of the efficiency of production.[623] Such interpretations could find support in Article 15.2 which provides that "each Member shall, promptly after the date on which the Agreement enters into force for it, inform the Committee of measures in existence or taken to ensure the implementation and administration of the Agreement". The TBT Committee stressed that such statements could assist Members "in meeting their obligations under the Agreement, by enabling them to take stock of their existing legislation and institutional structure for the implementation and administration of the Agreement".[624]

It is important to note that Article 2.4 lays down the harmonisation obligation under the TBT Agreement. Article 2.4 states that "where technical regulations are required and relevant international standards exist or their completion is imminent, Members shall use them, or the relevant parts of them, as a basis for their technical regulations except when such international standards or relevant parts would be an ineffective or inappropriate means for the fulfilment of the legitimate objectives pursued". Article 2.4, which has been considered by the Appellate Body as a "central provision of the TBT Agreement"[625], applies not only to the "preparation and adoption" of technical regulations but also to the "application" of existing measures adopted prior to 1 January 1995. This requires that WTO Members, in their decision-making process with regard to a new TBT measure or an existing one, must seek international standards that might be wholly or partially relevant for the product or measure under consideration. The existence of a relevant international standard obliges the WTO Member to base its measure on this standard, except in cases where the latter is found ineffective or inappropriate for the Member's objective. Article 2.4 extends the same obligation to an international standard the adoption of which is imminent. In such an instance, the WTO Member must equally use the 'imminent' international standard as a basis for its new or revised TBT measure. The Panel in EC-Sardines, later supported by the Appellate Body, upheld that "the word 'imminent', the ordinary meaning of which is 'likely to happen without delay', is not intended to limit the scope of the coverage of technical regulations to the ones that have yet to be adopted. Rather, the use of the word 'imminent' means that WTO Members cannot disregard a relevant international standard whose completion is imminent with respect to their existing technical regulations".[626] From this angle, Article 2.4 established a "continuing obligation for existing measures", referring to "technical regulations generally and without limitations".[627]

623 Appellate Body Report, EC-Sardines, para. 215.
624 Committee on Technical Barriers to Trade, 2000, para. 6.
625 Appellate Body Report, EC-Sardines, para. 208.
626 Panel Report, EC-Sardines, para. 7.74.
627 Appellate Body Report, EC-Sardines, para. 205.

b. General obligations

The TBT Agreement lays down obligations for Members with regard to the preparation, adoption and application of technical regulations with respect to their central government bodies, as well as local government and non-governmental bodies. Most provisions are structured in a way to contribute to the avoidance of unnecessary obstacles to trade and the elimination of arbitrary and discriminatory treatment.

Article 2.1 states that, in respect of technical regulations, Members shall ensure that "products imported from the territory of any Member shall be accorded treatment no less favorable than that accorded to like products of national origin and to like products originating in any other country". Appropriately applied, this requirement must avert undue discrimination by preserving the competitive opportunities of products originating in any Member.[628]

It appears as underlined by the Panel in EC-Sardines that the TBT Agreement, like the GATT, accords a degree of deference with respect to domestic policy objectives which Members wish to pursue but, at the same time, shows less deference to the means which Members choose to employ to achieve their domestic policy goals.[629] It is worth noting that the second sentence of Article 2.5 established that, whenever a technical regulation is prepared, adopted or applied for one of the legitimate objectives explicitly mentioned in Article 2.2 and is in accordance with relevant international standards, it shall be a rebuttable presumption that it does not create an unnecessary obstacle to international trade.

Article 2.4 of the TBT Agreement requires Members to use existing international standards or those whose completion is imminent, or relevant parts of them, as a basis for their technical regulations. In case of a supposed violation of this provision, the complaining Member seeking the ruling of inconsistency has the burden of proof. This requires proving that the alleged international standard has not been used as a basis for the challenged regulation and that it was effective and appropriate to fulfil the legitimate objectives pursued by that regulation.[630]

As further established by Article 2.4, departing from international standards is allowed when the standards are an ineffective or inappropriate means for the fulfilment of the legitimate objectives pursued. As explained by the Panel in EC-Sardines, "an ineffective means is a means which does not have the function of accomplishing the legitimate objective pursued, whereas an inappropriate means is a means which is not specially suitable for the fulfilment of the

628 Panel Report, US-Tuna II (Mexico), para. 7.456.
629 Panel Report, EC- Sardines, para. 7.120.
630 Appellate Body Report, EC-Sardines, para. 275.

legitimate objective pursued". The Panel further clarified that 'effectiveness' must be examined with regard to the results of the means employed, while 'appropriateness' relates more to the nature of the means.[631]

At another level, WTO Members must ensure that the maintenance of technical regulations is consistent with the conditions that gave rise to their adoption. If the circumstances or objectives no longer exist, or in the event they can be addressed in a less trade-restrictive manner, Article 2.3 requires Members not to maintain the relevant technical regulations. This requirement puts on Members an ongoing obligation to reassess their technical regulations so as to eliminate or amend them with regard to the evolution of the circumstances and objectives underlying the regulations.[632]

To further prevent obstacles to trade, WTO Members are required by Article 2.8 to specify, wherever appropriate, their technical regulations based on product requirements in terms of performance rather than design or descriptive characteristics. Such an approach leaves maximum freedom to technical development[633] and prevents "the creation of unnecessary obstacles to trade by requiring that products requirements be laid down in functional terms".[634] In case a dispute arises, the complainant carries the burden of demonstrating that it would be appropriate to specify a particular technical regulation in terms of 'performance', rather than in terms of design or descriptive characteristics.[635]

With regard to standards, the Code of Good Practice for the preparation, adoption and application of standards (hereinafter Code of Good Practice) in Annex 3 of the TBT Agreement occupies a central position. Article 4.1 of the TBT Agreement states that Members shall ensure that their central government standardising bodies, the local government and non-governmental standardising bodies within their territories as well as the regional standardising bodies, of which they or one or more of the bodies within their territories are members, accept and comply with the Code of Good Practice. Pursuant to Annex 3(B), the Code of Good Practice "is open to acceptance by any standardizing body within the territory of a WTO Member, whether a central government body, a local government body, or a non-governmental body; to any governmental

631 Panel Report, EC-Sardines, para. 7.116. It results that an inappropriate means may still be an effective means. Likewise, a relevant international standard found to be effective does not automatically qualify as an appropriate means. This view was also confirmed by the Appellate Body which stated that the two words have different meanings. Therefore, it is conceptually possible that an effective measure is inappropriate and an appropriate measure is ineffective (See Appellate Body Report, EC-Sardines, para. 289).

632 Panel Report, EC-Sardines, para. 7.81. The Panel also emphasised that this obligation equally applies to technical regulations enacted before the entry into force of the TBT Agreement.

633 ISO/IEC Directives 2004.

634 Panel Report, US – Clove Cigarettes, paras. 7.481–7.482.

635 Panel Report, US – Clove Cigarettes, paras. 7.490. Note that in this dispute the Panel, following the approach developed in several other cases (for example EC-Sardines, EC-Tube and Pipe Fittings), defined 'appropriate' as 'proper', 'fitting', or 'suitable'.

regional standardizing body one or more members of which are Members of the WTO; and to any non-governmental regional standardizing body one or more Members of which are situated within the territory of a Member of the WTO". In case of acceptance of the Code of Good Practice, the TBT Agreement provides a presumption of compliance in its Article 4.2 that stipulates: "Standardizing bodies that have accepted and are complying with the Code of Good Practice shall be acknowledged by the Members as complying with the principles of this Agreement".

Substantively, the Code of Good Practice contains obligations these standardising bodies are under while preparing, adopting or applying standards. In this regard, the standardising body shall accord no less favourable treatment to products originating in the territory of any other WTO Member than that accorded to like products of national origin and to like products originating in any other country.[636] Likewise, the standardising body shall ensure that standards are not prepared, adopted or applied with a view to, or with the effect of, creating unnecessary obstacles to international trade.[637] Just like with technical regulations, international standards or their relevant parts are to be used as a basis for standards, except when they would reveal ineffective or inappropriate.[638] Standardisation bodies within a territory shall attempt to avoid duplication and overlap and shall also make every effort to achieve a national consensus on the standards they develop. In the same way, a regional standardising body shall make every effort to avoid duplication of, or overlap with, the work of relevant international standardising bodies.[639] Wherever appropriate, the standards shall be specified based on product requirements in terms of performance rather than design or descriptive characteristics.[640] Standardising bodies shall also comply with transparency obligations and publish at least once every six months about the standards it has adopted and the ones that are being prepared.[641] Furthermore, before a standard is adopted, the standardising body shall allow a period of at least 60 days for the submission of comments on the draft standard by interested parties within the territory of a Member of the WTO and take these comments into account in the further processing of the standard.[642]

As regards conformity assessment, in cases where a positive assurance of conformity with technical regulations and standards is required, Members shall ensure that their central government bodies prepare, adopt and apply their conformity assessment procedures in a non-discriminatory manner. This entails

636 TBT Agreement, Annex 3(D).
637 TBT Agreement, Annex 3(E).
638 TBT Agreement, Annex 3(F).
639 TBT Agreement, Annex 3(H).
640 TBT Agreement, Annex 3(I).
641 TBT Agreement, Annex 3(J).
642 TBT Agreement, Annex 3(L) & (N).

fair access for products originating in other Members with no less favourable conditions than those accorded to national suppliers or suppliers from any other countries and the avoidance of unnecessary obstacles to international trade. Care must be taken to ensure speed, transparency, equal treatment with regard to requests and confidentiality of information and the application of fees for the procedures. Also, Members must ensure that a procedure exists to review complaints concerning the operation of a conformity assessment procedure and to take corrective action when a complaint is justified.[643]

Members must make sure that their central government bodies use existing or imminent relevant guides or recommendations issued by international standardising bodies, or the relevant parts of them, as a basis for their conformity assessment procedures, except where, as duly explained upon request, such guides or recommendations or relevant parts are inappropriate for the Members concerned.[644] Members must also participate within the limits of their resources in the preparation by appropriate international standardising bodies of guides and recommendations for conformity assessment procedures with a view to achieving harmonisation on as wide a basis as possible.[645] When harmonisation becomes unfeasible because relevant international guides or recommendations do not exist, or in cases that the technical content of a proposed conformity assessment procedure is not in accordance with relevant international guides and recommendations, Members must ensure the early publication of such conformity assessment procedures when the latter may have a significant effect on the trade of other Members. Likewise, the products to be covered by these procedures, as well as a brief indication of their objective and rationale, shall be notified, through the Secretariat, early enough to enable comments and amendments.[646] Adopted conformity assessment procedures must be promptly published or made available to interested parties in other Members.[647]

7.3. LEVELLING DIFFERENCES THROUGH REGULATORY COOPERATION

There is now general acceptance that countries must cooperate to alleviate trade barriers in order to facilitate international trade. Regulatory cooperation becomes imperative due to the strong extra-territorial implications of national regulations and the increased awareness that the achievement of some national policy objectives might depend on careful consideration of the international

[643] TBT Agreement, Article 5.2.8.
[644] TBT Agreement, Article 5.4.
[645] TBT Agreement, Article 5.5.
[646] TBT Agreement, Article 5.6.
[647] TBT Agreement, Article 5.8.

context.[648] This need for coordinated activities, often referred to as regulatory rapprochement[649], entails a number of strategies that can be assimilated to a spectrum that begins with no rapprochement, moves to coordination[650], then to mutual recognition, and finally to the strongest level of rapprochement, harmonization.[651]

A 'no rapprochement' situation would perpetuate regulatory divergences among trading partners that would inevitably result in impediments to trade. Regulatory divergences obstruct imports and exports, create inefficiencies and increase costs for international business.[652] From the perspective of trade liberalisation, a global market functioning on a 'no rapprochement' basis would be the least preferred regulatory option. In such a context, information and adaptation costs would be very high[653] and destroy every incentive to trade at a global level.

7.3.1. REGULATORY COORDINATION

Regulatory coordination, sometimes referred to as alignment, is "the gradual narrowing of relevant differences between regulatory systems, often based on voluntary international codes of practice".[654] Coordination is a broad range of weak forms of rapprochement. The WTO approach to regulatory coordination includes international standard-setting, regulatory notification activities and bilateral dispute settlement.[655]

The success of regulatory alignment depends upon the quality of the international standard-setting system. The better the system works, the more useful the resultant standards will be in addressing unnecessary trade barriers.[656] Article 3.4 of the SPS Agreement states that Members shall play a full part, within the limits of their resources, in the relevant international organisations and their subsidiary bodies to promote within these organisations the development and periodic review of standards, guidelines and recommendations with respect to all aspects of SPS measures. Likewise, Article 2.6 of the TBT Agreement encourages Members' participation in the preparation by appropriate

648 OECD 2013, p86.
649 Caswell & Hooker 1996, p776.
650 Caswell & Hooker 1996, p775–776.
651 Caswell & Hooker 1996, p776.
652 Alemanno 2013, p3.
653 Moeniws 1999, p22. Information costs refer to costs incurred in research about the technical specifications and preferences of the importer. Adaptation costs are those engaged to modify domestic products to adapt them to the foreign market.
654 Hooker & Caswell 1999, p235.
655 Kastner & Douglas 2002, p290.
656 Wijkström & McDaniels 2013, p16.

international standardising bodies of international standards for products for which they either have adopted, or expect to adopt, technical regulations.

However, these provisions result in obligations for Members with regard to the standards developed by the international standard-setting bodies rather than with regard to their standard-setting procedures. These international bodies adopt standards according to their own procedures, which are not influenced by the WTO.

Members' cooperation in SPS and TBT Committees could contribute to regulatory convergence with regard to international harmonisation. These committees are forums that enable the discussion of Members' Specific Trade Concerns (STCs) in the context of disputes or trade negotiations and offer the opportunity to strengthen the implementation of the Agreements. Article 12 of the SPS Agreement entrusted the SPS Committee with various tasks with the regard to implementation of international harmonisation. For this purpose, the SPS Committee shall encourage the use of international standards, guidelines or recommendations by all Members by sponsoring technical consultation and study. The SPS Committee shall maintain close contact with the relevant international organisations and develop a procedure to monitor the process of international harmonisation and the use of international standards, guidelines or recommendations. These activities would increase coordination and integration between international and national systems and secure the best available scientific and technical advice for the administration of the SPS Agreement in order to avoid unnecessary duplication of effort.[657] The SPS Committee could also use the information generated by procedures of relevant international organisations to avoid duplication.[658] Lastly, pursuant to Article 12.6, the SPS Committee may, on the basis of an initiative from one Member, invite relevant international organisations or their subsidiary bodies to examine specific matters with respect to a particular standard, guideline or recommendation.

The TBT Committee has also served as a forum where Members' delegations can discuss specific trade concerns about particular laws, regulations or procedures that affect their trade, as well as implementation-related issues. In this way, its activity has equally covered international standards. About one third of all STCs raised in the TBT Committee are associated with international standards.[659]

It is worth mentioning that the work of the SPS and TBT Committees provide an opportunity for consultations in a transparent, multilateral setting of both a formal and/or informal nature. These discussions have in some cases

657 TBT Agreement, Articles 12.3 and 12.4.
658 TBT Agreement, Article 12.5.
659 Wijkström & McDaniels 2013, p5.

effectively facilitated the resolution of – or diffused at an early stage – issues arising between Members.[660]

7.3.2. EQUIVALENCE

a. Equivalence in the SPS Agreement

Despite the virtues of harmonisation and irrespective of Members' efforts to achieve this goal as far as possible, legitimate reasons can still justify differences in standards across countries. These differences could result from disparities in social objectives and priorities, in resource endowments or differences in the political economy of decision making, as well as the involvement of stakeholder groups in the policy process.[661] Moreover, differences in standards could also simply result from differences in climatic conditions. These factors can lead to a diversity of sanitary measures across countries, without necessarily inducing less protection with regard to health risks.

In reality, differentiation is a necessary part of any risk-based food safety system.[662] Therefore, the recognition of equivalence is an important provision for the levelling of differences in the regulatory regimes of Members, especially when structural conditions do not enable harmonisation or in the absence of international standards.

Equivalence can be defined as the acceptance of regulatory diversity in meeting common goals.[663] Equivalence appears to be the best alternative to reconcile the gaps resulting from the impossibility to harmonise in given circumstances. Under these conditions, the SPS and the TBT Agreements encourage Members to accept differing measures as equivalent to their own. The implementation of this cooperation at the international level would contribute to reduce the impact of regulatory differences among countries, thereby enabling a better regulatory convergence.

Article 4 of the SPS Agreement stipulates that Members shall enter into consultations with their counterparts, upon their request, "with the aim of achieving bilateral and multilateral agreements on recognition of the equivalence of specified sanitary or phytosanitary measures".[664] The exporting Member must provide reasonable access to the importing Member for inspection, testing and other relevant procedures for the recognition of equivalence. The equivalence may relate to specific measures about a product or categories of products, but it

660 WTO Agreements Series 2014, p29.
661 Hobbs 2010, p138.
662 Jaffee & Henson 2004, p3.
663 Hooker & Caswell 1999, p235.
664 SPS Agreement, Article 4.

can also be agreed upon a systems-wide basis, for instance systems of control or inspection.

In its work, the SPS Committee came up with some guiding principles to compensate the lack of clarity with regard to a time limit for the process of the recognition of equivalence.[665] Thus, the main guiding principles of the process of determining equivalence should be gradualness, reciprocity, non-discrimination and special consideration of historical trade. In the same way, the option of immediate eligibility for equivalence of low-risk products was suggested.[666] Furthermore, if, under normal circumstances, a procedure of recognition of equivalence should not exceed six months, historical trade ties between exporting and importing countries must lighten and accelerate the process. This alleviation is based on the confidence resulting from the familiarity the importing country acquired of the infrastructure and measures of the exporting country. Essentially, relevant information relates to the knowledge and confidence in the competent authority of the exporting Member, the existence of an evaluation and recognition of the product-related system of inspection and certification of the exporting Member and the available scientific information supporting the request for the recognition of equivalence.[667] To avoid discrimination, the determination of equivalence must be based on the measure or system actually enforced by the importing Member instead of theoretical and abstract regulations deriving from very high sanitary goals that are not implemented in practice.[668]

The establishment of an equivalence agreement does not interfere with the normal process of control of the importing Member. Necessary product control and sampling prior to marketing can still be conducted consistently. In that respect, in the event of emergency health problems, existing import prohibitions or similar measures shall apply without prejudice to the existence of equivalence agreements.[669]

---

665 All Members are encouraged to collaborate with the SPS Committee for the purpose of the implementation of the equivalence provision. The SPS committee developed guidelines on a number of issues related to equivalence. For instance, the SPS Committee came up in 2001 with the notification of the successful conclusion of bilateral equivalence agreements or arrangements, as well as information on countries' experience with regard to equivalence (Committee on Sanitary and Phytosanitary Measures, 2001a, para. 12). In the same spirit, the SPS Committee called for the development of guidance on the judgment of equivalence, which shall be entrusted to the Codex Alimentarius Commission (Committee on Sanitary and Phytosanitary Measures, 2001, para. 10). The Codex Alimentarius was prompt in satisfying that demand. In 2003, it adopted its guidelines on the judgment of equivalence (See Codex Alimentarius Commission, 2003). The guidelines should be read in conjunction with other relevant Codex texts, including in particular the Guidelines for the Development of Equivalence Agreements Regarding Food Import and Export Inspection and Certification Systems, CAC/GL 34–1999.

666 Committee on Sanitary and Phytosanitary Measures 2001b, para. 17.

667 Committee on Sanitary and Phytosanitary Measures 2004b, para. 5.

668 Committee on Sanitary and Phytosanitary Measures 2001b, annex para. 3.

669 Committee on Sanitary and Phytosanitary Measures 2001b, para. 18.

The recognition of equivalence must also be implemented within the spirit of Article 9 of the SPS Agreement, which requires technical assistance for developing countries Members. In the current situation, this assistance may, *inter alia*, aim at helping an exporting Member to identify and implement potential equivalent measures or measures likely to enhance market competitiveness.[670] Moreover, the recognition of equivalence may provide an opportunity for technical learning and assistance through the close cooperation and exchange of information. It requires close cooperation from both sides to enable its achievement.[671] In this regard, while the exporting Member's regulatory authorities gain more expertise about the regulatory systems of the importing Member, the officials of the importing Member gain familiarity with the regulatory system of the exporting Member and may learn alternative approaches to risk regulation.[672]

b. *Equivalence in the TBT Agreement*

Equivalence in the TBT Agreement is different from equivalence in the SPS Agreement due to the differentiation between technical regulations/standards and conformity assessment procedures. Thus, equivalence and mutual recognition can apply to technical regulations/standards and to inspection results, test reports and certificates of conformity issued by accredited laboratories in exporting countries.

Article 2.7 requires Members to give positive consideration to accepting as equivalent to their own technical regulations of other Members, even if these regulations differ from their own. This provision applies only in cases Members "are satisfied" that the foreign regulations adequately fulfil the objectives of their own regulations. It thus appears that, rather than putting an emphasis on the appropriate level of protection of the importing Member like in the SPS Agreement, the approach to equivalence in the TBT Agreement aims at equivalence with regard to the objectives of the regulation.

Similarly, whenever possible, results of conformity assessment procedures in other Members shall be accepted as equivalent, even when they are different, provided that Members are satisfied they offer an assurance of conformity with their own procedures.[673] Such recognition of equivalence might follow consultations enabling a mutually satisfactory understanding regarding, in particular, adequate and enduring technical competence of the relevant conformity assessment bodies in the exporting Member. This process aims at verifying compliance to ensure confidence in the continued reliability of their

670 Committee on Sanitary and Phytosanitary Measures 2001a, para. 8.
671 Prévost 2009, p751.
672 Idem.
673 TBT Agreement, Article 6.1.

results, for example by means of accreditation. The prior verification must also lead to the limitation of the acceptance of conformity assessment results to those produced by designated bodies in the exporting Member.[674] Accreditation with relevant guides or recommendations issued by international standardising bodies is an indication of adequate technical competence.

Furthermore, in Article 6.3, Members are encouraged, at the request of other Members, to be willing to enter into negotiations for the conclusion of agreements for the mutual recognition of results of each other's conformity assessment procedures. Commonly called Mutual Recognition Agreements (MRAs), these agreements can be negotiated with respect to specific regulations or can simply be voluntary arrangements between domestic and foreign conformity assessment bodies. Effective MRAs must take into consideration various criteria including a sound regulatory infrastructure, a sufficient volume of trade in specific sectors between the parties involved, tangible economic benefits; interest of stakeholders; support from key players; underlying compatibility in the regulatory systems of the potential MRA parties; and sufficient resources for MRA negotiation and implementation.[675] Where there are differences in the technical competence of the parties to a MRA, it might be convenient to resort to a step-by-step approach which could involve technical cooperation to obtain mutual benefits.[676]

c. *SPS and TBT equivalence principles in practice*

The most significant advantage of the equivalence principle is to facilitate trade while still allowing Members to preserve their regulatory autonomy. However, the approach to equivalence is decisive for the effective realisation of this advantage. For example, the choice for a product-related equivalence could allow flexibility to exporting Members, while systems-based equivalence would be more intrusive and costly to demonstrate.

From a practical perspective, problems arise essentially with regard to process standards since performance standards are easier to compare because they stipulate observable and/or testable attributes of finished products. However, process standards are necessary for the management of microbial risks inherent in products such as seafood, which makes it quite beneficial to seek equivalence in their markets.[677] However, there is a challenge related not only to the equivalence of different process standards themselves but also on how compliance with different standards is ascertained. As far as enforcement is concerned, there is more discretion with regard to process standards than

[674] TBT Agreement, Article 6.1.2.
[675] Committee on Technical Barriers to Trade 2003, para. 39.
[676] Idem.
[677] Roberts & Unnevehr 2005 p489.

performance standards, particularly due to the divergence of opinions between countries about institutional capacity and integrity.[678] The principle of equivalence is implemented differently across countries in accordance with their particular policy choices.

1° The EU approach to equivalence

In the view of the EU, the selection of the right instrument with regard to trade facilitation measures "will depend on the characteristics of the markets, the regulatory environment in the third country or region concerned and the willingness on the part of industries, regulators and other parties to achieve the agreed objectives.[679] Based on its own experience, the EU focussed on judgments of the equivalence of regulatory systems, particularly food inspection and certification systems, including conformity assessment procedures, which could lead to a further determination of equivalence for a wide variety of product standards and regulations.[680] Therefore, in practice, the EU does not have one approach to equivalence but many approaches, depending on the sectors and products involved. Equivalence assessments of the EU have been more used for sanitary measures, the core objective of which is health protection, than for technical regulations and standards for which a whole range of objectives are involved.[681]

In the fishery sector, the EU approach to equivalence is largely applied on a unilateral basis. In this way, the EU undertakes on its own initiative to evaluate the inspection and certification systems of exporting countries so as to determine whether they could be deemed equivalent to that of the EU.[682] The principle of equivalence in the fishery sector was already applied with Directive 91/493/EEC in which Article 10 stipulated that "provisions applied to imports of fishery products from third countries shall be at least equivalent to those governing the production and placing on the market of Community products". Currently, the principle is reflected in the General Food Law in Article 11, which stipulates that "food and feed imported into the Community for placing on the market within the Community shall comply with the relevant requirements of food law or conditions recognized by the Community to be at least equivalent thereto..." The EU underlines in a submission to the SPS Committee that Directive 91/493/EEC is intended to describe the system rather than the individual measures, and the EU approach has always emphasised the prerequisite need for an equivalent system before considering product equivalence.[683] This translates in practice into

678 Idem.
679 Commission of the European Communities 2001, p22.
680 Veggeland 2006, p53.
681 Veggeland 2006, p20.
682 Veggeland 2006, p50.
683 Committee on Sanitary and Phytosanitary Measures 2002d, p2.

a clear focus of the EU work on equivalence determinations on different aspects of food inspection and certifications systems.[684]

Based on compliance with EU food regulations, the successful completion of the one-way equivalence judgment leads to EU approval whereby the country concerned is placed on the list of approved countries. This approach tends to lighten the administrative burden and the costs related to the procedure for many countries. On-spot visits of EU experts provide an opportunity for an exporting country to prepare in advance to make available within a short period the documents required by the experts to assess the compliance of its systems with EU requirements.[685] In addition, it enables a clear emphasis on the shortcomings of the system in place in the exporting country, facilitating an improved focus on undertaking remedial measures.

More importantly, this one-way assessment of equivalence is beneficial for countries like Benin that are impaired by their lack of financial means and adequate expertise. On the one hand, it provides them with an opportunity to circumvent the burden of proof laid down in Article 4 of the SPS Agreement. In this regard, equivalence can only be granted by the importing country upon the objective demonstration by the exporting Member State that the implementation of its measures can lead to the attainment of the appropriate level of protection of the importing country.

Providing scientific evidence to satisfy this requirement could be extremely complex in a context where an exporting country is lacking the capacity to conduct a risk assessment to support its own domestic measures. The SPS Agreement did not stipulate any formal requirement for the 'objective demonstration' by the exporting Member. The SPS Committee later established that the exporting Member should give appropriate science-based and technical information to support its claim. In so doing, the exporting Member may refer to relevant international standards or risk assessments undertaken by the importing Member or another WTO Member. Although this provision might solve a dilemma for many countries, it does not entirely solve the burden of proof issue. A risk assessment is mostly context-dependent, and there must still be sufficient domestic expertise in the exporting country to adapt a 'ready-for-use risk assessment' to its own circumstances so that the subsequent measure would validly enable the attainment of the importing Member State's appropriate level of protection.

Beyond the apparent complexity of the burden of proof, the lack of clarity surrounding the level of protection of importing countries seems to be a greater

684 Veggeland 2006, p20.

685 In fact, for the EU itself, this method provides more reliability than a mere documentary assessment of the food control system, as previously carried out for many countries under Directive 91/493/EEC. This procedure would also involve much correspondence and a lengthy negotiation for third countries.

stumbling block in the process of the recognition of equivalence.[686] To better tackle this issue, an SPS Committee decision further elaborated on the subject so as to facilitate the implementation of the equivalence provision on the request of the exporting Member. Therefore, the importing Member is expected to explain the objective and rationale of its SPS measure and clearly identify the associated risks. Moreover, the importing Member should indicate the appropriate level of protection targeted by the measure, by providing evidence of the risk assessment conducted prior to the measure or a technical justification based on a relevant international standard, guideline or recommendation. Going even a step further, the SPS Committee's decision requires the importing Member to also provide any additional information that may assist the exporting Member in providing an objective demonstration of the equivalence of its own measure.[687]

On the other hand, although the TBT Agreement does not link equivalence to an appropriate level of protection, it does stipulate that an importing Member would grant equivalence only when it was satisfied that the foreign regulations adequately fulfil the objectives of its own regulations. Within this logic, it is quite obvious that an exporting country cannot provide evidence to support the achievement of a fictitious objective. Clearly defining the objectives of TBT regulations is therefore of paramount importance to ensure the practicality of the equivalence provision.

The EU itself has emphasised that, although it considers the recognition of equivalence with regard to the TBT Agreement a potentially powerful tool and a valuable instrument of trade facilitation, the complexity of the process could undermine its applicability. This complexity relates to many factors. First, the objectives of a regulation have to be clearly defined sector by sector, then an agreement must be reached on their equivalence and finally on their mutual acceptability. Secondly, any substantial revision or updating (for example, to take account of technical progress) would likely lead to a new determination and recognition of equivalence.[688]

In the same way, the EU identified that certain conditions must be fulfilled to facilitate the establishment of the TBT equivalence. First, the objectives of the technical regulations must be similar, if not identical, because a radical difference would render the determination of equivalence impossible and even harmonization would prove unfeasible. These objectives can be set out explicitly or they can be inferred from the regulations. Secondly, the regulations at one side should be able to meet the regulatory objectives of the other side and vice versa. Lastly, both parties must have confidence in the conformity assessment

686 Jayasuriya et al. 2006, p2. In this regard, developed countries also do have some practical difficulties. The US, for example, emphasised the inherent difficulties of linking SPS measures to the importers' appropriate level of protection. See Committee on Sanitary and Phytosanitary Measures 2000b.

687 Committee on Sanitary and Phytosanitary Measures 2001a, para. 2.

688 Commission of the European Communities 2001, p12.

infrastructure of each other, in terms of the technical competence, honesty, impartiality, and independence of the conformity assessment bodies.[689] In the context of the one-way assessment of equivalence, it is essentially the EU which seeks to ensure that it has enough confidence in the conformity assessment systems of the exporting country.[690]

It is worth mentioning that there is a complexity resulting from the frequent intertwining of the descriptive characteristics of technical measures and the regulatory objectives, which are not always specified.[691] Therefore, TBT equivalence potentially involves a more complicated process of identifying both legitimate objectives and parameters that can be used for comparison.[692]

In any event, in the context of the one-way assessment of the EU, the main steps to establish the 'ability to satisfy' either the appropriate level of SPS measures or the objectives of TBT regulations would be made by the EU, assuming the importing country provides necessary information.

In spite of the differences in approaches in both agreements, it is quite noticeable that none of them lay clear procedural rules leading to the establishment of equivalence. Neither the SPS Agreement nor the TBT Agreement places any obligation on WTO Members to reach an equivalence agreement with regard to their different domestic regulations. On the one hand, Article 4.2 of the SPS Agreement simply requires Members to 'enter into consultations upon request' with the aim of establishing equivalence. Although

689 Idem.

690 It is worth noting that the EU applied stricter rules for the conclusion of MRAs. Thus, the EU chose to establish MRAs only with governments of third countries, which are on a comparable level of technical development as the EU and moreover have a comparable approach concerning conformity assessment (European Commission, 2000, p63). As underlined by Veggeland (2006), MRAs presuppose the existence of a comparable level regarding the protection of health, safety, environment or other public interests. Unlike equivalence, EU's MRAs are based on the recognition of conformity assessment procedures instead of the acceptance of the equivalence of technical regulations, standards, or legislation. Yet, MRAs may pave the way for a more harmonised system of standardisation and certifications and more regulatory coherence and transparency between the involved parties. The EU has identified a number of important points with regard to the prospects of and difficulties in applying comprehensive MRAs and equivalence agreements. They refer *inter alia* to trade volume, political salience and political will, the level of development, political institutions and regulatory frameworks, and the need to balance the agreements. First, due to the cost-intensive character of the procedures there must be a substantial volume of trade to motivate them and they must be able to generate some returns either of an economic nature or rather of a political nature. Second, in cases economic gains from MRAs and equivalence agreements are not significant, political returns might be an extra incentive, and sometimes a prerequisite, for entering into negotiations. Third, there must exist in both countries a sufficient infrastructure and regulatory capacity to sustain the agreements. Fourth, it is important to consider organisational asymmetry and divergent regulatory cultures in the processes due to their potential to negatively impact the implementation of the agreements. Last, trade agreements should include sectors and products that are of interest to both parties.

691 Elvestad 2002, p17.

692 Idem.

lacking procedural rules, the SPS Agreement requires Members to accept equivalence in case the exporting Member objectively demonstrates the ability of its measures to attain the appropriate level of the importing country. Therefore, if this condition is fulfilled, there is an implicit obligation for the importing country to grant recognition of equivalence to the exporting country. However, the 'objective demonstration' is in itself quite challenging for most developing countries, and they must really have enough confidence in their regulatory systems to engage in such a process. Formal recognition of equivalence is equally challenging for developed countries. According to the SPS Committee, the weaker requirement in Article 4.2, as compared to that in Article 4.1, attests to the difficulty of negotiating formal equivalence agreements, as opposed to the *ad hoc* recognition of equivalence with respect to specific products or measures. This burdensome nature of procedures for the recognition of equivalence is particularly the case for formal equivalence agreements. Some importing Members, such as the US, are of the opinion that "the negotiation of formal equivalence agreements or determinations are too time consuming and resource intensive, imposing administrative burdens on both the importing and the exporting countries, whereas the gains in trade achieved thereby are limited".[693]

On the other hand, Article 2.7 of the TBT Agreement merely encourages Members to 'give positive consideration' to accepting foreign regulations as equivalent to their own. In this way, the equivalence provision in the TBT Agreement seems even weaker than in the SPS Agreement.[694] However, it might be quite helpful for developing countries to seek accreditation and/or participation for instance in inter-laboratories cooperation with prominent laboratories in developed countries to give more credibility to their testing systems.

A quite significant administrative burden related to equivalence determinations tends to undermine the expected benefits.[695] Moreover, diverse concerns are raised as to the real merits of the equivalence principle. Developed countries have informally expressed that the application of the equivalence principle will lead to discriminatory border controls between their products and those under equivalence agreements.[696] To overcome this obstacle, it would have been interesting for most trading partners to enter into equivalence agreements. However, the implementation of the equivalence principle has many difficulties,

---

693 See Committee on Sanitary and Phytosanitary Measures 2000b, para. 16.

694 Despite the constraining factor, Schroder (2011, p142) also underlined the fact that the equivalence in the SPS Agreement relies only on one objective, which is science, makes it easier than equivalence in the TBT Agreement because science is universal. In fact the equivalence assessment of SPS measures seems easier because it addresses only one type of goal related to protection levels that may be easier to harmonise.

695 This involves the evaluation of infrastructure, the overall programme design and implementation, and specific technical requirements. See Roberts & Unnevehr 2005, p491.

696 Hathaway 1999, p253.

and Members have concluded very few formal equivalence agreements. The recognition of equivalence granted by the EU to several countries, including developing countries, as regards their systems of control and inspection for fishery products, is a very notable step forward.

2° Recognition of equivalence: Benin's experience

After the on-spot visit by EU experts in Benin in 2002 to assess the equivalence of standards, it became apparent that a compromise could hardly be found to establish equivalence between the food production and certification systems in the EU and in Benin. First, the system in Benin was too impaired to even leave open the possibility to claim that the shrimp processing in the country or subsequent governmental controls would definitely lead to reasonable safety. Second, the differences between the EU and Benin systems were too extensive and the shortcomings too serious to leave room for reconciliation.

This is particularly relevant considering that recognition of equivalence by the EU has far-reaching consequences. On the one hand, equivalence between the two systems means that a health certificate issued by the Benin's competent authority would attest that an inspection had been performed according to EU requirements and that Benin's shrimps comply with the level of safety required on the EU market. Given the situation in 2002, this outcome was not attainable. On the other hand, the recognition of equivalence by the EU implies a significant reduction of physical controls of Benin's consignments at EU Border Inspection Posts. For example, as a result of the EU approach to recognising the equivalence of inspection and certification systems for fishery products, there was a reduction in the frequency of physical controls from 100% to 50 or 20%, depending on the risk level.[697] However, such alleviation could not be given to Benin at that moment without an inherent risk of allowing potentially unsafe food onto the EU market. Therefore, undertaking regulatory and institutional reforms in Benin was an absolute necessity for it to consider a potential for equivalence afterwards in order to regain access to the EU market.

Undertaking reforms to comply with EU requirements is rather widespread and usual. Many countries, both in Africa and in Asia have made 'adjustments' to their legislation for the purpose of establishing the equivalence that would give access to the EU market. Benin has followed that trend but in a rather different fashion. Due to the huge gaps between its legislation and the legislation of the EU, it was predictable that, unless a radical change occurred in the short-term, the EU would have issued a trade restrictive measure to protect its market from potentially unsafe shrimps from Benin. The regulatory efforts of Benin to cope with the inconsistencies revealed in its shrimp production and certification system, as well as its inability to rapidly set up a satisfactory

[697] Committee on Sanitary and Phytosanitary Measures 2002d, p3.

regulatory framework, led to the transplant of the EU law in its domestic legal order, supposedly due to the EU's influence.[698]

Many developing countries have underlined "that the process of recognition of equivalence is so costly and time-consuming that it is often easier to apply the same measure".[699] Some other developing country Members expressed concerns that instead of recognising the equivalence of differing measures, importing countries push demands for the recognition of equivalence so far that they result in a *de facto* request for the 'duplication' or 'sameness' of measures.[700] But the objective of the equivalence principle is to look for 'likeness' rather than 'sameness' of different rules with regard to some predetermined parameters.[701] However, the push for sameness of foreign rules by importing countries makes the procedure of the recognition of equivalence easier for the importing country because looking for identity in the rules rather than the identity of the effects is the simplest way to evaluate domestic policies.[702] The fact remains that if 'sameness' seems easier to implement than establishing 'equivalence' of different standards, its major disadvantage is to deprive Members of the flexibility in their choice of measures, thereby undermining the effectiveness of the equivalence provision.[703] As underlined by the Codex Alimentarius, one of the benefits of the principle of equivalence for an exporting country is the possibility offered to "employ the most convenient means in its circumstances to achieve the appropriate level of protection of the importing country".[704]

Considering this flexibility, an equivalence assessment is intended to establish the ability of two different measures to achieve the same appropriate level of protection or fulfil the same regulatory objectives. In this way, the recognition of equivalence does not target the harmonisation of measures to facilitate trade, but it could be seen as a means of harmonisation of regulatory objectives and appropriate levels of protection across countries.

7.3.3. HARMONISATION

Harmonisation is broadly defined as the process of making different domestic laws, regulations, principles, or government policies substantially or effectively the same or similar.[705] Annex A of the SPS Agreement clearly defines harmonisation as the establishment, recognition and application of common

---

698 This fact cannot be corroborated by any factual evidence.
699 Jayasuriya et al. 2006, p2.
700 See for example in this regard WTO, Doc. G/SPS/GEN/128, SPS and Developing Countries, Statement by Egypt at the meeting of 7–8 July 1999, para. 2.
701 Veggeland 2006, p2.
702 Mayeda 2004, p755.
703 Prévost 2009, p759.
704 Codex 2003, p1.
705 Mayeda 2004, p740.

sanitary and phytosanitary measures by different WTO Members.[706] One of the goals of the SPS Agreement is to promote the harmonisation of sanitary and phytosanitary measures on as wide a basis as possible so as to reduce the impact of different standards on international trade. For the purpose of harmonisation, Members are encouraged to base their measures on international standards, guidelines or recommendations.[707] As far as food safety is concerned, the standards, guidelines and recommendations established by the Codex Alimentarius Commission relating to food additives, veterinary drug and pesticide residues, contaminants, methods of analysis and sampling, and codes and guidelines of hygienic practice must serve as basis for the purpose of harmonisation.[708] The Codex has extensively worked on food safety related standards, covering areas such as equivalence, risk analysis, or traceability. The relevance of one or more Codex standard(s) for a case under consideration at the WTO is assessed on a case-by-case basis.

Article 3 of the SPS Agreement entitles Members to either base their measures on international standards under Article 3.1 or bring their SPS measures into conformity with international standards under Article 3.2. However, the emphasis on harmonisation must not undermine the right of Members to decide freely their appropriate level of protection. The Appellate Body in EC-Hormones held that the right of a Member to establish its own level of sanitary protection under Article 3.3 is an autonomous right and not an exception from the general harmonisation obligation under Article 3.1.[709] As such, Article 3.3 of the SPS Agreement states that Members may introduce or maintain SPS measures which result in a higher level of sanitary or phytosanitary protection than would be achieved by measures based on the relevant international standards, guidelines or recommendations as a consequence of a Member's appropriate level of protection or in case there is a scientific justification for the stricter measures. The adoption of these more stringent measures is allowed provided that the latter are not inconsistent with any other provision of the SPS Agreement. This provision gives room to Members for flexibility in the implementation of the harmonisation provision. In this regard, Article 3.3 is not an exception to Articles 3.1 and 3.2, but an autonomous right for Members to establish such a higher level of protection.[710]

Although the TBT Agreement does not provide any clear definition of harmonisation, it also requires Members, like in the SPS Agreement, to "use international standards as a basis" for their measures. WTO Members have a strong incentive to aim for the international harmonisation of standards. Promulgation by a Member of a sanitary measure that conforms to international

706 SPS Agreement, Annex A(2).
707 SPS Agreement, Article 3.1.
708 SPS Agreement, Annex A(3-a).
709 Appellate Body Report, EC-Hormones, para. 172.
710 Appellate Body Report, EC-Hormones, para. 104.

standards[711] offers the benefit of a rebuttable presumption of GATT and SPS-consistency for measures based on international standards. Likewise, in the TBT Agreement, when a technical regulation "is in accordance with relevant international standards, it shall be rebuttably presumed not to create an unnecessary obstacle to international trade".[712]

In contrast to the SPS Agreement, the TBT Agreement does not officially recognise any international standard-setting organisation that would serve the purpose of implementing the harmonisation provision. The TBT Committee stated the need to solicit input from a wide range of interests and develop principles that would ensure the quality of international standards. These principles refer to transparency, openness, impartiality and consensus, relevance and effectiveness, coherence and developing countries' interests to clarify and strengthen the concept of international standards under the TBT Agreement so as to contribute to the advancement of its objectives. The principles were developed in relation to the preparation, adoption and application of technical regulations by central government bodies (Article 2), procedures for the assessment of conformity (Article 5), and the Code of good practice for the preparation, adoption and application of standards (Annex 3).[713] In practice, the case-by-case determination of relevance also applies in disputes involving the TBT Agreement. In EC-Sardines, the Appellate Body confirmed the statement of the Panel that the ordinary meaning of the term "relevant" is "bearing upon or relating to the matter in hand; pertinent".[714] Therefore, to be a 'relevant international standard', a standard at issue in a dispute must 'bear upon, relate to, or be pertinent' to the regulation concerned.

Furthermore, Article 2.4 of the TBT Agreement requires the use of relevant international standards but also of 'relevant parts of them' as a basis for

711 An international standard is defined in the ISO/IEC Guide 2 as a standard that is adopted by an international standardisation/standards organisation and made available to the public.

712 TBT Agreement, Article 2.5. The use of international standards is promoted in Article 2.4 which stipulates that "where technical regulations are required and relevant international standards exist or their completion is imminent, Members shall use them, or the relevant parts of them, as a basis for their technical regulations except when such international standards or relevant parts would be an ineffective or inappropriate means for the fulfillment of the legitimate objectives pursued, for instance because of fundamental climatic or geographical factors or fundamental technological problems" (the same requirement is established by Article 5.4 as regards conformity assessment procedures, which also allows the same derogations). Interpreting Article 2.4 in US –Tuna II, the Panel stated that a claim related to this Article must be examined following three elements. First, the existence or imminent completion of a relevant international standard must be examined. Then the analysis should assess whether the international standard has been used as a basis for the technical regulation. Finally, it must be assessed whether the international standard is an ineffective or inappropriate means for the fulfilment of the legitimate objectives pursued (see Panel Report, US- Tuna II (Mexico), para. 7.627).

713 See Committee on Technical Barriers to Trade, 2000, para. 20 and Annex 4.

714 Panel Report, EC-Sardines, para. 7.68.

technical regulations, where the latter are effective and appropriate to meet the WTO Member's objective. It follows that in some instances, an international standard is not relevant in its entirety for the technical regulation at hand. The Appellate Body in EC-Sardines held that the examination of the relevance of the international standard must be limited to the parts that relate to the subject-matter of the challenged prescriptions or requirements. Nevertheless, the examination must be broad enough to cover all the relevant parts since it is not an option for the regulating Member to select only some of the relevant parts of an international standard.[715]

Endorsing harmonisation was meant to circumvent the substantial increase of trade transaction costs resulting from compliance with divergent SPS measures, as repeatedly reported by exporters.[716] The ability to rely upon a common authoritative source of food standards could also constitute an incentive to international harmonisation because it would imply less need to devote scarce national technical resources to the formulation and validation of unique national standards.[717] This process could be rather beneficial because it would remove the difficulty of differentiating between protectionist domestic standards and legitimate regulatory initiatives.[718]

It is worth noting that harmonisation can apply to any aspect or stage of the regulatory process, rather than just to the final outcome, in terms of a specific standard or regulation.[719] This means that the aim of regulatory cooperation in this sense is to harmonise the outcome rather than impose a pre-defined set of policies to which Members must comply.[720]

Harmonisation on the basis of international standards is interesting in several regards. Existing international standards have improved the functioning of food markets by improving the quality of regulation[721], leading to better trading opportunities. Moreover, international standards have the potential to increase world economic welfare, especially for low-income countries, by avoiding the inefficiency of segmented national markets following different standards, prevent conflicts about differences in standards, raise conditions

715 Appellate Body Report, EC-Sardines, para. 250.

716 Roberts & Josling 2011, p1.

717 Gascoine 1999, para. 4.

718 Mayeda 2004, p742.

719 Majone 2004, p9.

720 Alemanno 2013, p4. In his paper, Alemanno explains that due to the failure of the WTO framework to effectively mitigate negative trade effects, Member States are increasingly seeking other forms of regulatory cooperation. For example 'horizontal regulatory cooperation' is regulatory cooperation on cross-cutting issues such as risk assessment, impact assessment or cost-benefit analysis. This refers to the general analytical basis of regulation as opposed to the 'sector-specific' regulatory cooperation. According to Jaffee & Henson (2004, p8) these cross-cutting issues even received more attention and resources from international standards organisations than international standards *per se*, aiming at the development of common approaches to risk identification, assessment and management (meta-standards).

721 Roberts & Unnevehr 2005, p494.

for countries with lower standards, reduce costs of compliance for developing countries by reducing the number of standards with which they would have to comply[722], and result in greater ability at capacity building for developing countries.[723] Harmonisation facilitates international dialogue on technical issues because it generates a collective responsibility towards risk assessment[724] that could constitute a common incentive towards finding appropriate ways to approach risk regulation so as to avoid that it hinders international trade.

The use of relevant guides, standards and recommendations might circumvent many implementation-related issues. These instruments could serve as a basis for the recognition of the credibility and competence of conformity assessment bodies, thereby facilitating the acceptance of their results, and ultimately help ensure a harmonised approach to conformity assessment procedures.[725] The harmonisation of conformity assessments at the international level is an effective way of solving the difficulties arising from duplicate testing and/or certification of products that constitutes one of the major hurdles to cross-border trade.[726]

Yet the merits of harmonization have often been challenged. There are suspicions that international standards trample on national sovereignty and the freedom to set own domestic standards, resulting in the endorsement of international standards mostly driven by industry interests.[727] Pressure for downward harmonisation ensues, especially with regard to the SPS Agreement. since its primary purpose is to facilitate trade, and not to raise health and safety standards.[728] At the same time, there are concerns among developing countries that harmonization has been harnessed by industry interests in developed countries to generate 'complex, rigid and costly standards' aiming at realising their protectionist aims, leading to international standards that are of little use to Members at lower levels of development.[729]

---

722 Mayeda 2004, p751.

723 Charnovitz 2002, p12. Charnovitz stressed that international standards must be set at an appropriate level to actually raise welfare among countries. When a standard is too high for most of the world, it could slow down economic growth and lower incomes. Conversely, an improperly low standard could be counterproductive if it dragged down environmental or social conditions. To avoid these two extremes, many standards are recommended as minimums.

724 Banque Mondiale 2006, p18.

725 Committee on Technical Barriers to Trade 2000, para. 30. To effectively reach this goal, it is important that in the preparation of international standards, some criteria are taken into account such as trade needs, technical progress, and, according to Article 12.6, products of special interest to developing country Members.

726 ISO/UNIDO 2009, p12.

727 Du 2010, p296.

728 Silverglade 2000, p520. For Victor (2000), this downward harmonisation could be the result of a trade/industry bias that international standards could force countries with tight product standards to relax them. In that way, international standards would only mirror the lowest common denominator.

729 Prévost 2009, p321.

In addition, exclusive reliance on Codex Alimentarius standards could slow down the process of harmonisation. Due to underinvestment in the development of international standards, existing standards are insufficient or outdated.[730] Developing countries even expressed their concern that after 15 years of implementation of the SPS Agreement, the adoption of international standards has not been widespread enough to provide an effective platform for increasing market access as they had hoped.[731] In this regard, existing international standards are thought to be more effective at improving the quality of regulation than by reducing the transaction costs of exporting to different markets, making them more beneficial for consumers than exporters.[732]

Although the SPS Agreement is said to put more emphasis on harmonisation than the GATT[733], the fact remains that the SPS approach to harmonisation is also questioned. For instance, while the SPS Agreement encourages Members to ratify Codex standards, the WTO has no means of leveraging this adoption, except if a country's food safety system is challenged as an unscientific and an unjustified non-tariff barrier to trade.[734] Furthermore, despite the existence of many international standards, their actual influence on trade dispute resolution is still uncertain. For example, in the first three SPS disputes[735], although international standards were referenced in the resolution of each of them, none of the outcomes from the disputes were affected by the existence of an international standard.[736]

In EC-Hormones, the Appellate Body made clear that the SPS Agreement does not intend to create international standards, guidelines and recommendations with obligatory force and effect. Consequently, the requirement for Members to base their measures on international standards should not be equated to a requirement for Members to make their measures conform to international standards. In such a way, harmonisation in the SPS Agreement must be seen as "a goal, yet to be realized in the future".[737]

In contrast, it appears that the requirement to use international standards as a basis for technical regulations in the TBT Agreement is not a mere

730 Roberts & Unnevehr 2005, p492. According to these authors, the lack or obsolescence of international standards explains the low adoption rate of existing standards. For instance over the first four years of the SPS Agreement, partial or full acceptance of international standards as a percentage of total notified measures was highest for the lower-middle-income countries (38%), followed by high-income (22%), lower-income (20%) and upper-middle-income countries (17%). As Josling et al. (2004) stated, most SPS notifications from 1995 to 2002 specified that no international standard existed for the measure.

731 Roberts & Josling 2011, p2.

732 Roberts & Unnevehr 2005, p494.

733 Zleptnig 2010, p120.

734 Caswell & Hooker 1996, p777.

735 EC-Hormones, Australia-Salmon, Japan-Varietals.

736 Victor 2002, p19.

737 Appellate Body Report, EC-Hormones, para. 165.

encouragement, but it creates a mandatory requirement for Members.[738] However, the binding nature of that requirement depends on the scope granted to the definition of the phrase "as a basis for". In this respect, the Appellate Body upheld the Panel's view that "an international standard is used 'as a basis for' a technical regulation 'when it is used as the principal constituent or fundamental principle for the purpose of enacting the technical regulation".[739] This suggests that for one thing to be 'the basis for' another, there must be a strong and very close relationship between the two things.[740] At a minimum, these two things should not contradict each other.[741]

While opinions diverge as to the merits of harmonisation, it is still considered the strongest level of regulatory rapprochement.[742] The lack of harmonisation has been deplored as one of the major aspects that fuel contention because this lack of harmonization is the source of disparities that complicate the compliance efforts of small countries. For fish and fishery products, despite the existence of overlapping requirements, especially the increasing emphasis on application of HACCP, significant differences remain in food safety standards and conformity assessment procedures between the major importing markets (EU, US and Japan).[743] Through harmonisation, the same principles are expected to underlie most legislation, making it difficult to encounter divergences that could result in serious violations in different jurisdictions.

However, there would probably still remain some weaker countries that might fail, for some reason, to keep up with the pace. In such instances, international harmonisation issues would go well beyond the disadvantages underlined previously. In the specific case of Benin, the concern that appears important to answer is whether an adequate functioning of international standardisation bodies or an improved adhesion of developed countries like the EU to SPS and TBT harmonisation would play any role in eliminating or otherwise mitigating the adverse effects incurred in the fisheries sector. Such an analysis requires from the outset that one to refrain from any inference as to the validity or the actual updating of international food standards. The most appropriate approach is probably to dive back into the past in order to examine the normative trends

738 The Panel view on this matter actually answers a recurring issue. In fact the use of 'shall' and 'should' in the provisions of both SPS and TBT Agreements has been the object of much debate and criticisms. Most generally, 'shall' is assigned binding force, while 'should' is considered to be a mere recommendation that has no binding force. In any event, the invariable use of these two 'terms' has often been blamed with regard to the provisions of the SPS and TBT Agreements, since the lack of clarity renders the obligations weak and unenforceable. In EC-Sardines, the Panel decided to give strength to 'shall' by stating "the use of the word "shall" denotes a requirement that is obligatory in nature and that goes beyond mere encouragement." (See Panel Report, EC-Sardines, para. 7.110).

739 Appellate Body report, EC-Sardines, para. 243.

740 Appellate Body report, EC-Sardines, para. 245.

741 Appellate Body report, EC-Sardines, para. 248.

742 Caswell & Hooker, 1996, p776.

743 Henson & Jaffee 2006a, p597.

prevailing at the Codex Alimentarius at the moment the facts raising the current case between Benin and the EU were coming into play. This would help shed some light on whether the existence or relevance of international standards would have influenced food safety regulation in Benin. The observation that stands out is that, already in 1997, the Codex developed guidelines on principles such as risk analysis and quality assurance.[744] Likewise, guidelines were adopted for the monitoring of microbiological criteria for foods at any point in the food chain from primary production to final consumption[745], already suggesting a farm-to-fork approach to deal with food safety hazards better. In view of those parameters, countries are left with many options with regard to the regulatory choice that would ensure market access.

The acute need of technical resources and expertise can result in a dilemma as to the strategic option that must be followed by food exporters if they are to gain or sustain access to a high-value market. Some countries opt for a proactive approach, a forward-looking strategy to reinforce competitive advantage, while other countries adopt a reactive and defensive approach consisting mostly of adjustments to face adverse trade events.[746] In this process, a proactive approach consists of taking action before the entry into force of the relevant standard, taking into consideration the likely future evolution of standards. In contrast to the reactive approach, the proactive approach enables more flexibility due to a longer compliance period while minimising detrimental spillovers.[747] Complying with more stringent standards would therefore only necessitate incremental changes for producers and minor adjustments in public oversight arrangements.[748] The application and the results of those strategies depend on the focus of the food safety initiative.

a. Food safety regulation focusing on national needs

The first approach towards food safety regulation is to establish a food safety legislation in which the main focus is on national needs. This approach is not necessarily a response to the food safety regulation of importers and does not necessarily aim at international harmonisation, but it answers more food safety concerns arising from the domestic market. Therefore, it might serve the purpose of market access, but strengthening competitiveness is not its primary focus. From the outset, focusing on national needs seems the most reasonable regulatory choice in the sense that it enables national needs, national priorities

---

744 Codex, Guidelines for the Design, Operation, Assessment and Accreditation of Food Import and Export Inspection and Certification Systems, CAC/GL 26-1997, 1997.

745 Codex, Principles for the Establishment and Application of Microbiological Criteria for Foods, CAC/GL 21-1995, 1995.

746 Rios & Jaffee 2008, p57.

747 Henson & Jaffee 2006a, p612.

748 Jaffee & Henson 2004, p13.

and economic constraints, as well as domestic institutional capacities to be integrates efficiently. In addition, this option enables a better convergence of national regulatory policies, which is important to ensure a greater commitment of stakeholders and guarantee an easier implementation of the measures adopted.

However, even if the required capacities to validly concretise the policy goals were available, the development of purely national standards might at times be too focused on national needs and impede international market access.[749] This is all the more true when the level of development associated with the awareness of consumers does not require a very high level of protection and a constant monitoring to face emerging risks. Since in Benin the Law 84–009 on the control of foodstuffs adopted in 1984 was never implemented until 2002, this suggests that the combination of factors –consumers' awareness, major food crisis, political will – that must give rise to its implementation were never met. It can also be inferred that there was never a compelling need, for example to comply with importers' requirements, which called for the implementation of the law.

In such a context, domestic needs of regulation would certainly fall below the level of standardisation at a global level. Even though international standards might appear outdated in some circumstances, they would anyway be more stringent because they are subject to an ongoing review process, as opposed to continual lethargy as in the case of Benin. A fact that further complicates the case of Benin is that Law 84–009 was not only obsolete but there was no apparent effort to ensure its implementation. From this perspective, focusing solely on national needs might equal a deliberate choice of marginalisation, as compliance with international standards has become a key to market access.

b. *Food regulation focusing on international standards*

Seeking a better and realistic balance between national and international features would lead to the adoption of an outward-looking strategy, which also takes into consideration national institutional capacities. As a matter of fact, there is now global realisation that standards and National Standardization Bodies (NSB) can no longer stand alone and there must be an integrated technical mix of the components of the quality infrastructure – conformity assessment, accreditation, metrology and standards – for a successful cross-borders trade.[750]

This scenario implies that, regardless of EU law, Benin took the necessary steps to comply with the international guidelines mentioned earlier and to establish an adequate institutional framework to ensure their implementation. However, if that was the case, the country would not have been in a situation in which there was almost a complete absence of food legislation and quality

749 ISO/UNIDO 2008, p15.
750 ISO/UNIDO 2008, p3.

infrastructure in 2002 at the moment of the first FVO inspection. This proactive approach would have induced a whole different perspective. First, the FVO report would not have revealed such serious shortcomings and would have resulted in less categorical conclusions. Second, a subsequent upgrading procedure to the FVO's inspection would not have revealed such an arduous and time-consuming task and would not have necessitated so many resources at once.

But the issue is slightly more delicate than this. In analysing this scheme, it is important to factor in the difficulties faced by Benin during the upgrading process, which appears not to be fully completed even after a decade and substantial technical assistance from many donors. If, in addition, account is taken of the status of international standards, the situation is made even more complex. International standards are mostly set by developed countries, representing more the interests and circumstances of these industrialised nations.[751] This greater emphasis on developed countries' needs places a disproportionate burden on developing countries due to the entailed higher costs of compliance.[752]

Seen in this light, it becomes less evident that aiming at complying with relevant international standards would have also been an easy task for Benin. This regulatory choice without an underlying internal demand would quite likely fail to bring about the significant progress expected. Moreover, adopting Codex standards would not necessarily result in market access because most developed countries do not implement Codex standards due to their unwillingness to disrupt their long established control systems.[753] In the current case, even when Benin would have adopted Codex standards following an SPS/TBT harmonisation scheme, further steps would have been required to gain access to the EU market.

---

751 This illustrates the fact that most developing countries do not have the capacity to take part in all the meetings of international standard-setting bodies. Developing countries have often complained about the issue. But it is important to realise that developing countries might not necessarily be interested in the development of every single international standard, especially when countries have only a narrow and export-based industrial production (World Trade Report, 2005, p94). This view finds an interesting support in Article 2.6 of the TBT Agreement. This article requires Members to "play a full part, within the limits of their resources, in the preparation by appropriate international standardizing bodies, of international standards for products for which they either have adopted, or expect to adopt, technical regulations". Therefore developing countries must not aim at participation in the activities of international standard-setting bodies in general, but their participation should result from the interests at stake for their trade objectives. The aim of related technical assistance should also be more narrowly defined to be more beneficial and efficient.

752 Mayeda 2004, p751.

753 Majone 2004, p8. According to Majone, it was initially felt that Codex standards, especially provisions on food additives, contaminants and hygiene requirements, were developed to provide developing countries with ready-made standards that they could adopt. Therefore, developing countries assumed that adopting these standards would lead to access to developed countries' markets, but this result did not occur.

c. Food safety regulation focusing on importer's standards

Another strategic approach towards food safety regulation consists of responding reactively after compliance issues have been identified. In cases of low standards, compliance issues are never related to a failure to adopt international standards. As mentioned earlier, neither the SPS Agreement nor the TBT Agreement places an obligation on countries to adopt international standards. Article 3.3 of the SPS Agreement stipulates that the only obligation is to provide scientific justification in cases of the adoption of stricter standards. This means that if a country chooses for some reason to have less stringent standards or cannot afford the adoption of the relevant Codex standard, there would be no violation *vis-à-vis* WTO law. Therefore there would be no legal sanction and that country would not run the risk of legal action from another country either. The lack of compliance in this instance would only expose this country to a risk of marginalisation, which is not a desirable outcome for any country.

Thus, when compliance issues are invoked, they usually refer to higher-value market standards, and call for regulatory and institutional changes in the exporting country. However, in a market like the EU whose standards are recognised as being higher than international standards, the situation falls outside the ambit of the 'customary' form of harmonisation advocated in the SPS and the TBT Agreements. These agreements call for harmonisation "on the basis of international standards", rather than harmonisation with the importer's standards. Would the EU requirement that exporter's regulation must be at least conform to its own regulation amount to a violation of the harmonisation provision in the SPS and TBT Agreements? In this respect, it is important to recall that harmonisation is not a legally binding requirement and countries have the right under specific conditions to adopt stricter standards than international standards. While in the SPS Agreement stricter norms must be backed up by scientific evidence or result from the appropriate level of protection, in the TBT Agreement WTO Members might overlook harmonisation when international standards are inappropriate or ineffective to achieve their legitimate objectives.

In fact, the EU conformity requirement has had an important impact on food safety regulation as regards fish and fishery products. Many developing countries, despite their weak food safety management capacity, have managed to put in place the necessary regulatory, technical and administrative arrangements to meet EU demanding standards.[754] This meant that these countries upgraded their standards of hygiene in the capture, processing, transportation, and storage of fish and fishery products to a level at least equivalent to the level within the

---

754 Jaffee & Henson 2004, p12. According to these authors, the number of countries achieving List I status increased from 27 to 83 from 1997 to 2003 and more than half of these are low or lower-middle income countries.

EU.[755] Similarly, it means that the EU has enough confidence in its public control systems to grant them a status that translates into reduced physical inspections at EU borders.

In this way, the objective of trade liberalisation through harmonisation is virtually attained because many countries have – at least in principle – similar food safety regulatory policies and quality infrastructure. This situation enables fisheries trade not only between these countries and the EU, but also between these countries themselves, making it also easier for them to access the markets of other countries with equally stringent requirements. Therefore, the EU conformity provision could be seen as a kind of harmonisation that is pulling many countries forward as far as fisheries safety is concerned.

However, the major difference between these two approaches remains that the SPS/TBT harmonisation is 'a goal' while 'EU harmonisation' is compulsory. The EU conformity requirement places exporting countries in a 'do or die' scenario that involves strict compliance with its requirements. Mindful of the ongoing threat of exclusion for non-compliance, most stakeholders, especially private sector operators, make sure to put in place a system enabling oversight. In this way, these countries can keep track in a timely manner of changes in the EU legislation in order to make the necessary adjustments. This has resulted in a spontaneous awareness of the EU legislation in the visited countries such as Senegal and Benin.

In Benin, food business operators and officers of the competent authority could more spontaneously mention EU Regulation 178/02 and its main regulatory requirements than make reference to the corresponding law in domestic legislation. In this current instance, the situation does not translate into a real problem because the two laws are similar, but it reflects the obvious orientation of the shrimp processing food chain that has no real incentive to comply with the domestic law.

Put differently, this could result in a situation where a foreign law is applied in a country in disregard of the domestic law due to the interests at stake. In other areas of law this could lead to serious implications in terms of violations and the violators could be held liable for their breaches. However with regard to food law, the trend on the international market nullifies this occurrence. EU requirements appear to even rule out the possibility that countries whose laws have different outcomes could gain access to the EU market.

The fact remains that in situations where conformity is privileged, differences in procedures may still be admitted in the two jurisdictions provided that the choice of measures in the exporting country ensures the attainment of the appropriate level of protection or the regulatory objectives of the importing country. In this instance, could procedural differences still lead to a significant violation of the domestic law for an operator that focuses on the implementation

755 Jaffee & Henson 2004, p12.

of the foreign law? In the current state of the international food safety and quality regulation, this end result would be quite unlikely. In fact, even when the choice of measures would be different, the actual farm-to-fork monitoring of the entire process of production and control cannot ignore some customary basic principles, like food hygiene.

But the risk, which is even quite accurate in the case of Benin, is that, as regards food safety standards, there is often in some developing countries, the existence of a dual track system depending on the targeted market. Therefore, it is widespread that there is a gap between food standards for the food chains for domestic or foreign markets.[756] This results in an 'artificial harmonisation' of food standards on the international market. This kind of harmonisation does improve trade, but it does not contribute to the improvement of food safety overall. Nor does it contribute to the ultimate goal of trade liberalisation that is providing higher levels of welfare to the citizens of trading partners, because it still leads to trade losses and other socio-economic adverse effects.

The current trend on the global market shows a shift away from complete harmonisation in the form of uniformity of rules towards more flexible options that would better accommodate national interests.[757] Indeed, significant hurdles arise from regulatory cooperation that compromises the principle of regulatory sovereignty or leads to standards insufficiently tailored to certain national needs.[758] Harmonisation through the uniformity of rules has shown its limits in the case of Benin and the EU. However this type of harmonisation was neither 'based on' international standards nor a 'flexible' approach as required by the SPS and TBT Agreements.

7.4. TOWARDS THE ELIMINATION OF DISCRIMINATION

Although based on an exception to the general principles of the GATT, the SPS Agreement is designed to include the fundamental obligation of non-discrimination underlying the WTO Agreements. Therefore, the avoidance of discrimination is a basic requirement that appears either implicitly or explicitly throughout the SPS Agreement. Where identical or similar conditions prevail, Members must avoid arbitrary or unjustifiable discrimination, including between their own territory and that of other Members.[759] Similarly, while deciding their appropriate level of protection, Members shall avoid arbitrary or unjustifiable distinctions applying to different situations, if such distinctions

756 Jayasuriya et al. 2006, p3.
757 OECD 2013, p54.
758 OECD 2013, p89.
759 SPS Agreement, Article 2.3.

result in discrimination or a disguised restriction on international trade.[760] This section first outlines the provisions on the determination of the appropriate level of protection and then assesses consistency in the EU approach.

7.4.1. AVOIDING DISCRIMINATION RELATED TO THE APPROPRIATE LEVEL OF PROTECTION

Sanitary measures adopted by Members must be derived from their appropriate level of protection[761], which is defined as the level of protection a Member deems appropriate to protect health within its territory. The appropriate level of protection reflects a particular country's public health goals in term of management of risk[762] and all sanitary measures adopted with regard to a particular sector must contribute to its attainment.

Determining the level of health protection in a given situation is a prerogative of the WTO Member concerned[763] and constitutes an "undisputed right".[764] The Appellate Body in Australia-Salmon held that the determination of the level of protection is an integral part of the decision-making process that "logically precedes and is separate from the establishment or maintenance of the SPS measure".[765] However, because it is rarely clear that enacting legislatures consider the determination of the desired level of protection and the measure itself as two separate processes, the idea of a readily ascertainable appropriate level of protection for a particular SPS risk is most often a fantasy.[766] In addition, the SPS Agreement does not contain any explicit obligation to determine the appropriate level of protection, making its determination an implicit duty for Members.[767] This creates a loophole that enables Members to adopt SPS measures without necessarily going through the step of determining their appropriate

---

760 SPS Agreement, Article 5.5.

761 The SPS Agreement mentions that many Members refer to the appropriate level of protection as the "acceptable level of risk" (Annex A(5)). According to some authors, this reflects the sensitivity of the issue. Atik (2011) stated that relating these two concepts both aids and hinders at the same time the understanding of the definition because the notions, even though they are interchangeable, do not indicate the same coverage. The acceptable level of risk addresses residual SPS risk experienced in the territory of the WTO member (once an SPS measure is in place), whereas the appropriate level of protection measures the protection an SPS measure provides. Therefore, his analysis concludes that a 'higher' ALoP corresponds to a smaller acceptable level of risk.

762 Hathaway 1999, p 251.

763 Appellate Body Report, Australia-Salmon, para. 199.

764 Appellate Body Report, EC-Asbestos, para. 168.

765 Appellate Body Report, Australia-Salmon, para. 203.

766 Atik 2011, p14.

767 Appellate Body Report, Australia-Salmon, para. 205. The same paragraph further underlines that such an implicit obligation can be seen through several provisions of the SPS Agreement, in particular paragraph 3 of Annex B, Article 4.1, Article 5.4 and Article 5.6 of the SPS Agreement.

level of protection.[768] In any case, while determining their appropriate level of protection, Members must satisfy the requirements related to consistency, risk assessment, and they must adopt the least restrictive trade measure.

7.4.2. ASSESSING CONSISTENCY IN THE EU APPROACH

The right granted by the SPS Agreement to freely determine the appropriate level of protection must be balanced within the more global framework of the disciplines of the Agreement and must under no circumstances constitute a disguised restriction on trade. In that respect, while exercising their regulatory autonomy, Members should take into account the objective of minimising negative trade effects[769] and aim at consistency both in the determination and the application of their appropriate level of protection. This means that "each Member shall avoid arbitrary or unjustifiable distinctions in the levels it considers to be appropriate in different situations, if such distinctions result in discrimination or a disguised restriction on international trade".[770]

A closer look at the consistency-provision (Article 5.5) subjects its violation to a three-pronged test. The first element requires that distinctions must exist in appropriate levels of protection adopted by a Member in different situations. The Panel in EC-Hormones stated that the scope of "different situations" that can be compared under the consistency-provision includes situations dealing with the same substance and those involving the same adverse health effect.[771] In Australia-Salmon, the Appellate Body held that comparable situations with regard to Article 5.5 are those involving either the same or a similar disease or involving the same biological and economic consequences.[772]

The second element reveals that these levels of protection exhibit arbitrary or unjustifiable differences in the treatment of the different situations. The answer to the question whether arbitrary and unjustifiable differences or distinctions in levels of protection established by a Member do in fact result in discrimination or a disguised restriction on international trade is not straightforward, and must

---

768 Atik (2011, p6) has explained the situation. According to him, "What Members actually do (at least in context of dispute settlement) is promulgate idiosyncratic measures and then *ex post* seek to justify them by telling a story of careful legislative deliberation (which likely never happened) in which (1) the international standard was rejected for failing to provide for an appropriate level of protection and (2) the idiosyncratic measure was selected as it does in fact achieve that level of protection. A first order check on the plausibility of such an account would be to simply compare the respective levels of protection of the idiosyncratic measure with that of a measure consistent with the international standard. The claim would clearly fail if the idiosyncratic measure does not achieve at least a marginally greater level of protection than does the measure based on the international standard".

769 SPS Agreement, Article 5.4.

770 SPS Agreement, Article 5.5.

771 See Panel-Report, EC-Hormones (US), para. 8.176.

772 Appellate Body Report, Australia-Salmon, para. 146.

be sought in the particular circumstances of each individual case.[773] In the same report, the Appellate Body held that the situations exhibiting different levels of protection cannot be compared unless there are comparable, that is, unless they present some common elements or elements sufficient to render them comparable. It would not be rational to compare and search for arbitrariness in situations that are totally different from one another.[774]

The last element requires that the measure embodying the differences identified results in discrimination or a disguised restriction on international trade.[775] It is worth mentioning that the three elements are additional and cumulative in nature and must be demonstrably present to establish a case of violation.[776] It follows that the second element alone would not suffice to establish a violation of the consistency provision. But as the Appellate Body further explains, the presence of that element operates practically as a 'warning' signal that the measure at issue might be either discriminatory or a disguised restriction on international trade.

EU requirements with regard to third countries seem to suggest that the assessment of equivalence is, not conducted taking into account the appropriate level of protection in itself, but rather the appropriate level of protection as reflected in the relevant regulations. Although this approach is not fully in line with the provisions of Article 4 of the SPS Agreement, its application would be desirable to avoid discrimination and is even recommended by the case law. In this regard, the food regulation of the EU is equally demanding for domestic and foreign products alike. Since the application of the consistency provision cannot be validly tested in the context of an individual country, some responses would be found in other jurisdictions.

With respect to third countries, they must all be subject to the assessment of equivalence procedure to be allowed to export to the EU. Differences in sanitary measures can result from the nature of inconsistencies observed in the given exporting countries. Generally speaking, suspension measures refer to one food business operator or may apply to a whole country if the latter is unable to provide sufficient guarantees of production and certification according to standards at least equivalent to EU standards. The fact remains that, according to Directive 91/493/EEC, some low risk countries were granted List I status, while other authorised countries were put on List II, with restricted access to the EU market. It follows that some countries on List I can be degraded depending on the circumstances and end up on List 2, which is a far more lenient measure than an outright import ban. Is it then possible that some countries receive more

773 Appellate Body Report, EC-Hormones, para. 240.
774 See Appellate Body report, EC-Hormones, para. 217.
775 Appellate Body Report, EC-Hormones, para. 214.
776 Appellate Body Report, EC-Hormones, para. 215.

favourable treatment despite inconsistencies of a similar level of severity as those of other countries?

From the outset, one can notice that the case of Benin is rather peculiar. Despite the serious shortcomings denoted in 2002 and the recommendations made by the FVO inspection team to the European Commission to take safeguard measures against Benin, no formal EU decision had been taken to prohibit or even limit Beninese shrimp exports. On the contrary, Benin, on its own initiative, decided to suspend its exports temporarily until corrective actions were undertaken. Going even further, Benin decided on the destruction of all old shrimp stocks, supposedly under EU pressure. This latter action seems to be an isolated case of such a drastic measure, which, considering the circumstances, cannot even be directly attributed to the stringency of EU sanitary measures. However, a measure of unilateral export suspension following an FVO inspection was also carried out in neighbouring Togo in May 2003.[777] An FVO inspection conducted in October 2002 pointed out that "the competent authority of Togo was absolutely not able to guarantee and certify the conformity of products exported to the EU under the requirements of Directive 91/493/EEC".[778] The inspection team had then recommended that the EU Commission "consider the need to take protective measures commensurate with the identified deficiencies in the sanitary control system of Togo".[779] However, just like in Benin, the EU did not officially take any action against Togo until the voluntary suspension was decided for shore processing plants eight months later.[780]

However, on many occasions, the competent authorities of the third countries that were inspected took less strict measures to comply with FVO recommendations. In Senegal, for instance, in 1996 the competent authority

777 Commission Européenne 2007a, p3.

778 Commission Européenne, 2002, p4. Togo has several fishery product sectors exporting to the EU. The sector of frozen products is the most important. In 2001, Togo exported about 1,000 tons that were directly landed in Portugal and about 1,500 tons were exported to countries such as Portugal, Spain, Belgium, Greece, and the Netherlands. About 210 tons of smoked fish were also exported to France, the United Kingdom, Belgium, Germany, and the Netherlands. Small quantities of lobster (about 16.5 tons) were also exported.

779 Commission Européenne 2002, p11.

780 These deficiencies were underlined by a third FVO mission in Togo. The first inspection conducted in 1996 had identified shortcomings referring in particular to the absence of legislation, the insufficiency of analyses carried out by the only laboratory with obsolete equipment, the lack of a rapid alert system, and the lack of implementation of HACCP principles (FVO report VI/1939/96-FR). Therefore, Togo was put on the List II of Decision 97/296/EEC in April 1997. The second FVO inspection in 2000 highlighted that the legislation was still not equivalent to that of the EU, except for the legislation on fishing vessels. Moreover, many deficiencies were reported with regard to the implementation (insufficiently equipped laboratory, absence of good laboratory practices, shortcomings regarding business plants agreements, etc). The FVO then suggested that Togo should not be put on the List I and must provide guarantees for remedial actions. But, during the third mission in 2002, the FVO reported that the situation had worsened despite slight improvements with regard to the legislation.

suspended about 20 processing plants that used to export to the EU. The FVO then reported a lack of rigour with regard to the granting and withdrawal of agreements with processing plants. In the same way, in 2007 Togo withdrew 15 freezer vessels from the list of potential exporters due to their refusal to take part in the sanitary and technical audit programmes organised by the competent authority of Togo.[781] However, even though these actions were triggered by FVO inspections, they are largely voluntary, and can hardly be qualified as EU sanitary measures. At best, they are unilateral acts of the involved third countries intended to ensure compliance with EU requirements.

In a few cases, immediate EU measures were taken as a result of deficiencies. During a mission in Togo in 2000, the FVO made a specific request for the suspension of the activities a processing plant that supplies smoked fishery products to the EU in which the hygienic conditions were deemed "unacceptable".[782] This request was made only in relation to that processing plant, even though the FVO reported that the other plants were also not in compliance, given that only one of them was implementing monitoring programmes according to HACCP plans.[783] In 2002, the competent authority also immediately suspended the activities of a fishing boat after the inspection of the FVO.[784]

However, the European Commission rarely took action with regard to the recommendations made by the FVO. Beyond the cases of Benin and Togo, in 2004 an FVO mission declared that Senegal was unable to control and certify fishery products in accordance with EU law. The health conditions in the fishery sector were impaired by "severe" shortcomings.[785] But after guarantees were provided that the FVO recommendations would be taken into account, Senegal remained on the list of countries authorised to export to the EU. In this regard, despite the improvements observed, in 2007 Senegal was still considered unable to certify products according to EU requirements and its control system was still deemed not compliant in 2010. But strikingly, the FVO mitigated its conclusions on these two occasions. In 2007, the FVO report supported that, given the

781 Commission Européenne 2007a, p3.

782 Commission Européenne 2000, p9.

783 Idem.

784 Commission Européenne 2002, p9.

785 Commission Européenne 2004, p9. The situation in Senegal deteriorated over the years. Already in 1996, the first FVO mission pointed out that the Senegalese food law was equivalent to Community legislation (Directive 91/493/EEC) except with regard to the criteria for the quality of drinking water and tolerance levels for histamine and mercury (Document Réf. VI/1960/96). In addition, it was stressed that the Competetnt Authority had sufficient means to fulfil its responsibilities. Minor deficiencies were detected in the control system. A second mission in 1999 reported their improvement. The controls were then performed following the recommendations of the first mission, but there was no legal basis at the national level for the implementation of the European standards. This absence of domestic law certainly contributed to the deterioration of health conditions in the sector. Senegalese products were notified 12 times in the RASFF in 1998 and 1999.

progress already made, the type of exported products (fresh fish exported by air, fish, cephalopods, and frozen shrimps minimally processed), and considering the quality of official controls carried out in processing plants, "it is unlikely that these products pose an immediate and/or serious risk to the health of European consumers".[786] Likewise, the inspection report concluded in 2010 that "the impact of deficiencies is reduced by the fact that the majority of products exported to the EU consists of fish, cephalopods or whole shrimps, chilled or frozen".[787] Nevertheless, following the audit in 2010, Senegal was requested by DG SANCO to suspend the approval of new units, while its competent authority was urged to visit all approved processing plants and vessels and send individual inspection reports for review and evaluation.[788]

In general, similar observations were made in the four UEMOA countries – Benin, Togo, Ivory Coast, and Senegal – involved in the export of fishery products to the EU. While in Benin the food legislation was deemed equivalent to that of the EU in 2009, areas of non-compliance remained in the legislation of the other countries compared to the EU food law. But, at an earlier stage in 2002, while the legislation and the whole system of production and marketing in Benin were not deemed equivalent, no EU action was taken either against the processing plants, or against the country.

Considering these examples, the EU food law in its extraterritorial application does not seem to apply double standards. Inspection missions carried out in these mentioned third countries never revealed a perfect functioning of the certification system, let alone a perfectly compliant legislation. But, as long as these countries show a certain willingness to cooperate in bringing their laws and systems of production and certification to the level required by the EU, they are granted time and assistance to do so.

With respect to actual exports, foreign products are in principle subject to border inspections before being definitively allowed on the EU market. Differences will then appear regarding the frequency and the number of these controls, taking into account factors such as the trade history or special arrangements deriving from equivalence or mutual recognition. However, it cannot be directly inferred that these differences result from discriminatory practices. The differences observed are the result of the level of risk associated

---

786 Commission Européenne 2007b, p12. The deficiencies were referring in particular to compliance and hygiene (including in respect of storage temperature of fresh fishery products) to primary production (artisanal vessels, landing sites and ice plants) and official control (including inadequate training of staff and lack of accreditation of testing laboratories).

787 Commission Européenne 2010, p19.

788 Commission Européenne 2013a, p2. It is worth noting that the 2010's mission has reported deficiencies that were never detected by the CA of Senegal. These deficiencies refer to the unsatisfactory (or non-compliant) health status, incomplete HACCP in some processing plants, and self-control plans sometimes poorly implemented and ineffective. The individual visits requested were carried out by the CA and deemed satisfactory by the FVO.

with an exporting country, but more importantly they depend on the negative results of past controls that call for more caution to ensure the effective safety of products of this origin.

Nevertheless, some third countries seem to find the EU approach discriminatory, because there are no clearly established rules, but the measures taken just depend on the results of an FVO inspection conducted at a given time. In this way, there is always a possibility that differentiation left at the discretion of the EU can occur in more or less similar situations. Yet, looking through the cases developed earlier, it would be hard to support the view that certain measures taken sporadically against certain processing plants would be constitutive of arbitrary or unjustifiable discrimination leading to a violation of the consistency provision. This is all the more true since the visited countries are generally prompt in admitting the deficiencies reported by the FVO missions, which would add legitimacy to consequent safeguard measures from the EU.

Seen in this light, it becomes challenging to bring together cumulatively all the three conditions necessary to argue for an EU violation of the consistency provision. Furthermore, the mere proof of different treatment in different situations is not sufficient, even though it might provide a warning signal that the measure implemented could be discriminatory or constitute a disguised restriction on trade.[789] From the logic of market access, it is more interesting for these exporting countries to aim at upgrading their production and certification systems, than engaging in denying the obvious non-compliance which applies to each one of their individual cases.

In any event, at the current stage of the case-law on the SPS Agreement, it is quite unlikely that a claim of a violation of the consistency provision will result in a positive and decisive ruling in favour of gaining market access. In EC-hormones, the Appellate Body established that the consistency provision laid down in Article 5.5 must be read in context, taking into account the basic obligations of Article 2.3 of the SPS Agreement, which refers essentially to the avoidance of arbitrary and unjustifiable discrimination between Members. This step taken by the Appellate Body in explaining the consistency provision, far from strengthening that requirement, seems to provide a leeway for countries to escape an apparent burden. Drawing on the wording of Article 5.5 itself, the Appellate Body stated that the "the desired consistency is a goal to be achieved in the future"[790] by means, for example, of the development of guidelines to further the implementation of the article. Therefore, the consistency provision does not establish a legal obligation of the consistency of appropriate levels of protection and, furthermore, absolute or perfect consistency is not required, as Members frequently establish their appropriate level of protection on an ad hoc basis and

[789] Committee on Sanitary and Phytosanitary Measures 2005, G/SPS/36.

[790] Appellate Body Report, EC-Hormones, para. 213.

over time, as different risks present themselves at different times.[791] However, the Appellate Body's ruling in EC-Hormones does emphasise the immediate obligation to avoid arbitrary and unjustifiable inconsistencies in the levels of protection. Therefore, unjustified distinctions in levels of protection would lead to a violation of the consistency provision.

7.5. ASSESSMENT OF FOOD RISKS

Scientific evidence within the SPS Agreement must be gathered by means of a risk assessment, as appropriate to the circumstances, taking into account risk assessment techniques developed by the relevant international organisations. The phrase 'as appropriate to the circumstances has provided some flexibility about the criteria to be taken into account while assessing a risk. In its Australia-Salmon Report, the Panel confirmed the view of both Canada and Australia on the subject. On the one hand, Canada stated that the circumstances referred to in this article could be the source of the risk (for example a chemical contaminant) or the subject of the risk (whether human, animal or plant life or health is at stake). Australia, on the other hand, supports the view that the phrase 'as appropriate to the circumstances' "confers a right and obligation on WTO Member States to assess the risk, on a case-by-case basis, in terms of product, origin and destination, including, in particular, country specific situations".[792] Furthermore, the risk assessment requirement does not intend to put a burden on Members to base their measures on a risk assessment of the whole range of SPS measures existing before the SPS Agreement entered into force. In EC-Hormones, the Appellate Body held that the stipulation "as appropriate to the circumstances" intentionally gave a certain degree of flexibility to Members to satisfy the requirement of Article 5.1.[793]

The risk assessment requirement establishes science as a central yardstick for the lawfulness of SPS measures.[794] Risk assessment appears then to be a 'countervailing factor' to the freedom referred to in Article 3.3 to establish measures that results in a higher level of protection than achieved by international standards.[795] For food safety matters, risk assessment is defined as the evaluation of the potential for adverse effects on human or animal health arising from the presence of additives, contaminants, toxins, or disease-causing organisms in food, beverages or feedstuffs.[796] In this respect, a two-step test must be applied for the assessment of foodborne risks. First there must be an

791 Idem.
792 Panel Report, Australia-Salmon, para. 8.71.
793 Appellate Body Report, EC-Hormones, para. 129.
794 Zleptnig 2010, p361.
795 Appellate Body Report, EC-Hormones, para. 177.
796 SPS Agreement, Annex A, para. 4.

identification of the adverse effects on human health. Second, if such an adverse effect exists, the potential occurrence of these effects must be evaluated.[797] The SPS Committee identified that "for a risk to exist, there had to be a hazard, an adverse event, or something harmful that one feared. Secondly, there had to be some level of uncertainty associated with what was known about the probability and the consequences of the adverse event".[798] In the assessment of risks, "Members shall take into account available scientific evidence; relevant processes and production methods; relevant inspection, sampling and testing methods; prevalence of specific diseases or pests; existence of pest- or disease-free areas; relevant ecological and environmental conditions; and quarantine or other treatment".[799] In its EC-Hormones ruling, the Appellate Body held that there is nothing to indicate that this list of factors is intended to be a closed list.[800] Therefore other factors relevant to the case at hand might be considered while conducting the risk assessment.

The likelihood may be expressed either qualitatively or quantitatively and there is no requirement to establish a certain magnitude or threshold level of degree of risk.[801] In its EC-Hormones ruling, the Appellate Body rejected the limitation of the description of risk to strictly quantitative yardsticks. The Appellate Body sets out to clarify the approach adopted by the Panel to use 'probability' as an alternative term for 'potential'. Such an interpretation would mistakenly introduce a quantitative dimension to the notion of risk. Therefore, the Appellate Body underlines: "The ordinary meaning of 'potential' relates to 'possibility' and is different from the ordinary meaning of 'probability'. 'Probability' implies a higher degree or a threshold of potentiality or possibility".[802] This approach was confirmed by another ruling of the Appellate Body stating that "the assessment of risk need not be expressed in numerical terms or as a minimum quantification of the level of risk".[803]

A risk assessment does not have to come to a uniform conclusion that coincides with the scientific conclusion or view implicit in the SPS measure. Both 'mainstream' scientific opinions and opinions of scientists taking a divergent view can be set out in a risk assessment. Basing a measure on a divergent opinion coming from qualified and respected sources[804] may well reflect a reasonable relationship between an SPS measure and a risk assessment, especially in the

797 Appellate Body Report, US/Canada – Continued Suspension, para. 569.

798 Committee on Sanitary and Phytosanitary Measures, Risk Analysis, G/SPS/GEN/209, para. 12.

799 SPS Agreement, Article 5.2.

800 Appellate Body Report, US/Canada – Continued Suspension, para. 527; Appellate Body Report, Australia- Apples, para. 207.

801 Appellate Body Report, Australia-Salmon, para. 124.

802 Appellate Body Report, EC-Hormones, paras. 182–184.

803 Appellate Body Report, US/Canada- Continued Suspension, para. 569.

804 In its EC-Biotech report, the Panel sets out that an SPS measure reflecting a divergent opinion could be reasonably said to be based on a risk assessment provided that this divergent opinion

presence of life-threatening risks perceived to constitute a clear and imminent threat to public health and safety.[805]

In EC-Hormones, the Appellate Body held that the risk to be evaluated is not limited to "risk ascertainable in a science laboratory operating under strictly controlled conditions, but also covers risks in human societies as they actually exist, in other words, the actual potential for adverse effects on human health in the real world where people live, work and die".[806] Integrating such risks into the scope of risk assessment has been a subject of controversy in the case law. On the one hand, the Panel in the EC-Hormones case tried to delineate the coverage of risk assessment by excluding certain factors it deemed clearly not to belong to this discipline. The Panel then considered risk assessment as a scientific examination of data and factual studies, which must not be a political exercise involving a social value judgment made by political bodies. The Panel's analysis concluded that the steps to be taken after the assessment of the risk fall with risk management, which might involve social value judgments.[807] Following the same reasoning, the Panel held that the determination and application of the appropriate level of protection by a Member is part of risk management. This exercise follows the assessment of risk, which identifies the risks and their probability of occurrence that leads the Member to decide, on the basis of its own value judgments, when it can accept these risks.[808] Such an interpretation offers Members a wide range of possibilities with regard to the assessment of risks. On the other hand, some of the provisions of the SPS Agreement were purposefully left open. For example, as regards risk management principles, Members were only required to minimise the trade effects of their policies when choosing levels of risk reduction. Members considered it inappropriate for the SPS Agreement to be more prescriptive and deemed that the Codex Alimentarius would be a better forum for the development of best regulatory practices related to food safety.[809] Nevertheless a risk assessment must exclude from its scope risks resulting from theoretical uncertainty.[810]

The question remains how to draw the line between the assessment and management of risks? Despite the ruling of the Appellate Body that excluded the concept of risk management from the scope of the SPS Agreement for not having a textual basis, the broader concept of risk analysis (which encompasses risk assessment, risk management and risk communication) has often been used for the work of the SPS Committee. In this regard, risk analysis has been

is expressed in the risk assessment. Otherwise, this opinion would not 'sufficiently warrant' or 'reasonably support' the SPS measure (Panel Reports EC-Biotech para. 7.3060).

805 Appellate Body Report, EC-Hormones, para. 194.

806 Appellate Body Report, EC-Hormones, para. 187.

807 Panel Report, EC- Hormones I, para. 8.97 and 8.100.

808 Panel Report, EC- Hormones I, para. 8.97 and 8.100, para. 8.163.

809 Roberts & Unnevehr 2005, p488.

810 Appellate Body Report, EC-Hormones, para. 186.

defined as a systematic way of gathering, evaluating and recording information, which would lead to recommendations, positions or actions in response to an identified hazard.[811] Likewise, risk analysis, and therefore risk management, is an integral part of the work of the Codex Alimentarius. In this respect, the latter even established some working principles for food safety risk analysis.[812] These principles are intended to provide guidance to national governments for risk assessment, risk management and risk communication with regard to food-related risks to human health. In any case, risk analysis is a widely acknowledged concept, which is used on a daily basis by most Members. As mentioned earlier in this book, risk management, as part of risk analysis, is textually recognised and applied in EU food safety regulation.

From another perspective, a fundamental issue is how to attest to the relevance of a risk assessment. As regards standards of review applicable in dispute settlement proceedings, and considering the silence of the SPS Agreement, the Appellate Body ruled on the issue in the EC-Hormones dispute. It stated that Article 11 of the Dispute Settlement Understanding (DSU) bears directly on the matter of the standard of review for panels for the ascertainment and legal characterisation of facts under the SPS Agreement or under other covered Agreements.[813] Article 11 of the DSU requires a panel to "make an objective assessment of the matter before it, including an objective assessment of the facts of the case and the applicability of and conformity with the relevant covered agreements". Falling within this approach, the responsibilities as regards risk assessment in the SPS Agreement are clearly defined. While it is for the WTO Member to perform the risk assessment, the panel is vested with the task to ensure its review. This results from quite a simple logic according to which, while panels are poorly suited to engage in a *de novo* review, "total deference to the findings of the national authorities could not ensure an 'objective assessment of the facts' as foreseen by Article 11 of the DSU".[814] Consequently, the task of the Panel is not to assess the correctness of the risk assessment conducted by a Member but to determine instead whether this risk assessment is objectively justifiable, in other words supported by coherent reasoning and respectable scientific evidence.[815]

In any case, a review of a Member's risk assessment must follow a process of four steps.[816] At first, a Panel must identify the scientific basis upon which the SPS measure was adopted. The second step consists of verifying that the

---

811 Committee on Sanitary and Phytosanitary Measures, Risk Analysis, G/SPS/GEN/209, para. 11.

812 See Codex, Working Principles for Risk Analysis for Food Safety for Application by Governments, CAC/GL 62-2007, 2007.

813 Appellate Body Report, EC-Hormones, para. 116.

814 Appellate Body Report, EC-Hormones, para. 117.

815 Appellate Body Report, US/Canada – Continued Suspension, para. 590.

816 Appellate Body Report, US/Canada – Continued Suspension, para. 591.

scientific basis comes from a respected and qualified source, which can be considered 'legitimate science' according to the standards of the relevant scientific community.[817] At the third step, the particular conclusions drawn by the Member must be assessed so as to review whether they rely sufficiently on the scientific evidence, ensuring that the "reasoning articulated on the basis of scientific evidence is objective and coherent". Lastly, "the panel must determine whether the results of the risk assessment 'sufficiently warrant' the SPS measure at issue". The 'legitimacy' of the scientific basis relied upon must first be assessed, prior to any further review as regards the reasoning and the conclusions.[818]

There is no established and single way of reviewing a Member's risk assessment. As such, a Panel may review the risk assessment as a whole or base its overall conclusions on the analyses of the individual steps and factors reviewed, depending on the type and structure of the risk assessment and, if possible, the way a complainant presents and develops its claims.[819]

As regards temporal application, the requirement in Article 5.1 that SPS measures must be "based on" a risk assessment applies as long as the SPS measure concerned remains into force. In this regard, the Panel in EC-Biotech held that "both a risk assessment carried out before the adoption of a particular safeguard measure and a risk assessment carried out after its adoption could 'sufficiently warrant', or 'reasonably support', the maintenance of that measure".[820] Therefore, as it currently stands, until it actually comes before a WTO panel, there is no necessity for a country to go through the effort and expense of a risk assessment.[821]

It is also worth noting that, although measures must be based on a risk assessment, the SPS Agreement does not require Members to carry out their own assessment of risks. The objective justification of an SPS measure could be found in a risk assessment carried by another Member or an international organisation.[822] The SPS Agreement provides several disciplines through which the impact of differences in regulation could be reduced to the extent strictly necessary.

Despite its importance, the lack of procedural rules undermines the implementation of the risk assessment provision. There is no need to first

---

817 Appellate Body Report, Australia-Apples, para. 220.

818 Idem.

819 Appellate Body Report, Australia-Apples, para. 258. It is worth mentioning that the Appellate Body explained in this ruling that a Panel is not required to establish that each fault in a risk assessment is serious enough to undermine the entire risk assessment. In this regard, only a comprehensive analysis of all the steps and factors may help determine whether the conjunction of various flaws provides sufficient grounds for a risk assessment to violate Article 5.1 of the SPS Agreement.

820 Panel Report, EC-Approval and Marketing of Biotech Products, para. 7.3030.

821 Neugebauer 1999–2000, p1271.

822 Appellate Body Report, EC-Hormones, para. 190.

complete a risk assessment before determining a specific level of protection.[823] The determination of the appropriate level of protection can even at times be very important for conduct a risk assessment. In such cases where a Member chooses not to adopt an SPS measure based on an international standard because it seeks to achieve a higher level of protection than offered by the relevant international standard, its appropriate level of protection would affect the scope and method of its risk assessment. This means that the chosen appropriate level of protection might require the country "to perform certain research as part of its risk assessment that is different from the parameters considered and the research carried out in the risk assessment underlying the international standard".[824]

In any event, the appropriate level of protection can be expressed in a variety of ways, defining for example broad public health goals or representing a quantitative expression of the probability of an adverse public health consequence or an incidence of disease.[825] However, there is no obligation for Members to set the appropriate level of protection in quantitative terms. However, it must be defined with sufficient precision, avoiding "vagueness and equivocation"[826], without however excluding the possibility of setting it at a "zero risk" level.[827] The appropriate level of protection and the SPS measure must be clearly distinguished. While the appropriate level of protection is an objective, the SPS measure is an instrument chosen to attain or implement that objective.[828] In case a dispute arises, and following a failure of a Member to determine its appropriate level of protection, the level of protection may be established by panels on the basis of the level of protection reflected in the SPS measure actually applied.[829]

7.6. DISCIPLINES ON THE CHOICE OF MEASURES

7.6.1. ADOPTING THE LEAST TRADE-RESTRICTIVE SPS MEASURE

Under normal circumstances, once the appropriate level of protection is determined, the Member would move forward and, according to the risk identified, decide whether or not it must establish an SPS measure. In this respect, Article 5.6 states that "when establishing or maintaining sanitary

---

823 Panel Report, Australia-Salmon, paras. 8.125 and 8.126.
824 Appellate Body Reports, US/Canada – Continued Suspension, para. 685.
825 De Swarte & Donker 2005, p 825.
826 Appellate Body Reports, US/Canada – Continued Suspension, para. 523.
827 Appellate Body Report, Australia-Salmon, para. 125.
828 Appellate Body Report, Australia-Salmon, para. 200; see also Appellate Body Report in EC – Hormones, para. 214.
829 Appellate Body Report, Australia-Salmon, para. 207.

or phytosanitary measures to achieve the appropriate level of sanitary or phytosanitary protection, Member States shall ensure that such measures are not more trade-restrictive than required to achieve their appropriate level of sanitary or phytosanitary protection, taking into account technical and economic feasibility". Building on the footnote to Article 5.6, the Appellate Body in Australia-Salmon held that a three-pronged test must be applied to establish a violation of this article, with the understanding that the three elements applied cumulatively.[830] Thus, a measure is not more restrictive to trade than necessary unless there is another SPS measure, which is reasonably available, taking into account technical and economic feasibility, that achieves the Member's appropriate level of protection, and is significantly less restrictive to trade than the measure contested. A measure is reasonably available when the adopting Member has the resources or the technical capacity for its adoption and implementation. The alternative measure suggested must not imply a change of the appropriate level of the importing Member and must be significantly less trade restrictive than the questioned measure, considering the trade impacts of the two measures.

When health risks are detected, the importing country is entitled to adopt such measures as may be necessary to enable the preservation of its appropriate level of protection. In general, non-compliance can at first lead to border detentions and ultimately result in trade restrictions such as import bans.[831] Border rejections of consignments can be considered the most transparent measures because they mostly follow the detection of an actual health issue with the consignments. Border controls are to be taken very seriously as they are the last 'obstacle' to full market access. However it is practically impossible to conduct a check on all individual consignments arriving at the borders. That explains why some non-compliance is still found regarding products already released onto the market. In any case, depending on the severity of the risk detected, the detained container is in principle destroyed, re-dispatched or returned to the country of origin.

However, considering the normal procedure at the borders, when a serious risk to health is detected, it is clearly quite difficult to argue otherwise and seek a solution that would be less trade restrictive than a straight rejection of the consignments. In the case of Senegal for example, 40 notifications were issued in the RASFF from June 2010 to December 2012.[832] These notifications include 37 rejections of consignments at BIPs for various reasons: non-maintenance of the cold chain, altered organoleptic characteristics, exceeding accepted mercury levels, presence of enterobacteriacea, Pseudomonas spp. and aerobic

[830] Appellate Body Report, Australia-Salmon, para 194.
[831] Maertens & Swinnen 2009, p317.
[832] Senegal exported 43,000 tons and 35,000 tons of fishery products respectively in 2011 and 2012.

microorganisms. In 2011, fresh fishery products were rejected at the border because they originated from an unauthorised processing plant. Likewise, one alert and two information notifications were issued about fishery products exceeding accepted mercury levels. In these cases, protective measures will distort trade, even though these measures contain no protectionist intent.

When risks to health are detected with regard to products that are already on the market, the severity of the risk can lead to the recall of the products. These withdrawals apply to both EU and foreign products. The procedures in these cases are quite transparent as the related information is reported in the RASFF, including the country of origin of the products and the action taken subsequently. In August 2002, Spain issued a RASFF notification against Benin, reporting the detection of a high content of non-pathogenic micro-organisms (Enterobacteriaceae and aerobic mesophiles) in frozen shrimps. Although this was just an information notification, it led to the first FVO mission in Benin in October 2002. Other cases can lead to seizure or destruction depending on the severity of the health risk detected. Further actions could result in an outright ban on the product originating from the country concerned.

While the causes that lead to border rejections of consignments are more visible, the reasons that motivate an import ban can be very diverse. It is precisely this diversity that creates the potential for the adoption of measures on questionable grounds. As reported by the Panel in EC-Asbestos, an import ban is by its very nature the most restrictive market access measure.[833] In this regard, the SPS Agreement subjects its adoption to a 'necessity-test' previously mentioned, which entails a balance of three factors including the health protection goal of the measure, the reasonable availability of the measure and the choice of the least restrictive measure available.

In the current case, the situation is rather delicate since the EU did not decide on the suspension of Benin's shrimp exports. Benin decided to take such a categorical measure, out of the fear that the protective measure recommended by the FVO would definitely be an import ban. But, if an EU ban would have actually occurred, the trade restriction would then result from dysfunctions of the system of production and certification rather than have been based on proven evidence of health risks. Although many stakeholders in Benin felt that a suspension in the absence of proven health risks was unjust, the fact remains that systemic issues like dysfunctions in production and certification systems cast serious doubts as to the ability to provide safe products. Moreover, the Appellate Body in EC-Hormones held that it would be an error to limit the scope of risk assessment to matters susceptible to quantitative analysis by the empirical or experimental laboratory methods commonly associated with the physical sciences. The Appellate Body further stated that "some of the kinds of factors

833 Panel Report, EC-Asbestos, para. 8.49.

listed in Article 5.2 such as 'relevant processes and production methods' and 'relevant inspection, sampling and testing methods' are not necessarily or wholly susceptible of investigation according to laboratory methods".[834] In this regard, the risk to be evaluated in a risk assessment is not only the "risk ascertainable in a science laboratory operating under strictly controlled conditions, but also risk in human societies as they actually exist, in other words, the actual potential for adverse effects on human health in the real world where people live and work and die".[835] Seen in this light, the difficulties to effectively implement controls in the shrimp sector could actually give rise to legitimate measures taken by the EU to protect its consumers from these potential health issues.

7.6.2. LEAST TRADE-RESTRICTIVE TBT MEASURE

In 2003, the TBT Committee underlined the importance for regulators to consider the use of different approaches for the fulfilment of their legitimate objectives and to take into account the least-restrictive trade option available.

Article 2.2 stipulates that Members must ensure "that technical regulations are not prepared, adopted or applied with a view to or with the effect of creating unnecessary obstacles to international trade". "For this purpose, technical regulations shall not be more trade-restrictive than necessary to fulfil a legitimate objective, taking account of the risks non-fulfilment would create". There is a wide range of legitimate objectives, "*inter alia*: national security requirements; the prevention of deceptive practices; protection of human health or safety, animal or plant life or health, or the environment. In assessing such risks, relevant elements of consideration are, *inter alia*: available scientific and technical information, related processing technology or intended end-uses of products".

Consistency with this provision calls for a two-step analysis pursuant to which a technical regulation must first pursue a legitimate objective and then it must not be more trade-restrictive than necessary.[836] The Panel in US-Clove cigarettes stated that the identification of the objective pursued is the logical starting point as it serves as the reference point to further the analysis to check compliance with the second condition.[837] Members have the prerogative to decide which policy objectives they wish to pursue and the levels at which they wish to pursue them[838], keeping in mind that, "it would be entirely possible, both as a factual and a legal matter, for a single technical regulation to pursue more

834 Appellate Body Report, EC-Hormones, para. 187.
835 Idem.
836 Panel Report, US – Tuna II (Mexico), para. 7.388.
837 Panel Report, US-Clove cigarettes, para. 7.335.
838 Panel Report, EC-Sardines, para. 7.120.

than one objective".[839] But, assessing the legitimacy of the objectives pursued is the responsibility of Panels and the Appellate Body.[840]

The Panel in the US-Tuna II case examined the notion of trade-restrictiveness. The Panel adopted the views of both parties to the dispute (Mexico and US) and concluded that trade-restrictive measures include those that "impose any form of limitation of imports, discriminate against imports or deny competitive opportunities to imports".[841] Whether a measure is more trade-restrictive than necessary should be analysed in consideration of the risks non-fulfilment would create. The Panel in US-Tuna II (Mexico) established that this requirement integrates as part of the analysis "both the likelihood and the gravity of potential risks (and any associated adverse consequences)" that might arise in case of non-fulfilment of the legitimate objective pursued. In the view of the Panel, a less trade-restrictive measure that would entail greater risks of non-fulfilment would not be a valid alternative means of achieving the objective.[842] In any event, it is up to the complaining party to demonstrate that the conditions of a violation are met.[843]

At another level, Members must ensure that the maintenance of a technical regulation is consistent with the conditions that gave rise to their adoption. If the circumstances or objectives no longer exist, or in the event they can be addressed in a less trade-restrictive manner, Article 2.3 requires Members not to maintain the relevant technical regulations. This requirement puts on Members an ongoing obligation to reassess their technical regulations so as to eliminate or amend them with regard to the evolution of the circumstances and objectives underlying the regulations.[844]

7.6.3. ADOPTION OF PROVISIONAL MEASURES

When there is insufficient relevant scientific evidence, a Member may provisionally adopt sanitary or phytosanitary measures subject to compliance with four requirements established by Article 5.7 of the SPS Agreement. On the one hand, the adoption of such measures must meet two requirements: the measures must be imposed in respect of a situation where "relevant scientific information is insufficient" and must be adopted "on the basis of available pertinent information", including information from the relevant international organisations and other Members' SPS measures.

---

839 Panel Report, US-Clove cigarettes, para. 7.342.
840 Appellate Body Report, EC-Sardines, para. 286.
841 Panel Report, US-Tuna II (Mexico), para. 7.455.
842 Panel Report, US-Tuna II (Mexico), paras. 7.466–7.467.
843 Panel Report, US-Tuna II (Mexico), para. 7.388.
844 Panel Report, EC-Sardines, para. 7.81. The Panel also emphasised that this obligation equally applies to technical regulations enacted before the entry into force of the TBT Agreement.

On the other hand, the maintenance of provisional measures is also subject to two conditions: the Member must seek to obtain the additional information necessary for a more objective assessment of risk[845], and must review its measure(s) accordingly within a reasonable period of time.[846] The Appellate Body underlined in the Japan-Agricultural Products dispute that the four requirements are cumulative in nature and equally important for the determination of consistency with Article 5.7.[847]

Adopting a measure on the basis of available scientific information implies that a rational and objective relationship must exist between the information concerning a certain risk and the provisional measure adopted by the Member. This involves situations where there exists some evidentiary basis indicating the possible existence of a risk, but where relevant information is not sufficient to conduct a risk assessment according to the requirements set out in the SPS Agreement, particularly with reference to Articles 2.2 and 5.1.[848] Whether the provision in Article 5.7 operates as an autonomous right, or constitutes a mere exception to the general obligation of risk assessment (Article 5.1) and the obligation not to maintain a measure without sufficient scientific evidence (Article 2.2) has become issue. The Panel in EC-Biotech concluded that Article 5.7 creates a right vis-à-vis both Articles 2.2 and 5.1 of the SPS Agreement rather than an exception. In this sense, Article 5.7 operates as a qualified exemption from the obligation to base SPS measures on a risk assessment established under Article 5.1.[849]

In reality, such precision is of paramount importance due to its implications with regard to the allocation of the burden of proof. In the EC-Biotech case, the Panel held that "in cases where a complaining party alleges that an SPS measure is inconsistent with Article 5.1, it is incumbent on the complaining party, and not the responding party, to demonstrate that the challenged measure is inconsistent with at least one of the four requirements set forth in Article 5.7".[850] It is only after such non-compliance is established that Article 5.1 would be applicable

845 Situations where new scientific developments do not enable the Member that adopted a provisional measure to perform a new risk assessment with sufficient a degree of flexibility would still fall within the scope of Article 5.7 (See Appellate Body Reports, US/Canada-Continued Suspension, para. 701).

846 Concerns were expressed that certain emergency measures were becoming permanent measures. Therefore, it was suggested that Members should clearly indicate the period of application, including an end date, for all emergency notifications. (See Committee on Sanitary and Phytosanitary Measures 2008, p7). However, according to Prévost (2005, p6), Article 5.7 creates room for provisional measures to be taken even in circumstances where scientific uncertainty persists for a long time or where the risks at issue are expected to materialise only in the long term. Reconciling these two aspects can appear problematic in some cases such as the long-standing debate on Genetically Modified Organisms (GMOs).

847 Appellate Body Report, Japan – Agricultural Products II, para. 89.

848 Appellate Body Report, US/Canada – Continued suspension, para. 678.

849 Panel Report, EC-Approval and Marketing of Biotech Products, para. 7.2997.

850 Panel Report, EC-Approval and Marketing of Biotech Products, para. 7.3000.

to the challenged SPS measure. Likewise, a claim of violation under Article 5.1 must be sustained by a *prima facie* case of inconsistency with both Articles 5.1 and 5.7 established by the complaining party.[851]

As regards the requirement to "seek additional information", the case law noted the absence of explicit prerequisites regarding the type of information to be collected, a specific collection procedure or the actual results that must be achieved within that framework. Nevertheless, the Appellate Body in the Japan-Agricultural Products case underlined that since the aim of the provision is to allow the Member to conduct a more objective assessment of risk, "the information sought must be germane to conducting such a risk assessment".[852]

As far as the 'reasonable period of time' is concerned, there is no specific period of time allocated for a review of a provisional measure. The 'reasonable period of time' "must be established on a case-by-case basis, depending on the specific circumstances of each case, including the difficulty of obtaining the additional information necessary for the review and the characteristics of the provisional SPS measure".[853]

It remains quite unclear whether the adoption of provisional measures should be assimilated to the implementation of the precautionary principle. The Appellate Body conceded that in many ways, the SPS Agreement enabled the exercise of caution. In this respect, the precautionary principle is not only be found in Article 5.7 but also in the establishment of an appropriate level of protection higher (i.e. more cautious) than implied in international standards, guidelines and recommendations, as enabled by Article 3.3. In addition, the precautionary principle is reflected in the sixth paragraph of the preamble stating that furthering harmonisation must not lead to requiring Members to change their appropriate level of protection.[854] But, to what extent can legitimate caution be asserted? It would obviously be challenging to answer such a question without considering the particular circumstances of each case. The Appellate Body in EC-Asbestos noted that "a panel presiding over an SPS dispute should consider that governments are frequently overcautious where potentially irreversible risks to human health or life are concerned".[855] In any event, the Appellate Body stressed that "the principle has not been written in the SPS Agreement as a ground for justifying SPS measures that are otherwise inconsistent with the obligations of Members set out in particular provisions" of the Agreement.[856] Without taking any formal position on the issue of the precautionary principle that it considered "important but abstract", the Appellate Body held that the

851 Idem.
852 Appellate Body Report, Japan – Agricultural Products II, para. 92.
853 Appellate Body Report, Japan – Agricultural Products II, para. 93.
854 Appellate Body Report, EC-Hormones, para. 124.
855 Appellate Body Report, EC-Asbestos, para. 78.
856 Appellate Body Report, EC-Hormones, para. 124.

"precautionary principle, at least outside the field of international environmental law, still awaits authoritative formulation".[857]

In practice, it is not well defined what kind of measures could be considered as falling within the ambit of the implementation of the right to adopt provisional measures under the SPS Agreement. In general, EU import restrictions are decided for indefinite periods of time. Such measures must remain valid until the exporting country provide sufficient guarantees of an actual improvement in its production and certification system and after an FVO follow-up inspection is carried out to confirm their accuracy. In the event of an 'ordinary restriction' following an FVO inspection or a measure for the strengthening of border inspections on specific products, it appears clearly that it would be an error to invoke the adoption of provisional measures as established by Article 5.7 of the SPS Agreement. The adoption of such measures is certainly not motivated by a hypothetical insufficiency of relevant scientific evidence, but based on the assumption that dysfunctions in the system would undoubtedly lead to potentially unsafe food.

But with regard to import restrictions motivated by a 'perceived' threat like the cholera outbreak or the alleged use of chemicals to harvest fish in East Africa, the situation calls for more scrutiny. For both cases, the EU did not put forward any empirical evidence. No scientific evidence or data established the possibility of cholera-causing pathogens being transmitted to humans through fish consumption.[858] Likewise, the EU did not demonstrate any scientific proof that fish from Lake Victoria were poisoned as a result of the use of chemicals and a ban was decided in disregard of analyses conducted in Kenya to show the absence of contamination.[859] However, the lack of scientific evidence in this case cannot be imputable to gaps in the scientific knowledge that creates an impossibility to carry out the necessary analyses. Rather, these measures seem to be responses to emerging risks to deal with emergency situations. The EU approach did not show any willingness to conduct further research that would provide scientific grounds for the maintenance of the measures, definitively ruling out the possibility to qualify the measures on the basis of Article 5.7.

7.7. PUTTING EU MEASURES TO THE TEST

An examination of the dynamic of trade relationships between the EU and third countries shows that the EU became very active with regard to measures taken against third-country exporters after the creation of the FVO. Increasingly, countries had been subject to import restrictions that vary in duration

857 Appellate Body Report, EC-Hormones, para. 123.
858 Ochieng & Majanja 2010, p310.
859 Ochieng & Majanja 2010, p311.

depending on the reactivity capacity of the country concerned. The reasons for these decisions are substantially the same. They are often based on the inadequacy of third countries' laws whose provisions are frequently considered insufficient or inappropriate to be able to achieve a level of protection at least equivalent to the one of the EU. Furthermore, it may simply be the result of more or less serious shortcomings in the implementation of control procedures by the competent authority of the country concerned.

While Benin transplanted EU food law, the assessment conducted by the FVO concluded that Benin's law was equivalent to that of the EU. Despite the formal recognition of equivalence between the Members concerned, this situation would not trigger the equivalence provision, which requires that different measures be used to achieve the same level of protection.

The main issue would therefore be assessing whether identical measures are capable of achieving the same level of protection in two different contexts. This question is all the more relevant in cases where the laws in the two countries became 'harmonised' through a process of legal transplant from the part of the exporting country. Whether such transplanted laws can effectively result in the same level of protection in two different legal systems is very debatable. The level of protection is context-specific and identical SPS measures differ in their effect in different settings.[860] Holding this true, it becomes doubtful that the same types of legal issues will arise in both small and large jurisdictions if the cultural, economical, political, and legal cultures of the two jurisdictions are entirely different.[861] Considering that regulatory inconsistencies can arise from both the application of regulations and from divergences in the regulations and standards themselves, it can be inferred that two countries may share the same standards and still engage in different compliance and verification efforts.[862]

Obvious differences in the legal systems and the institutional frameworks in Benin and the EU are the first elements that could illustrate that the implementation and enforcement of the same law will definitely lead to differences in the levels of protection. Moreover, another important factor is the co-existence in Benin of two food chains in the shrimp sector, one for the domestic market and an export-oriented food chain. The fact remains that the same actors (fishermen, fishmongers) supply both the export-oriented sector and the domestic market. While following a farm-to-fork approach, it is expected that Good Hygiene Practices are implemented throughout the export-oriented food chain and no extra care is required for supplying the domestic market. Seen in this light, the expected results amount to achieving through the same stakeholders two different levels of protection according to the targeted market. Through these two food chains that are interconnected, it is quite unlikely to

860 Atik 2011, p9.
861 Mayeda 2004, p750.
862 OECD 2013, p54.

achieve the attainment of two levels of protection, one of which reaches the appropriate level of protection of the EU. This is particularly true considering the persistent shortcomings inherent to the shrimp export sector even a decade after the legal 'borrowing'. In any case, the attainment of the same level of protection with a measure borrowed from another jurisdiction is hardly attainable due to the vast array of factors that might influence the implementation and enforcement in the context of the transplanted law.

As a result, EU trade restrictions could still be legitimate despite even though the imported products are subject to the same regulation as domestic products. These rejections of consignments would not qualify as arbitrary or unjustifiable since there is evidence that the implementation of the food law in Benin would not achieve the level of protection of the EU.

At a more operational level, there is a claim that when safety issues are detected, fish consignments are rarely, if ever, recalled, and quality concerns are solved through private negotiations or arbitration[863], while no information is transmitted about these questionable products in the RASFF network. These 'behind-the-scene' arrangements could be discriminatory as they link the resolution of safety issues to the bargaining power and financial position of individual exporting plants.

In a more extended context, the case of the export of Nile Perch caught in Lake Victoria to the EU is a good illustration of the various reasons that may motivate import bans, while showing at the same time that the legitimacy of these import bans are sometimes questionable. This case involves three countries that share the exploitation of the lake: Uganda (43%), Kenya (7%)[864] and Tanzania (51%). Already in 1994, there was a rejection of the East African fish following the massacre in Rwanda. As a matter of fact, there were allegations that dead bodies of the human beings killed during the conflict were dumped in Lake Victoria.[865] Then, from 1997 to 2002, the Nile Perch industry faced EU import bans on grounds qualified as "allegorical meanings of the notion of fish safety".[866] Such a statement results from the fact that some of the EU measures

863 Ponte 2007, p64.

864 The case of Kenya was the most reported due to the small size of its industry that made this country more vulnerable to EU actions with regard to the Nile perch export. Kenya's industrial fish sector started in the mid-1980s and aimed at exporting Nile perch fillets to the EU. By 1996, there were 15 processing factories operating around Lake Victoria and in Nairobi. (See Henson et al. 2000b). Until that time, Kenya relied heavily on the EU market (70%), particularly on Spain (Noor, 2000, p6). It has been argued that the fishery industry in Kenya is one of the fastest growing non-traditional export products in Kenya and generates both private and public benefits. Nile Perch represents 90% of fishery product exports and the EU is the main destination (Nyangito et al. 2003).

865 Nyangito et al. 2003, p53.

866 Ponte 2007, p1.

were not sufficiently supported by scientific evidence but based on the poor performance of exporting countries' regulatory and monitoring systems.[867]

The first ban was applied in 1997 when during border inspections Spain and Italy detected the presence of Salmonella in the products coming from Lake Victoria. In this case, the ban applied only in these two countries. If this first restriction was based on the actual detection of unauthorised substances in the products, the second ban in January 1998 imposed by the EU itself was based solely on fears generated by an outbreak of cholera in East Africa. As a result, the EU decided that every consignment from the lake must be subject to border testing for Vibrio cholera and Vibrio parahaemolyticus. Since these tests were time-consuming, it simply amounted to a ban on chilled fish exports from the region. This EU-wide restriction that lasted until June 1998 was also extended to Mozambique. The EU import restriction lasted seven months during which the World Health Organization (WHO) gave evidence that there was no risk involved in exporting these fishery products.[868] The Director General of the WHO issued a 'Note Verbale'[869] explaining that, although at least 50 countries were affected by epidemic or endemic cholera since 1961, a cholera outbreak subsequent to trade in foodstuffs has never been reported. Likewise, the FAO reported that the cholera bacteria does not survive proper cooking or drying, and cooked, dried or canned products are considered safe with cholera transmission. In addition, epidemiological data suggest that the risk of transmission of cholera from contaminated imported fish is negligible. Only rare and sporadic cases of cholera have occurred in developed countries as a result of eating fish transported across international borders by individuals.[870]

Later on, the EU decided another ban in April 1999 following the reported use of chemicals for fishing in Uganda. This was coupled with poor sanitary conditions along the fishing beaches.[871] Uganda took the initiative to suspend its exports to the EU, pleading with the EU that it needed time to solve the problem.[872] The EU acknowledged Uganda's request but decided immediately to take its own import suspension measure that was also extended to Tanzania and Kenya, although the latter both adopted precautionary measures in an attempt to prevent contaminated fish from entering the food chain.[873] The allegations were never proven.[874] Furthermore, even if such rumours were true, there is evidence that it would have been technically impossible to capture Nile Perch using

867 Idem.

868 Ponte 2007, p56.

869 A note Verbale is formal document sent by the Director-General of the WHO to Member States.

870 Noor 2000, p8.

871 Nyangito et al. 2003, p52.

872 Ponte 2007, p57.

873 Henson et al. 2000b, p1163.

874 Rudaheranwa et al. 2003, p392.

that method because they are big predators that can grow up to 50 kilograms and they leave in deep waters.[875] This new episode had attracted considerable attention on fishery products from Lake Victoria, which became one of most scrutinised food items on the international market.[876]

While Uganda and Tanzania were able to rapidly improve their production conditions before the follow-up inspection, Kenya, which has the smallest industry, had more difficulties to adapt.[877] Consequently, while the first two countries were given List I status[878], Kenya had to settle for a place on List II and could reach List I status only in 2004. However, before the ban was lifted in November 2000, extensive inspections and analysis were carried out on fish and water samples.[879] These events are evidence that import bans can sometimes result from an overcautious approach towards food risk regulation. Although there were obvious shortcomings in these countries' food legislation and questionable practices in the enforcement of existing laws, most measures in the Nile Perch case were based on perceived risks to health and were not backed up by any scientific evidence as required by the SPS Agreement. Aiming at the adoption of the least trade restrictive measure would require considering the existence of other measures that could deal effectively with the alleged risks. According to the WHO, the best way to deal with food imports from cholera-affected areas is for importing countries to agree on GHPs during food handling and processing to prevent, eliminate or minimise the risk of any potential contamination and to set up consequent arrangements. This is in line with the alternative measure decided by the EU itself on the cholera-related ban that amounts simply to an amendment of the Health certificate requiring appropriate checks on fishery products to ensure their fitness for consumption and the absence of pesticide residues.[880] This alternative measure could have been implemented in a few days[881], enabling the avoidance of the import bans along with their economic and social consequences.

From this analysis, it can be inferred that, in most instances, there would often be an alternative measure to avoid specific sanitary measures, particularly for an outright import ban. In the case of Benin, increased control at EU

875 Ponte 2007, p57.

876 Nyangito et al. 2003, p53.

877 It is worth underlining that hygiene and quality problems were often detected in Kenya. After the bans, Kenya tried to develop standards on fish based on Codex Stan 165 and EU Directive 91/493/EEC. Therefore, during the FVO inspection, it was noticed that regulations existed to ensure the inspection of fish but the institutional framework was missing and there were overlaps in the mandate of responsible Departments.

878 In fact, the ban was lifted in July 2000, and Uganda was first placed on List II after having developed standard operating procedures for the competent authority, having achieved transparency, etc. Kenya was moved to List I in 2001. Tanzania was placed on List I in 2000 (See Ponte 2007, p57).

879 Nyangito et al. 2003, p52.

880 Noor 2000, p8–9.

881 Noor 2000, p6–8.

Border Inspection Posts could have been considered as an alternative measure until remedial measures were taken. The implementation of this option would obviously generate additional costs that Benin could not be able to bear. In this event, food safety diplomacy would be the means to ensure a probable arrangement between the EU and Benin. But again, negotiations on these grounds would be seen to be uncertain because the severity of the deficiencies in Benin provide reasons for genuine concerns from the EU.

In general, it is quite challenging to provide evidence that a questioned measure is more restrictive to trade than necessary. According to the Appellate Body, the burden rests on the complaining party to establish with scientific evidence[882] a *prima facie* case that an alternative measure meeting all required three elements is available.[883] First, this entails sufficient scientific and technical expertise that might not be readily available for developing countries like Benin. Even in case the latter would be able to effectively challenge some measures, putting together the necessary evidence might require a great deal of time and substantial damage would have occurred meanwhile. The allocation of the burden of proof can be problematic even for developed countries. In the Australia-Salmon case, the Appellate Body rejected Canada's argument that an alternative measure was available, asserting that its ability to achieve Australia's appropriate level of protection has not been scientifically established.[884]

7.8. TRANSPARENCY

The notification of measures required by the SPS and TBT Agreements is valuable for improved transparency and can further contribute to eliminate protectionism. Both the SPS and the TBT Agreements require Members to communicate their draft measures in a timely manner and enable other Members to make necessary comments. This procedure provides an opportunity for Members to exchange about their measures and, if appropriate, to make amendments to take into account particular interests of other Members. Access to, and exchange of information about each other's measures and experiences can contribute to regulatory learning and even improve national standards.

Furthermore, collaboration within the framework of the SPS and TBT Committees is an important aspect of how increased transparency can contribute to regulatory coordination. These committees have served as forums for Members to exchange implementation-related information. As such, the SPS and TBT Committees could be seen as forums that are useful as means for a

882 Appellate Body Report, Australia-Apples, para. 364.
883 Appellate Body Report, Japan-Agricultural Products II, para. 126.
884 Appellate Body Report, Australia-Salmon, paras. 210–213.

multilateral review of draft measures and a means of raising awareness.[885] This section provides insights on the provisions in the SPS and TBT Agreements pertaining to transparency.

7.8.1. IMPROVING MARKET ACCESS THROUGH SPS TRANSPARENCY

Given the requirements for compliance with exporters' food safety regulations, it has become essential to exchange reliable and timely information as regards sanitary measures, so as to help relevant importers take the necessary steps to sustain their market access. The SPS Agreement has made a significant contribution to the facilitation of such information exchange through its transparency provision. Article 7 requires Members to provide information and notify changes in their sanitary measures. Promptness in the publication is a major aspect of this process. Promptness enables interested Members to become acquainted with their trading partners' regulations and helps the initiator of the measure in its obligation to give a reasonable interval of time to importers to adapt their products and methods of production to its requirements.

Improved transparency would also give developing countries a better visibility of regulatory changes in their export markets, since they often lack resources to keep up adequately. Timely notification of new or modified SPS measures offers developing countries a virtual compliance period during which they could take steps to make necessary reforms as regards their legislation and their production and certification systems.

Substantially, whenever a measure departs significantly from an international standard, guideline or recommendation (or when such an international standard does not exist), and the regulation might have a significant impact on trade, the Member must notify the measure at an early stage, when comments and amendments could still be made and taken into consideration.

The aim of the transparency provision goes far beyond the mere notification of sanitary measures. In addition, each Member must establish an enquiry point that would provide answers to all reasonable questions from interested Members. The enquiry point must also provide relevant documents with regard *inter alia* to any sanitary regulation, any control and inspection procedures, risk assessment procedures, or the determination of the appropriate level of protection.[886]

In a similar fashion, Article 5.8 of the SPS Agreement creates an obligation for a Member to provide an explanation of the reasons underlying its SPS measure, when the measure is not based on relevant international standards, guidelines or recommendations, or such standards, guidelines or recommendations do not

---

885 Wijkström & McDaniels 2013, p10.

886 SPS Agreement, Annex C(3).

exist. Such a request for explanation may come from any other Member that has a reason to believe that the specific introduced or maintained SPS measure is constraining, or has the potential to constrain, its exports. Although this provision is not a subparagraph of the transparency provision, its wording makes it perfectly fit for the requirements of the transparency provision.[887]

In cases of emergencies or in the presence of an imminent health threat, a Member may lighten the notification procedural rules, provided that the Member communicates immediately about the regulation and its coverage, still allows other Members to make comments or request discussions, and takes both comments and results of discussions into consideration. The rationale for such an urgent adoption of sanitary measures must also be notified.

As is quite noticeable, the transparency notification is not meant to particularly tackle developing countries' market access issues but, through its requirements, the transparency notification puts an emphasis on developing countries' concerns, while implementing the provision. For example, the concept of "significant effect on trade of other Members" may refer to the effect on trade of one single SPS regulation or of a combination of various SPS regulations; to a specific product, group of products, or products in general; and to the effects on trade between two or more Members.[888] The transparency notification must include any significant import-enhancing and import-reducing effects on the trade of other Members. In the assessment of the potential effects on trade, the Member should take into account the value or other importance of imports, their potential development, and difficulties for third countries' producers to comply, specifically in developing countries.[889] In reality, this would amount to assessing the impact of any new market access' measure on the exporters of the product involved.[890]

Beyond WTO formal notifications, the information related to importers' requirements appears to be following an informal channel that seems to be very effective. In India, for example, local firms felt that importing firms are a better source of information about food safety measures in their respective countries than their local government departments and industry associations.[891] This observation also applies in the case of Benin. In fact, this is because the primary responsibility for food safety falls on the food business operators in the EU

---

887 It is worth noting that the provision of Article 5.8 is not intended to deal with dispute settlement situations. The Appellate Body in EC-Hormones underlined that "a Member State seeking to exercise its right to receive information under Article 5.8 would, most likely, be in a pre-dispute situation, and the information or explanation it receives may well make it possible for that Member State to proceed to dispute settlement proceedings and to carry the burden of proving on a *prima facie* basis that the measure involved is not consistent with the *SPS* Agreement." (See Appellate Body Report, EC-Hormones, para. 102).

888 Committee on Sanitary and Phytosanitary Measures, 2002c, para. 6.

889 Committee on Sanitary and Phytosanitary Measures, 2002c, para. 7.

890 Panel Report, Japan-Apples, paras. 8.313 and 8.314.

891 Jayasuriya et al. 2006, p5.

food law. Therefore, beyond the prior approval that must be given by the EU Commission for a particular exporting firm, EU food business operators, while importing from third countries, ensure that the exporting plants are fully aware of and implement EU food safety requirements. As underlined earlier, Benin's food business operators are more knowledgeable about the EU food law than the corresponding orders and decrees in the domestic law.

7.8.2. DISSEMINATION OF TBT INFORMATION

Through the provisions of the TBT Agreement, Members are required as much as possible to communicate information to other Members, notify their measures and take necessary steps to ensure transparency of their procedures.

Article 2.5 establishes that "a Member preparing, adopting or applying a technical regulation which may have a significant effect on trade of other Members shall, upon the request of another Member, explain the justification for that technical regulation". This requirement sets a compulsory mechanism requiring the regulating Member to supply information.[892]

Likewise, an agreement between two or more countries must be notified in the event it that may have a significant effect on trade. This provides an opportunity for other Members to request consultations with Members involved in that agreement so as to conclude similar agreements or give the possibility to take part in the existing agreement.[893] Furthermore, when a proposed technical regulation does not comply with relevant international standards, either because of differences in technical contents or the inexistence of relevant international standards, Members are required to take certain steps in terms of publication and notification, if the technical regulation may have a significant effect on the trade of other Members.[894]

With regard to the concept of a 'significant effect on trade of other Members', the TBT Committee had clarified that it might refer to the effect on trade of one technical regulation or procedure for conformity assessment only or of various technical regulations or procedures for the assessment of conformity in combination; in a specific product, group of products or products in general; and between two or more Members.

The assessment of such an effect should take into consideration a wide range of criteria, including the value or other importance of imports in respect of the importing and/or exporting Members concerned, whether from other Members individually or collectively, the potential growth of such imports, and difficulties for producers in other Members to comply with the proposed technical

892 Appellate Body Report, EC-Sardines, para. 177.

893 TBT Agreement, Article 10.7.

894 TBT Agreement, Article 2.9.

regulations. This might also include any significant[895] import-enhancing and import-reducing effects on the trade of other Members.[896]

In fact, Members' obligations with regard to the dissemination of relevant information is an important component of the mechanism set up by the TBT Agreement to minimise as far as possible the effect of regulation on market access. For example, as regards conformity assessment procedures, the TBT Committee suggests that a better exchange of information is a key in removing unnecessary duplication and therefore avoiding the creation of unnecessary obstacles to trade.[897] In this regard, Members are invited, on a voluntary basis, to share information on their experience in using relevant international guides and recommendations on conformity assessment, as well as in the various types of conformity assessment procedures and their conditions of application. This initiative would serve as a basis for the Committee to make recommendations aimed at ensuring the avoidance of the creation of unnecessary obstacles to international trade.

Consequently, at an early appropriate stage, Members must publish a notice to enable interested parties in other Members to become acquainted with the technical regulation. A notification of the technical regulation must be made through the Secretariat, clarifying its objective and rationale and the products covered. This notification must also be timely enough to enable the introduction and consideration of amendments and comments. Upon the request of other Members, the initiator of the technical regulation must provide particulars or copies and identify, whenever possible, the parts that deviate from relevant international standards. Lastly, the adopting Member must, without discrimination, allow reasonable time for other Members to make written comments, discuss them upon request and take them into account.

A Member is allowed to omit some of the steps related to notification and publication in cases that urgent problems of safety, health, environmental protection or national security arise or threaten to arise. However, this lightening is subject to the condition that an immediate notification must be made, copies of the technical regulation are provided upon request and the opportunity for comments and discussions is still given without discrimination.[898]

The actual adoption of a technical regulation must also lead to prompt publication or be made available otherwise so as to enable interested parties to become acquainted with them.[899] In this case, the initiator of the technical regulation must allow an "reasonable interval between the publication and the

895 The Panel in US-Clove cigarettes stated that 'significant' means "sufficiently great or important to be worthy of attention, noteworthy"; see Panel Report, US-Clove Cigarettes, paras. 7.529–7.531.

896 G/TBT/1/Rev.10, p19–20.

897 Committee on Technical Barriers to Trade, 1997, para. 29.

898 TBT Agreement, Article 2.10.

899 TBT Agreement, Article 2.11.

entry into force in order to allow time for producers in exporting Members, and particularly in developing country Members, to adapt their products or methods of production to the requirements of the importing Member".[900]

This obligation does not obstruct the procedure in emergency cases. The Ministerial Decision on Implementation-related Issues and Concerns stated that the phrase 'reasonable interval' should normally mean a period of not less than six months, except when this would be ineffective in fulfilling the legitimate objectives pursued.[901] Although this period of time was not embodied in the text of the TBT Agreement, the Panel in US – Clove cigarettes concluded on these grounds that the United States acted inconsistently with the provision of Article 2.12 "by not allowing an interval of at least six months between the publication and the entry into force of the technical regulation at issue".[902]

Lastly, Members must establish one or more enquiry points[903] capable of answering all reasonable enquiries[904] from other Members and interested parties in other Members and provide relevant documents regarding adopted or proposed technical regulations, standards and conformity assessment procedures.[905] The provision of information shall also cover the membership and participation of the Member or its relevant bodies in international and regional standardising bodies and conformity assessment systems, as well as in bilateral and multilateral arrangements within the scope of the TBT Agreement.

The circulation of copies of notifications to all Members and interested international standardising and conformity assessment bodies is the task of the Secretariat. The Secretariat must draw the attention of developing country Members to any notifications relating to products of particular interest to them.[906]

---

900 TBT Agreement, Article 2.12.

901 WT/MIN(01)/17, para. 5.2.

902 Panel Report, US-Clove cigarettes, para. 7.563–7.595.

903 According to Article 10.2, a Member may establish more than one enquiry point for legal or administrative reasons. In such a case, complete and unambiguous information must be provided on the scope of responsibility of each of them, and the Member must ensure the prompt conveyance of mistakenly addressed request for information.

904 The TBT Committee stressed that an enquiry would be 'reasonable' when it would be limited to a specific product, or group of products, as opposed to an enquiry referring to an entire business branch or field of regulations, or procedures for conformity assessment. (See Committee on Technical Barriers to Trade 2011, p34).

905 Article 10.5 requires developed country Members to provide translations of the documents (or summaries in case of voluminous documents) covered by a specific notification in the official languages of the WTO (French, English and Spanish), in cases other Members request so.

906 TBT Agreement, Article 10.6.

7.9. TACKLING DEVELOPING COUNTRIES' CONCERNS

The need for technical assistance for developing countries is one of the core principles recognised by Members in the preambles of both SPS and TBT Agreements. These Agreements acknowledged the special difficulties developing countries might encounter in complying with importers' measures and in the formulation and application of technical regulations, standards and conformity assessment procedures. Considering the consequences on access to markets, Members asserted their desire to assist developing countries in their endeavours with regard to these areas.

7.9.1. TECHNICAL ASSISTANCE

a. *Technical assistance in the SPS Agreement*

The seventh paragraph of the preamble to the SPS Agreement acknowledged, on the one hand, the special difficulties developing countries may encounter in complying with SPS measures of importing countries, which might negatively impact their market access ability. On the other hand, potential difficulties were also underlined with regard to the formulation and application of SPS measures in their own territory. From this perspective, Article 9 of the SPS Agreement states the commitment of Members to facilitate the provision of technical assistance to other Members, especially developing country Members, either bilaterally or through the appropriate international organisations.

Article 9 specifies a broad range of areas where this technical assistance can be provided, "*inter alia*, in the areas of processing technologies, research and infrastructure, including in the establishment of national regulatory bodies". Such technical assistance "may take the form of advice, credits, donations and grants, including for the purpose of seeking technical expertise, training and equipment to allow such countries to adjust to, and comply with, sanitary or phytosanitary measures necessary to achieve the appropriate level of sanitary or phytosanitary protection in their export markets". More specifically, in a bilateral setting, when a developing country Member needs substantial investments to comply with SPS measures of an importing Member, the latter "shall consider providing such technical assistance as will permit the developing country Member to maintain and expand its market access opportunities for the product involved".[907]

The Doha ministerial conference also addressed the issue of SPS technical assistance, with a particular focus on LDCs. Members were urged to provide,

---

[907] SPS Agreement, Article 9.2.

to the extent possible, the financial and technical assistance necessary to enable LDCs to respond adequately to the introduction of any new SPS measures with potential negative effects on their trade.[908] Similarly, technical assistance must be provided to LDCs with a view to responding to special implementation problems they might have with regard to the SPS Agreement.[909]

It is evident that circumstances and specific needs are not uniform across countries, and therefore a standardised approach cannot be applied indiscriminately for all Members that need technical assistance. The involvement of the beneficiaries, both in the public and the private sector, is also a major issue that will, or should, considerably influence the way the technical assistance is tailored in a particular country. In view of these factors, the Secretariat of the SPS Committee was assigned in 2000 with the mission to "prepare a paper outlining a possible typology of technical assistance needs to help Members decide which types of technical assistance action were most appropriate".[910] This initiative aims at helping beneficiaries of technical assistance to improve, through cooperation, their understanding of the SPS Agreement, implement the obligations, and fully benefit from the rights conferred. In view of this objective, technical assistance could be systematically classified in four broad categories: information; training; 'soft' infrastructure development; and 'hard' infrastructure development.[911]

With regard to "information", technical assistance aims at enhancing awareness and understanding of Members' rights and obligations under the SPS Agreement and can be addressed at a technical level[912], a policy level[913], or to the public, media and private sector.[914] 'Training' aims at giving a more specific understanding of the SPS Agreement or the WTO dispute settlement procedures and focuses on issues such as the determination of the appropriate

---

908 WTO Ministerial Conference, 2001, para. 3.6 (i).

909 WTO Ministerial Conference, 2001, para. 3.6 (ii).

910 Committee on Sanitary and Phytosanitary Measures 2000, para. 1.

911 Committee on Sanitary and Phytosanitary Measures 2000, para. 2.

912 This kind of technical assistance targets official directly responsible for the application of SPS measures. It can take the form of seminars and workshop aiming at giving a better understanding of the SPS Agreement's importance for international trade, so as to help these officials initiate an assessment of their needs for an appropriate implementation of the SPS Agreement.

913 This type of technical assistance targets officials responsible for the development of the regulatory framework. It focuses on policy issues related to core principles of the SPS Agreement such as the concept of an appropriate level of protection, the use of non-discriminatory or least trade restrictive measures. It also provides a better understanding of the work of international standard-setting organisations and consideration of ways and means for a more active participation of developing countries in the work of these organisations.

914 This form of technical assistance aims at facilitating the task of government officials in educating their traders and consumers with regard to their rights and obligations under the SPS Agreement. This results from the increasing attention that food safety issues required nowadays from all sectors.

level of protection, the recognition of equivalence or the implementation of transparency provisions. 'Infrastructure development' includes human and financial bilateral assistance by WTO Members to cover areas where substantial investments are needed for the exporting Member to comply with SPS measures. 'Soft' infrastructure development would provide technical assistance for instance for the development of national regulatory frameworks or for the formation of technical and scientific personnel. 'Hard' infrastructure development is provided to cover the need for equipment and infrastructure, such as laboratories, testing equipment, or processing and storage facilities.

It is worth noting that SPS technical assistance is not only the privilege of Members or the SPS Committee. As regards food safety, the Codex Alimentarius has been providing assistance to its Members in areas as diverse as updating food control laws and regulations, providing laboratory methods and improving laboratory practices, developing food control policies and procedures, or developing inspection, sampling and investigative procedures.

b. Technical assistance in the TBT Agreement

Provisions on technical assistance are not exclusively directed towards developing countries. Such assistance must generally be provided to all Members but with particular regard to developing countries. Quite noticeably, Article 11 of the TBT Agreement provides that the provision of technical assistance depends on the request of the Member needing it. Along the same lines, mutually agreed terms and conditions must be sought to satisfy the requirements of technical assistance. Moreover, under Article 11.8, Members are required to give priority to the needs of the least-developed country Members whenever they undertake activities related to technical assistance.

Hence, upon the request of other Members, and especially developing country Members, advice must be provided on the preparation of technical regulations, the establishment of national standardising bodies, the participation in the international standardising bodies, the establishment of regulatory bodies, or bodies for the assessment of conformity with technical regulations and the methods by which their technical regulations can best be met, the establishment of bodies for the assessment of conformity with standards adopted within the territory of the requesting Member.[915] Likewise, assistance must be provided regarding the steps that should be taken by producers of the requesting Member if they wish to have access to systems for conformity assessment operated by governmental or non-governmental bodies within the territory of the Member receiving a request for technical assistance.[916] Furthermore, whenever appropriate, Members must take such reasonable measure as may be available

915 TBT Agreement, Article 11.1–11.4.
916 TBT Agreement, Article 11.5.

to them to arrange for their regulatory bodies and their national standardising bodies to give relevant advice.[917]

From another perspective, WTO Members, which are also members or participants of international or regional systems for conformity assessment, shall advise and grant technical assistance to other Members about the establishment of the institutions and legal framework which would enable the latter or their relevant bodies to fulfil the obligations of membership or participation in such systems.[918]

The TBT Committee recognised the necessity of a demand-driven technical cooperation, and aims at seeking ways to achieve more effective cooperation and coordination among donors to target the needs identified by developing country Members better. In this regard, the Committee recognised some elements to focus upon, such as the assistance to developing countries in needs identification, the inventory and prioritisation by developing and least developed country Members of their specific needs in the TBT field, the enhancement of co-operation between donors, or the reassessment of technical assistance needs in light of agreed priorities.[919] A survey conducted by the TBT Committee revealed that due to the dynamic and sophisticated nature of technical regulations, standards and conformity assessment and transparency procedures, TBT-related technical assistance needs to relate to a wide range of areas, including the need for improved knowledge of the Agreement, effective implementation of the Agreement, exchange of experience among Members and bilateral cooperation, national and regional coordination; training for the development of human resources; improvement of infrastructure and capacity building; participation in the work of the Committee and other relevant regional and international organisations; and needs in relation to market access.[920]

Moreover, technical assistance must be delivered following a step-by-step approach that focuses firstly on the provision of knowledge and skill, and secondly on the development of TBT-related infrastructure.[921] To ensure an improved sustainability and dissemination of the knowledge, there is a need that some steps are taken by both parties involved. On the one hand, the beneficiary country must strive to strengthen its domestic institutions, the use of internal measures to complement the technical assistance and undertake awareness-raising activities for domestic stakeholders with regard to the TBT Agreement.[922] On the other hand, there is a need for the country that provides the technical assistance to ensure the monitoring, assessment and follow-up of the activities

---

917 TBT Agreement, Article 11.2–11.3.
918 TBT Agreement, Article 11.6.
919 Committee on Technical Barriers to Trade 2011, p37.
920 Committee on Technical Barriers to Trade 2003, para. 46.
921 Committee on Technical Barriers to Trade 2003, para. 50.
922 Committee on Technical Barriers to Trade 2003, para. 51.

involved.[923] Furthermore, the TBT Committee noted that for technical assistance to work effectively, its activities should be coordinated with other intergovernmental organisations with a particular focus on the development of human and institutional resources, especially with respect to conformity assessment procedures.[924] Finally, the TBT Committee underlined the valuable interest of south-south technical cooperation and regional approaches to ensure the effectiveness of technical assistance and the facilitation of experience sharing among Members with similar situations.[925]

c. *Applying technical assistance to the case of Benin*

The ability of technical assistance to truly contribute to trade liberalisation is impaired by several factors. The most important complaint is the failure of technical assistance programmes to appropriately address the daily challenges faced by developing countries, which result mostly from their level of economic development.[926] The approach adopted towards technical assistance is a significant element for its potential to bring about the expected benefits. Generally speaking, much of the technical assistance is reactionary rather than part of a general capacity building strategy.[927] This means that technical assistance is essentially provided once compliance problems have been detected. Such an approach could overlook important steps due to the pressure resulting from the possibility to loose market access.

In Benin, the need for technical assistance derived immediately from the FVO inspection in 2002 and was seen as a response to the shortcomings identified. While Benin committed to undertake reforms to comply with the EU food regulation, it asserted at the same time its inability to succeed without the assistance of the EU. From a TBT Agreement perspective, this request for assistance was a very important step taken by Benin since such a request is a necessary triggering factor. As regards the SPS Agreement, the importing WTO Member is required to consider providing technical assistance where substantial investments are necessary for compliance with its requirements, with the aim of "maintaining and expanding the market access opportunities of the product involved" for the exporting Member.

In both cases, the EU granted technical assistance to Benin through diverse programmes focusing exclusively on fishery products (for example SFP) or taking into account the fishery sector as one of the priority sectors for the countries concerned (i.e. UEMOA quality programme). Obviously, the usefulness of technical assistance cannot be questioned, especially in the case

923 Committee on Technical Barriers to Trade 2003, para. 50.
924 Committee on Technical Barriers to Trade 1997, para. 3.
925 Committee on Technical Barriers to Trade 2003, para. 52.
926 Noor 2000, p14.
927 Idem.

of a country like Benin where the needs for successful capacity building aiming at compliance with the EU law were enormous. It virtually amounted to starting the upgrading process from scratch, including legal reforms. After a decade, it also appears to be undeniable that many achievements could be underlined, and to a large extent, the technical assistance could be regarded as having positively contributed to the establishment of a legal and institutional framework able to ensure a food safety level that might possibly result in the appropriate level of protection of the EU.

However, even though the EU asserted after the FVO inspection in 2009 that the shrimp production and certification system in Benin was equivalent to its own, one cannot disregard the numerous deficiencies that the report still pointed out during the inspection. Despite the overall conclusion establishing the equivalence, when the areas are considered at individual levels, the FVO report emphasised that the control system and the functioning of factories could not be deemed equivalent to EU requirements. Consistently, the FVO report concluded that one could not consider that "the organization of the competent authority and the implementation of national provisions on which is based the control of fishery products intended for export to the EU were at least equivalent to EU requirements."

But the recognition of equivalence that followed this report and the approval for Benin to export its shrimps to the EU do not translate into effective gains of market access, considering that the shrimp export sector has been virtually "wiped out". Moreover, given the deficiencies still reported by the FVO inspection, there remains a reasonable doubt that the food safety level has actually improved, even for the export market.

Looking through both SPS and TBT Agreements, technical assistance programmes should aim at positively impacting market access opportunities of exporting countries. But in this instance this goal cannot materialise unless there is an effective improvement of the food safety level in the exporting country, leading to its ability to attain the appropriate level of protection or the legitimate objectives set by the importing country.

In any event, technical assistance programmes in Benin consisted in legal and institutional reforms that should enable a proper implementation and enforcement of the food law adopted.

1° Assistance for legal reforms

Sovereign countries enjoy autonomy of decision making for the establishment of their regulatory framework. This must also prove true even when legal reforms are triggered by non-compliance issues that call for major changes intended to provide the necessary regulatory background for coordinated activities that are aimed at attaining a certain level of protection. However, with regard to food safety and product standards, various elements seem to influence decision makers in the exercise of their regulatory autonomy. In Benin, the need for a more effective and updated food law was not induced by national needs for food safety, but rather motivated by economic incentives in the form of sustaining market access. In this context, the intended appropriate level of protection was that of the EU, and the resources expected to achieve it were to a large extent expected to be provided by the EU.

Legal reforms have mostly resulted in the borrowing of the EU food law in an attempt for Benin to achieve the recognition of equivalence of its law by the EU. Legal borrowing is not a new concept. In fact, lawmakers have prodigiously used 'borrowing' whereby foreign models are exploited, with minor modifications, rather than inventing entirely new rules.[928] Many developing countries in Africa have long relied upon laws 'inherited' from their former colonisers in diverse fields of regulation.[929] Food regulation systems in Africa are often based on laws adopted during colonial times that have not been updated[930] to take account of current trends and food safety hazards. These systems were also often inappropriate because they were adopted on an ad hoc basis as responses to problems of particular interest to colonial administrators.[931] Nevertheless, lawmakers tend to make borrowing from a particular legal system a habit, resulting from "a bias in favor of treating that system as the primary quarry for legal rules whenever local law is silent".[932]

This approach sheds some new light on the transplant of the EU food law into Benin legal order. A proper regulation was clearly non-existent and the 'borrowing' appeared to be the most readily available alternative to circumvent time and resource constraints. The fact remains that even though pressure from the EU was argued for this regulatory choice[933], the regulatory autonomy of Benin could not be claimed to have been undermined and there could be no allegation of a violation on the part of the EU.

Nevertheless, it would still be important to acknowledge the role played by the EU in assisting Benin in transplanting the EU food law. This brings back the fundamental issue of the core objective of technical assistance as

---

928 Wise 1990, p5.

929 According to Berkowitz et al. (2003), colonisation – as well as imperialism – have resulted in a massive transplantation of Western law in other parts of the world. In Benin, for instance, the civil code was for a long while a virtual copy of the French code until conflicting national circumstances, mostly resulting from domestic customary rules, led to essential changes. More generally, as underlined by Faure et al. (2010, p100), environmental regulation is also a good example where past efforts to assist developing countries relied upon the importation of legal schemes by colonial powers and the transplantation of regulatory models developed in the Northern Hemisphere.

930 Smith DeWaal & Robert 2005, p28.

931 Idem.

932 Wise 1990, p16.

933 Interview with a Directorate of Fisheries' official (competent authority), Cotonou, March 2011.

designed in the SPS and TBT Agreements. In this instance, technical assistance was 'successful' in 'harmonising' EU and Benin food laws, leading to the recognition of equivalence of the Benin food law by the EU in 2009. However, this recognition and subsequent approval did not translate into actual gains in market access, due not only to the ineffectiveness but also to other domestic circumstances resulting mostly from the level of development. Regulatory efforts should aim at designing regulation that is appropriate to the legal, economic, political, and social situations in which they must function.[934] In this regard, an internal development of law through a process of trial and error and the participation of interested stakeholders ensures a highly effective functioning of legal institutions. This suggests that the process of lawmaking, rather than the contents of legal rules, determines the effectiveness of legal institutions.[935]

But, from a deeper analysis, one could infer that the borrowing in itself could not be blamed immediately for the ineffectiveness of the transplanted law. Looking for guidance in foreign laws is still legitimate if it leads to a process that enables the weighing of different alternatives to adopt the framework that fits most domestic constraints. Moreover, the approach towards the legal transplant is decisive for its receptivity; that is the country's ability to give meaning to the imported law.[936] A foreign law can even be transplanted without requiring significant changes if adaptation has been carried out through an informed choice about alternative rules to adapt the law to local conditions. This process that implies extensive comparative research was not applied in Benin due mostly to the pressure resulting from the fear of being removed from the list by the EU. In any case, the roots of the ineffectiveness of law lie mostly in issues related to enforcement and implementation.[937]

In a food law context, beyond the mere existence of legal rules, only a good cooperation of stakeholders at various levels, supported by the necessary institutions, could ensure effective implementation. In Benin, the establishment of the supporting framework was almost entirely subject to foreign aid, resulting from the incapacity of governmental authorities to provide necessary resources and expertise. Moreover, considering the past records of weak implementation, it could be reasonably expected that a high-level transplanted food law would face problems of stakeholders involvement, especially in a field where the demand for law at the national level is rather weak. At the time, the demand for a food

---

934 Faure et al. 2010, p100.

935 Berkowitz et al. 2003a p190.

936 Berkowitz et al. 2003a, p179. According to these authors, familiarity with the legal system of origin is also a major indicator of the receptivity of legal transplant. When countries share the same legal history, the resulting familiarity with the transplanted legal concepts makes it unnecessary to proceed to major adaptations.

937 Faure et al. 2010, p105. As also underlined by Jayasuriya et al. (2006, p2), officials from developing countries complain that many countries do not provide the adequate technical assistance required by the SPS Agreement on a best endeavours basis.

law was only intended for the shrimp export sector, rather than being a nationwide demand for an improved food safety. The demand for law is a decisive criterion for its effectiveness; a high demand for law will trigger high voluntary compliance, leading a society to invest in the legal institutions necessary for upholding the legal order.[938] In the current case, the demand for the law was mostly focused on the industry (three processing plants), even if the government would benefit incidentally from maintaining market access.

The failure of the government to follow through on its commitment, not only towards the industry, but also with regard to the upgrading process is an indicator that there might be a lack of strong political will. In the long run, unless there is a radical change, this could hinder the proper implementation of the food law. Furthermore, the lack of consistency with regard to inspection and the absence of remedial measures following the detection of breaches also indicate shortcomings with regard to enforcement. It emerges that the effectiveness of the transplanted law is still an issue.

The combination of the ineffectiveness and the absence of an initial demand for the law could lead to more lethargy in Benin, especially if the conditions for resuming the activities of processing plants are not met in the short run. Society seems to have a remarkably high tolerance for unsuitable law[939], with the understanding in this case that the law is unsuitable for the needs of the domestic market.

It becomes evident that a better symbiosis between local needs and compliance requirements of the importing countries is crucial to ensure successful technical assistance. When legal transplant is the preferred option it should be carried out in such a way as to ensure a good fit of foreign with domestic law by making meaningful adaptations to imported laws to local conditions.[940] In any case, legal reforms must be driven by valid incentives. While maintaining market access is an important incentive, maintaining market access at all costs, at the detriment of the rightful legislative process and outside the framework of national policy objectives, should not be the leading incentive for major regulatory changes. Without a self-sustaining demand for legal innovation and change, the 'borrowing of law' will result in the 'transplant effect', which means that the legal order of the 'borrower' "would function less effectively than origins, or transplants that either adapted the law to local conditions and/or had a population that was familiar with the transplanted law".[941]

In this way, a subtle or informal imposition of its law by the exporting country is beneficial neither for the exporting country itself, nor for the importing country. The failure of the technical assistance to provide Benin with

---

938 Berkowitz et al. 2003, p189.
939 Wise 1990, p3.
940 Berkowitz et al. 2003a, p190.
941 Berkowitz et al. 2003a, p167.

better market access could also be seen as a waste of the EU's valuable resources, which would perhaps be better utilised in other areas. With regard to Benin, even though important steps have been taken for an improved food safety, at least in the fish export sector, internal efforts as well as external technical assistance have ultimately resulted in the collapse of the shrimp export sector. In this process, setting regulatory goals that are too high is one of the major factors that have contributed to the demise of the sector. One can therefore conclude that "legal reform viewed simply as technical assistance programs that can be implemented by having Western experts design good laws, are unlikely to produce the desired outcome, i.e. an effective legal order and economic growth and development".[942]

2° Replicating SPS and TBT infrastructure

The establishment of the adequate quality infrastructure for an effective implementation of the food legislation derives from the legislation itself. Transplanting the food safety regulation of the EU translated into the necessity to provide the right expertise and to put together the right institutions to carry out production and certification at a level equivalent to that of the EU.

This required major investments in training, laboratories, infrastructure to check raw shrimps' organoleptic characteristics, but also less costly actions such as the provision of the fishermen with isothermal boxes.

Training has been an essential part of the technical assistance provided to both private operators and public officials to compensate for the gaps in knowledge about the food law in general, but also about more technical fields related to food safety hazards. Providing training is important to proceed to the appropriate transfer of expertise required for building and sustaining the quality infrastructure. A good knowledge of food safety hazards is a prerequisite for the development and the implementation of an effective risk-based inspection system in which roles and responsibilities of stakeholders are carried out suitably.[943]

Due to the hazards associated with fishery safety, building institutional capacity must also integrate chemical and microbiological analyses of not only the shrimps but also their natural environment, including the water and sediments of relevant lakes and lagoons. In this regard, technical assistance also covered the construction and equipment of laboratories. However, these works were not completed mostly due to the lack of commitment of Beninese authorities, which did not make available their share of the upgrading budget in a timely manner, the lack of coordination between many technical assistance

---

942 Berkowitz et al. 2003a, p190.

943 FAO 2009, p11.

programmes (SFP, UEMOA Quality Program[944], BTSF, BTC, etc) and poor harmonisation between technical assistance programmes and governmental plans.

Furthermore, there was the need for the creation of an independent body that would have the mandate of providing independent scientific advice and communicating on existing and emerging risks, as carried out by the European Food Safety Authority (EFSA). The attempt to replicate the EFSA in Benin took a decade for its completion. Yet, the ability of the Benin Food Safety Authority (BFSA) to carry out its mandate effectively is rather uncertain. Beyond the insufficiency of resources at the national level, the nonexistence of a national demand for market surveillance and ongoing regulatory monitoring are major impediments for the successful functioning of this body.

3° Strategies for the improvement of technical assistance

The effectiveness of technical assistance is a much greater issue, even at the global level. A study conducted on six developing countries[945] found that technical assistance provided over many years to build both SPS and TBT-related infrastructures has been fragmented and has not been effectively integrated into national activities.[946] To be effective, food safety technical assistance must be considered in a larger context of national policy and development objectives. In this way, there would be more adhesion from the recipient stakeholders and a greater commitment from governmental authorities.

Capacity building must be seen as a gradual process that draws upon the intrinsic capacities and constraints of a given country. As emphasised by the TBT Committee, capacity building activities, either at the national or regional level, aimed at improving the technical infrastructure or the capacity to enforce (including with respect to market surveillance and product liability) should be consistent with national priorities and take into account the existing level of technical infrastructure development.[947] In addition, there is increasingly a need for a demand-driven technical assistance.[948]

The capacity building process can be viewed as a pyramid-shaped hierarchy that gathers different functions, with the understanding that 'lower' level functions are put in place ahead of functions further up in the pyramid. In a

[944] The Quality Program of the UEMOA subscribed to one of the most important rule advocated for effective SPS and TBT-related technical assistances. This Program aimed indeed at improving market access for the products that offered real export potential for the countries involved. For all these countries, the emphasis had been put on different sectors according to their prospects and their importance for the country.

[945] These countries are Jamaica, Kenya, Malaysia, Mauritius, Namibia, and Uganda.

[946] Gujadhur 2002, p35.

[947] Committee on Technical Barriers to Trade 2011, G/TBT/1/rev.10, p40.

[948] Committee on Technical Barriers to Trade 2000, G/TBT/9, p10.

sequential manner, these functions are: awareness and recognition of food safety issues and practices; application of basic "best" food safety practices in food production; coherent institutional structures for food safety planning, regulation and monitoring; technically-demanding risk management functions related to food safety; and food safety diplomacy.[949] Towards the base of the pyramid are the foundations of food safety management capacity, while functions towards the top are more sophisticated and are a response to the maturation of the industry that creates increasingly complex technical, administrative and political challenges resulting from access to higher-value markets.[950]

Following this approach, Benin, which directly targeted a higher-value market (EU market), skipped the staged process, moving directly to the top of the pyramid. Approaching the food safety issues faced by Benin in that way was certainly bound to fail due to the great gaps between the initial situation and the new policy goals, even though the financial support of a major donor was secured in the meantime.

The technical assistance in Benin was an absolute necessity if the possibility of recognition of equivalence by the EU was to be considered. But considering the results, it remains unclear whether the modalities for the success of the interventions were well defined. Evidently, numerous achievements can be pointed out to testify to the improvements with regard to regulatory and institutional frameworks in comparison to the initial state in 2002. However, due to the collapse of the shrimp export industry, the quality infrastructure is not being used because they were specifically developed for the shrimp export sector instead of food safety in general.

Even if the capacities for analysis may be used for other food products, the fact remains that most activities are still either halfway, or unutilised despite their completion. Most importantly, even though Benin gained approval to export its shrimps to the EU, this achievement does not result in effective market access, casting some doubts on the appropriateness of the technical assistance. It is important to note that, due to limited public capacity and underdeveloped food systems, the implementation of many food safety interventions in low-income countries is premature.[951] In this regard, the example of Benin is certainly a case in point. The trade-related technical assistance agenda might have been overly ambitious, and the stakeholders in Benin were not sufficiently prepared to ensure its full receptivity. Technical assistance programmes must take into account the differences between the needs and priorities of food importing and food exporting countries and avoid replicating developed countries' capacities by designing tailor-made solutions.[952]

---

949 Henson & Jaffee 2006a, p612.

950 Idem.

951 Unnevehr & Hirschhorn 2000, p32.

952 Gujadhur 2002, p35.

7.9.2. SPECIAL AND DIFFERENTIAL TREATMENT (SDT) OF DEVELOPING COUNTRIES

The specific needs of developing countries were accommodated in the GATT and several other agreements of the WTO. This initiative intends to take into consideration the intrinsic development constraints of these countries so as to provide a level playing field on the medium or long range for all countries engaged in international trade.

a. SDT in the SPS Agreement

Essentially, two main areas justify the need for Special and Differential Treatment in the SPS Agreement: the first area relates to the SPS agreement itself and addresses "the difficulties of developing countries to comply with the resource-intensive obligations and their lack of capacity to enforce their rights under the agreement".[953] The second area covers issues beyond the SPS Agreement and "relates to constraints on developing countries' ability to meet the SPS requirements of their trading partners".[954] In this respect, countries are required in Article 10.1 of the SPS Agreement to take into account the specific needs of developing countries while preparing and applying their SPS measures, especially in the case of least-developed Members. Where there is a possibility for the phased introduction of new SPS measures, the Special and Differential Treatment entails granting longer timeframes for compliance to those 'weaker' countries with regard to their relevant products in order not to jeopardise their export opportunities.[955]

The fourth ministerial conference held in 2001 clarified that the timeframe for compliance shall be understood to mean normally a period of not less than six months, taking into consideration the particular circumstances of the SPS measure and the actions necessary for its implementation.[956] In the same spirit, Members are required by the second paragraph of Annex B of the SPS Agreement to allow a reasonable interval – not less than six months[957] – between the publication of an SPS measure and its entry into force. This provision has been regarded as included in the Special and Differential Treatment provision[958], inasmuch as the reasonable adaptation of time is meant to provide time for producers in exporting Members, particularly in developing country Members, to adapt their products and methods of production to importing Members' requirements. On the one hand, this could mean substantial transformations

953 Prévost 2005, p7.
954 Idem.
955 SPS Agreement, Article 10.2.
956 WTO Ministerial Conference, 2001, paras. 3.1 and 3.2.
957 WTO Ministerial Conference, 2001, para. 3.2.
958 Prévost 2005, p8.

for business operators in developing countries as regards their production and processing systems, which may even include subsequent investments in infrastructure and workforce. On the other hand, upgrading might also imply changes in the legislation of some developing countries, including infrastructural modifications and significant restructuring in the control and inspection systems such as in the case of Benin. In any event, granting a phase-in period to developing countries to comply with new measures also intends meanwhile to protect their interests with regard to market access. Lost export opportunities would deprive them of important revenues, endanger their position on the global market, undermine their credibility, and might even require some additional costs to later regain lost markets.

However, the implementation of such a provision does not exclude the adoption of SPS measures to cover urgent circumstances, for which there is no possibility of a phased introduction. In these cases, upon the request of an interested developing country Member, the importing developed country shall enter into consultations with a view to finding a mutually satisfactory solution to specific problems detected by the developing country, while continuing to achieve the importing Member's appropriate level of protection.[959]

From another perspective, the SPS Committee is entrusted with the task of granting developing countries time-limited exceptions in whole or in part from obligations under the SPS Agreement. The implementation of this particularity will follow an express request from the beneficiary of the alleviation measure, taking into account its financial, trade and development needs.[960]

The binding nature of the SDT provision as laid down in Article 10.1 is not quite clear. Similarly, the particulars of its practical implementation are debatable. The case law undertook to clarify the provision by focusing on providing further explanation to the phrase "take account of developing country Members' needs". According to the Panel in EC-Biotech, one must refer to the ordinary meaning of the expression 'take account of', defined by the dictionary as 'consider along with other factors before reaching a decision'. Consistently, Article 10.1 cannot be considered to prescribe a specific result to be achieved or to provide that "the importing Member must invariably accord SDT in a case where a measure has led, or may lead, to a decrease, or a slower increase, in a developing country exports".[961]

Quite logically, it would be rather cumbersome to take account of the vast array of specific features inherent to all developing countries that might be affected by a particular SPS measure. This was acknowledged by several Members within the framework of a meeting of the SPS Committee in 2002. This debate was essentially the result of a proposal made by Egypt that contends that there

959 WTO Ministerial Conference, 2001, para. 3.1.
960 SPS Agreement, Article 10.3.
961 Panel Report, EC-Approval and Marketing of Biotech Products, para. 7.1620.

might be a better implementation of the SDT through enhanced transparency including a process of prior notification. In any case, concerns were expressed that it would be difficult for the Member notifying its measure to identify *ex ante* the specific exporting Members that may require SDT and adapt its measure accordingly, including the specific type of SDT it should provide in each case.[962]

In an attempt to solve that equation, a proposal by Canada suggested that *ex post* information on SDT is more beneficial in several respects. First, exporting Members would get more opportunities to identify the measures or elements thereof for which they wish to seek Special and Differential Treatment. This procedure can also enable greater transparency with regard to the response provided by the importing Member to the SDT request. Secondly, providing the information *ex post* is a better way to acknowledge that Special and Differential Treatment must be situation-specific, that is tailored to each Member's needs, the product considered, or the nature of the risk involved. Therefore, no conclusive information could be reported prior to thorough discussions between the two parties on the specific aspects for which assistance is required. Lastly, *ex post* information on SDT can foster more frequent and accurate reporting by importing Members and encourage exporting Members to request and secure Special and Differential Treatment.[963]

Eventually, in 2004 the SPS Committee adopted the Canadian proposal to enhance the transparency of the SDT.[964] The Canadian proposal establishes a procedure in eight steps, which, without prejudice to the rights and obligations of Members under Article 10.1, intends to facilitate the implementation of the SDT through an improved communication.[965] The procedure rests on the submission of a notification to the WTO secretariat by a Member preparing a new or a revision to an existing SPS regulation. The submission of the draft with the complete text of the regulation must be timely, meaning that the Members should allow a period of at least 60 days during which it is still possible to introduce amendments and consider related comments. This provides an opportunity for an exporting Member affected by the measure notified to contact the notifying Member to seek additional information in case it would have concerns about the content of the notification.

In case there are significant difficulties for an exporting Member, the latter could request an opportunity to discuss and resolve the issue with the notifying Member. This written request will lead to bilateral discussions to examine the

962 Committee on Sanitary and Phytosanitary Measures 2002b, para. 3.
963 Committee on Sanitary and Phytosanitary Measures 2002b, para. 7.
964 The Canadian proposal builds upon a proposal by Egypt to enhance transparency through the modification of the notification formats (See Committee on Sanitary and Phytosanitary Measures, 2002). The SPS Committee saw this proposal as only one step towards the resolution of the implementation problems related to the Special and Differential Treatment and also agreed to consider other proposals and possible actions.
965 Committee on Sanitary and Phytosanitary Measures 2004-a, p1.

best possibilities to address the issue with regard to the special needs of the developing country. To solve the issue, the notifying Member could use three possibilities or a combination thereof: a change in the measure to be applied on a Most Favoured Nation (MFN) basis; the provision of technical assistance to the exporting Member; or the provision of SDT, provided that such an option requires the equal application of the differential treatment to all developing country Members.

It is worth noting that, in addition to the normal period for comments, an exporting developing country may require a 30-day extension to compensate for delays in receiving and translating the notification or serve the need for further clarification. Nevertheless, even after a measure has entered into force (or after the entry into force of an emergency measure), the identification of significant compliance difficulties by an exporting Member may still lead to a request for discussions.[966] This request triggers again the mechanism for bilateral discussions and may also lead to one of the solutions mentioned above.

In any event, the outcome of bilateral discussions should always be promptly submitted to the WTO secretariat in the form of an Addendum to the original notification. If relevant, the form of the SDT provided must be indicated. In the case there is none, the reasons for the denial must be clarified and the Addendum must mention whether technical assistance or any other solutions were provided instead.

A revised version of this procedure was adopted in 2009, which placed the burden on the exporting developing Member to identify for the notifying Member the specific problems arising from the measure or the specific reasons why it cannot ensure compliance by the implementation date.[967]

Furthermore, developing countries' needs cannot be given absolute priority in the process of weighing and balancing the various interests at stake for the adoption of an SPS measure. Other legitimates interests, including interests of consumers and environment, can rank at the same level as developing countries' interests. Therefore, the absence of SDT at the end of the process is not *prima facie* evidence of a failure to comply with Article 10.1.[968] Moreover, Article 10.1 does not stipulate any obligation for the developed country, initiator of an SPS measure, to mention, demonstrate or document the manner in which it has taken into account the interests of its developing countries trading partners.[969] On the contrary, it is incumbent on the Complaining Party – in this case the developing country – "to adduce evidence and argument sufficient to raise a presumption" of failure by the developed country to take its special needs into account. The TBT Committee shall review the implementation of the procedure periodically

966 Obviously, this right is stronger when no time or an insufficient period of time was provided for comments.

967 Committee on Sanitary and Phytosanitary Measures, 2004-a, p3.

968 Panel Report, EC-Approval and Marketing of Biotech Products, para. 7.1621.

969 Panel Report, EC-Approval and Marketing of Biotech Products, paras. 7.1623, 7.1624.

in light of Members' experiences. In this regard, the TBT Committee is granted the ability to modify, suspend or terminate the procedure at any time in its implementation in view of Members' experiences.[970]

b. SDT in the TBT Agreement

SDT provisions in the TBT Agreement are specially tailored to developing countries' needs. Requirements for SDT build upon the recognition of special problems, including institutional and infrastructural problems, which may be faced by developing countries regarding TBT measures. Substantially, Members are required by Article 12.1 to provide differential and more favourable treatment to developing country Members, not only through the provisions laid down in Article 12 but also the relevant provisions of other articles of the Agreement. SDT aims at developing an approach underpinned by the need to avoid creating unnecessary obstacles to the expansion and development of exports by developing countries. This approach would ensure that special development, financial and trade needs of developing country Members are taken into account in the implementation of the Agreement, both nationally and in the operation of the Agreement's institutional arrangements. Moreover, SDT requires in Article 12.7 that Members take into account, as part of their obligations of technical assistance, the stage of development of requesting Members, in particular least-developed country Members.

In this logic, developing country Members should not be expected to use international standards as a basis for their technical regulations or standards, including test methods, which are not appropriate to their development, financial and trade needs. Similarly, they may adopt measures aimed at preserving indigenous technology and production methods and processes compatible with their development needs.[971]

Members, for their part, must ensure that international standardising bodies examine the possibility of and, if practicable, prepare international standards concerning products of special interest to developing country Members. Likewise, reasonable available measures must be taken to ensure "that international standardizing bodies and international systems for conformity assessment are organized and operated in a way which facilitates active and representative participation of relevant bodies in all Member States, taking into account the special problems of developing country Members"[972]

Beyond the obligations on Members, through Article 12.8, the TBT Committee is allowed to grant developing countries, upon their request,

[970] Panel Report, EC-Approval and Marketing of Biotech Products, para. 7.1622.
[971] TBT Agreement, Article 12.4.
[972] TBT Agreement, Articles 12.5–12.6.

specified, time-limited exceptions in whole or in part from their obligations under the TBT Agreement.

7.10. DISPUTE SETTLEMENT

Trade disputes over food safety and product standards might arise between countries due to several factors: the imposition of new or stricter standards, differences in the adoption and implementation of standards[973], domestic economic considerations, domestic public's risk perception, and domestic government's willingness to embrace intergovernmental regulatory coordination.[974]

At the same time, the continuation of several unresolved public policy issues constitutes a major challenge. These concerns could refer to varying approaches to risk management, especially with regard to economic analysis and the role of non-economic factors in risk management, controversy surrounding the role of standards, and the capacity and authority of regulatory agencies.[975] In this context, some countries in Africa claim, for example, that the SPS agreement is not implemented well essentially due to the lack of adequate SPS information about their targeted markets, the arbitrary or discriminatory application of SPS measures, the use of SPS measures to disguise trade restrictions, and the lack of efforts from developed countries to monitor the extraterritorial effect of their SPS measures.[976]

In the event of a contention, Article 11.1 provides for consultations and dispute settlement under the SPS agreement in Articles XXII and XXIII of GATT 1994, as elaborated and applied by the Dispute Settlement Understanding (DSU). The same holds true for the TBT Agreement in which Article 14.1 also places consultations and disputes settlement under the auspices of the Dispute Settlement Body, pursuant to the provisions of Articles XXII and XXIII of GATT 1994. This implies that SPS and TBT disputes must follow the 'normal' dispute settlement mechanism of the WTO.

In a nutshell, a dispute arises when a trade policy measure adopted by one Member is considered by another Member to be inconsistent with relevant WTO obligations. A procedure of dispute resolution begins with a request for consultations by a Member with another one. Only the failure to reach a satisfactory solution on the issue of concerns through bilateral consultations, or unsuccessful attempts to consult, would lead to adjudication. This stage starts by a request for the establishment of a dispute panel. The panel investigates the

---

973 Roberts & Unnevehr 2005, p478.
974 Kastner & Douglas 2002, p284.
975 Roberts & Unnevehr 2005, p477.
976 Nyangito 2002, p8.

specific circumstances of the case, reviews the factual and legal aspects of the case and issues a report on the complaint and the trade conflict involved. In cases of SPS and TBT-related disputes, the panel should seek advice from experts when scientific or technical issues are involved at the request of the parties to the dispute or at its own initiative.[977] With regard to SPS disputes, relevant international organisations could also be consulted for such expertise.

Both parties to the dispute can appeal the findings of the Panel on points of law. In such an instance, the case is brought before the Appellate Body that reviews the legal aspects of the Panel's reports. The report of the Appellate Body is considered final. Therefore, the ruling of the Appellate Body Report is binding and must be implemented by the Members concerned. Consequently, a case of non-compliance constitutes a violation of the DSU, which requires prompt compliance with the recommendations or rulings of panels or the Appellate Body within the framework of a dispute settlement procedure.[978] When it is impracticable for the respondent to bring its measure into conformity with the covered agreement immediately, the Member can be granted a reasonable period of time to ensure compliance with the recommendations or rulings. Failure to bring the measure found inconsistent into conformity within a reasonable period of time can lead to temporary measures such as 'voluntary compensation'[979] or a suspension of concessions.[980]

In reality, the primary goal of the dispute settlement system is not to make rulings but to secure the withdrawal of measures that are found to be inconsistent with a provision. Therefore, solving disagreements through consultations between the Members involved is promoted throughout the whole dispute settlement process, so as to reach a mutually agreed solution between parties to the dispute. Even when the first consultations have failed, a case that has evolved to the establishment of a panel or the Appellate Body can still be settled through consultation and mediation.

Quite interestingly, Members can resort to an informal procedure of dispute settlement to circumvent the heaviness of the formal procedure. This informal procedure enables Members to use the SPS Committee as a forum to attempt to solve their disagreements. In fact, the meetings of the SPS Committee that, in principle, occur three to four times a year, as representatives of all Members, enable Members to pursue the implementation of the transparency provision.

977 SPS Agreement, Article 11.2, TBT Agreement, Article 14.2.

978 DSU, Article 21.

979 A voluntary compensation is not a monetary payment but a benefit offered by the respondent such as a tariff reduction, which is equivalent to the benefit that has been nullified or impaired as a result of the measure of the respondent.

980 The suspension of concessions must be authorised by the Dispute Settlement Body, generally in the same sector as that in which there was nullification or impairment (Cross-retaliation can occur under certain circumstances). The level of concessions must be equivalent to the level of nullification or impairment.

At those meetings, Members can obtain information and clarification on the SPS measures of their trading partners and get an opportunity to discuss their consequences on their market access opportunities. This procedure proved to be valuable in solving bilateral contention over SPS measures.

As regards proceedings under the SPS Agreement, one important issue is certainly the allocation of the burden of proof. Generally speaking, the Appellate Body ruled that "the initial burden lies on the complaining party, which must establish a *prima facie*[981] case of inconsistency with a particular provision of the SPS Agreement on the part of the defending party, or more precisely, of its SPS measure(s) complained about. When that *prima facie* case is made, the burden of proof moves to the defending party, which must in turn counter or refute the claimed inconsistency".[982]

As emphasised by the Appellate Body in EC-Hormones, the complaining party is thus not responsible for providing proof of all facts raised during the dispute settlement proceedings. The complaining party bears "the burden of proving its case" and the respondent "must prove the case it seeks to make in response".[983] It follows that, despite the significant investigative authority of the panel[984], under no circumstances must it 'make the case' for the complainant. In other words, the authority of the panel cannot be used "to rule in favor of a complaining party which has not established a *prima facie* case of inconsistency based on specific legal claims asserted by it".[985]

In any case, many developing countries lack the confidence and resources to start legal proceedings against major trading countries. Due to the length of the procedure and the required financial, legal and technical resources, there is a need to have a strong case to pursue complaints. Benin for example would not engage in such a procedure, considering the significant shortcomings impairing its food production and certification system. Moreover, the allocation of the burden of proof is a major impediment for a country like Benin. It would certainly be very inconvenient and costly to seek foreign expertise to 'make a case'.

However, when faced with limited resources to make adequate use of the WTO dispute settlement system, developing countries can seek legal advice on all procedural and substantive issues through the Advisory Centre on WTO law

981 A *prima facie* case is one which, in the absence of effective refutation by the defending party, requires a panel, as a matter of law, to rule in favour of the complaining party presenting the *prima facie* case (See Appellate Body Report, United States-Shirts and Blouses, p14).

982 Appellate Body Report, Japan-Agricultural Products II, para. 122; see also Appellate Body Report, EC-Hormones, paras. 97–98.

983 Appellate Body Report, Japan-Apples, para. 154.

984 In order to make an objective assessment of the case before it, the panel may need to seek information and technical advice from scientific experts or consult other relevant international organisations. This process is only intended to help the panel understand and evaluate the evidence submitted and the arguments made by the parties.

985 Appellate Body Report, Japan-Agricultural Products II, para. 129.

(ACWL). The ACWL is an organisation, independent of the WTO, that aims to provide developing countries and LDCs with the legal capacity necessary to fully benefit from the instruments available in WTO law. Such assistance covers opinions on legal issues arising in WTO decision making and negotiations or on measures taken or contemplated by the WTO Member or LDC seeking legal advice. A developing country or an LDC can also refer to the ACWL to obtain legal advice on another WTO Member's measures that the former is considering challenging under the WTO dispute settlement procedures.

The ACWL provides its assistance to developing countries and LDCs at low or subsidised costs. As an LDC, Benin, unlike developing countries Members, is not required to join the ACWL and does not need to contribute to the ACWL's Endowment Fund. In Benin's situation, the ACWL's assistance is potentially essential to analyse and guide actions that could contribute to minimising the impacts on the shrimp trade with the EU. Furthermore, ACWL is also mandated to guide countries like Benin in their choice of measures with regard to WTO law. Resorting to such an organisation could help to prevent adverse legal transplants.

7.11. IS BENIN FOOD LAW WTO COMPLIANT?

In order to comply with EU requirements, Benin has undertaken reforms that led to the transplant of EU law into its domestic legal order. This kind of 'harmonisation' is *a priori* beneficial because it provided Benin with a law which, if properly implemented and enforced, would enable the attainment of a high level of protection with regard to food hazards. While the food law refers to all food products, the implementation efforts in Benin itself are focused on fishery products intended for the EU market, rather than initiatives for the overall improvement of the food safety regime in Benin. Evidence shows that even in the fishery sector several shortcomings must still be addressed to attain a high level of protection.

However, transplanting EU food law implies that, as much as the EU is demanding with regard to third countries, Benin has become equally demanding with its trading partners within the spirit of its law. This means that a third country that intends to export food products to Benin must be able to implement food safety measures from a farm-to-fork approach, following the compulsory requirements of traceability, implementation of HACCP principles or risk analysis. In addition, such a country must have a competent authority vested with sufficient capacity and expertise to conduct inspection and certification at a level satisfactory enough to reach the food safety objectives of Benin. This also entails that accredited laboratories must exist in such a country to conduct trustworthy and impartial analyses.

But this is simply the depiction of the ideal situation in which Benin was itself able to accurately implement the law. The fact remains that the capacities to implement the food safety law adopted by Benin are still not fully in place after a decade of technical assistance. Considering the shortcomings still plaguing its production and certification system, Benin itself runs the risk to be found violating some requirements of the SPS and TBT Agreements. Article 2.3 of the SPS Agreement stipulates that "Members shall ensure that their sanitary and phytosanitary measures do not arbitrarily or unjustifiably discriminate [...] between their own territory and that of other Members". Similarly, Article 2.1 of the TBT Agreement stipulates that Member shall ensure that products imported from the territory of any Member shall be accorded treatment no less favourable than accorded to like products of national origin. Yet, despite the existence of stringent norms at the national level in Benin, with regard to the domestic market, domestic producers are subject to lax standards – if any. As a result, third countries producers would be asked, in principle, to comply with stricter norms than the domestic producers, resulting in discrimination. However, this analysis should be put into perspective. The facts have shown that Benin has only been able to implement the food legislation in relation to fishery products destined for the EU market. Moreover, even by choosing to devote all its efforts to this particular niche, many gaps in implementation and enforcement remain. Therefore, the same lax approach is likely to extend to imported food products. This means that, while the legislation imposes strict requirements on third countries that intend to export to Benin, in practice these countries might not be asked to comply with such stringent requirements. In this case, it would be rather inconceivable that a trading partner raises a claim against Benin for discrimination between domestic and foreign products.

In any event, in the current circumstances, it is doubtful that Benin would implement its requirements with regard to third countries in the same way as was carried out by the EU. The expertise and resources are not available to conduct inspections to verify the conformity or equivalence of the legislation of all third countries willing to export food products to Benin, especially considering that Benin imports most of the food consumption needs of its citizens.

With regard to scientific evidence, Article 2.2 of the SPS Agreement requires that food safety measures are based on scientific principles and are not maintained without sufficient evidence. The implementation of this provision is challenging for many developing countries like Benin due, once again, to the lack of local expertise and resources. But, owing to the provisions of the SPS Agreement, it is made possible for Benin to adopt its food legislation on the basis of the risk assessment conducted by the EU. However, since the EU food law is considered more stringent than relevant international standards, it implies that the food law in Benin is equally stringent and results therefore in a higher level of protection than measures based on international standards, guidelines or recommendations. While this is not a violation of the SPS Agreement as long as the measures are supported by scientific evidence, Benin must also be able to provide an explanation of the reasons of its measures when so requested by a Member, which is, or could be, constrained by Benin's measures. Failing this due to a lack of expertise would be a violation of Article 5.8 of the SPS Agreement.

Lastly, in principle, sanitary measures adopted by Members must reflect the appropriate level of protection they deem fit to their particular circumstances. In the case of Benin, transplanting the EU law has practically resulted in endorsing the level of protection apparent in the measures applied by the EU, as well as EU's regulatory objectives. Setting an appropriate level of protection through this process is not *per se* a violation with regard to the SPS Agreement. However, it is important to recall that food safety is not a primary concern for the domestic food market, and the current technological advancement does not enable the proper implementation of the food legislation. This implies that such a high level of protection might be neither necessary nor desirable to satisfy consumer preferences on the domestic market. In such a context, opting for the appropriate level of protection currently required by the food safety regulatory framework would be hard to defend with scientific evidence matching Benin's domestic features.

7.12. CONCLUSION

With the technological development, the improvement of living standards and increasing awareness, expectations for food safety will absolutely be intensified in the future. Regulating food safety, and even aspiring to a high level of protection, is allowed and encouraged by the WTO as long as the rules regarding consistency, risk assessment and transparency are complied with. Therefore, it is quite unlikely that the EU will in the future lower its food safety requirements as regards developing countries. Enabling longer timeframes and providing technical assistance for compliance seem the most readily available alternatives to avoid that food safety requirements become obstacle to developing countries trade. Yet, none of these solutions worked out well in the case of Benin.

In countries such as Benin, domestic-level concerns are far more detrimental than EU restrictions. Internal dysfunctions of food safety systems coupled with limited awareness as regards food safety issues sustain the circumstances for the inapplicability of laws. Moreover a system in which controls are only performed sporadically and sanitary measures are taken only to face major crises is not likely to stimulate the compliance of food business operators. In this regard, EU requirements and their effects on Benin are only a triggering factor for the collapse of the shrimp export industry. In the initial situation in 2002, the same compliance issues could have been raised if Benin would target another industrialised market such as the United States' market. The lack of compliance with mere hygiene rules would be and remain an issue on any high-quality food market. In this way, the SPS or the TBT Agreements would quite unlikely provide avenues to escape the requirements of the EU.

However, the issue of consistency requires consideration. In some cases like in Benin, the EU fails to take consequent measures when proven severe dysfunctions are reported in the food production and certification system. In other cases, like in East Africa, the EU decides on import bans on the mere suspicion that a cholera outbreak might end up affecting the safety of fishery products from Lake Victoria. Moreover, the EU ultimately approved Benin as a safe source of fishery products, although the relevant FVO report acknowledged that serious deficiencies still remain in the production and system. These examples show that in some instances, the EU adopts an overly cautious approach, while in others it refrains from taking consistent measures. Provided that a high level of protection motivates all EU food safety measures, genuine health concerns like in the case of Benin should not be compromised in the face of evidence of the unreliability of a food safety system. In the current case, this lax approach is in favour of Benin since the EU never officially banned Benin's exports. But, from a more general perspective, this inconsistency in approach could be the cause of concerns for developing countries.

However, the allocation of the burden of proof makes it difficult for developing countries to engage in litigation proceedings. The lack of expertise and internal capacity to conduct risk assessments and demonstrate equivalence[986], the costs associated with this type of litigation, fears of retaliation and the uncertain benefits which may be derived from such challenge all contribute to the reluctance of developing countries to make use of the dispute settlement proceedings.[987]

Nevertheless, it should be noted that all trade frictions should not necessarily lead to formal dispute settlement procedures. These formal procedures encourage Members to settle their issues through consultations. Alternatively, the work of the Committee provides a forum for Members to raise their specific trade concerns. This kind of regulatory cooperation could contribute to pre-empting trade concerns that arise between Members, whether informally at a bilateral level, formally in the Committee or even in a dispute settlement context.[988] Specifically, the SPS Committee agreed on several guidelines that help to reduce arbitrariness in Members' actions. Interestingly, the SPS Committee further adopted a procedure on 9 July 2014 to encourage and facilitate the resolution of specific sanitary and phytosanitary issues among Members.[989] Voluntary in

---

986 Henson & Loader 2001, p97.

987 Broberg 2009, p28.

988 WTO Agreement Series TBT 2014, p32.

989 Committee on Sanitary and Phytosanitary Measures, 2014.

nature, this procedure aims at assisting Members to reach mutually satisfactory solutions on specific SPS issues. While the procedure is not legally binding, it enables any Member(s) at any time to request consultations with another Member(s) regarding any SPS measure(s) within the meaning of the definition in Annex A(1) of the SPS Agreement. Upon the acceptance of the consultation request by the responding Member, the consulting Members will agree on a Facilitator, which would normally be the Chairperson of the Committee, unless otherwise decided by the consulting Members. With the agreement of the Members, the Facilitator may suggest one or more possible ways forward in an attempt to resolve the concerns. Furthermore, developing country Members, and in particular least-developed country Members, may request assistance from the WTO Secretariat to promote their understanding of the use and functioning of the procedure. These alternative means of dispute resolutions provide avenues to alleviate the constraints related to the formal dispute settlement proceedings and are especially valuable for developing countries.

The fact remains that when countries are aware that the gaps in their legislation and food systems are too great, even in comparison with the international standards of reference, the best approach to manage compliance issues seems to be the use of WTO technical assistance provisions to enhance their capacity. The EU itself has set provisions for cooperation in development in Articles 177 and 178 of the EC Treaty, committing to foster sustainable economic and social development of developing countries and their smooth and gradual integration into the world economy.

CHAPTER VIII
CONCLUSION

This book has examined the influence of sanitary measures on international food trade, taking as an example the case of Benin, a least developed country, which intends to export shrimps to the EU. Specifically, the book contrasts the example of two entities, different from the standpoint of their ability to legislate effectively to prevent and/or eliminate potential and proven food safety risks. On the one hand, even though confronted with issues of lack of resources and expertise, Benin found itself faced with a requirement to have a satisfactory food safety system, according to the standards of the EU, its exclusive export market. On the other hand, the EU is committed to holding its trading partners to the same high standards applicable to food business operators on its own market. Through such an analysis involving two entities with conflicting challenges and local contingencies, the ultimate aim of this book was to examine to what extent and by what mechanisms the SPS and the TBT Agreements can provide effective solutions to safeguard the trade interests of Benin while preserving the legitimate food safety objectives of the EU.

8.1. FOOD SAFETY AS A MAJOR ISSUE IN BENIN

Developing the shrimp export chain is a major challenge for Benin, because this commodity represents the only important food product with a promising export potential for the country. For Benin, ensuring access and sustainability to the international food market implies compliance with international standards and more specifically compliance with EU food safety and quality measures.

Even though this condition is well acknowledged in general, taking steps towards compliance reveals challenges for many developing countries due to the resources and expertise necessitated to carry out related activities. Nevertheless, a study conducted on six developing countries[990] concluded that developing countries are not unable to meet SPS measures and 'when SPS or TBT requirements threaten their economic interests, the countries are willing

[990] Jamaica, Kenya, Malaysia, Mauritius, Namibia and Uganda.

and able to take action'.[991] Most developing countries do maintain effective SPS control over some of the most immediate and important health risks.[992]

Food safety requirements of major importers like the EU have been catalysts for many developing countries, including in Africa. Countries such as Uganda, Kenya and Senegal have upgraded their food safety laws and systems to satisfactory levels to regain or sustain their access to the EU fishery products market. The fact remains that, in some cases, the situation is not as positive as it may seem. Kenya, for example, experienced the effect of EU trade restrictions acutely in the form of loss of exports, high compliance costs and diverse socio-economic consequences. Looking solely at the global picture or the final outcome leads often to losing sight of major setbacks encountered by many developing countries on the upgrading path. Therefore the catalytic effect of stringent importers' food safety standards is often primarily tarnished by a more or less lengthy period of time where standards are clearly barriers to exports.

While the case of Benin could fit into this scheme, the current situation with regard to market access is contrary to the habitual patterns. The obligation to comply with EU requirements was in itself a catalyst for food safety reforms in Benin. This need for compliance acted like a constraining factor that triggered the regulatory process for an improved management of food safety risks in Benin. As a result, legal reforms were followed by institutional capacity building aimed at providing the adequate infrastructure for an effective implementation and enforcement of the food safety law. Even the empowerment of a competent authority as required by the EU was rather beneficial to impulse a more adequate task redefinition and coordination within the public institutions involved in food safety activities. Although the requirement for a trustworthy competent authority has often been considered a bottleneck in countries where governmental action is weak and unreliable, it remains an incentive for countries like Benin to avoid inaction and seek solutions for issues of overlaps, duplication of efforts and gaps in enforcement.

The upgrading process has undoubtedly served as a catalyst that resulted in the recognition of equivalence granted by the EU, upon the attainment of a satisfactory level of compliance with EU requirements. However, from the perspective of the trade impacts of compliance issues, EU requirements triggered a process that led to the collapse of Benin's shrimp export industry. At first glance, adverse effects could be attributed to the stringency of EU requirements. The EU demand for conformity or equivalence left little policy space to Benin, especially in the face of the threat of an imminent EU ban. The combination of these factors pushed Benin towards choices that proved subsequently too ambitious in relation to national capacities.

991 Gujadhur 2002, p32.
992 Idem.

Furthermore, a deeper analysis of the food safety situation in Benin shows that many other causes contributed to the failure of reforms to bring about a better trade outcome. First, the serious dysfunctions pointed out by the FVO in 2002 were not only the results of the absence of adequate food safety laws in Benin but were also and mostly the consequences of the poor implementation and enforcement of existing laws. This fact is indicative that the same compliance issues would have arisen with regard to any other high-value market targeted by Benin. In reality, the compliance gap could undeniably point to discrepancies even with regard to international standards, considering that current basic risk regulation tools such as HACCP principles were non-existent. Recurring issues of lack of resources, the lack of adequate infrastructure and organisational problems related to public administration also impeded the upgrading process.

Secondly, the small size of the sector, its exclusive reliance on the EU market and the total dependence on international donors to undertake reforms weighed heavily and contributed to the rapid decline and the ultimate collapse of the shrimp export sector. While trade with neighbouring countries is not very developed, targeting other high-value markets could not be envisaged due to the ban on exports decided by the government.

Thirdly, one of the most significant challenges was and remains the lack of demand for intricate food legislation on the domestic market. This has resulted in a *de facto* creation of two different food chains in the shrimp sector. The first food chain is intended for the export market and is required to comply with EU requirements, while the second food chain supplies the domestic market and functions in a virtual 'no-standards' system. This situation becomes more complex considering that the same grassroots actors are still involved in these two food chains. It appears therefore delicate to reach a clear-cut separation that ensures compliance of the export-oriented food chain with strict food safety requirements. In this regard, unless sufficient awareness is raised and regular controls are organised, it remains doubtful that the current 'compliant law' will enable the attainment of the expected food safety level.

From a more general perspective, and without questioning the importance of developing a legal and institutional food safety framework, it may be important from the standpoint of the rationalisation of resources and prioritising regulatory steps to weigh the actual contribution of shrimp exports to development objectives in Benin. According to studies[993], there is no demonstrable correlation (either positive or negative) in sub-Saharan Africa between fish trade and national economic development and/or wellbeing indicators. Several reasons could substantiate this conclusion. First, the contribution of fishery exports is too small relative to the rest of the national economy and the revenues generated in most countries are not large enough to impact the macro-economy. Even

993 Béné 2008, p6, 13–14.

in more well-off countries, the revenues generated by the fishery sector do not impact the overall economy due to the absence of effective redistribution mechanisms.

In Benin, statistical data suggest that, despite the shrimp exports suspension, production did not decrease subsequently. This implies that the amounts of shrimps previously delivered to the shrimp processing plants are currently being sold either on the local market or the regional market. The direct effect of this trade redirection results from the structure of the shrimp market in Benin. Contrary to the trend in the shrimp export sector, operators supplying the domestic market rely upon artisanal practices mostly developed in the informal economy. Therefore, even though shrimp fishing and trade are not fully disrupted, most activities and operators would escape State control, resulting in a loss of earnings in tax revenue and hard currencies.

From a food safety perspective, the direct consequence is the difficulty to motivate these small-scale operators to comply with food safety measures. The possibility of rejection of their supplies by the processing plants' collectors was a sufficient incentive to compel the operators to comply with minimum hygiene rules. With the collapse of the shrimp export industry, the basis for the progressive development of a reliable food safety system in the fisheries sector is undermined. Therefore, it would take a strong commitment from the competent authority to preserve the achievements.

8.2. COMPLIANCE STRATEGIES

The ability of many developing countries to gain recognition and approval from the EU indicates that the appropriate level of protection sought by the EU is not out of reach if countries put the right strategies for compliance in place. In this process, seeking proactive compliance either with international standards or importers' standards is a major step, because it helps to solve the issue of timeframe given for compliance with new sanitary measures. Proactive compliance also provides more opportunities to seek alternative ways to achieve compliance. Nevertheless, a reactive approach towards compliance could also lead to suitable regulation if ways are found to accommodate the needs arising from the level of development better.

It is evident that the level of protection currently provided by the EU food law was the outcome of an evolutionary process. Countries like Benin must take into account that the gradual tightening is also dependent upon the evolution of their market structure. Market access strategies should be more oriented towards drawing advantages from the provisions of SPS and TBT Agreements to the improve food safety situation in developing countries.

8.2.1. LEGAL TRANSPLANT

Borrowing or looking for guidance in other jurisdictions is not a new concept[994] and is not *per se* an unsuitable approach to lawmaking. Countries like Benin have long relied on law from their former colonisers and such initiatives proved useful in some contexts to address regulatory deficits at given times and/or settle various societal issues. However, in the field of trade, and particularly trade-related food safety issues, there remains a significant difference with regard to usual legal transplant patterns. For example, while the Civil Code in Benin applies equally in all society segments, this Code could accommodate differences resulting from customary law that responded to needs inherent to local cultural and societal values. The legal transplant related to the food law was equally considered a solution to a specific issue at a given time. However, unlike the Civil Code, the leading incentive was not originally to find a solution to intrinsic domestic issues. Rather, the legal transplant was seen as an answer to issues of non-compliance with EU requirements. Despite being somewhat a solution to a domestic market access challenge, the finality of this transplant is more to satisfy the societal demands of a foreign jurisdiction.

This means that this process fails to take into account a fundamental factor for a successful legal transplant. The lack of a national demand for the law is a major determinant to its legality; that is the ability of the recipient country to give meaning to the transplanted formal legal order and to apply it within the context of its own socioeconomic conditions.[995] Regulatory efforts should target achieving a fitness of regulations to legal, economic, political, and social situations in which they must.[996] In this endeavour, the process of lawmaking rather than the contents of legal rules determines the effectiveness of legal institutions.[997] Development of law through a process of trial and error, innovation and correction involving the participation of interested legal and economic stakeholders tends to bring about highly effective legal institutions.[998] This argument does not exclude the possibility of a legal transplant. Although social and economic differences between the donor and the recipient's systems are not an insuperable obstacle to a legal transplant[999], the latter must target a proper adaptation of the foreign model to local circumstances. Extensive prior research coupled with a broad compatibility with the pre-existing legal order indicates an informed choice and can induce a better receptivity of the transplanted law.[1000] In the case of Benin, the adaptation process was lacking

994 Wise 1990, p5.
995 Berkowitz et al. 2003a, p179.
996 Faure et al. 2010, p100.
997 Berkowitz et al. 2003a, p189.
998 Idem.
999 Wise 1990, p5.
1000 Berkowitz et al. 2003a, p189.

predominantly due to the lack of resources and the time pressure resulting from the threat of an official EU ban.

In any case, the quality of the transplanted law and its fitness with domestic circumstances is a significant determinant of its effectiveness and hence responsiveness. The ability of Benin to ensure responsiveness is questionable. Responsiveness involves the maintenance of institutional integrity while taking into account new problems, new forces in the environment, new demands, and expectations.[1001] While the EU adapts its law and institutions in the face of scientific and market development, Benin has no underlying internal incentive to sustain an oversight leading to a continuing enactment of optimal laws and subsequent institutions.

Furthermore, beyond the issues related to the lawmaking process itself, it is important to underline that the existence of laws is meaningless unless proper implementation and enforcement is ensured. Only an effective enforcement could contribute to behavioural changes that increase compliance.[1002] The second FVO mission in Benin has pointed out some failures in implementation and enforcement that suggest the ineffectiveness of the transplanted food law.

Weak capacity of a State was a major issue in the capacity building process in Benin, and this limitation largely undermined the effectiveness of the legal transplant in Benin's context. In any case, it is futile to expect that an effective transplant strategy will have a direct or immediate impact on economic development.[1003]

8.2.2. INSTITUTIONAL REFORMS

It is claimed that for most of the SSA countries in general, the stringency of the EU standards has become neither a significant barrier to trade nor a significant catalyst for proactive action.[1004] Due to their lack of adequate food access, many countries in the African Region give a lower priority to the development of food control systems.[1005] This has translated in Benin in the weak implementation and enforcement of its food law that dated back to 1984. Observing similar situations, a study conducted in 2008 concluded that it would be more accurate to refer to a management problem than to a compliance problem for most African food chains.[1006]

1001 Selznick 1992, p336.
1002 Faure et al. 2010, p100.
1003 Berkovitz et al 2003b, p192.
1004 Rios & Jaffee 2008, p69.
1005 Smith DeWaal & Robert 2005, p27.
1006 Rios & Jaffee (2008) reported that the analysis of the levels of total aflatoxins recorded by the notifications revealed that, overall, most African groundnuts exporting countries would face difficulties in providing safety assurance even if the Codex standard were to be applied. They underlined that "Though there could be reduction of intercepted product and associated

A growing body of literature also supports that health and safety standards should not necessarily result in bottlenecks for developing countries. In fact, if it is considered from a strategic perspective, compliance with standards should enable developing countries to reap the benefits deriving from high-value markets or minimise the associated threats.[1007] Although the lack of resources is often alleged for most compliance issues, the implementation of certain steps towards compliance does not necessarily require high investments. In Benin, raising proper awareness about basic hygiene rules in the food supply chain or overall awareness with regard to food safety and its implications for health and trade was attainable without requiring unaffordable costs.[1008]

Assuming that the political will was lacking to upgrade the public institutional framework, the shrimp export industry could at first take some steps towards its own compliance with at least some basic food hygiene principles and then find appropriate ways to stimulate – or demand – governmental action, and also include small-scale actors. Furthermore, it is obvious that, as participants in international trade, the exporting processing plants are used to undertaking market surveillance strategies to remain competitive. Logically, these strategies should enable them to stay informed about safety and quality issues as they evolve on the international market.

At a country level, the lack of awareness with regard to EU requirements could not be argued as an obstacle for compliance. Major requirements of the EU food legislation, such as those on food hygiene or the development of HACCP principles already existed for fishery products for a long time, deriving from Directive 91/493/EEC, which came into force on 1 January 1993. Since EU approval was granted to Benin after a documentary assessment in 1998, it could be inferred that Benin has had plenty of time to take some basic steps to ensure compliance with EU law.

---

transaction costs, application of the less stringent Codex standard would primarily benefit these countries and suppliers that have effectively implemented systems to prevent and control aflatoxin along the food chain and that have developed other competitive advantages in the groundnut product trade".

1007 Henson & Jaffee 2006b, p5.

1008 For example, the possibility of a contamination of fresh shrimps resulting from the unloading on the surface of wooden canoes was only pointed out by the FVO mission in 2002. This shortcoming could be easily solved by the use of isothermal boxes on board of fishing canoes. Yet, the provision of isothermal boxes to the fishermen has been subject to technical assistance programmes which, moreover, did not manage to complete that task. Similarly, raising overall awareness with regard to food safety and its implications for health and trade could be undertaken. For instance, only 33% of the fishermen were aware of the shrimp exports moratorium. Among these, only 40% of the fishermen and 45% of fishwives were reported to be aware that compliance issues were the cause of the shrimp export suspension. These results are indicative that general awareness about compliance issues is relatively low among small-scale actors although they are at the roots of the export supply chain (Houssa & Verpoorten 2013, p21).

From this analysis, it appears that, despite the existence and opportunities of many channels to get food safety and quality information, proactive actions to comply with mere basic hygiene rules were never triggered, neither by the industry nor by the competent authority.

This is suggestive that, without a compelling need, voluntary compliance with SPS and TBT measures would take a long time to be achieved in some countries like Benin. Seen in this light, the provisions of the EU that demand conformity or equivalence puts a burden on developing countries, but it is also pulling many of them forward by setting the ground for undertaking actions to ensure compliance with essential safety and quality standards. In this regard, only the threat of a ban led Benin to initiate reforms and apply for technical assistance.

In any case, seeking access to higher-value markets solely for the sake of gaining hard currencies is not a sufficiently motivated incentive to build up a food safety framework. Given that market access for food businesses currently amounts to compliance with food safety requirements of major importers, it becomes imperative not to consider these two elements as two different objectives to be achieved separately. Improving food safety at the national level along with improving competitiveness should both work together as contributing to trade expansion and improving access to foreign markets. The case of Benin, where capacity was built solely for improving market access at the detriment of initiatives to trigger improved food safety at the national level, could compromise the success of food safety initiatives and the improvement in the quality of infrastructure. Furthermore, it is essential that sufficient awareness be raised as regards food safety risks to stimulate voluntary compliance from the actors involved in the food supply chain. Therefore, developing countries must see food safety as a public health policy rather than a trade expansion tool.

8.3. ATTEMPT TO SOLVE FOOD SAFETY ISSUES THROUGH REGIONAL COOPERATION

There is much value in regional cooperation to overcome food safety challenges, especially in the context of UEMOA countries. Undeniably, regional cooperation offers avenues for solving certain issues arising solely from the lack of resources at an individual country level. The general trend showed that, within the UEMOA, the results of such cooperation are rather limited. When countries are already engaged in an upgrading process at the national level, such as Senegal and Ivory Coast, they are more likely to derive substantial benefits from regional cooperation. By contrast, in the case of countries such as Benin and Togo, regional cooperation has not had a significant impact on the food safety level, and it has therefore not contributed to improving their market access.

This suggests that the extent to which countries reap benefits from this regional cooperation is also dependent upon the true motivation that underlies their food safety regulatory steps. If regional cooperation aims at providing support to existing efforts at the national level, the gains are more likely to be meaningful. Conversely, if regional cooperation is perceived as an initiative to solve national food safety issues, it fails to achieve the expected results. It appears that regional cooperation is only beneficial when the conditions are met at the national level to foster an actual development of food safety initiatives. Moreover, the success of this cooperation will depend essentially on the level of commitment of Member States. Many UEMOA countries fail to provide the UEMOA Commission with agreed upon financial means[1009], slowing down and jeopardising the functioning of the Union.

Developing regional cooperation has proven very effective for the countries of the UEMOA, especially with regard to the development of the quality infrastructure. Owing to the success of the UEMOA quality programme, a similar technical assistance initiative is now extended to the ECOWAS. Weak regulators can become stronger by networking with other weak actors.[1010] Therefore, Benin and other neighbouring countries would benefit from increasing their cooperation, so as to compensate each other's weaknesses. Through collective actions, regional cooperation could be a valuable tool to improve participation in SPS Committee meetings and in the activities of international standard-setting organisations.[1011] This kind of cooperation would alleviate the financial burden for individual countries and provide them with a better visibility and awareness on the international scene. In addition, networking in this way is an important step towards the development of international standards that are more considerate to their specific circumstances. In fact, if standards become more 'accessible' from the perspective of developing countries, there would be a greater willingness to proactively adopt international standards. As underlined earlier, if Benin would have had international standards in place, the upgrading process would have necessitated fewer adjustments and would have been less costly and time-consuming.

Seeking to overcome food safety challenges through regulatory cooperation is also a valuable initiative, especially with regard to building institutional capacity. This kind of cooperation provides a solution for the lack of resources and expertise at the level of individual countries. For such an initiative to be viable, it is essential that the cooperation focus on real priority sectors for the economic needs and the development of the country concerned. For example, Burkina Faso and Niger have no interest in the export of fishery products. Therefore, even if these countries earnestly desire the overall expansion of the

1009 Interview with a UEMOA official, Ouagadougou, March 2011.
1010 Faure et al. 2010, p128.
1011 Henson et al. 2000a, p73.

UEMOA, it is obvious that they would not be inclined to invest their scarce resources in a case predominantly involving fishery products.

Furthermore, a high commitment that leads to regular financial contributions, even if minimal, would ensure the realisation of planned activities to reach the objectives. But, most importantly, it would help not to expect external help to carry out the mission of the Union. Relying mainly on technical assistance to achieve the goals would be a major impediment for this kind of cooperation.

8.4. ASSESSING THE LEGITIMACY OF THE EU APPROACH

One of the mainstays of the SPS and TBT Agreements is the acknowledgment of the regulatory autonomy for Member States. By virtue of this autonomy, the EU can define its appropriate level of protection and food safety objectives within the limitations provided for this purpose. Following the same logic, measures taken to meet this level of protection are presumed legitimate as long as these measures are not found discriminatory or insufficiently supported by scientific evidence.

In its extraterritorial dimension, the current EU food safety legal regime has undeniably had more or less disastrous consequences for many fishery product exporting developing countries. The food law has become more stringent, setting stricter responsibilities and principles for both food business operators and competent authorities, shaping procedures for compliance and domestic decision making.

But this extraterritorial application must be relativised. *Stricto sensu*, the EU food law only affects third countries to the extent that their food business operators engage in trade relations with the EU and intend to market food within the EU. Therefore, it remains difficult to argue that the EU food safety regime violates the principle of state sovereignty.[1012] The EU does not intend to apply its measures directly to food business operators in third countries or to replace their competent authorities in enforcing relevant laws. Seen in this light, the EU food law does not trample on the regulatory autonomy of third countries.

However, by looking beyond this seemingly simplistic interpretation, requirements of compliance or equivalence of third countries legislation with the one of the EU before they can gain approval is in itself restricting the freedom attached to sovereignty. In this way, EU law is actually dictating to third countries the results that must be attained by their food safety law. Therefore, it can be inferred that the regulatory autonomy of third countries is constrained as

1012 Broberg 2009, p27.

to the choice of measures made to reach their food safety objectives. For example, the application of HACCP principles is not optional for food business operators in third countries, and it is not conceivable that a third country's authorities draft a regulation that would not integrate the application of these principles.

The fact remains that food safety principles, such as traceability or even HACCP principles, are nowadays commonly recognised by international standard-setting bodies such as the Codex Alimentarius, and sovereign countries can no longer disregard these principles, irrespective of their choice to export to the EU market. Even though these international standards are of a voluntary nature, their development is often the result of concerted efforts of many countries involved in international trade. Therefore, these standards are likely to reflect the scientific trends and risk perception and mitigation expectations at a given moment. In this way, international standards could serve as a pertinent starting point for countries in their national regulatory activities. For developing countries, using international standards could help to avoid devoting their scarce resources to duplicate work already done by international experts.[1013]

The decision to participate in the international food trade is already in itself a constraining factor for sovereign countries, because it makes them parts of a collective commitment to protect human life or health from food consumption risks.

The approach chosen to ensure compliance with EU law is still subject to the regulatory autonomy of each Member State. Choosing to develop an own set of laws that fits domestic needs or deciding for a legal transplant cannot *per se* be blamed on EU requirements. But, once again, this decision is constrained by the threat of trade restrictions, the lack of technical capacity, expertise and resources, and the magnitude of the gaps between the initial law and the requirements of the EU law. In this respect, reacting reactively was the major issue for Benin in its endeavour to ensure compliance with the EU food law.

In any case, despite the temporary losses resulting from diverse trade restrictions taken by the EU, with the corollary of economic and social effects, these strict EU measures were catalysts for many countries to update their often-outdated system. The catalytic effect depends to a large extent on the discrepancies existing between the initial food safety system of the developing countries and the requirements deriving from the EU food safety regime. When the gaps are enormous, like in the case of Benin, the ability to rise swiftly to a satisfactory level of compliance is greatly undermined. Undertaking a few adjustments appears then to be insufficient to tackle the compliance issues.

The regulatory autonomy acknowledged by the WTO appears in some cases a double-edged principle. In this regard, the EU cannot be held responsible for measures taken by Benin as a sovereign State. Although stakeholders of

1013 WTO Agreements Series SPS 2014, p25.

the shrimp export sector and even some international experts have mentioned EU pressures on Benin to decide voluntarily on the export suspension and the destruction of old shrimp stocks, it is difficult to legally blame the EU for these behind-the-scenes actions, if any. Therefore, even if EU requirements triggered the shrimp export suspension, this voluntary moratorium by Benin is the main factor that prompted the collapse of the sector.

At first glance, the EU approach to food safety regulation seems to cast suspicions of protectionism given that the same requirements are applied within the EU and to third countries. Even the controls carried out in third countries for assessing the equivalence of their production and certification systems are legitimised by the SPS Agreement, although they seem to reflect an supremacy of the EU over the weaker countries involved with it in trade relationships.

Yet, differences in approaches seem to appear in measures due to EU controls, calling into question the consistency in the implementation and enforcement of the food law. Although competent authorities of EU Member States could also be inspected for compliance with EU requirements, they benefit from a *de facto* presumption of compliance resulting from their EU membership. By contrast, third countries' competent authorities must 'prove' compliance with EU requirements to obtain approval for their exports of fishery products to the EU. In this regard, thanks to the one-way equivalence assessment of the EU, third countries are released from the burden established by the SPS Agreement to demonstrate through their own scientific evidence the equivalence of their systems with EU requirements. While this alleviation is extremely valuable for developing countries, it is not certain whether it results in effective and non-discriminatory market access across countries.

As far as fishery trade is concerned, EU controls and approval procedures indicate some flaws. First, in many cases, EU measures translated into an overcautious approach towards risk regulation. Fish exports from East Africa is a case in point showing that suspicions of potential risks could lead to unsubstantiated trade restrictions. Secondly, the major issue with regard to EU trade restrictions relates to the fact that the EU bases its measures on dysfunctions in the production and certification systems rather than actual health risks. In so doing, an excessive focus is put on the assessment of equivalence of the exporter's food law, disregarding the actual conditions of production and certification. This approach has some legitimacy considering that only an adequate legislation enables the implementation of appropriate actions to achieve a certain regulatory goal. However, the approach also bears the risk that export approval is granted to a country which, despite the equivalence of its legislation with that of the EU, is technically unable to guarantee the level of protection of the EU. The case of Benin illustrates this emphasis on the equivalence of a third country's legislation. Despite persistent inconsistencies with regard to the institutional framework and the conditions of production in

Benin, the EU has given its approval on the basis of the equivalent legislation and the guarantees to further pursue the capacity building process.

Basing the recognition of equivalence solely on the conformity of the laws is unreliable to effectively ensure safe products. Likewise, a too cautious approach to food risk management appears to create a zero tolerance scheme. Although setting the appropriate level of protection at zero risk is allowed by the WTO jurisprudence, this must be the result of a rigorous scientific process and not merely the outcome of an overcautious approach applied on a case-by-case basis with regard to risks likely to arise.

While in some cases, dysfunctions in the systems of production and certification sometimes lead to trade restrictions, in other cases, like Benin, the severe dysfunctions revealed did not give rise to any EU measures. Similarly, giving approval back to Benin, despite persistent deficiencies, is likely to undermine the legitimacy of the EU approach. This legitimacy is weakened by the inconsistencies between the results reported and the actions taken by the EU Commission. Genuine health concerns should not be compromised in the face of evidence of the unreliability of a food safety system of a given third country.

However, findings of a violation with regard to consistency depend on many parameters. Differences in approaches should be assessed with regard to the comparability of the risks involved. It is therefore important to determine whether the risk from cholera outbreaks is comparable to risks from pathogens in shrimps. Moreover, the extent to which these differences could be legitimate must also be analysed.

The fact remains that neither the SPS Agreement nor the TBT Agreement make it an obligation for importing countries to actually conclude equivalence agreements with their trading partners. It follows that establishing equivalence agreements with weak developing countries appears to be a trade-friendly approach, which in fact might be more damaging for the EU itself than for the involved beneficiary countries. In the case of Benin, after the EU gave its approval for export in February 2005, Benin was mentioned four times in the RASFF in spite of the dramatic decrease in quantities of exported shrimps. Moreover, in 2009, the second FVO mission still pointed out that the food safety system in Benin remained unreliable even though Benin's law is currently 'equivalent' to EU law. Under these circumstances, the recognition of equivalence on dubious grounds allows a loophole in the EU's system that could result in potentially harmful products on its market.

Consistency could also be analysed from the standpoint of the appropriate level of protection and not merely the SPS measure as it is applied in practice. An overemphasis on caution like in the Nile Perch case suggests a very strict level of protection. By contrast, a compromising approach like in the Benin case indicates a less stringent level of protection. Although the determination of the appropriate level of protection falls within the regulatory autonomy of Members, the SPS Agreement advocates the avoidance of arbitrary or unjustifiable discrimination in its application. But also in this case, differences in treatment do not necessarily result in discrimination and could be justified according to the particular circumstances of each case, including the risks involved.

Proving non-compliance or sustaining a claim of violation of the necessity principle is quite complex, and these options might not be readily available for developing countries due to their lack of resources and capacities. Furthermore, the situation is further complicated by the actual dysfunctions plaguing the systems of many of the developing countries' cases analysed with regard not only to international standards but concerning EU food law.

The former EU's approval system had an interest in accommodating countries that did not fully comply with EU requirements. In this regard, some of these countries could still benefit from a partial access to the EU market through an approval on 'List II'. The increased stringency of EU requirements ruled out this possibility and countries like Benin could simply face EU import bans, should the EU decide to take measures against them. The current EU system put more emphasis on technical assistance. But while this is very interesting to improve the food safety level in importing developing countries, the involved countries could lose market access when the necessitated reforms are time-consuming and costly. In this regard, the obligation to seek the least trade-restrictive measure could lead the EU to consider the possibility to keep this distinction to further facilitate trade. This strategy could be seen as an alternative to giving a longer timeframe for compliance with new laws. This solution could be supported by increased border controls on the beneficiary countries' consignments to enable the EU to preserve its appropriate level of protection.

8.5. DOES WTO LAW MATTER FOR BENIN SHRIMP EXPORTS TO THE EU?

While advocating trade liberalisation in accordance with WTO general principles, the SPS and TBT Agreements provide a framework to protect the health and life of human beings by allowing countries to take measures that satisfy the appropriate level of protection resulting from their sovereign choices. However, these agreements also provide mechanisms to avoid abusive or discriminatory regulation of health risks. Member States are therefore obliged to take account of provisions of consistency, transparency, risk assessment or necessity. In this way the SPS and TBT Agreements can be seen as providing the framework to set boundaries that restrict, at least in theory, the regulatory autonomy of Member States with regard to setting their appropriate level of protection, their food safety objectives and subsequent measures. Furthermore, these agreements also offer the opportunity to ensure cooperation between

Members within the framework of the SPS/TBT Committees and international standard-setting organisations. The work of the SPS/TBT Committees has enabled developing countries to raise and solve some of their concerns about specific issues. This helped reduce the difficulties faced by developing countries to make use of the dispute settlement proceedings. Considering these benefits, it can be inferred that the existence of the WTO is certainly very effective to prevent that international food trade takes place under anarchic circumstances where the supremacy of the strongest countries leads to their standards being imposed in an unconstrained way in the weaker players.

However, can the SPS and the TBT Agreements contribute to reducing trade barriers when compliance issues arise? With regard to the SPS Agreement, differences in treatment are allowed as long as they are not arbitrary or unjustifiable. Likewise, differing TBT measures could be justified on the grounds of legitimate regulatory objectives. Genuine health concerns and lawfully decided measures may not be lowered even for the sake of integrating a developing country Member in the world food trade. But, in the specific case of developing countries, developed Members can provide special and differential treatment and technical assistance to help them ensure compliance. However, while developing countries can apply for such mechanisms, the framing of the provisions make them voluntary and failure to comply does not give developing countries an entitlement to raise a claim of violation and start a procedure accordingly.

Currently, a country that is lagging too far behind with regard to compliance with basic food safety requirements cannot expect to benefit from the advantages of the WTO agreements to sustain market access. Although trade liberalisation is the major goal of the WTO, trade interests do not seem to take precedence over the protection of life and health. Developing countries must then seek ways to benefit from technical assistance and differential treatment to improve their food safety level, thereby improving their market access.

The lack of knowledge about the WTO agreements and the inability to distinguish between consistent and inconsistent measures are also major concerns for developing countries. The lack of resources and expertise are significant bottlenecks for a country like Benin for establishing a *prima facie* case of violation. In this regard, the assistance of institutions like the ACWL is praiseworthy. By providing legal advice, training and support to developing countries and LDCs, this institution could contribute to making WTO instruments more readily accessible to weaker countries.

Moreover, several factors are not conducive to a claim of violation from Benin. First, acknowledging the deficiencies pointed out by the FVO mission constitutes tacit proof of non-compliance with EU measures. Secondly, the voluntary export suspension and the destruction of old shrimp stocks are evidence of serious dysfunctions in the shrimp production and certification system.

From an SPS and TBT Agreements' perspective, the 'sudden' compulsion to comply with EU food safety requirements has an otherwise catalytic effect. Although instruments, such as special and differential treatment and technical assistance, were available to lessen the effect of EU food safety measures, Benin did not make any use of them prior to the FVO inspection. The pressure and the need to comply have triggered the mechanism to seek the use of the Special and Differential Treatment and the Technical Assistance. In this regard, SPS and TBT were then not helpful for improving market access although the instruments were available for Benin to make the benefit of these provisions a reality.

8.6. PARTICIPATION IN INTERNATIONAL STANDARD-SETTING ORGANISATIONS' ACTIVITIES

Many impacts of SPS measures on developing countries that are often highlighted are of a general character and do not necessarily apply to many individual States. It is widely asserted that the lack of resources and expertise to participate in standard-setting organisations is an important issue in the way of developing countries to effectively benefit from harmonisation, because the international standards are inappropriate or irrelevant to their interests or circumstances.[1014] While this statement is largely accurate, its significance must certainly be put into perspective when considered at a micro-level. Participation in international standards organisations' activities should only be desirable if it is meaningful for the country concerned. International trade interests of many developing countries are focused on a few selected products and seeking and delivering technical assistance to improve participation in standard-setting organisations should also put an emphasis on these areas accordingly. It is obvious that constraints related to their level of development will always take precedence over other needs the benefits of which are not immediately tangible. In Benin for instance, 43% of children are chronically malnourished.[1015] In such a context, which policy choice must Benin make between taking action against the malnutrition of children and participating in a Codex meeting on shrimp standards? Even though Benin does have an interest in international shrimp trade, its current lack of expertise clearly predicts that it would not add much value to the debate and would probably not be able to defend its interests, should the need arise. Therefore, it appears that the issue of participation in the works of standard-setting organisation is not especially relevant in the context of

[1014] See for example Jensen 2002, p23.

[1015] World Bank, World Bank to Help Benin Fight Widespread Malnutrition among Mothers and Children, World Bank press release, 2013.

Benin.[1016] If this participation does not translate into actual improvements in the shrimp production and certification system, mere participation cannot have the slightest influence on market access.

However, in these cases, the provisions on technical assistance could be very important in solving the apparent dilemma. If technical assistance is provided not only to cover the costs of participation in international standard-setting organisations' meetings, but also in assisting in the preparation for these meetings, the participation of Benin would be highly desirable. Both SPS and TBT Agreements encourage participation in international standard-setting organisations. Furthermore, taking into account a wide range of interests is the best way to set the most consensual international standards.

8.7. LESS STANDARDS OR MORE ASSISTANCE?

Technical assistance in itself, as underlined by many scholars and reiterated by many developing countries, is one of the most important tools to build food safety and quality framework and institutions in weaker economies so as to provide them with improved market access.

However, with regard to Benin, technical assistance has failed to reach its goal as a market access improvement tool. Despite significant investments from many projects and the recognition of equivalence by the EU, Benin is no longer able to export to the EU due to the collapse of the shrimp export sector. This unforeseen outcome is not entirely imputable to flaws in the technical assistance programmes. First, undertaking reforms reactively following the detection of non-compliances in the food safety and quality system leaves little room for weighing different policy alternatives and making choices that are most suitable for the domestic circumstances. In this case, by transplanting the EU food law, Benin has set the bar extremely high considering the huge discrepancies between its initial situation in 2002 and the new regulatory objectives 'inherited' from the EU law. Secondly, an exclusive reliance on technical assistance to create and enhance food safety-related institutions is a major impediment in the upgrading process. Moreover, the persistent lack of resources, the lack of commitment from Benin's authorities, their failure to solve structural and organisational problems of existing domestic institutions, the small size of the industry, and its exclusive

1016 Irrespective of this opinion, it is of paramount importance for Benin to take part in a meeting for setting standards for "gari". "Gari is the finished product obtained by artisanal or industrial processing of cassava tubers. The processing consists of peeling, washing and grating of the tubers, followed by fermentation, pressing, fragmentation, granulation, drying if necessary, sifting and suitable heat treatment. Gari is presented as flour of variable granule size." (Codex STAN 151–1989). The production of gari is deeply engraved in the culture of a few countries in West Africa and they are the best placed to contribute to establishing standards with regard to their traditional methods of producing gari.

dependence on the EU market have all contributed to the failure to complete the works initiated and the ongoing implementation and enforcement issues.

This case seems to be contrary to the various theories that advocate that the allocation of longer compliance time and the provision of technical assistance might be the most important solutions for the lack of resources of developing countries to comply with food safety and product standards. It is important to recall that food safety and product standards will always exist with or without the WTO and its agreements on SPS and TBT.[1017] Avoiding SPS and TBT measures is therefore impossible, as they are expected to even increase due to the technological advancement, consumer preferences and lobbying from professional organisations.

The lack of resources in some developing countries is an undeniable reality, and it does truly constitute an obstacle to the improvement of food safety systems. Therefore, the application of these countries for assistance is a justifiable initiative, considering that technical competences are actually missing at the national level while the need for improvement is desirable, if not compulsory for market access. Seeking more assistance, or improved technical assistance, is certainly a valuable tool for facilitating compliance with standards, but its effectiveness will depend for a large part on the commitment of the recipient country to reach higher goals of health and life protection. The success of technical assistance programmes is largely dependent upon the ability of the recipient country to take the right steps during the process and to demonstrate the capacity and the leadership to spend the money wisely.[1018]

While seeking assistance is important to solve the issues of a lack of resources and expertise, care should be taken that this process does not become a convenient excuse for developing countries to evade their responsibilities with regard to their own development and to shift the burden onto their developed trading partners. Benin is primarily the first responsible for finding appropriate ways to ensure and sustain market access. Technical assistance could definitely be one of these ways, but setting the grounds for the success of the intervention lies with Benin itself. It is incumbent on Benin to raise the awareness of operators and consumers about food safety risks and hazards, to find adequate solutions for the organisational issues related to the organisms involved in the management of food safety, to establish the appropriate coordination between several donors or several projects from the same donor, to ensure that training activities are delivered to the right stakeholders, and to take charge for the proper management and the sustainability of the quality infrastructure delivered. The daily challenges for operational food safety systems cannot be solved through technical assistance.

1017 Lemessa & Esmael 2010, p19.

1018 Eade 1997, p142.

It is of paramount importance for developing countries to clearly define the policy objectives on the basis of which they engage in SPS/TBT related upgrading. The interest of trade for development is widely acknowledged and seeking international market access is legitimate for its positive repercussions on the economy. However, while taking some regulatory and institutional steps to ensure compliance with importers' food safety requirements, whether the focus is on market share or on food safety, would certainly influence the choice of compliance strategies.

Seeking market access in itself offers a vast array of options to traders to cope with the constraints and challenges of different potential markets. This possibility of alternative options is likely to enable the avoidance of decisions that are not beneficial. The selection of the most effective strategy to cope with urgent needs of compliance will indubitably depend upon a proper consideration of many factors. There is a need for a cost-benefit analysis that must consider the timeliness of heavily investing in an upgrading process with regard to the expected benefits. In so doing, a few questions must be answered. Are the government and the private sector at the same pace and willing to commit as much as necessary to obtain market access in that particular sector? Answering this question is important in this context since a properly functioning and effective competent authority is a prerequisite for the recognition of equivalence by the EU, regardless of the performance of food business operators. Are the resources available to cover the on-going costs necessary for maintaining the upgraded quality infrastructure? If this analysis leads to the realisation that undertaking reforms, even the least costly ones, requires external funding, or worse still that the operational budget must be provided from external aid, it might be more appropriate to consider solutions that are more accessible from the perspective of one's circumstances. When major upgrades are needed and resources are scarce, trade redirection (to less demanding markets) might be the best provisional option to avoid marginalisation. Seeking access to or expansion of alternative markets at domestic or regional levels would enable sufficient time for weighing different policy options during the decision-making process. In this regard, lower prices on alternative markets would be offset by the avoidance of compliance challenges and costs.[1019] In the case of Benin, choosing for these lower prices could have moreover helped to avoid the destruction of shrimp stocks in 2005 and, most importantly, the current collapse of the shrimp industry.

It is worth underlining that other factors also exert an influence on the outcome of foreign assistance. First, the multiplicity of donors pursuing many and sometimes inconsistent objectives in innumerable assistance projects, under a plethora of conditions, can be overwhelming for the recipient country.

1019 Jaffee & Henson 2004, p13 & 16.

Secondly, the natural volatility and uncertainty of foreign aid make it difficult for recipient governments to plan their budgets.[1020]

8.8. LIMITS TO THE RESEARCH

This research addressed and assessed food safety issues from the perspective of shrimp trade between the EU and Benin. In this regard, it focused on the issues that were of concern within that framework. Therefore, this book does not intend to examine all the issues arising from the implementation of the SPS and TBT Agreements exhaustively, but specifically addressed those issues that were more relevant to the case under consideration. It follows that some principles of utmost importance, such as the rules of transparency, are touched upon only to the extent that they add some meaning to this particular debate. Similarly, the aspects related to the adaptation to regional conditions are overlooked in their entirety by the current research.

Furthermore, certain fishing practices are nowadays a threat to the sustainability of halieutic resources. In Benin it is asserted that some fishing methods can produce wastes in the lakes that are likely to influence the microbiological quality of the water and hence the quality and growth of the fresh shrimps. Even though the depletion of resources is also an issue for the expansion of the shrimp export industry in Benin, this dimension does not affect the present research and the compliance problems studied in any way and would not have impacted the outcome of this book. For the same reason, this research does not cover the EU legal framework to combat Illegal, Unreported and Unregulated fishing (IUU).

Lastly, even though the scope of the WTO agreements does not extend to private stakeholders, private food standards have lately become trade obstacles in the field of food safety and food quality. Their ability to impede trade has even increased because their monitoring and enforcement is now increasingly performed through third-party certification. Due to the importance acquired by these private food standards, there are lately often on the agenda of the meetings of the SPS and TBT committees. However, this research does not cover the related issues because private food standards have never raised concerns for shrimp processing plants in Benin. In any case, they remain an interesting topic for further research.

[1020] Eade 1997, p143.

SUMMARY

The recent increased emphasis on food safety regulations has stirred much debate for their effects on exporting countries. While an optimistic vision acknowledges standards as catalysts, there is an on-going controversy that food safety and quality requirements hinder developing countries' exports because several standards and methods of enforcement are protectionist and discriminatory and are thought to be more stringent than necessary to reach the appropriate level of protection or the policy objectives of the importer. Furthermore, even beyond all discriminatory intent towards imports, the growing intricacy of food safety and product requirements, the lack of harmonisation, the prohibitive costs of compliance, and some evidence such as total or partial import bans contribute to fuelling the debate because they sustain the view that a lack of compliance often leads directly to marginalisation. Therefore, the lack of compliance is believed to be even more detrimental due to the loss of exports and the adverse socioeconomic effects in the exporting country. For products such as fisheries that are considered extremely sensitive due to their ability to carry diseases or the ease of cross-contamination during the production process, relying on the sole capacity of processing plants to ensure compliance with exporters' requirements is no longer sufficient to attest to their reliability in supplying foreign markets. The ability of national authorities to certify compliance becomes then a key factor in ensuring market access.

This research contrasts the development of food safety policies and institutions in two different contexts. It first considers the European Union (EU) food law from the perspective of analysing an importer's requirements. Secondly, the research focuses on the case of Benin, which, as an exporter to the EU, had to undertake many reforms to comply with EU requirements. Lastly, the rules of the Agreement on the Application of Sanitary and Phytosanitary Measures (SPS Agreement) and the Agreement on Technical Barriers to Trade (TBT Agreement) are considered for their potential impact on food safety regulation in both the EU and Benin. Within this context, this doctoral research tries to answer the question: *are there conflicts between food laws at the EU, Benin, and WTO's levels of governance and, if so, is it possible to achieve a reconciliation between divergent requirements?* The main objective of the research is to ascertain whether WTO rules could be used as leverage to avert a potential 'overregulation' from the EU while enabling the EU to legislate adequately to avoid adverse effects from an overly lax food safety system in Benin.

On the one hand, an insight into the European Union (EU) food law underlines that the current EU food law, which appears to set stringent requirements, was the result of a gradual process that responds to the contingencies and the needs in furthering the harmonisation scheme aiming at the completion of a single EU market. Likewise, diverse food crises led to the strengthening of the food law to help provide an enhanced level of protection on the EU market. The focus then shifted from the mere realisation of the internal market to an increased emphasis on policies for an improved food safety system within the EU. These policies introduced a fundamental differentiation that set even stricter requirements for sensitive products such as fishery products. As a result, the extraterritorial application led to a prior approval scheme that governs fishery products exporting third country access to the EU food market.

On the other hand, food safety regulation in Benin revealed scattered measures spread through many legal instruments. The former food safety system was plagued with many issues that resulted in poor implementation and enforcement. These issues encompass the inconsistency between the provisions of laws and their implementing decrees, leading to redundancies and incoherencies, overlapping mandates, conflicts of jurisdiction, and the absence or weak accountability of authorities empowered to investigate and record violations of food safety requirements. In the aftermath of the first EU Food and Veterinary Office (FVO) inspection in Benin, the acute shortcomings revealed and the strong desire to avoid an EU import ban were catalysts to major reforms both at legislative and infrastructural levels. The goal of these reforms was essentially to sustain the shrimp exports sector, which comprised merely three processing plants that used to export exclusively to the EU. Due to the limited resources, the upgrading process was carried out relying almost exclusively on external donors. Despite the upgrading efforts, the small size of the shrimp export industry, the lack of appropriate capacity in terms of inspection, monitoring and analysis, the fragmentation of stakeholders' responsibilities, the absence of incentives to implement food safety requirements for the domestic market, and recurrent financial and technical problems were and remain major impediments to the proper implementation of the food law in Benin.

From another perspective, eight West African countries, gathered within the West African Economic and Monetary Union (UEMOA), undertook to develop a food safety framework at the regional level to overcome their difficulties. Such a regulatory convergence aimed at building on their respective strengths and the similarities in their legal and administrative frameworks to address the technical and financial issues that are major stumbling blocks for proper food safety systems. In this regard, many donors invested in several national programmes for legal reforms and capacity building in recent years to help UEMOA countries comply with international standards. This regional cooperation enabled the development of many institutions and networks to ensure a synergy of stakeholders in Member States.

At the international level, the SPS and TBT Agreements acknowledge the sovereignty of WTO Members in deciding the level of protection they deem appropriate in their own territory with regard to managing food risks. Likewise, both Agreements set up provisions to circumscribe the regulatory autonomy of Members to avoid that this freedom serves the purpose of protectionism or excessively precautious approaches to food safety regulations. In this respect, Members must comply with disciplines on consistency, necessity, risk assessment, and transparency.

This research examines the approaches towards food safety regulation in both the EU and Benin. Contrary to the EU, the current Benin food safety regime developed in a rather reactive approach, consisting mainly of replicating EU food safety policies and institutions. The recurring lack of resources at the national level made it a great challenge for Benin to move from a virtual absence of law to high-quality legislation such as the EU food law. Despite major improvements, the process of regulatory and institutional reforms eventually had some finance-related difficulties and delays that led to the collapse of the shrimp export industry.

While borrowing or looking for guidance in other jurisdictions is not *per se* an unsuitable approach to law-making, a national demand for the law is a major determinant of its applicability within the context of the socioeconomic conditions of the recipient country. As far as food safety is concerned in Benin, this approach revealed its limits because the adaptation process was lacking, predominantly due to the lack of resources and the time pressure resulting from the threat of an official EU ban. This reveals that, for successful legal transplants, the recipient country must strive for a proper adaptation of the foreign model to local circumstances to ensure effectiveness and responsiveness. This research underlines that responsiveness might reveal an issue in Benin due to the weak capacity of the State and the lack of underlying internal incentives to sustain oversight leading to a continuing enactment of optimal laws and subsequent institutions.

Furthermore, looking through the cases of fishery products exporting countries in West Africa, this research showed that costs of compliance do not affect all countries equally. Because structural differences are not homogeneous across countries, major disparities may appear in standard setting and implementation. The reactivity of countries in the face of compliances issues is also largely dependent upon the trade interests at stake for a particular country. When the stakes are high, the reactivity and the commitment of domestic stakeholders also tend to be higher, resulting in a better outcome. While some countries like Senegal and Ivory Coast tend to have a better reactivity in the face of non-compliance detected by the FVO, others like Benin and Togo are slower in undertaking reforms. In fact, the importance of the trade volume, the size of the industry, and the 'quality' of the pre-existing food safety system before proven compliance issues are of major importance for the ability and the time needed to upgrade to a satisfactory level. High-quality food safety standards then become catalysts, contributing to building capacity to ensure higher safety standards for the fishery products for the export supply-chain, which might later result in positive spillovers on the domestic market. However, standards act as barriers for smaller industries, especially when they rely heavily on only one outlet market like Benin.

This research contends that better results could have been achieved in Benin through more efficient ways of designing food safety policies and strategies. Only a clear definition of food safety objectives that includes a development on the domestic markets is likely to create the impulse necessary for an efficient and sustainable development of food safety frameworks. The regulation of food risks by public authorities must also be sufficiently considerate of the needs and constraints of the private sector to accommodate the socio-economic development of their private sectors and domestic markets better, leading to the adoption of more realistic standards. Moreover, the development of food safety for export markets, with the vision that this strategy will have spillover effects on domestic markets, will remain an illusion as long as primary issues on domestic markets are not addressed first.

This research also underlines that, while taking some regulatory and institutional steps to ensure compliance with importers' food safety requirements, whether the focus is on market share or on food safety, would certainly influence the choice of compliance strategies. There is a need for a cost-benefit analysis that must consider the timeliness of investing heavily in an upgrading process with regard to the expected benefits. Such an analysis must take into account the level of commitment of both public of private actors and the resources available for the maintenance of the upgraded quality infrastructure. When major upgrades are needed and resources are scarce, trade redirection (to less demanding markets) might be the best provisional option to avoid marginalisation. Seeking access to or expansion of alternative markets at domestic or regional levels would enable sufficient time for weighing different policy options during the decision-making process.

With regard to the EU, the tendency of an overly cautious approach seems to take precedence over the allegations of protectionism in the fishery sector. In many cases, the EU based its measures on suspicions of health issues, such as a cholera outbreak in East Africa, rather than actual health risks related to fishery products. As a result, some countries suffered EU bans on grounds that were later proven unsubstantiated. In other cases, EU trade restrictions were based on dysfunctions in the production and certification system of developing countries, on the assumption that reasonable doubts exist about the ability of such systems to provide end products that comply with EU requirements.

This research further questions the effectiveness of the EU approach in protecting its consumers. While the EU approach seems perfectly equipped to monitor food risks both with regard to EU products and products originating from third countries, the legitimacy of the EU approach in ensuring proper controls over the food safety system of third countries is, in some cases, undermined by the inconsistencies between the results reported by FVO's inspectors and the actions taken by the Commission. An excessive focus of the EU approach on the equivalence of the legislation seems to pay little regard to third countries' actual compliance with respect to implementation and enforcement. In Benin, the recognition of equivalence was established and the approval to import to the EU was granted even though many issues remain unaddressed, some of which are dependent on external aid for their completion. Seen in this light, if the shrimp export sector was still functional, the EU's approval would allow a loophole in its own system that could result in potentially harmful products entering its market. In this regard, genuine health concerns should not be compromised in the face of evidence of the unreliability of a food safety system of a given third country.

The research also argues that the SPS and TBT Agreements undeniably contribute to limiting Members' regulatory autonomy to avoid unnecessary trade obstacles. However, some requirements, such as the allocation of the burden of proof, make it difficult for developing countries to engage in litigation proceedings. For example, the lack of expertise and internal capacity to conduct risk assessments and demonstrate equivalence, or the costs associated with this type of litigation, hinder the willingness of developing countries to make use of the dispute settlement proceedings. In this regard, the assistance of institutions like the ACWL is praiseworthy. By providing legal advice, training and support to developing countries and LDCs at low or subsidised costs, this institution could contribute to making WTO instruments more readily accessible to weaker countries. Furthermore, mechanisms, such as consultations between WTO Members or the work of SPS and TBT Committees, provide alternatives for Members to raise their specific trade concerns. It is also interesting to underline that the SPS Committee provides an alternative means of disputes resolution that offers avenues to alleviate the constraints related to the formal dispute settlement proceedings.

The fact remains that trade interests do not seem to take precedence over the protection of life and health. Genuine health concerns and lawfully decided measures may not be lowered even for the sake of integrating a developing country Member in the world food trade. When countries are aware that the gaps in their legislation and food systems are too great, even in comparison with the international standards of reference, the best approach to manage compliance issues seems to be the use of SPS/TBT technical assistance provisions to enhance their capacity. Enabling longer timeframes and providing technical assistance for compliance seem the most readily available alternatives to avoid that food safety requirements become insurmountable obstacles to developing countries' trade. However, none of these solutions worked out well in the case of Benin. In countries such as Benin, domestic-level concerns are far more detrimental than importers' restrictions. Internal dysfunctions of food safety systems coupled with limited awareness as regards food safety issues maintain the conditions for the inapplicability of laws. In this regard, EU requirements and their effects on Benin were only a triggering factor for the collapse of the shrimp export industry.

When technical assistance is provided, it is important to keep in mind that its effectiveness will depend for a large part on the commitment of the recipient country to reach higher goals of health and life protection. While seeking assistance is indisputably valuable for many countries, care should be taken that this process does not become a convenient excuse for developing countries to evade their responsibilities with regard to their own development and to shift the burden onto their developed trading partners. Benin is primarily responsible for finding appropriate ways to ensure and sustain market access. Technical assistance could definitely be one of these ways, but setting the grounds for the success of the intervention lies with Benin itself. Raising awareness, setting the appropriate administrative structures, finding the appropriate coordination between several donors or several projects from the same donor, taking charge of the proper management and the sustainability of the quality infrastructure delivered, and letting the demand for food law and controls grow domestically are all incumbent on recipient countries themselves. The daily challenges for operational food safety systems cannot be solved through technical assistance. It is similarly important to ensure that technical assistance programmes developed at the regional level are not redundant next to national programmes. When necessary, complementarity must be sought between these programmes, which could even facilitate their implementation.

The case of Benin suggests that without a compelling need (such as EU requirements), voluntary compliance with SPS and TBT measures would take a long time to occur in some countries. Seen in this light, the provisions of the EU legislation that demand conformity or equivalence create a burden for developing countries, but they are also pulling many of them forward by setting the ground for undertaking actions to ensure compliance with essential safety and quality standards. This case perfectly illustrates that equivalent legislation can result in largely differing outcomes (differing levels of protection) in different countries, when the challenges and local contingencies are fundamentally in conflict.

POLICY DOCUMENTS, GUIDELINES AND REPORTS

BENIN

République du Bénin/Ministère du Développement Rural 2000
République du Bénin/Ministère du Développement Rural, Déclaration de Politique de Développement Rural, 2000.

République du Bénin- PNUD Bénin 2008
Republique du Bénin- PNUD Bénin, Plan d'action du Programme de Pays (PAPP) 2009–2013, entre le Gouvernement du Bénin et le Programme des Nations Unies pour le Développement, 2008.

République du Bénin/Délégation de la Commission Européenne au Bénin 2009
République du Bénin/Délégation de la Commission Européenne au Bénin. Assistance technique pour une étude diagnostique sur le développement du secteur privé au Bénin et l'Identification d'un Projet de Compétitivité et Croissance sous le 10ème FED. Diagnostic de la filière crevette. Demande de prestation 2009/220203 version 1., 2009.

AFRICA

Economic Commission for Africa 2010
Economic Commission for Africa, Assessing Regional Integration in Africa IV: Enhancing Intra-African Trade, 2010.

Economic Commission for Africa/African Union 2007
Economic Commission for Africa/African Union, Economic Report on Africa. Accelerating Africa's Development through Diversification, *UNECA*, 2007.

EUROPEAN UNION

EC Court of Justice 20/02/1979, Case 120/78, Rewe-Zentrale AG v Bundesmonopolverwaltung fur Brantwein (Cassis de Dijon), ECR 1979.

Judgment of the Court (Fifth Chamber) of 14 July 1983. – Criminal proceedings against Sandoz BV. Case 174/82, European Court reports 1983 Page 02445.

Judgment of the Court of 12 March 1987. - Commission of the European Communities v Federal Republic of Germany. - Case 178/84.

Commission of the European Communities, Completing the Internal Market: White Paper from the Commission to the European Council, COM(85) 310 final, 1985.

Commission of European Communities, Communication from the Commission to the Council and to the European Parliament, Completion of the Internal Market: Community legislation on foodstuffs, COM (85) 603 final, 1985.

Commission of the European Communities, Council Resolution on a New Approach to Technical Harmonization and Standards, OJ C 136/1, 1985.

Commission of the European Communities, Commission Green Paper on the Principles of Food Law in the European Union, COM (1997) 176 final, 1997.

Commission of the European Communities, Communication from the Commission to the Council and the European Parliament - Mutual recognition in the context of the follow-up to the action plan for the single market, COM(1999) 299 final, 1999.

Commission of the European Communities, White paper on Food Safety, COM (1999) 719 final, 2000.

Commission of the European Communities, Communication from the Commission on the Precautionary principle, COM (2000) 1, 2000.

European Commission, Directorate-General XXIV Consumer Policy and Health Protection- Food and Veterinary Office, Food and Veterinary Office Annual Report April 1998- March 1999, 2000.

Commission Européenne 2000
Commission Européenne, Rapport Final Concernant une Mission au Togo du 28 Février au 3 Mars 2000 Visant à Evaluer les Conditions de Production et d'Exportation des Produits de la Pêche, DG SANCO/1162/2000-MR Final, 2000.

European Commission 2000
European Commission, Guiding Principles on and a Vade mecum for the management of agreements on mutual recognition of conformity assessment, Commission staff working document, 2000.

Commission of the European Communities 2001
Commission of the European Communities, Implementing Policy for External Trade in the Fields of Standards and Conformity Assessment: A Tool box of Instruments, Commission Staff Working Paper SEC (2001)1570, 2001.

European Commission, Health and Consumer Protection Directorate-General, Food and Veterinary Office, FVO annual report 2001, 2002.

Commission Européenne 2002
Commission Européenne, Rapport Final Concernant une Mission Réalisée au Togo du 14 au 18 Octobre 2002 Concernant les Conditions de Production et d'Exportation

vers l'Union Européenne des Produits de la Pêche, DG(SANCO)/8698/2002 - MR Final, 2002.

Commission Européenne 2003
Commission Européenne, Rapport concernant une mission en République du Bénin du 7 au 11 Octobre 2002 concernant les conditions de production et d'exportation vers l'Union européenne des produits de la pêche, DG(SANCO)/8719/2002 - MR Final, 2003.

Commission Européenne 2004
Commission Européenne, Rapport final concernant une mission réalisée au Sénégal du 7 au 15 septembre 2004 afin d'évaluer les conditions de production et d'exportation des produits de la pêche vers l'Union Européenne (Décision 96/355/CE de la Commission), DG(SANCO)/7152/2004 - RM Final, 2005.

European Commission 2004
European Commission, From farm to fork. Safe food for Europe's consumers, European Communities, 2004.

Judgment of the Court (First Chamber) of 9 June 2005- HLH Warenvertriebs GmbH (C-211/03) and Orthica BV (C-299/03, C-316/03, C-318/03) v Bundesrepublik Deutschland.

Commission Européenne 2006
Commission Européenne, Bénin, Profil Environnemental du Bénin. Contrat Spécifique n°2006/120030 FWC BENEF - lot 6. Rapport Final - Provisoire, 2006.

European Commission 2006
European Commission/Directorate-General for Health and Consumers, The Rapid Alert System for Food and Feed (RASFF), Annual report 2005, 2006.

EFSA, EFSA Risk Communications Strategy and Plans, 2006.

European Commission 2007
European Commission/Directorate-General for Health and Consumers, the Rapid Alert System for Food and Feed (RASFF), Annual report 2006, 2007.

Commission Européenne 2007a
Commission Européenne, Rapport d' une Mission Effectuée au Togo du 23 au 27 Avril 2007 afin d'Evaluer les Contrôles de Santé Publique et les Conditions de Production des Produits de la pêche Destinés à l'Exportation vers l'Union Européenne, DG (SANCO)/2007–7566 - RM Final, 2007.

Commission Européenne 2007b
Commission Européenne, Rapport d'une mission réalisée au Sénégal du 17 au 27 Avril 2007 afin d'évaluer les conditions de production et d'exportation des produits de la pêche vers l'Union Européenne (Décision 96/355/CE de la Commission), DG(SANCO)/2007 - 7511- RM final, 2007.

European Commission/Directorate-General for Health and Consumers, Guidance document on the implementation of certain provisions of Regulation (EC) No 852/2004 on the Hygiene of Foodstuffs, SANCO/1731/2008 Rev.6, 2009.

European Commission 2009a

European Commission, Report from the Commission to the Council and to the European Parliament on the experience gained from the Implementation of the Hygiene Regulations (EC) No 852/2004, (EC) No 853/2004 and (EC) No 854/2004 of the European Parliament and of the Council of 29 April 2004, European Communities, 2009.

European Commission 2009b

European Commission, Directorate-General for Health and Consumers, The Rapid Alert System for Food and Feed (RASFF) of the European Union, 30 years of keeping consumers safe, European Communities 2009.

Commission Européenne 2010

Commission Européenne, Rapport d'une Mission Effectuée au Sénégal du 27 Avril au 06 Mai 2010 afin d'Evaluer les Systèmes de contrôle en Place Régissant le Production des Produits de la Pêche Destinés à l'Exportation vers l'Union Européenne, DG(SANCO) 2010-8545 - RM FINAL, 2010.

European Commission 2010

European Commission, Communication from the Commission on Trade, growth and world affairs, trade policy as a core component of the EU's 2020 strategy, COM (2010)612, 2010.

European Commission/Directorate-General for Health and Consumers, the Rapid Alert System for Food and Feed (RASFF), Annual report 2010, 2011.

European Commission 2011

European Commission/Directorate-General for Health and Consumers, The Rapid Alert System for Food and Feed (RASFF), Annual report 2010, 2011.

Commission Européenne 2013a

Commission Européenne, Rapport d'Un Audit Effectué au Sénégal du 22 Janvier au 01 Février 2013 afin d'Evaluer les Systèmes de Contrôle en Place Régissant la Production des Produits de la Pêche Destinés à l'Exportation vers l'Union Européenne, DG(SANCO) 2013-6708 - RM FINAL, 2013.

Commission Européenne 2013b

Commission Européenne, Rapport d'Un Audit Effectué en Côte d'Ivoire du 22 Janvier au 01 Février 2013 afin d'Evaluer les Systèmes de Contrôle en Place Régissant la Production des Produits de la Pêche Destinés à l'Exportation vers l'Union Européenne, DG(SANCO) 2013-6706 - RM FINAL, 2013.

OTHER INTERNATIONAL ORGANIZATIONS

ISO/IEC Directives, Part 2: Rules for the structure and drafting of International Standards, Fifth edition, 2004.

Codex 1969
Codex, General Principles of Food Hygiene, CAC/RCP 1-1969, Adopted 1969. Amendment 1999. Revisions 1997 and 2003.

Codex 1995
Codex, Principles for Food Import and Export Inspection and Certification, CAC/GL 20-1995, 1995.

Codex 1997a
Codex, Principles for the Establishment and Application of Microbiological Criteria for Foods, CAC/GL 21-1995, 1995.

Codex 1997b
Codex, Guidelines for the Design, Operation, Assessment and Accreditation of Food Import and Export Inspection and Certification Systems, CAC/GL 26-1997, 1997.

Codex 1999
Codex, Principles and Guidelines for the Conduct of Microbiological Risk Assessment, CAC/GL-30, 1999.

Codex 2003
Codex, Guidelines on the Judgment of Equivalence of Sanitary Measures associated with Food Inspection and Certification Systems, CAC/GL 53-2003, 2003.

Codex 2003b
Codex, Guidelines for Food Import Control Systems, CAC/GL 47-2003, 2003.

Codex 2003c
Recommended International Code of Practice. General Principles of Food Hygiene; CAC/RCP 1-1969, Rev. 4-2003.

Codex 2006
Codex Alimentarius, Principles for Traceability/Product Tracing as a Tool within a Food Inspection and Certification System, CAC/GL 60-2006, 2006.

Codex 2007
Codex Alimentarius, Working Principles for Risk Analysis for Food Safety for Application by Governments, CAC/GL 62-2007, 2007.

Codex 2008
Codex, Guidelines for the Validation of Food Safety Control Measures, CAC/GL 69 - 2008, 2008.

WORLD TRADE ORGANIZATION

WTO 2001
WTO, Decision of 14 November 2001 on Implementation-related Issues and Concerns, WT/MIN(01)/17, Ministerial Conference fourth Session, Doha, 9 - 14 November 2001, 2001.

WTO, Trade Policy Review, Report by Benin, Burkina Faso and Mali, Annex 1 Benin, 2010.

Committee on Sanitary and Phytosanitary Measures 2000
Committee on Sanitary and Phytosanitary Measures, Technical assistance Typology – Note by the Secretariat, G/SPS/GEN/206, 2000.

Committee on Sanitary and Phytosanitary Measures, Risk Analysis, G/SPS/GEN/209, 2000.

Committee on Sanitary and Phytosanitary Measures 2000b
Committee on Sanitary and Phytosanitary Measures, *Equivalence, Submission of the United States to the Committee on Sanitary and Phytosanitary Measures*, G/SPS/GEN/212, 2000.

Committee on Sanitary and Phytosanitary Measures 2001a
Committee on Sanitary and Phytosanitary Measures, Decision on the Implementation of Article 4 of the Agreement on the Application of Sanitary and Phytosanitary Measures, G/SPS/19, 2001.

Committee on Sanitary and Phytosanitary Measures 2001b
Committee on Sanitary and Phytosanitary Measures, Equivalence, G/SPS/GEN/268, 2001.

Committee on Sanitary and Phytosanitary Measures 2002a
Committee on Sanitary and Phytosanitary Measures, Comments on the Canadian Proposal. Statement by Egypt at the Meeting of 7–8 November 2002, G/SPS/GEN/358, 2002.

Committee on Sanitary and Phytosanitary Measures 2002b
Committee on Sanitary and Phytosanitary Measures, Enhancing Transparency of Special and Differential Treatment within the SPS Agreement, Submission by Canada, G/SPS/W/127, 2002.

Committee on Sanitary and Phytosanitary Measures 2002c
Committee on Sanitary and Phytosanitary Measures, Recommended Procedures for Implementing the Transparency Obligations of the SPS Agreement (Article 7)-Revision, G/SPS/7/Rev.2, 2002.

Committee on Sanitary and Phytosanitary Measures 2002d
Committee on Sanitary and Phytosanitary Measures, A Practical Example of Implementation of the Principle of Equivalence, Submission by the European Communities, G/SPS/GEN/304, 2002.

Committee on Sanitary and Phytosanitary Measures 2004-a
Committee on Sanitary and Phytosanitary Measures, Procedure to enhance Transparency on Special and Differential Treatment in favour of Developing Countries, Decision by the Committee G/SPS/33, 2004.

Committee on Sanitary and Phytosanitary Measures 2004-b
Committee on Sanitary and Phytosanitary Measures, Decision on the Implementation of Article 4 of the Agreement on the Application of Sanitary and Phytosanitary Measures, Revision, G/SPS/19/Rev.2, 2004.

Committee on Sanitary and Phytosanitary Measures 2008
Committee on Sanitary and Phytosanitary Measures, Workshop on Transparency held on 15–16 October 2007, Note by the Secretariat, G/SPS/R/47, 2008.

Committee on Sanitary and Phytosanitary Measures 2014
Committee on Sanitary and Phytosanitary Measures, Procedure to Encourage and Facilitate the Resolution of Specific Sanitary and Phytosanitary Issues among Members in accordance with Article 12.2.

Committee on Technical Barriers to Trade 1997
Committee on Technical Barriers to Trade, First Triennial Review on the Operation and Implementation of the Agreement on Technical Barriers to Trade, G/TBT/5, 1997.

Committee on Technical Barriers to Trade 2000
Committee on Technical Barriers to Trade, Second Triennial Review on the Operation and Implementation of the Agreement on Technical Barriers to Trade, G/TBT/9, 2000.

Committee on Technical Barriers to Trade 2003
Committee on Technical Barriers to Trade, Third Triennial Review on the Operation and Implementation of the Agreement on Technical Barriers to Trade, G/TBT/13, 2003.

Committee on Technical Barriers to Trade 2011
Committee on Technical Barriers to Trade, Decisions and Recommendations adopted by the WTO Committee on Technical Barriers to trade since 1 January 1995 (Revision), Note by the Secretariat, G/TBT/1/Rev.10, 2011.

WTO CASES

Panel Report, Australia-Salmon
Panel Report, *Australia – Measures Affecting Importation of Salmon*, WT/DS18/R and Corr.1, adopted 6 November 1998, as modified by Appellate Body, WT/DS18/AB/R, DSR 1998:VIII, 3407.

Panel Report, EC-Approval and Marketing of Biotech Products
Panel Reports, *European Communities – Measures Affecting the Approval and Marketing of Biotech Products*, WT/DS291/R, WT/DS292/R, WT/ DS293/R, Corr.1 and Add.1, 2, 3, 4, 5, 6, 7, 8 and 9, adopted 21 November 2006.

Panel Report, EC-Asbestos

Panel Report, *European Communities – Measures Affecting Asbestos and Asbestos-Containing Products*, WT/DS135/R and Add.1, adopted 5 April 2001, as modified by Appellate Body Report, WT/ DS135/AB/R, DSR 2001:VIII, 3305.

Panel report, EC-Hormones (Canada)

Panel Report, *EC Measures Concerning Meat and Meat Products (Hormones), Complaint by Canada*, WT/DS48/R/CAN, adopted 13 February 1998, as modified by Appellate Body Report, WT/DS26/ AB/R, WT/DS48/AB/R, DSR 1998:II, 235.

Panel Report, EC- Sardines

Panel Report, *European Communities – Trade Description of Sardines*, WT/DS231/R and Corr.1, adopted 23 October 2002, as modified by Appellate Body Report, WT/ DS231/AB/R, DSR 2002:VIII, 3451.

Panel Report, EC- Trademarks and Geographical Indications (Australia)

Panel Report, *European Communities – Protection of Trademarks and Geographical Indications for Agricultural Products and Foodstuffs, Complaint by Australia*, WT/ DS290/R, adopted 20 April 2005, DSR 2005:X-XI, 4603.

Panel Report, US Poultry

Panel Report, *United States – Certain Measures Affecting Imports of Poultry from China – Report of the Panel*, WT/DS392/R, adopted 25 October 2010.

Panel Report, US-Tuna II (Mexico),

GATT Panel Report, *United States – Restriction on Imports of Tuna*, 3 September 1991, unadopted, BISD 39S/155.

Appellate Body Report, Australia-Apples

Appellate Body Report, *Australia – Measures Affecting the Importation of Apples from New Zealand* – WT/DS367/AB/R, adopted 17 December 2010.

Appellate Body Report, Australia-Salmon

Appellate Body Report, *Australia – Measures Affecting Importation of Salmon*, WT/DS18/ AB/R, adopted 6 November 1998, DSR 1998:VIII, 3327.

Appellate Body Report, Canada – Continued Suspension

Panel Report, *Canada – Continued Suspension of Obligations in the EC – Hormones Dispute,* WT/ DS321/R, adopted 14 November 2008, as modified by Appellate Body Report, WT/DS321/AB/R.

Appellate Body Report, EC-Asbestos

Appellate Body Report, *European Communities – Measures Affecting Asbestos and Asbestos-Containing Products*, WT/DS135/AB/R, adopted 5 April 2001, DSR 2001:VII, 3243.

Appellate Body Report, EC-Sardines

Appellate Body Report, *European Communities – Trade Description of Sardines*, WT/ DS231/AB/R, adopted 23 October 2002, DSR 2002:VIII, 3359.

Appellate Body Report, EC-Seal Products
Appellate Body Report, *European Communities – Measures Prohibiting the Importation and Marketing of Seal Products* – AB-2014–1 – AB-2014–2 – Reports of the Appellate Body, WT/DS400/AB/R – WT/DS401/AB/R, adopted 18 June 2014.

Appellate Body Report, Japan-Agricultural Products II
Appellate Body Report, *Japan – Measures Affecting Agricultural Products*, WT/DS76/AB/R, adopted 19 March 1999, DSR 1999:I, 277.

LEGISLATION

BENIN

Order of 1 March 1907 regulating river fishing in the waters of the Colony.

Decree of 15 May 1914 in French West Africa promulgating the decree of 12 April 1914 regulating the fishing and industrial exploitation of the whale in French colonies.

Decree of 29 July 1924 prohibiting fishing in French West Africa performed using explosives, poisons or other drugs.

Decree No. 207 of 30 January 1950 banning the use of firearms or explosives as a means of fishing.

Decree No. 204 of 1 October 1964 establishing a control of fishery products and the conditions of marketing of these products.

Law No. 65-10 of 23 June 1965 banning trawling and generally the practice of any fishing using towed gears within territorial waters of Dahomey.

Order No. 20/PR/MDRC/SP of 25 April 1966 laying down the general regulation of fishing in inland waters of Dahomey.

Decree No. 183/PR/MDRC of 25 April 1966 implementing the ordinance No 207/PR/MDRC/SP of 25 April 1966 laying down the General regulation of fishing in inland waters of Dahomey.

Order 68-38/PR/MTPTPT of 18 June 1968, Code of Merchant Marine as amended by order of December 9, 1969 69-49/PR/M.AE.

Decree No. 152 MDRC/ S.P. of 16 September 1970 on the removal of "acadjas" from the lake Ahémé and lagoons of Ouidah and Grand Popo.

Interministerial Decree No. 5/MDRC/MEF of 16 January 1974 regulating the fishing and marketing of lakes and lagoons' shrimps of Dahomey.

Order No. 76-49 of 10 September 1976 establishing the National Committee of Fisheries.

Decree No. 85-233 of 10 June 1985 relating to statements and prior authorizations for the production and marketing of foodstuffs.

Decree No. 85-238 of 14 June 1985 organizing the search and establishment of offences to the law No. 84-009 of 15 March 1984 on the Control of Foodstuffs, and regulating administrative actions taken under that law.

Decree 85-239 of 14 June 1985 on the functions, composition and functioning of the Technical Committee for the Control of Foodstuffs.

Decree No. 85-241 of 14 June 1985 on additives used in foods, levels of contaminants and undesirable substances in these foods, materials in contact with the food, and cleaning of these materials.

Decree No. 85-243 of 14 June 1985 on the hygiene of production and marketing of foodstuffs.

Law No. 87-015 of 21 September 1987 on the Code of Public Hygiene.

Order No. 0056/MET/DGM/DEP/DMM/SRD of 13 November 1989 laying down the terms and conditions of registration of canoes and trawlers in the Republic of Benin.

Order No. 0056/MET/DGM/DEP/DMM/SRD of 13 November 1989 laying down the terms and conditions of registration of canoes and trawlers in the Republic of Benin.

Law No. 90-005 of 15 May 1990 setting the terms for the exercise of commercial activities in the Republic of Benin.

Constitution of the Republic of Benin, Law 90-32 of 11 December 1990 laying down the Constitution of the Republic of Benin.

Decree No. 550 MDR/DCAB/CC/CP of 6 October 1994 prohibiting the slaughter of animals in the slaughterhouse of Bohicon.

Order No. 070/MDR/DC/CC/CP of 12 March 1997 on fishing regulations on the old lagoons (Toho - Todougba - Ahouangan - Dati).

Law No. 98-030 of 12 February 1999 laying down a framework law on the environment in the Republic of Benin.

Decree No. 98-215 of 11 May 1998 on quality assurance of fishery products in Benin.

Law No. 97-029 of 15 January 1999 on the organization of communes in the Republic of Benin.

Decree No. 2001-094 of 20 February 2001 laying down quality standards for drinking water in Benin.

Order No. 418/MAEP/D-CAB/SGM/DA/DP/CSRH/SA of 07 April 2003, carrying verification of good practices of laboratory of fishery products, OJ No 20 of 15/10/2003.

Order No. 419/MAEP/D-CAB/SGM/DA/DP/CSRH/SA of 07 April 2003, laying down limit values of total volatile basic nitrogen, trimethylamine and histamine in fishery products, OJ No 20 of 15/10/2003.

Order No. 421/MAEP/D-CAB/SGM/DA/DP/CSRH/SA of 07 April 2003, establishing the conditions for granting licenses and approval for establishments on land, vessels and isothermal facilities for fishery products, OJ No 20 of 15/10/2003.

Order No. 424/MAEP/D-CAB/SGM/DA/DP/CSRH/SA of 07 April 2003, defining the hygiene conditions in establishments on land, OJ No 20 of 15/10/2003.

Order No. 425/MAEP/D-CAB/SGM/DA/DP/CSRH/SA of 07 April 2003, laying down the limit values of lead, mercury and cadmium in fishery products, OJ No 20 of 15/10/2003.

Order No. 426/MAEP/D-CAB/SGM/DA/DP/CSRH/SA of 07 April 2003, Setting the definition of hygiene conditions on board fishing vessels and factory vessels, OJ No 20 of 15/10/2003.

Order No. 427/MAEP/D-CAB/SGM/DA/DP/CSRH/SA of 07 April 2003, setting out the quality of waters used in establishments on land for the treatment of fishery products, OJ No 20 of 15/10/2003.

Decree No. 114 of 09 April 2003, laying down the quality assurance of fishery products in the Republic of Benin, OJ No. 20 of 15/10/2003.

Order No. 2004-087/MAEP/D-CAB/SGM/DRH/DP/SA of 22 January 2004 listing cleaning and disinfection products authorized in establishments on land, ships and isothermal installations of fishery products, OJ No 22 of 15/11/2004.

Order No. 2004 – 1101/MAEP/D-CAB/SGM/DRH/DP/SA of 3 August 2004 laying down limit values of additives authorized in the processing of fishery products, OJ No. 22 of 15/11/2004.

Order 2005 No 3068/MAEP/D-CAB/SGM/DRH/DP/SA of 2 November 2005 concerning materials and objects intended to come into contact with fishery products, OJ No. 11 of 01/06/2005.

Order 2005 No. 3069/MAEP/D-CAB/SGM/DRH/DP/SA of 2 November 2005, setting the limits of organohalogen substances and other molecules of pesticides in fishery products, OJ No. 11 of 06/01/2006.

Order 2005 No 3477/MAEP/D-CAB/SGM/DRH/DP/SA of 22 November 2005 defining hygiene conditions on board fishing pirogues, OJ No. 11 of 06/01/2006.

Interministerial Order No. 1683/MFE/MAEP/D-CAB/D-CAB/DRF/DP/SA of 30 December 2005 implementing fees of control and monitoring of products and fishing facilities, OJ No. 11 of 06/01/2006.

Order No. 0334/MAEP/D-CAB/SGM/DRH/DP/SA of 11 October 2007 establishing conditions for export, import and distribution of fishery products in the Republic of Benin, OJ No. 9 of 01/05/ 2008.

Order No. 0362/MAEP/D-CAB/SGM/DRH/DP/SA of 30 October 2007 laying down maximum levels for certain contaminants in foodstuffs in the Republic of Benin, OJ No. 9 of 01/05/2008.

Order 2008 No. 086/MAEP/D-CAB/SGM/DRH/DP/SA of 18 March 2008 laying down organization rules, procedures for quality control, safety and traceability of fishery products, OJ No. 9 of 05/01/2008.

Order 074/MAEP/D-CAB/SGM/DRH/DP/DE/SA Order of 26 February 2009 laying down specific rules for the organization of official controls on products of animal origin intended for human consumption.

Order 075/MAEP/D-CAB/SGM/DRH/DP/DE/SA of 26 February 2009 laying down general principles and requirements of food law, of food security, and laying down procedures in matters of food safety.

Order 122/MAEP/D-CAB/SGM/DRH/DP/DE/SA of 23 March 2009, laying down hygiene of foodstuffs.

Order 123/MAEP/D-CAB/SGM/DRH/DP/DE/SA of 23 March 2009, laying down specific hygiene rules for food of animal origin.

Order 133/MAEP/D-CAB/SGM/DRH/DP/DE/SA of 23 March 2009 laying down rules for official controls to verify compliance of the legislation on animal feed and foodstuffs with the provisions on animal health and welfare.

UEMOA

Additional Protocol No. 2 pertaining to UEMOA Sectoral policies.

Additional Act 05/99 of 8 December 1999 adopting the Common Industrial Policy of the UEMOA.

Decision No. 05/99/CM/UEMOA on the adoption of the special regional programme for food security in the WAEMU member States (PSRSA/UEMOA).

Regulation 01/2005/CM/UEMOA of 04 July 2005 on the scheme of harmonization of activities of accreditation, certification, standardization and metrology in the UEMOA.

Regulation 01/2006/CM/UEMOA of 23 March 2006 establishing and laying down operating procedures of a Veterinary Committee within the WAEMU.

Decision 12/2006/CM/UEMOA of 29 June 2006 adopting the program of restructuring and upgrading of the industry of WAEMU Member States.

Regulation 04/2007/CM/UEMOA of 6 April 2007 establishing and defining the operating procedures of the Consultative Committed on the Harmonization of policies and laws of Member States with regard to fisheries and aquaculture.

Regulation 06/2007/CM/UEMOA of 6 April 2007 adopting the management plan of agricultural priority sectors in the UEMOA.

Regulation 007/2007/CM/UEMOA of 23 March 2007 on Safety of Plants, Animals and Foods in the UEMOA.

Regulation 03/2010/CM/UEMOA of 21 June 2010 laying down the harmonization scheme of activities of accreditation, certification, standardization and metrology in the UEMOA.

EU LAW AND DIRECTIVES

Treaty establishing the European Economic Community, EEC Treaty of 25/03/1957, not published in the Official Journal.

Council Directive 62/2645/EEC of 23 October 1962 on the approximation of the rules of Members States concerning the colouring matters authorized for use in foodstuffs intended for human consumption, OJ 115, 11/11/1962, pp2645–2654.

Council Directive 64/433/EEC of 26 June 1964 on health problems affecting intra-Community trade in fresh meat, OJ 121 of 29/07/1964, p. 2012–2032.

Council Directive 73/437/EEC of 11 December 1973 on the approximation of the laws of the Member States concerning certain sugars intended for human consumption, OJ L 356, 27.12.1973, p. 71–78.

Council Resolution of 17 December 1973 on Industrial Policy, OJ C 117, p. 1–14.

Council Directive 74/409/EEC of 22 July 1974 on the harmonization of the laws of the Member States relating to honey, OJ L 221, 12/8/1974, p. 10–14.

Council Decision 84/133/EEC of 2 March 1984 introducing a Community system for the rapid exchange of information on dangers arising from the use of consumer products, OJ L 070 of 13/03/1984.

Council Resolution on a New Approach to technical Harmonization and standards, OJ C136/1, 1985.

Council Directive 88/344/EEC of 13 June 1988 on the approximation of the laws of the Member States on extraction solvents used in the production of foodstuffs and food ingredients, OJ L157/28 of 24/06/1988.

Council Directive 88/388/EEC of 22 June 1988 on the approximation of the laws of the Member States relating to flavourings for use in foodstuffs and to source materials for their production, OJ L184/61 of 15/07/1988.

Council Decision 88/389/EEC of 22 June 1988 on the establishment, by the Commission, of an inventory of the source materials and substances used in the preparation of flavourings, OJ L184/67 of 15/07/1988.

Council Directive 89/662/EEC of 11 December 1989 concerning veterinary checks in intra-Community trade with a view to the completion of the internal market, OJ L 395 of 30/12/1992, p. 13–22.

Council Directive 89/107/EEC of 21 December 1988 on the approximation of the laws of the Member States concerning food additives authorized for use in foodstuffs intended for human consumption, OJ L40/27 of 11/02/1989.

Council Directive 90/425/EEC of 26 June 1990 concerning veterinary and zootechnical checks applicable in intra-Community trade in certain live animals and products with a view to the completion of the internal market, OJ L 224 of 18/8/1990.

Council Directive 90/675/EEC of 10 December 1990 laying down the principles governing the organization of veterinary checks on products entering the Community from third countries, OJ L 373 of 31/12/1990, p. 1–14.

Council Directive 91/492/EEC of 15 July 1991 laying down the health conditions for the production and the placing on the market of live bivalve molluscs of 22/07/1991, OJ L268 of 24/09/1991, p 1–14.

Council Directive 91/493/EEC of 22 July 1991 laying down the health conditions for the production and the placing on the market of fishery products, OJ L268 of 24/09/1991, p15–34.

The Maastricht Treaty, Provisions amending the Treaty establishing the European Economic Community with a view to establishing the European Community of 7 February 1992, OJ C 191, 1992.

Council Directive 92/48/EEC of 16 June 1992 laying down the minimum hygiene rules applicable to fishery products caught on board certain vessels in accordance with Article 3 (1) (a) (i) of Directive 91/493/EEC, OJ L 187, 7/7/1992, p. 41–44.

Council Directive 92/59/EEC of 29 June 1992 on general product safety, OJ L 228 of 11/11/1992, pp 24–32.

Council Regulation (EEC) No 2913/92 of 12 October 1992 establishing the Community Customs Code, OJ L302 of 19/10/1992, p 0001 – 0050.

Council Directive 93/43/EEC of 14 June 1993 on the Hygiene of Foodstuffs, OJ L 175 / 1, 19/07/1993.

Council Decision 95/408/EC of 22 June 1995 on the conditions for drawing up, for an interim period, provisional lists of third country establishments from which Member States are authorized to import certain products of animal origin, fishery products or live bivalve molluscs, OJ L 243 of 11/10/1995, p. 17–20.

Regulation (EC) No 2232/96 of the European Parliament and of the Council of 28 October 1996 laying down a Community procedure for flavouring substances used or intended for use in or on foodstuffs, OJ L299/1 of 23/11/1996.

Council Directive 97/78/EC of 18 December 1997 laying down the principles governing the organization of veterinary checks on products entering the Community from third countries, OJ L 24 of 30/1/1998.

Commission Decision 97/296/EC of 22/04/1997 drawing up the list of third countries from which the import of fishery products is authorized for human consumption. OJ L 122 of 14/05/1997, p. 21–23.

Council Decision 98/603/EC of 19 October 1998 amending Decision 95/408/EC on the conditions for drawing up, for an interim period, provisional lists of third-country establishments from which Member States are authorised to import certain products of animal origin, fishery products or live bivalve molluscs, OJ L 289 of 28/10/1998, p. 36–36.

Council Regulation (EC) No 104/2000 of 17 December 1999 on the common organization of the markets in fishery and aquaculture products, OJ L17/22 of 22/01/2000.

Commission Regulation (EC) No 466/2001 of 8 March 2001 setting maximum levels for certain contaminants in foodstuffs, OJ L 77/1 of 16/3/2001.

Regulation (EC) No 1049/2001 of the European Parliament and of the Council of 30 May 2001 regarding public access to European Parliament, Council and Commission documents, OJ L154/43 of 31/05/2001.

Commission Decision 2001/635/EC of 16 August 2001 amending Decision 97/296/EC drawing up the list of third countries from which the import of fishery products is authorized for human consumption, OJ L 221/56.

Commission Decision 2001/675/EC of 20 August 2001 amending Decision 97/20/EC establishing the list of third countries fulfilling the equivalence conditions for the production and placing on the market of bivalve molluscs, echinoderms, tunicates and marine gastropods, OJ L236/16 of 5/09/2001.

Commission Decision 2001/699/EC of 19 September 2001 concerning certain protective measures with regard to certain fishery and aquaculture products intended for human consumption and originating in China and Vietnam, OJ L251/11 of 20/10/2001.

Commission Regulation (EC) No 2065/2001 of 22 October 2001 laying down detailed rules for the application of Council Regulation (EC) No 104/2000 as regards informing consumers about fishery and aquaculture products, OJ L278/6 of 23/10/2001.

Commission Decision 2001/881/EC of 7 December 2001 drawing up a list of border inspection posts agreed for veterinary checks on animals and animal products from third countries and updating the detailed rules concerning the checks to be carried out by the experts of the Commission, OJ L326 of 11/12/2001.

Regulation (EC) No 178/2002 of the European Parliament and of the Council of 28/01/2002 laying down the general principles and requirements of food law, establishing the European Food Safety Authority and laying down procedures in matters of food safety; OJ L31 of 01/02/2002.

Regulation (EC) No 852/2004 of the European Parliament and of the Council of 29 April 2004 on the hygiene of foodstuffs, OJ L 139/1 of 30/4/2004.

Regulation (EC) 853/2004 of the Parliament and the Council of 29 April 2004 laying down specific hygiene rules on the hygiene of foodstuffs, OJ L139/55 of 30/4/2004.

Regulation (EC) No 854/2004, of the European Parliament and of the Council of 29 April 2004 laying down specific rules for the organization of official controls on products of animal origin intended for human consumption, OJ L 139 of 30/4/2004.

Regulation (EC) No 882/2004 of the European Parliament and of the Council of the 29 April 2004 on official controls performed to ensure the verification of compliance with feed and food law, animal health and animal welfare rules, OJ L 191 of 28/5/2004.

Regulation (EC) No 2230/2004 of 23 December 2004 laying down detailed rules for the implementation of European Parliament and Council Regulation (EC) No 178/2002 with regard to the network of organizations operating in the fields within the European Food Safety Authority's mission, OJ L 379/64 of 24/12/2004.

Commission Regulation (EC) No. 208/2005 of 4 February 2005 amending Commission Regulation (EC) No. 466/2001 as regards polycyclic aromatic hydrocarbons OJ L34/3 of 8/2/2005.

Commission Regulation 2073/2005 of 15 November 2005 on microbiological criteria for foodstuffs, OJ L 338/1 of 22/12/2005.

Regulation (EC) No 2074/2005 of 5 December 2005 laying down implementing measures for certain products under Regulation (EC) No 853/2004 of the European Parliament and of the Council and for the organization of official controls under Regulation (EC) No 854/2004 of the European Parliament and of the Council and Regulation (EC) No 882/2004 of the European Parliament and of the Council, derogating from Regulation (EC) No 852/2004 of the European Parliament and of the Council and amending Regulations (EC) No 853/2004 and (EC) No 854/2004, OJ L 338/27 of 22/12/2005.

Council Directive 2006/52/EC of 5 July 2006 amending Directive 95/2/EC on food additives other than colours and sweeteners and Directive 94/35/EC on sweeteners for use in foodstuffs, OJ L 204/10 of 26/7/2007.

The Treaty on the Functioning of the European Union (TFEU), OJ C115/47 of 09/05/2008.

BIBLIOGRAPHY

Ababouch et al. 2005
Ababouch, L., Gandini, G. & Ryder, J., Causes of Detentions and Rejections in International Fish Trade, *FAO Fisheries Technical Paper.* No. 473. Rome, FAO, 2005.

Ababouch 2006
Ababouch, L., Assuring Fish Safety and Quality in International Fish trade, *Marine Pollution Bulletin* No 53, 2006, pp 561–568.

Abila 2003
Abila, R. O., Food Safety in Food Security and Food Trade, Case Study: Kenyan Fish Exports, 2020 vision for food, agriculture and the environment, *Focus 10, Brief 8 of 17,* 2003.

Africa Research Bulletin, 2011
BENIN: Challenges Ahead. *Africa Research Bulletin: Economic, financial and Technical Series.* Vol 48, Issues 4, 19081A-19081C, 2011.

Akyoo & Lazaro 2008
Akyoo, A. & Lazaro, E., Institutional Capacity for Standards Conformity Assessment. A Case Study on Spices in Tanzania, *DIIS Working Paper,* Danish Institute for International Studies, 2008, pp1–40.

Alemanno 2006
Alemanno, A., The Evolution of European Food Regulation, Why the European Food Safety Authority is not a EU-style FDA, in What's the Beef, the contested governance of European food safety, C. Ansell and D. Vogel eds, *Bocconi legal research working paper,* 1007451, 2006.

Alemanno 2007
Alemanno, Trade in food. Regulatory and Judicial Approaches in the EC and the WTO, *Cameron May Ltd,* 2007.

Alemanno 2007b
Alemanno, A., Science and EU Risk Regulation The Role of Experts in Decision-making and Judicial Review, Young Researchers Workshop on Science and Law, Scientific Evidence in International and European Law, *ISUFI,* Italy, 2007.

Alemanno 2009
Alemanno, A., Solving the problem of scale: The European Approach to Import Safety and Security Concerns; in Import Safety: Regulatory Governance in the Global Economy, *Cary Coglianese, Adam Finkel, David Zaring, eds.,* University of Pennsylvania Press, 2009.

Alemanno 2013

Alemanno, A., Is there a Role for Cost-Benefit Analysis Beyond the Nation-State? Lessons from International Regulatory Co-operation, In the Globalization of Cost-Benefit Analysis in Environmental Policy, *Michael A. Livermore & Richard L. Revesz eds*, forthcoming, 2013.

Amaskane 2010

Amaksane, M., Appui aux Systèmes d'Information sur les Mesures Sanitaires et Phytosanitaires au Bénin, Rapport de Mission Projet MTF/BEN/053/STF (Mission du 17/03/2010 au 07/04/2010), *FAO*, 2010.

Anders & Caswell 2009

Anders S. & Caswell, J., Standards as Barriers versus Standards as Catalysts: Assessing the impact of HACCP Implementation on US Seafood Imports, *Amer. J. Agr. Econ.* 91(2) 2009; pp 310–321.

Arcuri 2012

Arcuri, A., Law and Economics of the SPS Agreement: A critical perspective, *Rotterdam Institute of Law and Economics (RILE) Working Paper Series*, 2012.

Atik 2011

Atik, J., On the Efficiency of Health Measures and the 'Appropriate Level of Protection in Research Handbook on Environment, Health and the WTO, Denise Prévost & Geert Van Calster, eds., Edward Elgar, 2012; Loyola-LA Legal Studies Paper No. 2011-43, 2011.

BafD/OECD 2006

BafD/OECD, Perspectives Economiques en Afrique 2005–2006 Bénin. *Banque Africaine de Développement/Organisation de Coopération et de Développement Economique*, 2006 pp147–161.

Baldwin 2000

Baldwin, R. E., Regulatory Protectionism, Developing Nations and a Two-Tier World Trade System, *Brookings Trade Forum*, 2000, pp. 237–280.

Banque Mondiale 2006

Banque Mondiale, La Problématique Sanitaire et Phytosanitaire au Niger, *La Banque Mondiale, ESSD/Afrique*, 2006.

Bayili 2003

Bayili, J., Programme pour la Mise en Place d'un Système d'Accréditation, de Normalisation et de Promotion de la Qualité au sein de l'UEMOA (EU/RAF/01/001), Coordination Technique du programme, Synthèse Générale des rapports techniques Sur l'état des lieux détaillé de la situation des pays de l'UEMOA en matière d'accréditation et de certification, *ONUDI/UEMOA/UE*, 2003.

Beghin & Bureau, 2001

Beghin, J. C. & Bureau J.C.,Quantification of Sanitary, Phytosanitary, and Technical Barriers to Trade for Trade Policy Analysis, *Centre for Agricultural and Rural Development* Iowa State University *Working Paper 01-WP 291,* 2001, pp 1–35.

Béné 2008
Béné, C., Global Change in African Fish Trade: Engine of Development or Threat to Local Food Security?, *OECD Food, Agriculture and Fisheries Working Papers*, 10, OECD publishing, © OECD. doi:10.1787/230215206300.

Berkowitz et al. 2003a
Berkowitz, D., Pistor, K. & Richard, J.F., The Transplant Effect, *The American Journal of Comparative Law*, 51(1), 2003, pp. 163–203.

Berkowitz et al. 2003b
Berkowitz, D., Pistor, K. & Richard, J.F., Economic Development, Legality, and the Transplant Effect, *European Economic Review*, 47(1), 2003, pp 165–195.

Bernauer & Caduff 2006
Bernauer, T., & Caduff, L., Food Safety and the Structure of the European Food Industry, in What's the beef? The Contested Governance of European Food Safety, *C. Ansell and D. Vogel eds*, 2006, pp 81–95.

Blanc 2003
Blanc, F., Rapport Final/ Appui à l'Autorité Compétente Numéro de Projet JVCS: 80.2935.01_002, Mission du 26 Juin – 5 Aout 2003, Benin Module 1-A Requete de services N° 4/05/03/BEN, *Secretariat Général du Groupe des Etats ACP-Amélioration de l'Etat Sanitaire des Produits de la Peche dans les Etats ACP et les PTOM REG./70021/000 – 8.ACP.TPS.137, 1748/R/01/C*, 2003, pp105.

Bossche (van den) et al. 2005
Bossche, van den. P., Prévost D. and Matthee, M., WTO Rules on Technical Barriers to Trade, *Maastricht Faculty of Law Working Paper 2005/6*, 2005.

Broberg, 2009
Broberg, M., European Food Safety Regulation and the Developing Countries; Regulatory Problems and Possibilities, *DIIS working Paper 2009:09*, Standards and Agro-food exports (SAFE), 2009.

Brown 2005
Brown, O., EU Trade Policy and Conflict, *International Institute for Sustainable Development*, 2005.

BTC 2011
BTC, Appui au Développement des Filières Halieutiques du Bénin, BEN0601311. Rapport Final. 2011.

Business Africa 2011
Business Africa, The Republic of Benin Briefs, *Newsletter ISSN 1563–4108*, 2011.

Buzby & Unnevehr 2003
Buzby J. C., & Unnevehr, L., International Trade and Food Safety, Economic Theory and Case Studies, *Agricultural Economic Report* 828, 2003.

Buzby & Unnevehr 2004

Buzby J. C., & Unnevehr, L., Food Safety and International Trade, *Issues in Diet, Safety and Health/ Agriculture Information* Bulletin Number 789–1, 2004.

Caffagi 2010

Caffagi, F., New Foundations of Transnational Private Regulation, EUI Working Papers, RSCAS 2010/53, *Robert Schuman Centre for Advanced Studies Private Regulation Series*-04, 2010.

Caldeira, et al., 2010

Caldeira, E., Rota-Graziosi, G. & Foucault, M., Decentralisation in Africa and Fiscal Competition: Evidence from Benin, *CIRANO – Scientific Publications* 2010s-35, 2010.

Caswell & Hooker 1996

Caswell, J. A. & Hooker, N. H., HACCP as an International Trade Standard, *American Journal of Agricultural Economics*, 1996, pp775–779.

Chalmers et al. 2010

Chalmers, D., Davies, G., & Monti G., European Union Law – Cases and Materials, Second edition, Cambridge University Press, 2010.

Charnovitz 2002

Charnovitz, S., International Standards and the WTO, The George Washington University Law School, *Public Law and Legal Theory Working Paper*, 2002.

Crosnier & De Bondy 1967

Crosnier, A. & De Bondy, E., Les Crevettes Commercialisables de la Cote-Ouest de l'Afrique Inter-tropicale. Etat de nos Connaissances sur leur Biologie et leur Pêche en Juillet 1967, *Initiations- Documentations Techniques No 7*. Office de la Recherche Scientifique et Technique d'Outre-Mer (ORSTOM), 1967.

CTA 2003

CTA, The EC Traceability and Equivalence Rules in the Light of the SPS Agreement: A Review of the Main Legal Issues, *O'Connor and Company*, 2003.

DaSilva-Glasgow & Bynoe 2012

DaSilva-Glasgow, D. & Bynoe, M., Strategic Response to Evolving Food Safety Standards: A Case Study of Guyana's Fish Export Sector, *Estey Centre Journal of International Law and Trade Policy*, 2012, pp 201–215.

Decaluwe & Robichaud 2008

Decaluwe, B., & Robichaud, V., Trade Policy and Poverty in Benin: A General Equilibrium Analysis. *Poverty and Economic Policy Research Network Working Paper No. MPIA-2008-14*. 2008.

Degbey 2004

Degbey J.B., Plan d'Actions National des Pêches, Ministère de l'Agriculture, de la pêche et de l'Elevage, 2004.

Diaz Rios & Jaffee 2008
Diaz Rios, L. B. & Jaffee, S., Barrier, Catalyst, or Distraction? Standards, Competitiveness, and Africa's Groundnut Exports to Europe, *Agriculture and Rural Development Discussion Paper*, World Bank, 2008, pp 1–83.

Dominguez & Foster 2011
Dominguez, C. & Foster, V., Benin's Infrastructure: A Continental Perspective. *World Bank Policy Research Working Paper Series No. 5689*, 2011.

Dossou et al. 2010
Dossou, J., Tobada, P., Sedogbo, Y. A., Mama, D., Tossou S., Ouikoun, G., Laleye, P., & Capo-Chichi, B., Impacts de la Pollution de l'Environnement sur la Qualité Sanitaire des Crevettes Capturées sur les Pêcheries du Lac Nokoué, *Annales de la faculté des Lettres, Arts et Sciences Humaines de l'Université d'Abomey-Calavi*, 16(1), 2010, pp120–133.

Du 2010a
Du, M. M., Reducing Product Standards Heterogeneity through International Standards in the WTO: How Far across the River? *Journal of World Trade*, 2010, pp 295–318.

Du 2010b
Du, M. M., Standard of Review under the SPS Agreement after EC-Hormones II, *International and Comparative Law Quarterly*, 59, 2010, pp. 441–459.

Eade 1997
Eade, D., Capacity-Building. An Approach to People-centered Development, Oxfam development Guidelines, Oxfam UK and Ireland, 1997.

Fafchamps & Gabre-Madhin 2001
Fafchamps, M. & Gabre-Madhin, E., Agricultural Markets in Benin and Malawi: The Operation and Performance of Traders, *World Bank Policy Research Working Paper* No. 2734, 2001.

FAO 1999
FAO, The importance of Food Quality and Safety for Developing Countries, 25th session of Committee on World Food Security, Rome, 31 May – 3 June 1999, *FAO*, 1999.

FAO 2003
FAO, The State of Food Insecurity in the World. Monitoring Progress towards the World Food Summit and Millennium Development Goals. Rome: *Food and Agriculture Organization*, 2003.

FAO 2008
FAO, Vue Générale du Secteur des Pêches National, République du Bénin, Fishery and aquaculture country profiles, *FAO*, 2008.

FAO 2009
FAO, Guidelines for Risk-based Fish Inspection, *FAO Food and Nutrition Paper 90*, 2009.

FAO/WHO 1997
FAO/WHO, Risk management and food safety, *FAO Food and Nutrition Paper 65*, 1997.

FAO/WHO 1998

FAO/WHO, The Application of Risk Communication to Food Standards and Safety Matters, 1998.

FAO/WHO 2004

FAO/WHO, Regional Office for Africa, 'Developing and Maintaining Food Safety Control Systems for Africa - Current Status and Prospects for Change', presented at the FAO/WHO Second Global Forum of Food Safety Regulators, Conference Room Document 32, *Food and Agriculture Organization and World Health Organization*, Bangkok, Thailand, 12–14 October 2004, 2004.

Faure et al. 2010

Faure, M., Goodwin M., & Weber, F., Bucking the Kuznets Curve: Designing Effective Environmental Regulation in Developing Countries, *Virginia Journal of International Law*, 51, 2010, pp95–157.

Fazil 2005

Fazil, A. M., A Primer on Risk Assessment Modelling: Focus on Seafood Products, *FAO Fisheries Technical Paper- T462*, 2005.

Féral & Coulibaly 2004

Féral F. & Coulibaly H., Programme Spécial Régional pour la Sécurité Alimentaire des Etats Membres de L'Union Economique et Monétaire Ouest Africaine. Rapport de Synthèse des Rapports des Experts Internationaux concernant le Cadre Juridique et Institutionnel de la Sécurité Sanitaire des Aliments et des Contrôles, les Moyens et l'Organisation Pratique de la Surveillance et des Contrôles, les Moyens d'Analyse en Laboratoire et la Décentralisation et la Société Civile face à la Sécurité Sanitaire des Aliments. Projet UTF/UEM/001/UEM- Projet TCP/RAF/075, 2004.

Gascoine 1999

Gascoine, D., Harmonisation, Mutual Recognition and Equivalence - How and What Is Attainable?, presented at the *Conference on International Food Trade Beyond 2000: Science-Based Decisions, Harmonization, Equivalence and Mutual Recognition* (Food and Agriculture Organization of the United Nations, Melbourne Australia) 11–15 October 1999.

Gavard 2006

Gavard, P., Elaboration d'un Plan de Surveillance des Contaminants Environnementaux du milieu Aquatique au Bénin, Cameroun et Togo, Projet no. 46/07/06/FWA/SC1, Rapport de Mission du 7 Novembre au 10 Décembre, SFP-ACP/OCT, 2006.

Gebrehiwet et al. 2007

Gebrehiwet, Y., Ngqangweni S., & Kirsten, J.F., "Quantifying the Trade Effect of Sanitary and Phytosanitary Regulations of OECD Countries on South African Food Exports." *Agrekon*, 2007, 46(1), p. 23–39.

Gruszczynski 2006

Gruszczynski, L., Science in the Process of Risk Regulation under the WTO Agreement on Sanitary and Phytosanitary Measures, *German Law Journal*, 2006, pp 371–398.

Guimarães 2012
Guimarães, M.H., Non-Tariff Measures in The European Union: Evidence from the Agri-Food Sector, *Agricultural Economics Review*, 13(2), 2012, pp 21–34.

Gujadhur 2002
Gujadhur, S. K., Technical Assistance for SPS Measures Protect Health, Not Trade, *International trade Forum*, 3, 2002, pp31–35.

Hartzenberg 2011
Hartzenberg, T., Regional Integration in Africa, World Trade Organization, *Staff Working Paper ERSD*, 2011.

Hathaway 1999
Hathaway, S., Management of Food Safety in International Trade, *Food Control 10*, 1999, pp 247–253.

Henson 2003
Henson, S., Food Safety in Food Security and Food Trade, Food Safety Issues in international Trade, 2020 vision for food, agriculture and the environment, *Focus 10, Brief 5 of 17*, 2003.

Henson et al. 2000a
Henson S.J., Loader R.J., Swinbank, A., Bredahl, M. & Lux N., Impact of Sanitary and Phytosanitary Measures on Developing Countries, *University of Reading*, 2000.

Henson et al, 2000b
Henson, S; Brouder, A. & Mitullah, W., Food Safety Requirements and Food Exports from Developing Countries: The case of Fish Exports from Kenya to the European Union, *Amer. J. Agr. Econ.* 82 (5), 2000, pp1159–1169.

Henson & Jaffee 2006a
Henson, S. & Jaffee, S., Food Safety Standards and Trade: Enhancing Competitiveness and Avoiding Exclusion of Developing Countries, *The European Journal of Development Research*, 2006, pp.593–621.

Henson & Jaffee 2006b
Henson, S. & Jaffee, S., A Strategic Perspective on the Impact of Food Safety Standards on Developing Countries, Invited paper for presentation at the International Association of Agricultural Economists Conference, 2006.

Henson & Loader 2001
Henson, S. & Loader, R., Barriers to Agricultural Exports from Developing Countries: The Role of Sanitary and Phytosanitary Requirements, *World Development*, 29(1), 2001 pp. 85–102.

Henson et al. 2001
Henson S., Preibisch K. & Masakure O., Review of Developing Country Needs and Involvement in International Standards-Setting Bodies, *Centre for Food Economics Research*, 2001.

Henson et al. 2004
Henson, S., Saquib, M and Rajasenan, D., Impact of Sanitary Measures on Exports of Fishery Products from India: The Case of Kerala. *Agriculture and Rural Development Discussion Paper*, World Bank. 2004.

Hoffman & Harder 2010
Hoffman, S., & Harder, W., Food Safety and Risk Governance in Globalized Markets, *Resources for the future discussion paper*, 09(44), 2010.

Hooker & Caswell 1999
Hooker, N. H. & Caswell, J. A., A Framework for Evaluating Non-Tariff Barriers to Trade Related to Sanitary and Phytosanitary Regulation, *Journal of Agricultural Economics*, 1999, pp234–246.

Houndekon 1992
Houndekon, B., Conservation et Commercialisation des Produits de Pêche Lagunaire, Proceedings of the symposium on post-harvest fish technology, *FAO*, 1992.

Houndekon et al. 2003
Houndekon, V., Fagbohoun, L., & Ekue. C., Rôle de la Pêche Artisanale dans les Economies des Pays de l'Afrique de l'Ouest: Etude du cas du Bénin. *Organisation des Nations Unies pour l'Alimentation et l'Agriculture-* Programme pour des Moyens d'Existence Durables dans la Pêche en Afrique de l'Ouest. 2003.

Houssa & Verpoorten 2013
Houssa, R., & Verpoorten, M., The Unintended Consequence of an Export Ban: Evidence from Benin's Shrimp Sector, *CRED Working Papers Series* 1304, 2013.

Hornsby 2009
Hornsby, D. J., WTO Effectiveness in Resolving EU-US Trade Conflict, *Transatlantic Strategy Forum Working paper*, 2009.

ISO/UNIDO 2008
ISO/UNIDO, Fast Forward- National Standards Bodies in Developing Countries, 2008.

ISO/UNIDO 2009
ISO/UNIDO, Building Trust- The Conformity Assessment Toolbox, 2009.

ISO/UNIDO 2013
ISO/UNIDO, National Standardization Bodies in Developing Countries, Fast Forward, second edition, ISO Central Secretariat, 2013.

Jaffee & Henson 2004
Jaffee, S. & Henson, S., Standards and Agro-Food Exports from Developing Countries: Rebalancing the Debate, *World Bank Policy Research Working Paper* 3348, 2004, pp1–44.

Jaiswal 2003
Jaiswal, A. K., WTO Agreement on SPS: Strategic Implications, *Economic and Political Weekly*, 2003, pp4737–4742.

Jayasuriya et al. 2006

Jayasuriya, S., Maclaren, D. & Mehta, R., 'Meeting Food Safety Standards in Export Markets: Issues and Challenges Facing Firms Exporting from Developing Countries', Presented at the conference *IATRC Summer Symposium: Food Regulation an Trade: Institutional Framework, Concepts of Analysis and Empirical Evidence*, 2006, pp1–10.

Jensen 2002

Jensen, M. F., Reviewing the SPS Agreement: A Developing Country Perspective, *Centre for Development Research Working Paper* 02.3, 2002.

Jooste et al. 2003

Jooste, A., Kruger, E. & Kotzé, F., Standards and Trade in South Africa: Paving Pathways for Increased Market Access and Competitiveness, in Wilson, JS, Abiola VO, Standards and Global Trade: A voice for Africa. *World Bank*, 2003 pp235–370.

Josling & Roberts, 2011

Josling, T. & Roberts, D., Measuring the Impact of SPS Standards on Market Access, *International Food and Agricultural Trade Policy Council*, 2011, pp 1–10.

Josling et al. 2004

Josling, T., Roberts, D. & Orden, D., Food Regulation and Trade: Towards a Safe and Open Global System, Selected Paper prepared for presentation at the *American Agricultural Economics Association*, 2004.

Kadigi et al. 2007

Kadigi, R.M.J., Mdoe, N.S.Y., Senkondo, E. & Mpenda, Z., Effects of Food Safety Standards on the Livelihoods of Actors in the Nile Perch Value Chain in Tanzania, *DIIS Working Paper* no 2007/24, 2007.

Kaeser & Bau 2007

Kaeser S. & Bau B., The UEMOA Quality Programme. A Novel Regional Approach at UEMOA for the Implementation of Compliance related Business Environment Reform: Lessons for Future Donor Interventions, Creating Better Business Environments for Enterprise Development – African and Global Lessons for More Effective Donor Practices, Africa Regional Consultative Conference, 2007.

Kastner & Douglas 2002

Kastner, J. & Douglas, P., The SPS Agreement: Addressing Historical Factors in Trade Dispute Resolution, *Agriculture and Human Values*, 2002, pp283–292.

Kastner & Pawsey 2002

Kastner, J.J. & Pawsey, R.K., Harmonising Sanitary Measures and Resolving Trade Disputes through the WTO-SPS framework. Part I: a Case Study of the US-EU Hormone-treated Beef Dispute, *Food Policy*, 2002, pp 49–55.

Kuchenmüller et al. 2013

Kuchenmüller T., Abela-Ridder B., Corrigan T. & Tritscher A., World Health Organization Initiative to Estimate the Global Burden of Foodborne Diseases, *Rev. sci. tech. Off. int. Epiz*, 32 (2), pp 459–467, 2013.

Lamb 2006

Lamb, R. L., Rent Seeking in US-Mexican Avocado Trade, *Cato Journal*, 2006, pp159–177.

Lawogni & De Sadeleer 2002

Lawogni, A. & De Sadeleer, N., Droit de l'environnement au Bénin, Code Officieux de l'Environnement, *Centre d'étude du droit de l'environnement*, 2002.

MacMaoláin 2007

MacMaoláin, C., EU Food Law. Protecting Consumers and Health in a Common Market, *Hart Publishing*,2007.

Maertens & Swinnen 2009

Maertens, M. & Swinnen, J., Food Standards, Trade and Development, *Review of Business and Economics*, 2009, pp 313–326.

Magalhães 2001

Magalhães J., Sanitary and Phytosanitary Issues and the SPS Agreement, *China/FAO Citrus Symposium*, 2001.

Majone 2004

Majone, G., The Internationalization of Regulation: Implications for Developing Countries, *Centre on Regulation and Competition Working Paper Series*, 57, 2004.

Maldonado 1998

Maldonado C., Secteur Informel: Fonctions Macro-économiques et Politiques Gouvernementales- Le cas du Bénin, Document de recherche S-INF-1–18, *OIT*, 1998.

Marre 2001

Marre, B., Rapport d'Information Déposé par la Délégation de l'Assemblée Nationale pour l'Union Européenne sur la Sécurité Alimentaire Européenne, 2001.

Mayeda 2004

Mayeda, G., Developing Disharmony? The SPS and TBT Agreements and the Impact of Harmonization on Developing Countries, *Journal of International Economic Law*, 7(4), 2004, pp737–764.

Meulen (van der) & Velde (van der) 2008

Meulen (van der), B. & Velde (van der), M., European Food Law Handbook, *Wageningen Academic Publishers*, 2008.

Mialet 2010

Mialet S., Appui aux Systèmes d'Information sur les Mesures Sanitaires et Phytosanitaires au Bénin, Projet STDF 127, Rapport de mission, Mission du 2 au 13 août 2010, 2010.

Mitchell 2003

Mitchell, L., Economic Theory and Conceptual Relationships Between Food Safety and International Trade, *International Trade and Food Safety /AER-828*, 2003, pp10–27.

Mitchikpé et al. 2001

Mitchikpé, C.E.S., Atègbo, E.-A. D., Fanou, J.A. & Nago, M.C. Consommation Alimentaire des Ménages Urbains au Bénin. Alimentation, Savoir-faire et Innovations en Agroalimentaire en Afrique de l'Ouest. *CERNA, CIRAD*, 2001.

Moeniws 1999
Moeniws, J., Information versus Product Adaptation: The Role of Standards in Trade. Working paper, *University of California*, San Diego, 1999, p1–40.

Muhammad et al. 2001
Muhammad,S., Singh, S., Ekanem, E., Tegegne, F., & Akuley-Amenyenu, A., Exports from Developing Countries and Food Safety Concerns, *Journal of Food Distribution Research*, 2001, pp133–139.

Neeliah et al. 2011
Neeliah, S. A., Goburdhun D. & Neeliah, H., The SPS Agreement: Barrier or Catalyst?, *Estey Journal of International Law and Trade Policy*, 2011, pp 104–130.

Neugebauer 1999-2000
Neugebauer, R., Fine-Tuning WTO Jurisprudence and the SPS Agreement: Lessons from the Beef Hormone Case, *Law and Policy in International Business*, 1999-2000, pp1255–1284.

Nguyen & Wilson 2009
Nguyen, A. V. T. & Wilson, L. W. N., Effects of Food Safety Standards on Seafood Exports to US, EU and Japan, *Paper presented at the Southern Agricultural Economics Association Annual Meeting*, 2009, p1–20.

Noor 2000
Noor, H., Sanitary and Phytosanitary Measures and their Impact on Kenya. *EconNews Africa*, 2000.

Nyangito 2002
Nyangito, H., Post-Doha African Challenges in the Sanitary and Phytosanitary and Trade Related Intellectual Property Rights Agreement, *KIPPRA Occasional Paper*, 2002.

Nyangito et al. 2003
Nyangito, Olielo and Magwaro, Improving Market Access through Standards Compliance: A Diagnostic and Road Map for Kenya in Wilson, J.S, Abiola V.O, Standards and Global Trade: A voice for Africa. *World Bank*, 2003, pp 1–64.

Ochieng & Majanja 2010
Ochieng, D.A. and Majanja D.S., Sub-Saharan Africa and WTO Dispute Settlement: the Case of Kenya, Dispute Settlement at the WTO: The Developing Country Experience., Gregory C. Shaffer and Ricardo Meléndez-Ortiz eds, Cambridge University Press 2010.

OECD 2006
OECD, Étude Régionale Relative aux Opportunités Economiques de Développement de la Crevetticulture en Afrique de l'Ouest, Club du Sahel et de l'Afrique de l'Ouest Coopération économique Sud/Sud, 2006.

ONUDI 2005
ONUDI, Initiative pour le Renforcement des Capacités Commerciales/ Programme Qualité UEMOA, Accréditation, Certification, Normalisation, Métrologie,

Promotion de la qualité- Contribution à l'Etude du Droit lié à la Qualité dans l'Espace UEMOA, UE/ONUDI/UEMOA, 2005.

O'Rourke 1998
O'Rourke, R., *EC Food Law*, 1st eds, 1998.

Othman 2007
Othman, N. M., Food Safety in Southeast Asia: Challenges Facing the Region, Noraini Mohd Othman, *Asian Journal of Agriculture and Development*, 4(2), pp 83–92.

PAM 2009
PAM, Analyse Globale de la Vulnérabilité, de la Sécurité Alimentaire et de la Nutrition (AGVSAN) - République du Bénin (données de novembre et décembre 2008). *PAM*, 2009.

PASP 2007
PASP, Plan de Relance de la Filière Halieutique. Diagnostic de la Filière Crevette - Rapport de l'Expert International à Court Terme, 2007.

Pauwelyn 1999
Pauwelyn, J., The WTO Agreement on Sanitary and Phytosanitary (SPS) Measures as Applied in the First Three SPS Disputes: EC-Hormones, Australia-Salmon and Japan-Varietals, *Journal of International Economic Law*, 1999, pp 641–664.

Ponte 2004
Ponte, S., Standards and Sustainability in the Coffee Sector: A Global Value Chain Approach, *International Institute for Sustainable Development*, 2004, pp1–49.

Ponte 2007
Ponte, S., Bans, Tests, and Alchemy: Food Safety Regulation and the Uganda Fish Export Industry, *Agriculture and Human values*, 24, 2007, pp179–193.

Prévost 2005a
Prévost, D., What Role for the Precautionary Principle in WTO Law after Japan-Apples? *Economic Policy and Law, Journal of Trade and Environment Studies*, 2005. pp 1–14.

Prévost 2005b
Prévost, D, 'Operationalising' Special and Differential Treatment of Developing Countries Under the SPS Agreement, *South African Yearbook of International Law*, 2005, pp. 82–111.

Prévost 2009
Prévost, D., Balancing Trade and Health in the SPS Agreement: A Development Perspective, *Wolf Legal Publishers*, 2009, pp 1234.

Prévost & Matthee 2002
Prévost, D. & Matthee M., The SPS Agreement as a Bottleneck in Agricultural Trade between the European Union and Developing Countries: How to Solve the Conflict, *Legal issues of Economic Integration*, 2002, pp43–59.

Roberts 1998
Roberts, D., Preliminary Assessment of the Effects of the WTO Agreement on Sanitary and Phytosanitary Trade Regulations, *Journal of International Economic Law*, 1998, pp 377–405.

Roberts & DeKremer 1997
Roberts, D. & DeKremer, K., Technical Barriers to US Agricultural Exports, *Economic Research Service*, USDA, 1997.

Roberts & Josling 2011
Roberts, D. and Josling, T., Tracking the Implementation of Internationally Agreed Standards in Food and Agricultural Production, *International Food & Agricultural Trade Policy Council*, 2011, pp 1–10.

Roberts & Unnevehr 2005
Roberts, D. and Unnevehr, L., Resolving Trade Disputes Arising from Trends in Food Safety Regulation: the Role of the Multilateral Governance Framework, *World Trade Review*, 2005, pp 469497.

Rudaheranwa et al. 2003
Rudaheranwa, N., Matovi, F. & Musinguzi, W., Enhancing Uganda's Access to International Markets: A Focus on Quality, in Wilson, J.S. and Abiola, V. S. (eds) Standards and Global Trade: A voice for Africa, 2003, pp371–426.

Sédogbo 2004
Sédogbo A. Y., Impact de la Pollution Environnementale sur la Qualité des Crevettes Capturées au Bénin: Cas des Pêcheries du Sud du lac Nokoué, Mémoire de fin d'étude d'ingénieur de travaux, EPAC/Université d'Abomey-Calavi/Bénin, 2004.

Selznick 1992
Selznick, P., The Moral Commonwealth: Social Theory and the Promise of Community, *The Regents of the University of California*, 1992.

Shafaeddin, 2007
Shafaeddin, M., SPS Measures Lead to High Costs and Losses for Developing Countries, Third World Network, Briefing Paper 38, 2007.

Silverglade 2000
Silverglade, B. A., The WTO Agreement on Sanitary and Phytosanitary Measures: Weakening Food Safety Regulations to Facilitate Trade? *Food & Drug Law Journal*, 2000, pp517–524.

Skogstad 2001
Skogstad, G., The WTO and Food Safety Regulatory Policy Innovation in the European Union, *Journal of Common Market Studies*, 39(3), 2001, pp 485–505.

Slorach 2002
Slorach, S. A., Integrated Approaches to the Management of Food Safety throughout the Food Chain, at FAO/WHO Global Forum of Food Safety Regulators Marrakesh, Morocco, 28–30 January 2002, 2002.

Smith DeWaal & Robert 2005
Smith DeWaal, C. and Robert, N., Global and Local: Food Safety Around the World, *Centre for Science in the Public Interest*, 2005.

Snyder 2006
Snyder, F., Toward an International Law for Adequate Food in *La sécurité alimentaire-Food security and food safety*,1st ed., Martinus Nijhoff Publishers, 2006.

Society of Toxicology, 1998
Society of Toxicology, Risk Assessment: What's it all about? *Society of Toxicology's Newsletter*, Communiqué, Special Issue, p. 9, 1998.

Stewart & Johanson 1999
Stewart, T.P. & Johanson D.S., The SPS Agreement of the World Trade Organization and the International Trade of Dairy Products, *Food and Drug Law Journal*, 1999, p. 55–72.

Système des Nations Unies Benin 2008
Système des Nations Unies Benin, Bilan Commun de pays (common Country Assessment) Bénin, 2008.

Thorn & Carlson 1999–2000
Thorn, C. & Carlson, M., The Agreement on the Application of Sanitary and Phytosanitary Measures and the Agreement on Technical Barriers to Trade, *Law and Policy in International Business*, 1999–2000, p. 841–854.

Transparency International 2010
Transparency International, Corruption Perception Index 2010 Results, *Transparency International*, 2010.

UE/ONUDI/UEMOA, 2005
UE/ONUDI/UEMOA, Initiative pour le Renforcement des Capacités Commerciales/ Programme Qualité UEMOA, Accréditation, Certification, Normalisation, Métrologie, Promotion de la qualité- Contribution à l'étude du droit lié à la qualité dans l'espace UEMOA, UE/ONUDI/UEMOA, 2005.

UEMOA 2008
UEMOA, Lancement de la Composante UEMOA du Programme Qualité Afrique de l'Ouest, La Semaine de l'UEMOA/Bulletin Hebdomadaire de l'UEMOA No 200, 2008.

Union Européenne- Afrique de l'Ouest 2002
Union Européenne- Afrique de l'Ouest, *Diagnostic Stratégique des Filières Agro-industrielles, Rapport Bénin*, 2002.

UNCTAD 2007
UNCTAD, Voluntary Peer Review of Competition Policy: West African Economic and Monetary Union, Benin and Senegal, UNCTAD/DITC/CLP/2007/1(Overview), 2007.

UNCTAD 2011
UNCTAD, The Least Developed Countries Report 2008, Growth, Poverty and the Terms of Development Partnership, *United Nations*, 2008.

UNDP 2005
UNDP, Sub-Saharan Africa- the Human Costs of the 2015 'Business-as-usual' Scenario, *United Nation Development Programme*, 2005.

Unnevehr 2003
Unnevehr, L. J., Food safety in Food Security and Food Trade, Overview, 2020 vision for food, agriculture and the environment, Focus 10, Brief 1 of 17, 2003.

Unnevehr & Hirschhorn 2000
Unnevehr, L. & Hirschhorn, N., Food Safety Issues in the Developing World, *World Bank Technical Paper No 469*, 2000.

Unnevehr et al. 2003
Unnevehr, L., Haddad, L., & Delgado C., Food Safety in Food Security and Food Trade, Food Safety Policy Issues for Developing Countries, Focus 10, Brief 17 of 17, 2003.

Unnevehr & Jensen 1999
Unnevehr, L. J. & Jensen, H. H., The Economic Implications of Using HACCP as a Food Safety Regulatory Standard, *Food policy* 24, 1999, pp 625–635.

Vapnek & Spreij 2005
Vapnek, J., & Spreij, M., Perspectives and Guidelines on Food Legislation, with a New Model Food Law, *FAO*, 2005.

Varzakas & Jukes 1997
Varzakas, T. & Jukes, D., Globalisation of Food Quality Standards: the Impact in Greece, *Food Policy*, 1997, pp. 501–514.

Veggeland 2006
Veggeland, F., Trade Facilitation Through Equivalence and Mutual Recognition: The EU Model, *Centre for Food Policy/Norwegian Agricultural Economics Research Institute*, 2006.

Victor 2000
Victor, D. G., The Sanitary and Phytosanitary Agreement of the World Trade Organization: An Assessment after Five Years, *NYU International Law and Politics* 32, 2000, pp 865–939.

Victor 2002
Victor, D. G., WTO Efforts to Manage Differences in National Sanitary and Phytosanitary Policies, *UCIAS Edited Volumes*, 1/7, 2002.

Vos 1999
Vos, E., Institutional Frameworks of Community Health and Safety Regulation. Committees, Agencies and Private Bodies, *Oxford Hart Publishing*, 1999.

Vos & Wendler 2006
Vos, E., Wendler, F., Food Safety Regulation at the EU Level, Food Safety Regulation in Europe/A Comparative Institutional Analysis, *E. Vos and F. Wendler eds.*, 2006, p65–138.

Watson 2001
Watson, A., The Evolution of Western Private Law, *The John Hopkins University Press*, 2001.

Weidong 2006
Weidong, C., Food Safety and Trade: How to Decide the Appropriate Level of Food Safety? Comparative Study of Trade Dispute Settlement about Food Safety in the WTO and the EC, La sécurité alimentaire/ Food Security and Food Safety, Ahmed Mahiou and Francis Snyder editions, 2006, pp 725–752.

WHO 2004
WHO, Food and Health in Europe, a New Basis for Action, *WHO Regional Publications European Series*, 96, 2004.

Wilson & Abiola, 2003
Wilson, J. S., Abiola V.O., Standards and Global Trade: A Voice for Africa, *World Bank*, 2003.

Wise 1990
Wise, E. M., The Transplant of Legal Patterns, *The American Journal of Comparative Law*, 38, 1990, pp 1–38.

World bank 2011
World Bank, Benin: Country Brief, 2011.

World Bank 2013
World Bank, World Bank to Help Benin Fight Widespread Malnutrition among Mothers and Children, *World Bank Press Release*, 2013.

Zarrilli 1999
Zarrilli, S., WTO Sanitary and Phytosanitary Agreement: Issues for Developing Countries, *Trade-Related Agenda, Development and Equity (T.R.A.D.E) Working Papers*, South Centre, 1999.

Zleptnig 2010
Zleptnig, S., Non-Economic Objectives in WTO Law: Justification Provisions of GATT, GATS, SPS and TBT Agreements, *Nijhoff International Trade Law Series*, 2010.

CURRICULUM VITAE

Kévine Kindji Garspard (born in Cotonou, Benin in 1981) studied Law in Cotonou from 2004 to 2008. She obtained a master's degree in corporate law and judicial careers. She joined in 2010 the Maastricht Institute for Transnational Legal Research (METRO) in Maastricht University to conduct her doctoral research.

www.ingramcontent.com/pod-product-compliance
Ingram Content Group UK Ltd.
Pitfield, Milton Keynes, MK11 3LW, UK
UKHW051919100926
8556IPUK00021B/1262

9 781780 683287